PREFACE TO
WORLD LITERATURE

BY THE SAME AUTHOR

PREFACE TO WORLD LITERATURE

BY

ALBERT GUÉRARD

PROFESSOR OF GENERAL AND COMPARATIVE LITERATURE
STANFORD UNIVERSITY

NEW YORK
HENRY HOLT AND COMPANY

TO MY STANFORD STUDENTS

Die Luft der Freiheit weht

CONTENTS

PART THREE

MAIN PROBLEMS IN WORLD LITERATURE

APPENDICES

FOREWORD
SPIRIT AND METHOD OF THIS WORK

I received once a belated theme with the dedication:

I was very much impressed with the sincerity as well as with the courtesy of this homage. Now it is my privilege to return the compliment. This book is dedicated to the many hundreds of students who, for the last fifteen years, have collaborated with me in its preparation. Through symposia, essays and quizzes, through questions, objections and suggestions, through many private interviews, they have provided the very substance of this work. Even the few who remained obstinately silent and aloof have helped me. Many are the points I have elaborated until I could force at last some gleam of response: in the clarification of my thought, my reluctant auditors had a vital share. Many times also have I struggled to drive away from pleasant young faces the happy smile which betrays a wandering mind; until I had victoriously restored the expression befitting an earnest scholar: to wit, one of gentle worry and slight bewilderment.

This should suffice to indicate the nature of this work. It is the consolidated report of a prolonged laboratory experiment. My primary aim was not to transmit information; still less to propound a doctrine; and least of all to communicate my own prejudices. The study of literature is an effort to think honestly about literature—to think till it hurts, for pain is the test of all honest thinking. Out of such pain rises a strenuous joy: the purest no doubt, the least disappointing that this earth is able to afford.

There is no Art of Thinking so simple as that of old Descartes. From him we shall borrow the first precept of our method: Never to accept anything as true unless it appears to us clearly and evidently to be such. Many iridescent theories vanish at the prick of this plainest and sharpest of rules. The converse, more paradoxical, is worth bearing in mind: Never to reject anything as false when it is clearly and manifestly in accord with our experience. Our experience tells us that literature, from the nursery to the graduate school, is *World literature*; that the Bible, Grimm's *Fairy Tales*, *The Three Musketeers*, *Les Misérables*, not to mention the *Iliad*, the *Divine Comedy*, *Don Quixote* and *Faust*, are part and parcel of our heritage. Yet we reject this self-evident fact in favor of the national and departmental convention; we assume that literature must be divided into self-contained units, English, German or Italian, each ruled sternly and absolutely by some specialist. Starting from common experience, we shall consider "foreign" masterpieces not as alien, but as our very own. For us, the essential line of cleavage will not lie between Slav, Latin and Teuton, or between ancient and modern, but between the quick and the dead. Our field is *living literature*. It may or may not include the best-seller of yester eve; and no book will be barred out simply because it appeared twenty-five hundred years ago and five thousand miles away.

This conception of World Literature implies three consequences, which will be our three guiding principles, and which we shall name Humanism, Individualism, and Pragmatic Relativism.

By Humanism, we mean, not the grammarian's delight, nor the austere faith of an Irving Babbitt, but simply our belief in the essential unity of mankind. This is the first lesson—as it is the first condition—of World Literature. If Socrates or Plato, if the author of *Job* or that of *Ecclesiastes* are at times closer to me than my next-door neighbor, is it not in virtue of a human quality which transcends all minor differences?

But this Humanism does not lead us to admit that all men are equal and interchangeable. On the contrary, it brings out the fact that, within the range of their common human nature, all men are different. No discipline emphasizes this fact so strongly as does literature. Government imposes upon us *general* rules, dictated, it is to be hoped, by the *general* will and *general* interest. Science seeks *general* laws, and morality *general* principles. Religion expounds the *universal* truth. Art alone asserts the uniqueness of the individual.

With such a conviction, it would be vain to hope for absolute rules, laws, principles or dogmas in literature. The individual is the sole creator, and the individual is the sole judge. But this radical Individualism need not commit us to utter skepticism and anarchism. We have, it must be remembered, refused to deny those things which palpably exist. Group resemblances and group differences are among them. So, between the human race as a whole and the unique individual self, there are intermediate entities. These are the conditions of human society: races, languages, nations, social strata, economic interests; and the framework of literature: tendencies, schools, *genres*, periods. Perhaps these things are mere conventions; perhaps they are delusions; but a delusion firmly entertained is a fact for which men will work and die. Nothing that has power can be an empty name.

So, in a realistic, experimental spirit, we are willing to examine all the divisions and classifications that have been established among men and between the works of men. We reject every *a priori* rejection. But if we accept these notions as having some kind of reality, we are not bound to accept them uncritically as exclusive and absolute. We shall attempt to analyze them. And this process will, almost invariably, lead us to the same two conclusions. The first is that simple terms cover a variety of meanings, and that these meanings are not always reconcilable. We need more words than we have at our disposal to denote all the things that we have in mind when we speak of *love, genius, poetry, religion.* The tyranny of words is due to their looseness. The second is that, when we have defined our categories more accurately, when we have elaborated a neatly logical gridwork of terms and notions, in other words when we have built up a *system,* we find that it fails to coincide exactly with the moving, organic complexity of known reality. These two conclusions determine what we call Pragmatic Relativism: classifications, abstract thoughts should not be ignored; they are excellent instruments, and we should train ourselves to handle them with skill; but they are instruments merely, and not ultimate verities.

A Few Practical Words of Warning

We are aware that this method is more confusing to the young mind than a neat array of firm definitions and iron-bound classifications. Our first aim is to make the student conscious of this very confusion. But be sure that confusion is not the final goal. We shall

not rest satisfied when we have turned ideas that were vaguely clear
into ideas that are clearly vague. Our one hope is to challenge the
student to find out his own way. Beyond that challenge, our assistance will mostly consist in pointing out a few pitfalls.

The purpose of this book is to induce every reader to compose—for
his own use, not for publication—another one of the same kind. We
offer merely an incentive and a pattern. For instance, we discuss lists
of standard books; but it is for *you* to draw up the list of what you
have read, and to decide what you propose to read. We analyze the
nature and the formation of taste; but everyone should write the
biography of his own taste. We give in an appendix a Critic's Glossary,
the indispensable tool chest for any serious thought about literature:
but everyone must make sure that he knows his own tools, that he
uses his own vocabulary with a certain degree of definiteness and
consistency.

With this aim in view, the reader will perhaps be able to overcome
two apparent difficulties in this study: the first in the realm of thought,
the second in the domain of facts.

Each chapter presents some essential problem in World Literature;
but elucidation frequently consists in dispelling false simplicity. No
theory is stated without a respectful but determined challenge. So
every issue is the proper subject for a debate. Involved as dogmatic
exposition, each chapter will be found practical enough as an arsenal
for a discussion. Do not simply read: discuss. If you are not fortunate
enough to belong to a class or to a club, if you cannot find a partner
in this game, then follow Ernest Renan's example in his *Philosophical
Dialogues,* and start a debate between two lobes in your brains.

To clarify the process, for each chapter a Summary has been prepared which presents the gist of the argument; but it must be remembered that it is the discussion, and not the outline, that offers any
educative value.

The second difficulty relates to facts. We come together with personal experiences which do not coincide. Of the many authors and
books mentioned in this "Introduction," not a few, no doubt, will be
total strangers. Be not dismayed: one of the aims of this study is to
combat the notion that culture consists in knowing a particular set of
classics. No scholar, at the end of a learned career, is familiar with
all the books "that every child should know." In literature as in
science, we are all gathering pebbles by the seashore.

This book is not a Survey of World Literature; but, as no general idea is offered without some definite illustration, a vast number of facts had to be quoted. Yet the thought itself should be clear without the fact; and it would be highly desirable if, for the facts adduced in this "Introduction," each reader would substitute others from the fund of his own experience. Every college freshman has read enough to discuss intelligently the basic problems of World Literature: a few plays, a few novels, a few poems, will suffice for a start. Even a film could serve to illustrate *mimesis, hamartia, catharsis* and all the profundities of Aristotle. *For a start:* it is definitely understood, of course, that any student who takes up this work is pledging himself to read books, many books, good books, and difficult books. But do not believe that erudition must precede any attempt at intelligent criticism. Knowledge and reasoned appreciation should start together and progress hand in hand.

In the course of this study, we shall have to traverse the whole field of literature several times, starting from different points. This involves repetitions, which I have not sought to avoid. It involves also apparent contradictions, for which I do not apologize. These contradictions indicate in some cases problems which could not be thoroughly canvassed in this (comparatively) brief survey; in other cases, they reveal difficulties which I have not been able to resolve in my own mind. I am still taking as well as offering courses in World Literature. This is a report on work in progress: not a lengthy epitaph on the gravestones of dead masterpieces.

A. G.

Stanford University,
Jan. 15, 1940

CHAPTER I

WHAT IS WORLD LITERATURE?

THE EXPRESSION World Literature originated with Goethe. Our work could hardly be placed under a nobler or more fitting patronage. For Goethe is a perfect illustration of the conception that he named; to define his spirit is to define our subject. The supreme exponent of German culture, he was able to look beyond the political and linguistic boundaries of his tribe. Nothing human was alien to him. He considered the treasure house of mankind as his legitimate heritage; he enjoyed the masterpieces of ancient Greece and Rome, and those of modern France, Italy, Spain and England as well; he even sought to bridge the gulf between Oriental and Occidental cultures. Everywhere he assumed the freedom of a son of the house; he gave so convincing an interpretation of *Hamlet* that our critics accepted it for generations with scarcely a challenge. As he freely received, no less freely did he give. He had all Europe for his audience. Twice at least, in his early tale of frustration and despair, *The Sorrows of Young Werther*, and in the first part of his mighty philosophical drama, *Faust*, he reached, not scholarly and critical readers alone, but the multitude. For years before his death, his position as the head of European letters was unquestioned. Other prophets have arisen in his Germany, whose message can hardly be reconciled with Goethe's ideal; but the spirit that shone in Weimar shall outlive the fret and fury of our day.

There is some danger, however, in claiming Goethe as our master. It might foster the notion that World Literature is a formidable subject, fit only for such a titan of culture as he, or, at second-hand, for his learned disciples. We might as well

3

imagine that religion is the exclusive privilege of St. Paul, St. Augustine, St. Thomas Aquinas, Martin Luther, with their following of professional theologians. We know that on the contrary, religion is a fact of common experience, not denied to the common man. So it is with World Literature. It is not reserved for a supercilious élite, doctors of philosophy or cosmopolitan sophisticates. We all read and enjoy World Literature in the same way as a character in Molière, Monsieur Jourdain, the *would-be gentleman*, had been talking prose all his life—without being aware of it. *World Literature begins, not in the graduate school, but in the nursery.* Our children are told immemorial tales, the fairy lore of all ages and climes. They do not object to the Grimm Brothers because they were Germans, to Charles Perrault because he was French, to Hans Christian Andersen because he was a Dane. The same blissful openness of heart and mind still prevails when they graduate from the nursery. *The Swiss Family Robinson, Heidi, Pinocchio,* are great favorites, although they were not born under the Stars and Stripes. Adolescent America finds delight in *The Three Musketeers* and *Monte Cristo,* by that lusty dusky giant among storytellers, Alexandre Dumas; and youngsters still enjoy Jules Verne, even though many of his anticipations are now back numbers.

The common man retains this freedom from prejudice until he is taught better—I mean until he is taught worse. Adults are quite unconscious of national frontiers in the literary field. If there be but one book in the lone cabin, it will be the Book, the *Bible,* with its hoard of strange beauty as well as divine wisdom, a whole library of incomparable range within the covers of a single volume; and that book came to us down the ages, through men who spoke alien tongues and lived under alien skies. In the last century, the common man again was thrilled by the romances of Eugène Sue, *The Mysteries of Paris* or *The Wandering Jew;* he still enjoys, without the benefit of a university education, Victor Hugo's epic of redemption and social pity, *Les Misérables.* Among our best-sellers, read for sheer pleasure and not as class assignments, are many works of foreign origin: *Quo Vadis?* by Sienkiewicz, *The Four Horsemen of the Apocalypse* by Blasco Ibáñez, Ludwig's *Napoleon*, Remarque's *All Quiet on the Western Front*, Vicki Baum's *Grand Hotel*, Fallada's *Little Man, What Now?* World Literature, for the average reader, is not a theory, but a condition.

As our knowledge of literature expands, we realize more clearly that the best which has been thought and said in the world is not limited to our own bewildered generation, and to our terse and colorful American language. We become aware, not only of the best-sellers of today, but of those perennial good-sellers which are called the classics. Some day Homer swims into our ken; and Dante's *Divine Comedy*, and Goethe's *Faust*, and Tolstoy's *War and Peace*. Ignore these summits of human achievement, or grant them grudgingly a subordinate place, and you will stunt and warp the growth of your mind. This is not true only of the classics which rose to fame ages ago; anyone genuinely interested in contemporary literature has to get acquainted with Anatole France, Marcel Proust, Pirandello; with d'Annunzio, Gorky, Maeterlinck; with André Gide, Thomas Mann, Unamuno; with Jules Romains, Stefan Zweig, Ortega y Gasset.

From these plain facts, a plain conclusion must be drawn. *Literature should be taught as Literature in English, not as English Literature.* A selection there must be; but the basis of our selection should be excellence. It is far more important for us to know world masterpieces than to clutter up our minds with the names of local mediocrities. In the self-education which should continue throughout adult life, it would be wise to be guided by the same rule: let us read and enjoy the best, wherever the best may be found.

This simple suggestion may strike some readers as a willful paradox. We are used to a fairly rigid division into self-contained departments—English, Classical Languages, Modern Languages, History, Philosophy; and the disruption of these time-honored boundaries strikes us as a major heresy, like the confusion of the Three Powers in the Constitutional State. It would be well to remember that departments were made for man, and not man for departments. Above all, we should bear in mind that "time-honored" divisions are, in certain cases, surprisingly recent. In the long perspective of history, the study of literature from a strictly national point of view is a thing of yesterday. For centuries, the accepted approach was through the Humanities, that is to say through the Greek and Latin classics. When the present writer was a high-school boy in France, the same master taught French, Latin and Greek: the three formed a single whole. This long tradition is fading, but it has not completely disappeared. If Latin is still so extensively studied in America, it is not for utilitarian purposes, and not even for its very great intrinsic merits, but as the keystone of our culture. Latin may no longer be the indispensable bond among the nations; but few will deny that the disruption of Europe's spiritual unity involves a tragic loss.

The division of literature into separate language departments is defended on the plea that definite knowledge demands specialization. It is hard enough to know, accurately and intimately, a single literature, and that our own; it is out of the question even for a prodigy to take all literature as his domain. Such an attempt can lead only to shallowness, concealed at best under a pleasing film of generalities. As Professor C. H. C. Wright of Harvard put it with good-humored banter, the study of World Literature is apt to be "a breathless attempt to keep up with God and H. G. Wells."

This indicates a danger, not a radical impossibility. I agree with the professional scholars: the age of encyclopedic geniuses is past. But we must specialize far more than the departmental division would indicate. It is in fact impossible to know everything about a single literature. No man is expected to be a first-hand authority on *Beowulf* and James Joyce, extreme links in an enormous chain. In all cases, there must be selection, renunciation, and finally a confession of ignorance. We move in a little circle of trembling light; beyond that, a brief penumbra; and then, darkness absolute.

But, however limited our field may be, if we want to investigate it with any degree of thoroughness, we shall not be able to restrict it to national boundaries. Every great English writer had some foreign ancestor in the spirit, more important in shaping his art and thought than many of his English predecessors and contemporaries. No one could be a Chaucer scholar without some knowledge of Chaucer's French and Italian sources. A student of Milton will have to peer into Hebraic, Greek, Latin and Italian literatures. This is true even of our own darkly nationalistic age. We cannot fully understand Arnold Bennett without a knowledge of the influence of Maupassant, Edith Wharton without Paul Bourget, Katherine Mansfield without Chekhov, James Branch Cabell without Anatole France, George Bernard Shaw without Ibsen and Voltaire.

It may be contended, however, that foreign influences act only as modifiers of the national tradition, which remains the fundamental element. An Anglomaniac Frenchman like Voltaire remains a Frenchman all the same; a Gallophile and Gallicized Briton like Gibbon is none the less a thorough Briton. One man or one nation may borrow from another a set of terms, a doctrine, a technique, perhaps a new shade of thought or feeling; the underlying reality is unchanged. There are few things in literary history more dramatic than the success of Lord Byron on the Continent. Poets everywhere forsook their national masters to follow the lead of the prestigious English rebel. But Byron was so successful only because the Continent, through Rousseau, through Goethe and Schiller in their earliest works, through Chateaubriand, had independently reached the stage of Byronism.

Granted; but this only brings out the fact that all great literatures go through very much the same phases, almost at the same time. In other words, this emphasizes the unity of European culture. Within that unity, there are two sets of differences. The first are historical, and are manifested in the *periods;* the second are geographical, and separate the *nations.*

Between these two sets, nationality has the advantage of possessing a definite legal existence. Every man is registered as belonging to a nation, whereas the "spirit of the time" is but a shadowy sovereign. So we think more naturally of Edmund Spenser, for instance, as "an Englishman of the Renaissance" than as "a man of the Renaissance who happened to live in England." Yet, in the domain of culture, the period may actually be more real, more significant than the nation. There is greater resemblance among the European minds of a given age, such as the Enlightenment, than between a medieval Englishman and his distant mid-Victorian posterity. If you examine an old portrait, you will first of all be conscious of the period to which it belongs. It is only on closer scrutiny that you may be able to detect the nationality of the subject. There are fashions in clothes, but also fashions in expression and in modes of thought, which sweep the whole Western world. The proper unit for detailed study, then, would be a phase of civilization— the Romantic Revolt, for instance, or the Realistic Reaction— rather than any national group.

Nor should we fail to take into account, in pre-war Europe at any rate, the existence of class distinctions more rigid than national boundaries. For frontiers, now so sharply drawn, were long uncertain; what seems to us a vestige of feudal chaos survived into the Classical Age, and even after the French Revolution. Alsace, for instance, could at the same time be under the French crown and yet remain connected in many ways with the Holy Roman Empire. Less than a hundred years ago, Neuchâtel was still both a Prussian principality and a part of republican Switzerland. But, if a member of the nobility might hesitate about his national allegiance, he had no doubt whatever about his own rank, and the abyss that separated him from a commoner. Traces of such a state of mind can be found even in our own days. On the battlefield, all classes will fight with equal heroism for king and country. On the morrow, an aristocrat will give his daughter in marriage to a foreign aristocrat rather than to a plebeian of his own country.

This condition has a bearing upon literature. Members of the upper class, because they lived the same kind of life, inspired and enjoyed everywhere the same kind of art. Chrétien of Troyes, master of chivalric romance in the second half of the twelfth century, provided all Europe with patterns of refined love. Early in the sixteenth century, it was Baldassare Castiglione who, in his *Courtier*, defined the aristocratic ideal, for Englishmen and Frenchmen as well as for Italians. The spread of French literature under Louis XIV and Louis XV was due, not exclusively to its classic perfection, but in a large measure to the social prestige of Versailles and the Paris salons.

On the other hand, the common people also mingled with their kind across the uncertain border; they swapped stories, edifying or broadly satirical, on the market place and the fair ground, or along the pilgrimage routes. This prevented the formation of narrow regionalism, even in those days when communications were precarious and indeed perilous. It explains why the folk epic, *Reynard the Fox*, achieved such universal currency, and why the very same merry tales and farces, apparently home-grown and racy of the soil, are found in practically every land. There was a time when Christendom was a single pyramid, made up of the same social layers.

We must be cautious, however, not to over-emphasize the cleavage between these layers. There was, inevitably, a large amount of interpenetration. Lords, and even ladies, in all likelihood, enjoyed the rough-and-tumble humor of the populace. The "lower orders" have always craved for an insight into the magic existence of their "betters." There are, therefore, twilight zones between the cultures of the various classes, just as there are intermediate regions—Belgium, Switzerland—between the clashing worlds of Latin and Teuton. But the social class constitutes none the less a "climate" which influences literature more definitely than does the nation.

If the nation were but the political state, our demonstration would be fairly conclusive. But the idea of nation is complex. Ideally, the nation should be a territorial unit, under the same rule and *speaking the same language*. A genuine nation with a multiplicity of tongues, like Switzerland, is a miraculous exception.

Nowhere is this complete identity of linguistic and political boundaries fully attained. There are still many non-Germans within the Reich, and many Germans without. The English-speaking world is divided into two nations, and the Spanish world into twenty. France, so often supposed to be the model of a conscious nation, "one and indivisible," has to struggle even yet to impose linguistic unity within her European borders. It is perhaps because every nation is still in the making that national feeling is everywhere running so high.

From the point of view of culture, the *language group*, when it does not coincide with the political, is by far the more important factor. Indeed, in the study of what we call "national" literatures, the strictly political division is usually ignored. No one would think of eliminating Jean Jacques Rousseau from French literature because he was a citizen of Geneva. At the time when Germany was torn into hundreds of principalities, her literature was one—and great. In the nineteenth century, no *Anschluss* was required to bring the Austrian Grillparzer into the fold; and the Swiss Gottfried Keller is a German of the spirit. It would be an evil day for America if all the great British writers since the Revolution were voted *aliens*.

We may still maintain that a *language* is not the best natural unit for the study of literature; that the *period*, the *social class*, perhaps also the *theme* or the *kind*, would provide a better framework. But an artificial barrier, like a Maginot line of fortification, may be a formidable obstacle. World Literature is hampered by language differences far more than the other arts or than the sciences. Even mathematicians and chemists suffer through the lack of a common medium; but their basic symbols, at any rate, are universal, and the findings of Swedish or Italian research may be accurately checked in an American laboratory. The painting, the sculpture, and especially the music of foreign groups may at times demand special initiation; but their essential conventions, if not world-wide, are at any rate pan-European. Chinese music may be meaningless to us; but we can understand Debussy or Sibelius without the need of a translation. On the contrary, even for the most receptive and sensitive mind, the very best book in an unknown tongue is dead.

This difficulty can never be fully overcome. A universal language is a very remote possibility; and many lovers of literature doubt whether it would be clear gain.[1] We are imprisoned within the confines of our own speech: a frontier harder to cross than the bristling border between two hostile countries. *Yet World Literature does exist:* Germany knows Shakespeare, and England knows Goethe. There is no more striking proof of Western unity than this victory, however incomplete, over what might seem an impassable barrier.

At all times there were men, merchants and diplomats, whose business it was to cross the frontier. Many of these were not wholly impervious to culture; yet their influence on literary intercourse has not been very great. More important are those adventurous spirits for whom a barrier is a challenge. They are not equally numerous in every age and nation, and especially they are not evenly successful. In periods of serene self-satisfaction, conformity and tradition prevail: Boileau knew something of Italian and Spanish writers, but only to scorn them; the literatures of the North, for him, were lost in Cimmerian darkness; everything that was not bathed in clear, classical light vanished from his sight. But there are self-critical moments when eternal conformity grows wearisome. These are not necessarily times of decadence, self-depreciation and despair. They may be on the contrary periods of eagerness and

[1] Prophecy and objection apply to a *universal* language, not to a neutral *auxiliary* language.

hope, true *Renaissances,* with all the proud and joyous connotations of that word. It is the most vigorous ages that dare to travel and to borrow. A culture afraid of the least wind from across the border is confessing decrepitude.

There is therefore a fitful but unceasing process of interchange between national cultures. The balance of spiritual trade may shift with brutal suddenness; then the infiltration of foreign thoughts and phrases turns into an invasion; and the conservatives are appalled at what seems to them a catastrophe. Thus, in France, the irruption of Italianism in the sixteenth century was resented and denounced; so was the Romantic cult for English and German poets two hundred years later; or, at the end of the nineteenth century, the craze for Russian novelists and Scandinavian dramatists. Such a reaction is wholesome, when it seeks to check a mere vogue, the passing favor attaching to forms, tricks or poses; no master is good simply because he is foreign. But, on the other hand, no influence is bad simply because it is new and different. It is foolish to reject a gift from abroad on the plea that it is "alien to our spirit"; if it were so alien, our spirit would reject it automatically. The fact that Englishmen in the eighteenth century appreciated French wit simply proves that French wit was not un-English. Anglo-German romanticism would not have fructified so magnificently on French soil, if that soil had not been ready for such a crop. A foreign influence simply liberates us from artificial limitations, and reveals to us our own possibilities.

This process of international borrowing comprises several phases, which may or may not be carried through by the same man. The first step is obviously the *actual learning of foreign languages.* This is indispensable, but by no means sufficient. Many professional linguists, traders, scholars, teachers, interpreters, do not help very directly in the diffusion of foreign literatures. Two keys are needed, and if the first is, inevitably, knowledge, the second must be *appreciation.*

Thus one pioneer forces the barrier, takes hold of foreign

treasures. He must now bring them back to his own people. This is done through *translation, propaganda,* and *conscious imitation:* three methods which do not invariably follow in the same order. To take a concrete case, Voltaire knew English, appreciated Shakespeare, revealed the very existence of Shakespeare to the general public in France, and showed, in his tragedies, faint but distinct traces of Shakespearian influence. But it was reserved for an obscure hackwriter, Letourneur, to give the first translation; for a forgotten dramatist, Ducis, to bring out the first stage versions; while it was not until a whole generation later, about 1825, that the full impact of Shakespeare's power was felt in France, with Vitet, Vigny, Dumas and Victor Hugo. The process of assimilation, which in this case remains very incomplete, took nearly a hundred years. Coleridge, to give another example, traveled in Germany, translated from the German (in particular Schiller's *Wallenstein*), and showed in his philosophy and criticism the unmistakable influence of German thought. In Carlyle, all the various stages of the process are found. He knew German, appreciated German, translated Goethe's *Wilhelm Meister*, imitated, in his *Sartor Resartus*, the style of the German romantic humorists, appointed himself the chief propaganda agent for German culture; in many of his pages, we do not know whether we are hearing Germany expressing herself with a Scotch burr, or Scotland with a German accent. It was William Archer who translated and staged Ibsen; but it was George Bernard Shaw who made himself, in his own irrepressible way, the apostle of Ibsenism. A crop of "would-be Ibsenians" was followed by a crop of "Ibsenians without knowing it": all that remained lacking was an English Ibsen. The very last stage, most important of all, and hardest to define, is that of *complete absorption. Madame Bovary* was the pattern that innumerable modern novels followed; but writers and public no longer realize their obligation to Gustave Flaubert.

This study of international influences is technically known as *Comparative Literature*. The term, thus restricted, is a misnomer. There is scarcely any valid kind of criticism that is not based upon comparison: comparison between authors in the same field, comparison with earlier work of the same author, comparison with "standards" which are themselves the result of comparison: Aristotle's *Poetics*, founded on the examination of all the Greek plays known to him, is a perfect example of the "comparative" method. To trace influences is "comparative," even when the writers concerned used the same language. What Keats consciously owed to Milton, for instance, is as well worth examining as what he borrowed from Boccaccio.

It is not invariably futile to fight against a misleading word; once the glorious period of St. Thomas Aquinas was known as "the Dark Ages"; now that expression is seldom used by reputable historians. So we register our protest against the term *Comparative Literature;* and we must confess in the same breath that we have no better one to suggest. Rightly or wrongly named, Comparative Literature is an extensive and fascinating subject. It tends to break down our inevitable tendency to parochialism. It places masterpieces in their proper line of descent, and among their peers. When we take it for granted that Milton is the product of European culture as a whole, and a factor in European culture, our understanding of Milton will be greatly deepened.

The weakness of Comparative Literature is that it emphasizes the accident of individual foreign influences, and minimizes the deeper reality of common elements. It does not much matter whether a thing was said first in English and then in French, and whether the Frenchman knew that the Englishman had said it before; what does matter is that both wanted and tried to say the same thing. The men who revealed England to eighteenth-century France, ahead of Voltaire and Montesquieu, were, as individuals, of secondary importance; they merely proved that the developments of England and France were then so synchronized that communications between the two could be established even through mediocrities. In other terms, *Comparative Literature* would be an extremely minor branch of study, if it did not lead to *General Literature*; and by that we mean the consideration of literary problems beyond the national field, such as period, theme, school, kind, spirit. This was the ambition of the Danish critic Georg Brandes in his *Main Currents in Nineteenth Century Literature*. It is interesting to note that the French masters who have created a very active school of Comparative Literature, Fernand Baldensperger, Paul Hazard, Paul Van Tieghem, are all advocates of the wider conception.

Certain authorities choose to establish a four-fold division: Universal Literature, World Literature, Comparative Literature, General Literature. *Universal Literature*, in this scheme, stands for the fullest possible expansion of our field: it embraces all literatures, of all ages, in all languages, without insisting on their unity or their relations. *World Literature* is limited to those works which are enjoyed in common, ideally by all mankind, practically by our own group of culture, the European or Western. In both these cases, the word *Literature* applies to a body of literary works, not to their critical study. *Comparative Literature* and *General Literature*, on the contrary, are methods of approach. The first is concerned with the mutual influences between various national literatures; the second with those problems which are present in the literature of every epoch and every country. We do not deny the validity and the convenience of these distinctions. But they should not be over-emphasized. They do not represent four separate branches of learning; they deal with the same material and use the same mental disciplines. They are four aspects of a single subject: *literature*.

SUMMARY

Goethe was the godfather of World Literature. But this exalted patronage might give a wrong impression: World Literature begins in the nursery, not in the graduate school. The most modest readers have access to World Literature, in the form of the Bible, even when they have never heard of the term. World Literature is, "not a theory, but a condition."

The division of literature into national compartments or departments, English, French, German, etc., is recent and not eternal. For centuries, the approach to the study of literature was through the ancient Classics, and the unity of Western Culture was fully recognized.

Within that unity, there are two sets of differences: in space and time, *nations* and *periods*. From the cultural point of view, the periods, although not so sharply defined, are actually more real than the nations, and form a better unit for study. Even the social classes are more influential in this respect than political geography. Repeatedly, the aristocracy of Europe enjoyed the same or similar books very much at the same time; and popular literature also had common themes and a common spirit throughout the Continent.

The unity of European literature is veiled, but not destroyed, by language differences. These create barriers worse even than military frontiers; yet there are explorers who venture beyond the border, and bring back the products of other groups. The study of these international influences is technically known as *Comparative Literature:* a misnomer, for most forms of criticism, in one way or another, make use of the comparative method.

For the sake of clearness, we shall then distinguish:

1. *Universal Literature:* the sum total of all writings in all languages at all times.

2. *World Literature:* the body of those works enjoyed in common, ideally by all mankind, practically by our own Western group of civilization.

3. *Comparative Literature:* the study of relations, in the literary field, between different national or linguistic groups.

4. *General Literature:* the study of problems common to all literatures; this study might also be called *Principles of Criticism;* it finds its best examples in the works which belong to World Literature.

CHAPTER II

THE INDISPENSABLE INSTRU-MENT: TRANSLATION

THE FIRST key to World Literature is the learning of foreign languages. But it is a key so unwieldy that most of us, it must be admitted, renounce every hope of possessing it. Languages are actively studied in American high schools and colleges; but seldom are they thoroughly mastered. The pressure of technical and utilitarian subjects is too great; and even greater is the competition of sports and social pleasures. "We are so busy being human," said a youth in self-defense, "that we have no time for the humanities."

The situation could be remedied to some extent if the study of languages were frankly directed to the acquisition of a reading knowledge. To write and speak French or German with correctness, elegance and facility is indeed a heavy undertaking. It must remain a privilege and a luxury. The utilitarians, on their own chosen ground, are right: not one high school graduate in a thousand will have any practical need of writing and speaking any language but his own. On the contrary, a reading knowledge can be acquired with comparatively little effort, and the results it yields are immediate as well as abundant. There is no clerk in a country store whose life would not be enriched if he had direct access to the treasures of another literature. It would give him the exhilaration of release and of spiritual adventure, the welcome sense that the world is not a dismal interminable conglomeration of Gopher Prairies. It would enable him to look upon Gopher Prairie with critical eyes; and by critical, we mean understanding rather than depreciative: "What should they know of Gopher Prairie, who only Gopher Prairie know?"

For that deepening of experience, it is not necessary to be a Cardinal Mezzofanti, who spoke fifty or sixty languages with ease, and was acquainted with many others. The mastery of even a single foreign tongue is sufficient to break down the wall of provincialism. The reform we advocate, shifting the emphasis from the languages in themselves to the literatures they convey, has to face one great moral objection: it would make easy, and even pleasant, a branch of study at present proverbially hard. Our puritanical conscience balks at what might seem a capitulation to slackness. But the puritanical conscience is not always the best guide in matters of pedagogy; and a class in literature can be made as exacting, and if required, as forbidding, as a class in elementary grammar.

But even if the possession of several languages remained a necessary qualification for a scholar and a gentleman, it would not suffice. World masterpieces are found in more languages than even the professional philologist can be expected to master. Rare indeed are the men of culture who can read in the original, and with literary enjoyment, books in Chinese, Sanskrit, Arabic, Hebrew, and even Greek or Russian. It is an inexorable fact that our main line of approach must be through translation.

Nothing is so stubborn as a fact; but the refusal to face a fact may, for generations, be just as stubborn, and appear successful. To the present day, there are excellent scholars who decline to recognize the validity of any literature in translation. If we were to believe them, we should have no right to be moved by the beauty of the English Bible; it would have been better for Keats if he never had opened Chapman's Homer; it was a mistake for Chapman to translate Homer at all; and we should deny ourselves the illicit pleasure of reading Tolstoy or Dostoevsky in any language but the original Russian. I am hardly exaggerating: I have a letter from a great American critic, who happens to know Russian, but not German. He has stoically deprived himself of the great experience of reading *Buddenbrooks* and *The Magic Mountain*, although the perspicuous beauty of Thomas Mann's style survives particularly well the ordeal of translation.

However, it would not be safe to dismiss as absurd the opinion of men whose achievements and judgment we are bound to respect. Their reluctance to accept translation as genuine literature, although excessive, is not difficult to understand. The literary experience, whether in creation or appreciation, requires the intimate fusion of matter and form. The true poetical note is absolutely unique; the same feeling, expressed in different words, no longer is quite the same feeling. It is the exquisitely personal accent that creates *style*; and honest writing, without style, is business or science, but not literature.

There is profound truth in this contention. But it should not be turned into a rigid dogma; for in literature, truth, no less than beauty, depends on delicate and elusive shades rather than upon hard and fast distinctions. There are cases in which translation stands condemned; there are others in which, however inadequate, it will serve; there are others still in which the gain is immeasurably greater than the loss.

It is on the lowest level that the impossibility of translation is most apparent: hardly any pun can be rendered into another language. In French, *Pierre* means both Peter and a rock; in English, the identity disappears. Rostand's *Cyrano de Bergerac* is a crackling machine-gun fire of puns, including the aggravated kind known as *à peu près*, or near-pun. The play was none the less a brilliant success in many languages. Rough equivalents did the trick. What signified was not the actual pun, a poor thing at best, but the punning spirit, an evidence of insolent gaiety and bravado, as prominent a feature in Cyrano's picturesque figure as his waving plume or his enormous nose.

Almost as untranslatable as the pun is the melody of words. If a poem is sheer music in the material sense, if sound is emphasized at the expense of thought or feeling, then the magic disappears when the medium of expression is changed. Swinburne's alliterations, excessive even in English, would become nonsensical in French. Edgar Poe's *The Bells* would turn into a jarring jingle. The opulent rhymes and sprightly rhythms of Théodore de Banville, which, in French, have a lovely, lightsome, fantastic effect, would, in any other language, seem mere verbal acrobatics. There again, the loss is small: no poem is supreme by virtue of music alone. If literal translation is an impossibility, imitation remains open, provided it be deemed worth while.

There is, however, a subtler, less obtrusive kind of music which is the very essence of poetry, and which evaporates in transposition. The lines

> Break, break, break,
> On thy cold gray stones, o sea!

have in their absolute simplicity the true Tennysonian ring, which is not to be despised. George du Maurier, in his delightful *Vers Nonsensiques à l'Usage des Familles Anglaises*, offered this rendering:

> *Cassez vous, cassez vous, cassez vous,*
> *O mer, sur vos froids gris cailloux!*

which is literally perfect, and perfectly ludicrous. This is willful parody; but it clearly indicates a line which translation can hardly attempt to cross without self-destruction. The difficulty is not the same in every language and with every poet; and there may be translators whose miraculous gifts push back the limits of possibility; but, if the danger line is flexible, it is none the less inexorable.

It would be idle to deny that certain authors can never be fully known in translation. Byron's obvious attitude made him a European figure; Shelley's unearthly music is appreciated abroad only by a handful of thorough scholars. All that most

Americans understand of Victor Hugo's verse is the resounding rhetoric. The marvelous orchestration, the poignant delicacy which constantly accompanies the enormous blare and is not drowned by it, the underlying sense of tragic mystery and awe, all this is lost on the foreign reader; so that Victor Hugo in World Literature remains the very great popular romancer of *Les Misérables,* rather than the supreme lyric and epic poet of *Contemplations* and *The Legend of the Centuries.*

However, Mark Van Doren's daring and very successful *Anthology of World Poetry* has proved that there was at least a craving for the enlargement of our lyrical experience beyond the confines of our native speech. Granted that the best of these efforts are adaptations rather than literal renderings; in the case of the *Rubáiyát* of Omar Khayyám *and* Fitzgerald, a hybrid, the fruit of remote collaboration, rather than even an adaptation; still we are the richer by this straining toward the unattainable. Goethe's *Wanderer's Nightsongs,* done into English by Longfellow, are not quite Goethe's, but they are better than anything else in Longfellow.

Poetry, or that poetical element which is the essence of all style worthy of the name, is music as well as sense. But the music does not necessarily reside in the words. The overtones which make expression truly great are in the soul, not in the voice. This may sound like idealistic nonsense: let us take a concrete illustration. There is magic in the distant sound of bugle or hunting horn in the woods at eve. On this obvious theme, Tennyson wrote *"The splendour falls . . ."* in *The Princess;* Alfred de Vigny, *The Horn.* Tennyson's lyric is a masterly technical achievement. He is coolly aware of the opportunities offered by the theme, and coolly determined to display the resources of his art. With the unerring selection of glamorous echoing words, with inner rhymes, alliterations, repetitions, he transcribes the effect of music with a skill we frankly—and coolly—admire. Tennyson is untranslatable: a transcription of this marvelous transcription would fall flat. It would be another *Cassez vous, cassez vous, cassez vous.* Vigny is not a virtuoso, but a stoic. We hear no audible music: we feel by inner response the deep vibrations of music in a grave and tender soul. The words are not indifferent; they are perfect in French, in their quiet restraint. But equally perfect words in English could restore exactly the innermost song that is in Vigny. This, of course, could be achieved only by a great poet, with the dramatist's gift of sympathetic insight; but it is not inconceivable. Vigny's poem is at least a candidate for World Literature; Tennyson's cannot leave its native soil.

The truth in this matter was expressed by the Greek critic Longinus many centuries ago: there is a sublimity which is inherent in the thought, and which therefore is universal. Longinus gave as an example: "Let there be light"—perhaps the first time the Bible was appreciated purely as literature. The stark majesty of these words stands unaltered in Hebrew, in Greek, in English; and it would lose nothing in Tagalog or in Esperanto.

In every great writer, there are verbal felicities, which must remain within the circle of the original language, and deeper notes, capable of appealing to all mankind. If the quips and pranks and spirited conceits cannot be translated, they may, in many cases, be imitated very much in the same vein; the call of the soul to the soul is direct, profound and universal. The Elizabethan clevernesses of Shakespeare are delightful because of their English accent. There are moments when Shakespeare is not "Elizabethan," not "English" and not "clever": he is Shakespeare. "To be or not to be," "The rest is silence," belong to the world.

So there is a *World Literature* even in the realm of poetry, which seems hopelessly divided by language barriers. The greatest French poet of our age, Paul Claudel, learned his art from the Bible, Walt Whitman, and perhaps even Nietzsche, not from Boileau, Lamartine, or Verlaine. American lovers of poetry are more deeply influenced by Villon, Baudelaire, Mallarmé, and, in a limited field, Heredia, than by certain American classics that every child knows by heart.

In the case of prose, the objection is slightly different. The harmonics and overtones which, it is alleged, belong to the language and cannot be translated, are not strictly musical, but cultural. Two words like *king* and *roi*, like *boy* and *garçon*, may be given as equivalent in the dictionary, but their connotations are different. He who was not brought up in the American scene, whose ears were not attuned to American speech, whose palate does not respond to American savors, will never fully understand American letters. Whatever lexicographers may say, no *flan au potiron* can ever hope to be *pumpkin pie*. Conversely, it is argued that no American can ever read a foreign book without inflicting upon it some distortion, at times frankly ludicrous.

That translation is impossible is one of those impressive assertions in which profundity is artfully blended with mystification. Every book is "translated" by every reader into terms of his own experience. When he comes across the word *hills*, his imagination, if it be vivid at all, will evoke the hills which are familiar to his eyes. The experiences of all Americans do not by any means coincide; much of the "American Scene" remains, geographically or socially, foreign to most of us. *Death Comes for the Archbishop*, by Willa Cather, is an American masterpiece, written by an American and for Americans; the scene is laid in America; the subject is an authentic part of American history. But, among the thousands who have read this great book with delight, many have never been within hundreds of miles of Santa Fe; there is nothing in their memory that corresponds with the austere and yet friendly majesty of its landscape; nothing that will give them a clue to Indian or Mexican mentality; nothing that will enable them to fathom the soul of a priest.

If we could appreciate only the things of our own daily life, we never could enjoy any book with a setting remote in space or time. All exotic, all historical, as well as all foreign, literature, would be sealed against us. Even the masterpieces of England, and Shakespeare's first of all, would be meaningless.

Fortunately, this is not the case. For the plain man as well as for the man of culture, literature is no mere reproduction of experience, but an extension and a deepening.

The desire for extension is obvious. We all crave to travel, in the spirit, beyond the circle of our petty cares; to reach strange lands of thought, and plow unknown seas; to associate with great kings, great lovers and great criminals. Adolescent romanticism if you like; but phonographic realism and sociological reports will never quite supplant it. The deepening of experience does not require that we should start from the humble details of our daily existence. On the contrary, it may be clear gain to brush them aside. It is good that our spirit should escape from its immediate environment, so that we may better realize what is profoundly and eternally human in ourselves. The first, and lesser, benefit of World Literature is to reveal to us the picturesque, the delightful variety of mankind. The greater benefit is to make us conscious of its fundamental unity.

When Jack Smith of Middletown translates Henry James into terms of Jack Smith's experience, there is an obvious wastage; still Jack Smith will be the richer even for his faulty reading. When Charles Grandgent or Melville Best Anderson, great Dante scholars, pondered over the *Divine Comedy*, there was, even for them, a loss. They could never know all that Dante knew, they could never see all that he had seen. To such a loss they were resigned; they thought only of the immeasurable gain. I may not catch in *Buddenbrooks* the fine details and the subtle shades which are obvious to a Lübeck burgher. But I see far more in *Buddenbrooks* than in many novels about my own California. It is not inconceivable that you will enjoy Victor Hugo's *Notre Dame* better than Sinclair Lewis's *Work of Art*, that matchless handbook for hotel managers. If such be the case, let no abstract dogma stand in the way of your legitimate enjoyment.

It must be confessed that many translations are bad; and so are not a few original works. Translation is a thankless task:

difficult, ill-rewarded, despised. For that reason, it is too often abandoned to hackwriters of doubtful competence. Because we have such a poor opinion of translations and translators, we are contemptuously tolerant of inferior work. *Traduttore, traditore:* translator, betrayer, is an ancient, but not ill-humored jibe; the poor devil is doing his best. And when Woodrow Wilson said: "To hear one's words translated is to witness the compound fracture of an idea," he did so with a smile. If we realized the essential part that translation must play in world culture, we should grow less scornful and more exacting.

No art is to be despised as parasitic because it depends upon some other art. All performers—conductors, instrumentalists, vocalists, actors—are only interpreters; the composer, the dramatist, alone can claim full originality. Yet a performer is an artist in his own right, and may be a great artist. He does not mechanically transmit a work of art: he interprets and re-creates it. Paradoxically, a singer may be greater than his song, an actor than the text he is using as his medium. Sarah Bernhardt gave some semblance of poetical life to the gaudy melodramas of Victorien Sardou, and Sir Henry Irving to even cheaper plays, like *The Bells.*

But if the common run of translations is poor, it should not be forgotten that the art has been practiced by the very greatest. Goethe and Schiller translated both masterpieces and trifles. In England, Chaucer, Milton, Dryden, Pope, Fielding, Coleridge, Carlyle, George Eliot, did not spurn the lowly craft. Nor is the tradition in abeyance; for among translators in the twentieth century could be mentioned the leaders in French literature, Maurice Maeterlinck, Paul Claudel, André Gide, Marcel Proust, Jules Romains;[1] in America, George Santayana, Ludwig Lewisohn, Van Wyck Brooks, Edna St. Vincent Millay. . . . The contributors of translations to Mark Van Doren's *Anthology of World Poetry* constitute a very creditable roll of fame.

---

[1] A striking example of *World Literature* was offered by the success, in Paris, of Ben Jonson's *Volpone,* adapted by Jules Romains and Stefan Zweig.

That great writers should consent to act as translators need not surprise us. In one respect, the translator's attitude is one of humility; he abdicates initiative; he is willing to serve, not to command. In another respect, translation means proud collaboration. What exultation if Goethe, at the height of his fame, had consented to accept our aid! Now that he can no longer help himself, we are free to impose our partnership upon him. But that partnership possesses to a high degree the same merits as co-operation with the living man. It compels us to attune ourselves to his thoughts, to his moods, to his familiar and unconscious tricks. We must create in ourselves a self after Goethe's image, before we can translate Goethe at all. Every word not of the obvious kind is a challenge. We have to surmise the exact shade that Goethe had in mind, even—sacrilegious thought!—when Goethe's mind had remained in a convenient haze. So every translation worthy of the name becomes an interpretation, a commentary, a criticism. Nothing should be more ennobling than this wrestling with a great spirit. Like Jacob with the angel, we can compel a blessing.

This great dignity of translation should be more fully recognized in our universities. We need advanced courses—and very arduous courses they would be—in thorough translation. A version of some foreign classic, combining scholarly care with literary merit, might very well be accepted in lieu of a Master's thesis. And, in self-defense against botchers, conscientious translators should band themselves into an effective guild. They should insist that the work even of their qualified members be submitted to a competent board of revision; the editors of the very best firms are notoriously slack in this respect. Authors, publishers, public, need to be protected against unscrupulous middlemen.

There is one advantage that a translation possesses over an original work: it can be amended, and if need be discarded and superseded. We may feel that Proust's last volumes were left in a very imperfect condition; but we have no right to correct or complete his manuscript. And, when a masterpiece grows archaic, like Chaucer's *Canterbury Tales*, we greatly hesitate (far more than our ancestors did) before attempting to modernize it. Classic rank imposes upon a text a frozen dignity perilously akin to death. With a translation, our freedom is restored. Professor Zeitlin, for instance, in his very fine edition of Montaigne's *Essays*, did not feel compelled to reprint Cotton's version *verbatim*. The French are still trying to translate Shakespeare: it is to be hoped that each new version is both more Shakespearian and more French than the last. It is meet that every century, nay every generation, should have its own Homer and its own Dante. T. E. Lawrence's *Odyssey* and W. H. D. Rouse's *Story of Odysseus*, in a most welcome fashion, have renewed the freshness of that great tale of adventure.

Our conception of World Literature, to sum up this long discussion, is but the negation of a negation. It is the refusal to accept as final, in matters of the spirit, the limitations of political allegiance or local dialect. Our field is *living literature*. Whatever quickens in us the sense of life is part of *our* literature, even though it was first said in Hebrew or in Greek. Conversely, a writer may still be active, and he may use the purest "American": if he means nothing to us, he is dead.

In thus defining the domain of literature without reference to the map, we are not preaching internationalism: we are only noting elementary and uncontroverted facts. It is those who would introduce the question of nationality into the esthetic field who are guilty of injecting a political element where it does not belong. This is as futile as to inject it into religion or science. In culture, internationalism is the basic fact. Isolation, *autarky*, is delusion or self-mutilation.

But this brand of internationalism is perfectly compatible with the highest patriotism. If we love our own community, we shall be all the more eager to enrich it with the best which has been thought and said in the world; and, reciprocally, we shall desire to contribute our best to the common hoard of mankind. There is no place in all this for an inferiority complex. English Literature, of which the American branch is no less vigorous and no less legitimate than the British, is, by universal consent, second to none. We give, and we are more than willing to give, fully as much as we receive. Let us have the freest trade in spiritual goods: we need not be afraid of an adverse balance.

SUMMARY

For World Literature to come into existence, the language barrier must be overcome. This cannot be done except through the acquisition of foreign languages—a formidable task, if by acquisition we mean thorough mastery. But a mere reading knowledge is far more accessible, and would bring abundant reward to every high school student.

However, not even professional scholars can know even all the major culture languages, and the indispensable instrument of World Literature is translation. But translation is still distrusted, and even despised. It is claimed that in art intention and form are inseparable, and that every translation is bound to destroy this vital unity.

Obviously no translation can render literally that which depends altogether upon the sounds of a particular language: puns or verbal music. Only equivalents can be offered. Lyric poetry is far more difficult to render into a foreign tongue than narrative or drama. Plain sense, on the other hand, can easily be translated; and, beyond plain sense, there is a poetry which lies in the ideas or feelings themselves and their association. This deeper poetry also can be translated: the supreme passages in the Bible and Shakespeare are universal in their appeal.

Every book, even in our own language and dealing with our own country, requires a *translation* from the terms of the writer's experience to those of the reader's. Fortunately, man is able to make such an adjustment, and to feel the human element under the infinite variety of forms. Without such a capacity, there could be no communication between man and man. It is the extension of this capacity that makes communication possible between age and age, nation and nation, language and language, and accounts for the undeniable existence of World Literature.

In spite of grievous handicaps, translation has been practiced by great writers in the past, and the tradition is not lost. It is an exacting but ennobling task to co-operate with a foreign genius, to attune yourself to his thought, and to make his words your words.

Translation offers one advantage over original work: it can more readily be corrected, perfected, brought up to date, by successive generations. Every age has, and should have, its new translation of Homer or Dante.

The essential thought of these two introductory chapters is that World Literature is the negation of a negation. It is the refusal to accept as final, in matters of the spirit, the limitations of political allegiance or local dialect. Our field is not this or that national literature, but *Living Literature*. Whatever quickens in us the sense of life is part of *our* literature, even if it was first said in Hebrew, Greek or German.

This is an internationalism of the spirit which is not merely compatible with the highest patriotism, but identical with it. We want to enrich our community with the best which has been thought and said in the world.

CHAPTER III

THE TREASURE HOUSE

CULTURE, like World Literature, is associated in our minds with Goethe, and is thus entitled to our reverence. In the English-speaking world, it was chiefly Matthew Arnold who gave the term its slightly wearisome authority. We shall strive, at a later stage, to consider with some fullness the idea of culture. At this point, we must first discuss a conception for which Arnold is often made responsible: namely, that culture consists in "getting to know the best which has been thought and said in the world."

Arnold offered several definitions of culture, and the best known of them does contain the dangerous phrase. But it is far more complex than that, so complex indeed and so sinuous that it gets positively tangled.[1] But the involved qualifications are forgotten, and the simpler idea still prevails in minds that are far from primitive: *Culture is to be found in a set of books.* Get the right books, read the right books—a quarter of an hour a day will suffice—and you will turn into a man of unimpeachable culture. The process of transmuting a five-foot shelf into "sweetness and light" is perhaps not quite so automatic.

The belief that culture is embodied in a Canon, or Authorized Collection, of the Best Books acquired its strength through

[1] "The whole scope of the essay is to recommend culture as the great help out of our present difficulties; culture being a pursuit of our total perfection, by means of getting to know, in all the matters which most concern us, the best which has been thought and said in the world; and through this knowledge, turning a stream of fresh and free thought upon our stock notions and habits, which we now follow staunchly but mechanically, vainly imagining that there is a virtue in following them staunchly which makes up for the mischief of following them mechanically." *Culture and Anarchy*, Preface.

analogy with that "Library of Sacred Literature" which we call the Holy Bible. These writings, and these alone, contain the words of eternal life. All others, excellent as they may be on their own plane, are secondary in both senses of the term. Either they treat of lower things; or, if they deal with religion, their light is borrowed from the only source of light.

This conception created a habit of thought which was transmitted, with hardly any attenuation, into the realm of secular literature.[1] The classics of antiquity were revered as a second revelation. Their rarity, their remoteness, their perfection, set them apart from all other books. No modern could attain greatness, except by recovering some fragment of ancient splendor. For centuries, our education was founded on that principle. "The Humanities" had no less definite a basis than "Divinity." Boileau, who was the literary conscience of classical France, would have defined culture in very simple and unequivocal terms: to know the classics of Greece and Rome. There was in him a strain of modernism, but he did not confess it to himself. When Perrault, in 1687, suggested that "moderns" could stand on their own feet and even challenge their masters, Boileau thundered against the blasphemer.

Our yearning for an authoritative list of World Literature is the interminable twilight of Boileau's ideal. It haunts us even today with nostalgic poignancy; for it stands so sure in such a serene light. Yet forces were at work in Boileau's own lifetime, which were to disrupt his admirably balanced culture. The enormous growth of literatures in the vernacular could no longer be ignored. The northern nations, less directly dominated by the spirit of Greece and Rome, asserted themselves. It was impossible, although such a great critic as Lessing attempted the task, to confine Shakespeare within the Aristotelian tradition. The revival of interest and pride in our own origins, in the primitive monuments of our national literatures, broke down the autocracy of Olympus. This revolution in

---

[1] It must be noted that already in Pagan Alexandria, there were authoritative lists of Best Books, or Canons of Classics.

thought, implicit in the isolated historian and philosopher Vico, gathered momentum throughout the eighteenth century; it found new power in the primitivistic teachings of Rousseau; it joined forces with the romantic quest for the picturesque; it became a definite doctrine with Herder. When "barbaric" works like the *Niebelungen* crashed their way into the urbane company of masterpieces, to draw a list of the "best books" became a formidable task. There was no longer any single criterion, dogmatic or traditional. The function of the critic was no longer to guard the gate, but to explore.

Still, the obstinate hope remained. The enormous and teeming chaos of the new world must be reduced to some kind of discipline. Who knows? Perhaps even the old discipline, the ancient hierarchy, with here and there a timely concession to the new elements, a commoner or a barbarian promoted to patrician standing. Hence the insistent demand for the official list of "the best which has been thought and said in the world," the books that are "necessary and sufficient," those "that every child should know": a list not so long as to discourage the busy modern man; catholic enough to reconcile all parties; yet definite enough to serve as an effective test of *culture*.

Of making many lists there is no end; but they need not be a weariness of the flesh. On the contrary, there are few more delectable parlor games. It is good, when studying World Literature, to come to some preliminary and flexible agreement as to the extent of the field. Any class or club interested in the subject would do well to begin with such a symposium. Even the isolated reader will find it profitable to take stock of his initial knowledge: the books he has read, those that he knows by reputation only, and which seem to him proper candidates for World Literature. Such a list does not claim objective and final value; it is open to constant revision. At any rate, the road into World Literature thus starts from your own doorsteps.

As we cannot conduct such a symposium with our readers, we shall take as our starting point Sir John Lubbock's once famous list, proposed in 1885. It may seem odd, in twentieth-century America, even to mention the opinion of a Victorian banker. But the task has never been attempted under more favorable circumstances. Sir John Lubbock, who was to become Lord Avebury, represented the educated general public at its very best. He wrote abundantly, but he was not a professional writer. He kept in close touch with University life, but he was not a cloistered Don. He was a man of affairs, a successful banker, a useful politician, and more than a mere popularizer in natural history. There was no aspect of English life to which he was a stranger. He did not draw up his list as a formidable fence for the protection of a social élite: he first offered it in an address before the Workingmen's College in London. He was too sensible to believe in his own inerrancy: he merely wanted to press the point that we should take thought in the selection of our reading. He started, as he had desired, a discussion in which the keenest minds in England took part. Matthew Arnold and Herbert Spencer refused to commit themselves. But Stanley the explorer and General Wolseley had their say; Swinburne and William Morris offered very thorough-going contributions; and John Ruskin joined the game with characteristic wrong-headedness and gusto. The names of the thirty-four participants evoke a rich, varied, well-integrated civilization: respectful of the past, looking into the future with friendliness, and without tormenting fear. If the task could have been done at all, no one had a better chance than Sir John Lubbock and his group of sane, earnest, educated gentlemen.

Yet, after a little over fifty years, Sir John's impressive effort strikes us as naïve, rather futile, and even a little ludicrous. Such is the liberating virtue of historical perspective. If Messrs. John Dewey, Owen D. Young, Robert Millikan, H. L. Mencken, Robert Frost, General Pershing and President Nicholas Murray Butler had sponsored such an undertaking in the nineteen thirties, we might still be ovcrawed. But it is almost certain that 1980 would smile.

Every list of this kind is open, in different measures, to the same objections. The first is the extreme difficulty of integrating Eastern cultures with our own. Sir John made at least a courageous attempt. He included Confucius, a French book about Buddha, the *Koran*, the *Mahabharata* and the *Ramayana*, Firdusi, and a book of Chinese odes. This is either too little or too much. If we want to get a true picture of man's cultural history, the East is woefully under-represented. If, on the contrary, the list is limited to those works which have directly contributed to the growth of our Western mind; or, more narrowly still, to those which are alive to us at this hour, then not one of the half-dozen books mentioned by Sir John is really indispensable. They belong to a Library of Useful Knowledge: they have no part in our literary experience.

In other words, the term *World Literature* is an obvious exaggeration. It simply betrays the arrogance of the West: *our* world is *the* world. There is no writing today that is genuinely world-wide, not even the Bible, although we strive to translate it into every tongue spoken by man. Only the merest fringe of the nearer East has genuinely influenced our art: those parts of the Bible which may be called Oriental in style and spirit, the *Arabian Nights*, and, almost by accident, Omar Khayyám.

Still, the term *World Literature* may be retained as the voicing of a distant hope. The universal appeal of certain silent films like Charlie Chaplin's confirms the impression which we get from the study of folklore: there are elements common to all mankind, which may form the basis of a genuinely world-wide literature. For lack of a common medium of expression, these universal elements are rudimentary; but they may be brought to fuller consciousness, through the World Literature that is in the making. In the meantime, it would be more accurate to call our field *Western* World Literature: a literature for Westerners, wherever they may be, and for Westernized Orientals.

A second, and perhaps more grievous, manifestation of the same egotism is the over-emphasis almost invariably given to our own literature. Lists which are supposed to represent the cosmopolitan outlook might have as their mottos, if not *Ourselves Alone!* or *Ourselves First, Last and All the Time!*, at any rate *Ourselves Above All Others!* Out of the hundred titles mentioned by Sir John Lubbock, only seven belong to modern continental literatures. He includes Sheridan and Southey, but not Ariosto, Calderón or Schiller. He has Kingsley's *Westward Ho!* but ignores Balzac altogether. He gravely ranks among the "Best Hundred" Gilbert White's fragrant but minor *Natural History of Selborne,* and Smiles's most edifying sermons on "rugged individualism," *Self-Help.* We surmise that he barely missed Martin Tupper's *Proverbial Philosophy.* This aggravated provincialism must have caused Matthew Arnold to smile or wince. But Sir John Lubbock was not the worst offender in the group: Ruskin protested against wasting one's time on any continental works. With the whole field of French literature spread before him, Ruskin sought entertainment in Gaboriau, an earlier and cruder Edgar Wallace, and decided that such reading was futile. His excuse must be the one Dr. Johnson so manfully offered for a wrong definition in his *Dictionary:* "Sheer ignorance, Madam."

This egocentric tendency is almost inevitable. Books in our own language and in our own tradition are more accessible in every sense: easier to buy, easier to understand. Let us acknowledge the fact, and not feel obliged to limit our quota of home-grown writers to one tenth of the total list, on the plea that there are at least ten great literatures in the West. Nothing that is profoundly human is provincial, even if it should happen to have originated in our own village. Still, if we are honestly seeking for "the best which has been thought and said in the world," it does seem a pity to have Smiles foisted upon us. There an international jury would be of assistance. We need some outside authority to tell us whether Keble's *Christian Year* ranks among "the best Hundred Books in the world," or among the best Hundred for members of the Established Church.

A Pan-European consensus might thus be reached. We believe that our common ancestors, the Greco-Roman classics, would emerge triumphantly; and that agreement would be easy on at least a dozen names in modern literatures. For the man who strives to rebuild Europe's shattered unity, this would be very profitable work. For us, who are seeking the literary experience at its best, it does not matter quite so vitally. Of course, Shakespeare is "World Literature"; but, if he were not, we should study and enjoy him all the same. Conan Doyle, on his chosen level, is undeniably World Literature; Robert Bridges is not; this is no reason why we should place *Sherlock Holmes* above *The Testament of Beauty*. We should not worry overmuch, unless we are professional Comparatists,[1] about the place of our own authors in the opinion of foreigners. We should acknowledge quite simply that we are most familiar with our own people, even when they are but modest folk. But we should avoid drawing up a list which implies a hierarchy of merit, and give the engaging Rev. Gilbert White, of Selborne, Surrey, a rank denied to the mighty Buffon.

The wiser course then might be, provisionally at least, to keep separate accounts: home-bred classics, foreign-born classics. This might save us from the opposite danger as well: a certain reluctance to acknowledge the merits of our own compatriots, because their popularity is too obvious. This is a pitfall into which the sophisticate is very apt to stumble. A cosmopolitan like André Gide finds it hard to admit the greatness of Victor Hugo; it is painful for him to agree with the man in the street. We can hardly hope to keep the two tendencies in fine and steady equipoise from the very first, and to be absolutely fair both to strangers and to our own people. Balance is achieved as the reward of long practice; and with the best critic it remains precarious.

The third objection to all lists of Best Books is that they confuse works which are supreme as literature, and works which have had a decisive influence upon civilization. Between the two sets, there is hardly any common measure. Few indeed are

[1] *Comparatist:* student of Comparative Literature.

the writings in which surpassing beauty is linked with the power to affect the thoughts and deeds of men. The Bible almost alone possesses this double virtue; Plato, in a limited sphere; perhaps also a few hybrids between philosophy and letters such as Rousseau and Nietzsche.

On the other hand, on what basis can we list together Shakespeare and the *Koran?* Shakespeare has enriched innumerable lives, but his name is linked with no system, no creed, no revolution, no reform. The *Koran,* for twelve centuries, has swayed hundreds of millions; to us, it means nothing as literature— less than the frankly frivolous *Arabian Nights.* Among the "great" books of the nineteenth century, we should certainly name Darwin's *Origin of Species* and Karl Marx's *Capital;* perhaps also Malthus' *On Population,* which in part inspired the other two. These authors could write; Karl Marx, in his pamphlets at least, is actually brilliant. But their most impressive works do not survive as art. We are not inferring that literature cannot be great unless it be "pure," and cannot be pure unless it be absolutely useless. But, without committing ourselves to the doctrine of Art for Art's Sake, we can safely assert that the power of Villon, Burns or Keats is not of the same nature as that of Darwin and Marx. And it is with literature as an art that we are dealing in this book.

The fourth difficulty in drawing a list of Best Books is to take proper account of the *time element.* Not that we believe the test of time to be infallible; mediocre works survive for generations; it seems almost impossible to get rid of Bernardin de Saint-Pierre's *Paul and Virginia,* and Dr. Frank Crane, late adviser in ordinary to the American public, recommended the insufferable *Abbé Constantin.* On the other hand, there must have been masterpieces which never had the chance they deserved. But, in a rough and ready manner, "time will tell." Now, it is exceedingly dangerous to place contemporaries on the roll of *World Classics.* Sir John Lubbock thought he had sufficiently protected himself against this difficulty by "purposely excluding works by living authors." [1] It was none the less venturesome to accord a place in his Pantheon to Keble, Grote, Green, Lewes, Kingsley, Bulwer-Lytton; all honorable men, no doubt, still remembered with faint and cool approval, but scarcely qualified to become members in the "Best Hundred" Club. Rostand, in *Cyrano de Bergerac*, riddles with deft irony the "immortality" conferred *ex officio* upon every French Academician:

> Here are Boudu, Boissat, and Cureau de la Chambre, Porchères, Colomby, Bourzeys, Bourdon, Arbaud. . . . Not one of these names
> shall ever perish! . . . What an inspiring thought!

I remember with delight, at the Paris Exposition of 1900, a Diorama of the Trans-Siberian Railway. Before your window, the scene unrolled itself with surprising realism; the sense of motion was extremely convincing. This effect was obtained by having a first band, in the immediate foreground, move at fairly high speed; a second one more slowly; the third and fourth more slowly still. So it is with the literary scene. There are works which seem to dash past us, and are gone with the wind. There are others which appear to travel with us for several seasons, perhaps for a decade; finally they too recede and disappear. Others still are the companions of our whole earthly journey; some were the friends of our fathers, and will remain with our sons.

Note that permanency is by no means the secret of delight. Like the child in R. L. Stevenson, we find keen pleasure in the sudden scene:

> And here is a mill, and there is a river:
> Each a glimpse, and gone for ever!

The unrelieved companionship of the same distant mountain for endless hours might grow positively tedious, however ma-

---

[1] He must have thought that the excellent Smiles was dead in 1885; but Smiles continued to practice *Self-Help* until 1904.

jestic the mountain. There is room in literature for Ogden Nash as well as for John Milton.

But, when we attempt in our turn the pleasant game of list-making, we must take into account the ever-varying perspective of the literary scene. Past and present is too rough a division. There is no "present": by the time I finish writing the word, it is already "past." There is no "past": either it disappears altogether, or it is still alive in our memory. As in the Trans-Siberian Diorama, we should have several bands unrolling at graded speeds; in the far background, almost motionless, Homer; next to us, flashing by with cheerful grin, Ring Lardner or Damon Runyon; and as many intermediate bands as we can afford.

This thought of "perspective in motion" raises many problems. Is Mount Homer an absolutely fixed point round which we revolve, or will the day come when the twin peaks *Iliad* and *Odyssey* are definitely left behind? In other terms, is immortality mere longevity? Philosophers of art might argue this subtle point with great profit; for the lover of art, it makes very little difference. Do not ask me whether Shakespeare is "good for all time," or only for a few paltry centuries. He will outlive us and our children's children, at any rate. An auditor anxiously asked Sir James Jeans: "Did I understand you to say that the world would come to an end in four hundred million years?"—"No," answered the lecturer; "I said four hundred *billion* years." The questioner sat down with a sigh of intense relief.

It is wisdom therefore to list separately the proved "classics" and the notables of today, who are merely candidates for classic rank. They may fool us one way or the other: trifles survive, while towering epics crumble; the merry tender tinkle of *Aucassin and Nicolette* still comes to us crystal-clear. We had better refrain from prophesying. Let us simply note down that Mr. Hervey Allen, for instance, finds great acceptance among his contemporaries, just as Honoré d'Urfé did in the early seventeenth century.

The great difficulty lies in the intermediate period, which may extend over fifty, and perhaps a hundred years. Shall I pledge myself to the belief that Ibsen is "immortal"? He might be part of the age which considered Herbert Spencer as the ultimate philosopher. Few writers won such unanimous acclaim as Guy de Maupassant. At forty, he was already a classic. At last, we had life itself, viewed with fearless eyes, depicted with faultless hand! Recently a young scholar enquired into the present fame of Maupassant. Some of his admirers had not read him in thirty years; they dare not touch the dust gathering round the idol, lest the idol turn out dust to the very core. We do not know.

To avoid excessive complication, however, we shall propose only two lists, "classics" and "contemporaries." By contemporaries, we understand those writers who were active in the post-war era—our own tragic quarter of a century. Naturally, there are many ambiguous cases. Edmond Rostand, Anatole France, Gabriele d'Annunzio, Gerhart Hauptmann, Maurice Maeterlinck, survived beyond the assigned date. But they added nothing essential to their message: they are of the world before the flood. André Gide and Marcel Proust did their most significant work before the war; but their fame and influence are post-war phenomena. In a symposium on contemporary literature, many of my students mentioned Stendhal and Dostoevsky. Their chronology was at fault; in the spirit, they were right. In the same way, a French Anthology of the New Poetry ignores many writers who, although *living*, are not *new*, but includes Charles Baudelaire and Arthur Rimbaud.

All lists which attempt to express a consensus are in fact the record of a compromise. No list contains books which are actually best for all men and by every possible test. Even if we omit as we propose to do, the "decisive" works which are not of a literary nature, the range of choice remains boundless, and the reasons for our preferences manifold. *Survival* is the most objective criterion; but there are many different ways of surviving. In some cases, the work is better known than the man.

Don Quixote is more alive than Cervantes, *Robinson Crusoe* than Daniel De Foe, and the *Imitation of Christ* stands with unimpaired power, even though Thomas à Kempis is but a dim figure. In other cases, it is the man, not the work, that we remember. Erasmus is the very symbol of the Renaissance spirit; historical romances and glowing biographies were written about him; but many well-educated people would not be able to mention offhand the *Colloquia* or the *Praise of Folly*. Voltaire is still with us, with his indomitable zest, his antics and grimaces, his sardonic grin, his biting wit, his vanity, his hatred of fanaticism, hypocrisy and cruelty, his burning thirst for universal knowledge; but we think we are doing well if we recall *Candide* and perhaps *Zadig*.

Some men are known by very few, and their cult is all the more intense for being almost a secret of the catacombs: Stendhal, Baudelaire, Rimbaud, Mallarmé, James Joyce, went through the esoteric stage. Others are enormously popular, but never achieve unqualified respect: Alexandre Dumas, Conan Doyle. Some are known on two levels for totally different reasons: Victor Hugo, in the eyes of the many, is a rival of Alexandre Dumas and of Eugène Sue; in the eyes of the few, a Seer, with the sacred primitive gift of transmuting religious awe into cosmic symbols. Cervantes, De Foe, Swift, among the most mature of writers, survive chiefly as the authors of juvenile fiction.

Apparent unanimity, we repeat, is at best a compromise; and—this is the last and most damning objection against any "safe and sane" list of best writers—it seldom is an honest compromise. Our sincerity is vitiated by inertia or laziness; we repeat the "right names" automatically, because it is easier than thinking for ourselves. It is vitiated by politeness, which is an anti-scientific virtue: "Oh, well! If you insist. . . . I do not want to make a fuss." It is vitiated more deeply by snobbishness, which in matters of art is the sin against the Holy Ghost. "Every scholar and gentleman votes for Homer. You vote for Homer, don't you? Unanimously carried." Every class in literature ought to begin with a study of Hans Christian Andersen's allegorical tale, *The Emperor's New Clothes.*

In the discussion of Sir John Lubbock's list, a few cracks appeared on the smooth surface of gentlemanly agreement. Max Müller started courageously: "If I were to tell you what I really think of the Hundred Best Books, I am afraid you would call me the greatest literary heretic or an utter ignoramus." Ruskin assumed the privilege of a prophet to be rude for the sake of righteousness. He referred to the "rubbish and poison of Sir John's list." He gave as a reason for striking out Grote's *History of Greece:* "because there is probably no commercial establishment, between Charing Cross and the Bank, whose head clerk could not write a better one, if he had the vanity to waste his time on it." Swinburne alluded to the "morbid development of intellectual presumption and moral audacity" of all list-makers; and thereupon proceeded to offer a particularly orthodox selection. William Morris showed perhaps the greatest courage: "I hope I shall escape boycotting at the hands of my countrymen for leaving out Milton; but the union in his works of cold classicism with Puritanism (the two things which I hate most in the world) repels me so that I *cannot* read him."

We must not believe that Victorian England alone was capable of free thought and dissent. In spite of our exacting cult of standardization, we do not lack independent spirits who refuse to be intimidated into conformity. A few years ago (Nov. 8, 1933), *The Nation* conducted a symposium on "Ten Indispensable Books I have never read." A number of outstanding writers and critics, Carl Van Doren, Harry Hansen, Branch Cabell, Ernest Boyd, H. L. Mencken, Burton Rascoe, George Jean Nathan, Ellen Glasgow, stood up before the assembly of the faithful, and confessed their sins of omission. H. L. Mencken, more of a classicist and a Puritan than William Morris, had actually read *Paradise Lost,* and what is more, *Paradise Regained:* "If Milton had written a *Paradise Lost Again,* I'd probably have read it too." But he "escaped" Dante (except the Doré illustrations), George Eliot, Dostoevsky, Jane Austen, *The Faerie Queene, Madame Bovary, Paul and Virginia,* and Goethe's *Faust* ("I tried twice, once in English and once in German, and had to give up both times"). Ernest Boyd, who wrote *Essays in Ten Literatures,* offers a list of "indispensable books which can be dispensed with" which is literally devastating. Almost all works of fiction, for a start. "As regards non-fiction, the process of elimination is obviously determined by the extent to which one has the courage of one's prejudices. Here is the list. Publius Vergilius Maro: *The Æneid;* Giovanni Boccaccio: *The Decameron;* Edmund Spenser: *The Faerie Queene;* John Milton: *Paradise Lost;* John Bunyan: *The Pilgrim's Progress;* Alexandre Dumas: *The Three Musketeers;* Victor Hugo: *Les Misérables;* Charles Dickens: *David Copperfield;* Walt Whitman: *Leaves of Grass;* and Mark Twain: *Huckleberry Finn.* Carl Van Doren gives "not the ten best books I have never read, but the first ten that came into my mind when I was asked to think about the matter. Various authors: The Bible; Dante: *The Divine Comedy;* Ariosto: *Orlando Furioso;* Cervantes: *Don Quixote;* Spenser: *The Faerie Queene;* Goethe: *Wilhelm Meister;* Carlyle: *The French Revolution;* Landor: *Imaginary Conversations;* Browning: *The Ring and the Book;* Nietzsche: *Thus Spake Zarathustra.*

"I cannot claim," confesses Carl Van Doren, "that I know nothing about them." Of course any man professionally interested in the study of literature has been compelled, at one time or another, to look into most of the great books of the world. The symposium might have been more conclusive, although less amusing and less easy to conduct, if the question had been: "What are the indispensable books which have failed to make any impression upon me?" The boy who reads the *Æneid* for the sole purpose of parsing, the youth who crams down *The Faerie Queene* in preparation for a quiz, the professor who dissects Marlowe for a thesis or a graduate course, have not actually "read" them at all.

It is easy to say that to glory in one's ignorance is but a conceited pose. The young are supposed to be iconoclastic: middle-aged critics like to assert their indomitable youth by making faces at the masters. It takes the self-confidence bred of success to admit that one does not know those books "that every schoolboy ought to know." "How smart I must be, to be what I am in spite of such appalling gaps in my information!"

But, as we are no cynic, we are inclined to give the critics mentioned above the full benefit of sincerity. They are not "showing off"; they are not pedants in reverse; in a manner which, to the conventional mind, may seem paradoxical and even frivolous, they are striving for the true ideal of Goethe. Culture is not a catalogue, but, in the terms of Matthew Arnold himself, "an inward operation." In literature, there can be no "experience" without some knowledge; but knowledge without experience is barren. The Renaissance, which set such store upon learning, also declared war upon pedantry. The pedant was a stock character in Italian and French comedy, and, in the following century, Molière made abundant use of the theme. Rabelais, himself an omnivorous scholar, derides the student from Limoges, with his uncouth crust of bookish erudition.

We are not attempting to prove that "it does not matter what we read." On the contrary, we fully agree with Sir John Lubbock—and with all educators from the dawn of schools—that our literary diet requires the most attentive care. If every book were as good as the next, our reading might as well be picked out by lot: we do not believe in such absolute democracy in the Republic of Letters. No: there are good books, better books, best books; but there is no single, exclusive and final list of the best. Our discussion may be summed up in three words: *complexity, relativity, inwardness*. There are thousands upon thousands of good books; more than any man could read, even if, very foolishly, he devoted his whole life to reading. They are good according to many different standards: mere pleasure, technical skill, information, edification, mystic power. They may be good for you, and not for me; good for you exactly at the present stage, but inaccessible yesterday and useless tomorrow; good for our fathers, and not for ourselves. The ultimate test of their being good or bad is their power to make *us* happier, better and wiser.

Now we may take up again Matthew Arnold's full definition of culture, and recognize the pith under its apparent clumsiness. "Getting to know the best which has been thought and said in the world" is only a means to "our total perfection." But it is not a direct, still less an automatic means. It enables us "to turn a stream of fresh and free thought upon our stock notions and habits." In other words, it is not, like mere knowledge, a burden, however precious; it is a mode of release.

Arduous may be the process of culture: culture means tilling, and tilling is hard work. But the result is *ease*. The man of culture is the one who does the right thing easily. Therefore culture is neither rebellion nor timorous conformity, for both of these are painful. The fruit of a "liberal" education, through the "liberal" arts, it means liberation.

Liberation from the obvious handicaps of rude speech, rough manners, unkempt appearance, ignorance of essentials: this is the lowest level of culture, but it should not be scorned. Liberation from childish worries and childish vanities. Liberation also from the meaner aspects of worldly cares: how hard it is for those who are too intently engaged in the struggle for bread or gold to be thoroughly cultivated!

It means chiefly liberation from that sense of inferiority which leads either to diffidence or to assertiveness. The man of culture neither shrinks nor blusters. He feels that he can meet anyone in the land on terms, not of equality, but of mutual respect. No culture is genuine if it makes either for arrogance or for servility.[1]

SUMMARY

Matthew Arnold's definition of culture includes the famous phrase: "getting to know the best which has been thought and

[1] Lists of Notable Books in World Literature will be found in the Appendix.

said in the world." There is a constant desire to possess an authoritative list of classics indispensable to culture. We want to have a Canon of Secular Literature, as we have a Canon of Sacred Writings. For a long time, the established masterpieces of Greece and Rome, revered almost as a second Revelation, provided such a collection. In the last two centuries, our field has increased enormously. But we still crave for a convenient and approved selection of the *Best Books*.

Every study group, every individual, will have to draw up such a list to meet particular conditions and needs. All that we shall attempt to do in this chapter is to discuss the method of approach. We use as our starting point—and merely as a starting point—the list proposed by Sir John Lubbock in 1885, and discussed by a notable group of educated Englishmen. We hope thus to free ourselves from the prejudices of the present moment.

As a result of this discussion, we note that the precautions to be observed are the following:

1. We should frankly recognize that our so-called World Literature is Western Literature; the masterpieces of the East have not yet been fully integrated with our tradition.

2. As we are tempted to over-emphasize the importance of our own national literature, it would be safer to list foreign books separately.

3. We are apt to confuse books which are supreme as works of art, and books which have had a decisive influence upon civilization, like Darwin's *Origin of Species;* it is only with literature as an art that we are dealing in this work.

4. It is almost impossible to apply the same standards to long-established authors, and to our own contemporaries. To meet this difficulty, we propose to have two lists: before our own times, and our own times, with the outbreak of the World War as the dividing point. Even then, there is an intermediate period (two generations before 1914) in which values are still very uncertain.

Such a list is based on the idea of *survival*. But there are

many ways of surviving. Sometimes the author is better remembered than the book, sometimes it is the reverse.

Survival itself depends on *common consent;* but such consent
is never unanimous. Max Müller, Ruskin, William Morris,
expressed very heretical views. Fifty years later, a group of
American writers discussed "the ten indispensable books which
they had never read," with amusing and amazing results.

Our conclusion is that no list is necessary and sufficient for
culture. Commenting on Matthew Arnold's *full* definition, we
arrive at the conception that culture is not a burden of knowledge, but a means of liberation. It "turns a stream of fresh and
free thought upon our stock notions and habits." It frees us
from servile fears.

CHAPTER IV

LITERARY BIBLES

LIFE, in a crisis, compels us to effect a ruthless simplification. Many things we deemed "indispensable" in our days of ease have to be discarded in times of stress. We do not carry a complete wardrobe in a knapsack, nor the whole pharmacopeia in an emergency kit. What library would you take on a journey through darkest Africa? There is no sharper test of what is, in our estimation, "the best which has been thought and said in the world."

It happens that this curious test is not hypothetical. In three famous instances at least, the question had to be faced, and the result was made known to the world.[1] Napoleon Bonaparte in 1798, Stanley in 1874-1877, Theodore Roosevelt in 1909-1910 had their traveling libraries. Stanley started with "three loads, or about 180 lbs. weight": a goodly supply. The process of selection, as he blazed his way through the uncharted and hostile continent, was dramatic in the extreme:

As my men lessened in numbers, stricken by famine, fighting and sickness, one by one [the books] were reluctantly thrown away, until finally, when less than 300 miles from the Atlantic, I possessed only the Bible, Shakspeare, Carlyle's *Sartor Resartus*, Norie's Navigation, and the Nautical Almanac for 1877. Poor Shakspeare

[1] Bonaparte's Library (decidedly an epitome of World Literature) will be found in *Mémoires de M. de Bourrienne*, Vol. I, Ch. XXVI; Stanley's, in *The Best Hundred Books*, containing Sir John Lubbock's List and additional suggestions by Ruskin and others, New York, E. L. Kellogg & Co., 1887; Theodore Roosevelt's Pigskin Library, in *African Game Trails*, London, John Murray, 1910, appendix F-521-528; with very good remarks on Nationalism in Literature, and the vanity of all lists.

was afterwards burned by demand of the foolish people of Zinga. At Bonea Carlyle and Norie and Nautical Almanac were pitched away, and I had only the old Bible left.[1]

This leads us to the more searching question: if you were to be marooned on a desert island, with a single book, which one would you pick out? In the Anglo-Saxon group of civilization, at any rate, the answer, by an overwhelming majority, would be the same as Stanley's: "The old Bible." It is obvious that, in most cases, our choice would not be dictated by literary reasons. The sacred character of the Bible would be the first consideration. And the second would not be esthetic either, but national and even tribal. We should choose, not the Oriental Bible, a masterpiece filled with strange beauty and unrivaled power, but the English Bible, as the symbol of home and country, as the surest link with our lost world, as the single bond between all men of English speech, whatever may be their national allegiance, their Church membership, their party affiliation, their social standing. This fruit of the arid East is for us redolent of English earth. We venture the hypothesis that, for our second choice, we would hesitate between Shakespeare and Dickens. With a Dickens Omnibus in his hut, no modern Robinson Crusoe would be completely exiled from the Anglo-Saxon community.

But the selection of the Bible as our only companion would be justified also on purely literary grounds. With the Bible, no man in solitude would ever suffer spiritual starvation, even as an artist. For there is hardly any mood of man that is not reflected in its pages; and the variety of its themes and forms is infinite. This variety is dimmed for us by a triple veil. The first, of very little consequence, is the division into brief verses, which imparts a superficial sameness to Psalm and Chronicle, to epic and parable. The second—a veil of priceless beauty, but none the less a veil—is the quaintness and majesty of Jacobean diction. The third—a veil which we cannot wish away—is the

[1] *The Best Hundred Books*, p. 52.

uniformly reverent and uncritical attitude with which we approach passages of a totally different nature: ritual, statistics, genealogies, folklore, words of disenchantment, cries of despair. We are apt to read the Bible in a solemn drone of thought as well as voice. Its spiritual significance is not enhanced thereby, and its human appeal is all but ruined.

Many efforts have been made to give the Bible its rightful place among literary masterpieces. A new typographical arrangement may suffice to break the spell of drowsy custom, and reveal anews the living power of the ancient Word. A man whose list of "classics" were limited to the Bible could be *cultured*, even in the wordly sense. He would escape from the pettiness of daily cares; he would sharpen and deepen his own experience; he would ponder, with Job, over the most tragic problems of human destiny; he would have at his command an incomparable store of majestic images and vigorous words, wherewith to give color and sinew to the expression of his own thoughts. He would be, even in humblest station, a gentleman of the spirit.

The sheer convenience of an all-sufficient one-volume library has repeatedly tempted men to arrange other writings into *Bibles*. Both Jules Michelet and H. G. Wells, as prophets of democracy, toyed with the idea of a Bible of Mankind. Professor Richard Moulton, as an exponent of World Literature, propounded a fairly definite scheme, a Pentateuch of Bibles. What do we mean by a Bible? It is not every chance collection of books that deserves the hallowed name; in most cases, the modest term *Omnibus* would be more adequate. The test of a genuine "literary Bible" is two-fold: unity and variety. Variety: no essential need of man must be left unsatisfied. Unity: the "Bible" must offer from cover to cover the same spiritual atmosphere, even the same material tradition, so as to permit cross-references between its various parts; it must constitute *a country of the soul*.

The Holy Bible fulfills these two conditions. So does the Pagan Bible, the epitome of Hellenic culture, which, as we previously said, was long considered almost as a second revelation. Bind together the *Iliad* and the *Odyssey*; a full dozen plays by the four great dramatists, Æschylus, Sophocles, Euripides, Aristophanes; three or four of Plato's Dialogues; as a stiffening, the *Enchiridion* of Epictetus; as an ornament, the delicate poetic blossoms of the *Anthology*; Lucian, for no Bible is complete without a touch of irony; the historical background, as provided by Herodotus, Xenophon, Thucydides; Demosthenes as the god of eloquence; perhaps Plutarch, for he made definite for us the figure of the ancient Hero: the result would not be unwieldy, and it would be extraordinarily substantial. Just as the Holy Bible stands by itself, and does not need, in order to be appreciated, the enormous Hebraic and Christian literature that it inspired, so the Hellenic Bible is complete without the glorious train of imitations that it engendered: the whole production of Rome, and large elements in the modern world, down to Goethe's *Iphigenia in Tauris*.

So far, every reader will agree with Professor Moulton. As his third Bible, he proposes *The Divine Comedy* and *Paradise Lost* jointly. This suggestion is very tempting. Between the two poets, there is indeed a double bond of unity: the Christian faith and the Classic tradition. The medieval Florentine and the Englishman of the late Renaissance meet at the foot of the Cross, both with Vergil as their guide. It is this, however, that weakens their claim to form a genuine "Bible": intensely original as individuals, they did not discover a new "country of the soul." And, even if all their minor works were included, we doubt whether all-sufficient variety could be found in their pages. Our hypothetical Robinson Crusoe would have an ample supply of the dramatic, but perhaps not quite enough of the tender. While almost surfeited with sublimity, he would miss the homely touches, the direct contact with folk life and folk lore, that Homer and the Bible provide so abundantly. He would miss also the salt of wordly wisdom, which is found, not in the Greeks alone, but in *Proverbs* and *Ecclesiastes* as well. He would miss that shimmering light of irony which in Homer plays round the very gods, and in Plato hovers on the revered head of Socrates himself; that indulgent irony which suffuses the last chapter of *Jonah* and the gentlest of the parables. No man could live alone with two such angry and majestic prophets.

As a fourth Bible, we are offered Shakespeare, entire and alone. We are familiar enough with the thought; there are for sale sets of "the three essential books, The Bible, Shakespeare, and a Concise Dictionary." The unity of this Bible is undeniable; it resides in the personality, mysterious as it may be, of a single author. And there is a Shakespearian "country of the soul," which is not identical with Elizabethan England. Like English travelers in Tibet or Patagonia, the Shakespeare spirit carries its own atmosphere into unbelievable places: a blasted heath, a balmy night in Venice, Prospero's Island, a tavern in Cheapside, the coasts of Bohemia. It is a new land indeed; it borders on Christianity, Antiquity, and Medieval Romance; it borrows from all three, but it stoutly maintains its separate existence. The variety is that of life itself: a life tragic at the core even in its gayest moments, a life that reaches beyond the visible. It embraces Lear, Rosalind, Falstaff, Ariel. No need to expatiate on such a well-worn theme. The Robinson Crusoe who draws Shakespeare for solace on his desert island is not to be pitied.

The fifth Bible, in Professor Moulton's scheme, has for its center, not a man, but a theme: the Faust cycle. It is a wrestling with the eternal problem: What shall it profit a man to gain the world if he loses his soul? Faust is one of the three great Romantic myths in whom this conflict is illustrated. The second is Don Juan, and the third Napoleon: for the man of flesh and blood, the realistic administrator and strategist, became a symbol within a decade of his death. All three set out to "gain the world": through knowledge, through love, through power; three forms of conquests, three forms of selfishness, three ultimate failures. For all three "lose their souls": at least it is not through their own merits that they are redeemed.

This would form an admirable nucleus for a Bible. But, as

Goethe's *Faust* might be too slim for the purpose, Professor Moulton padded the collection with Marlowe's *Dr. Faustus*, Calderón's *El Mágico Prodigioso*, and Bailey's *Festus*. The result is highly artificial. Why read the same story four times over? And especially, why read *Festus* at all?

We beg leave to offer an amendment: keeping as a kernel the Faust motive, we might build round it a Goethean Bible. It could easily be reduced to a single volume of manageable size: I have on my shelves a fairly complete Goethe in 1200 double-column pages. The unity would be the Olympian spirit of Goethe. The variety would not consist, as in Shakespeare, in the intense and multitudinous creation of life: it would be found in the encyclopedic character of the work, and in the truly unique blend of Classicism, the Medieval spirit, the Renaissance, the Enlightenment and Romanticism. For good measure, it would offer also a glimpse of modern science. The key note of this Bible would be wisdom and culture; and, deepest of all, at the end of the first *Faust*, the sense that these, sovereign as they may be in the human sphere, will not suffice. To a Goethean Bible the Germans could have no objection; nor could the rest of the world, for in Goethe Germanism and humanity are fully reconciled.[1]

Can we descry, in the huge and shapeless mass of our Western writings, other Bibles to rank with the more definite of these? In comparison with our own Holy Bible, or the body of Greek classics, or the complete works of Shakespeare, every collection would seem heterogeneous, or vague, or incomplete. The vast body of medieval romance, with the Arthurian cycle as its nucleus, does indeed form "a country of the soul." Its very atmosphere is *romance*, that is to say *wonder*. Romance, in the most elementary sense, means discovery, adventure. This ele-

---

[1] Elaborating on a hint given above, it would be tempting to compile a Romantic Bible with Faust, Napoleon and Don Juan as the three heroes. The *Faust* we already have; for the Napoleon, *The Dynasts*, by Thomas Hardy, might serve. But there is so far no adequate *Don Juan*. Molière's play is a splendid indication, but far too hasty. There are tantalizing adumbrations in Byron, Musset, Baudelaire: but the theme is still inchoate.

ment we already found in the *Odyssey;* yet the whole spirit of
the *Odyssey* is different. Its background is curiously realistic;
Ulysses meets strange creatures and goes through weird experiences, but, through all his encounters with gods and monsters,
he remains a man of solid flesh, vigorous and shrewd, in the
clear-cut world of the Grecian seas. Medieval romance gives a
new quality to imagination; it creates, not fantastic shapes only,
but a fantastic atmosphere, a whole world of make-believe. In
a higher sense, romance means passion. Antiquity had known
Phaedra and Dido: but it was reserved for the poets of the
Tristan story to give us the theme of fateful love, irresistible,
justified by its very intensity, driving man and woman to bliss,
madness and death. In the highest sense, romance even touches
religion, and seeks alliance with mysticism. It takes us beyond
humdrum morality, and the cool intellectual intricacies of theology. It gives faith a richer, but a questionable glow; a mysterious radiance, as in the Grail stories, which is in part an inner
light, in part a half conscious trick. In chronicle of high deeds,
in love, in religion, romance is a waking and willful dream,
which makes dreaming the most real experience in life.

The appeal of this medieval cycle was intense. Unfortunately,
it never was embodied in perfect form: Chrétien of Troyes, best
known of the romancers, was but a clever novelist, writing fashionable tales in tripping measure. But the theme had great vitality. It reappeared, direct or suffused, in Malory, in Edmund
Spenser, in Shakespeare himself; among the moderns, in Tennyson, William Morris, Swinburne, Edwin Arlington Robinson; it reached its zenith in the music of Wagner. Such a Bible,
if it were constituted, would have undoubted unity of theme,
spirit, atmosphere. So definite is it in these respects that a few
lines, like the opening stanza in *La Belle Dame sans Merci,* suffice to carry us into the magic land. It would offer to our choice
an enormous variety of episodes. Yet it would lack the substantial variety of a true Bible. Released from the trammels of
sense, it loses itself into the impalpable. The bewildering adventures, without inner law, are capriciously monotonous. Knights

and ladies, however gaily they may be clad, are no more substantial than wizards and fairies. An unmitigated fare of medieval romance would soon make our Robinson Crusoe exceedingly sick; he would starve amid a marvelous profusion of sweets. This is a "country of the soul" indeed; but one in which man cannot live for long.

That is why our Bible of Romance could not stand by itself, but would need, as its corrective and complement, the *Bible of Ironic Naturalism*. This was felt already in the Middle Ages. By the side of high-flown romance flourished mocking tale and cynical farce. And not seldom did romance, in mid-air, suddenly seek the earth, laughing at its own broken flight. The first part of the *Romance of the Rose* is an allegory of refined love; the second an encyclopedia of bourgeois common sense. Chaucer added a rollicking cynical *Envoy* to his sad and sweet tale of patient Griselda. This culminates in *Don Quixote*, greatest of romances and satire on all romances. Let us repeat that mockery is but a corrective: even in *Don Quixote*, the supremacy of romance is not seriously challenged. Don Quixote is mad, and the fool of the story; but he is the noblest character in the book. We are half ashamed of ourselves for deriding his absurdities. The unavoidable "realism" of trivial care passes away, scorned and soon forgotten; the dream of Don Quixote still haunts us. We could thus imagine a contrasted Bible with Malory and Spenser at one end, Rabelais and Balzac at the other, and, in the center, mocking and wistful, Cervantes.

Unexpectedly enough, it is in the great tormented mystic Pascal that we find the pithiest expression of this counterblast to romance, this willful and brutal return to earth, this attitude of *ironic naturalism:* "Man is neither an angel nor an ass; he who poses as an angel makes an ass of himself." Stress the anti-romantic side, seek the ass, the ape, the swine in man, and you are led to cynicism, to Swift's savage picture of the loathsome Yahoos, to Aldous Huxley's Inferno, *Eyeless in Gaza.* Flippancy is but cynicism in lighter vein: we may be compelled to take the absurdities of humankind tragically, but we need not do them the honor of taking them seriously. Such was, for a period only, the philosophy of Anatole France.

But in Cervantes, as we have seen, derision had not wholly destroyed sympathy. And in Anatole France, Irony hardly ever lost touch with her sister muse Pity. The phrase "Irony and Pity" paid the penalty of universal success: it became so trite that for years it evoked in the reader an ironical or pitying smile. A smile is a marvelous contrivance: it may be the light which spontaneously registers understanding; it may indicate also the bland refusal to understand.

If Irony recedes, and Pity assumes command, then we have, if not a new "country of the soul," at least a new "climate." We might attempt, on that basis, to compile a *Bible of Social Pity.* Social pity is a feeling strikingly absent from ancient and medieval literature. The epic of the fighting caste, the courtly romance, the folk tale and farce, are equally harsh toward the plodding, stupid, long-suffering beast, the rustic, the boor, the hind, the clown. *Villanus,* the villein, became in modern English the villain, the scoundrel; in modern French *vilain* stands for mean and ugly. To be downtrodden was accepted as sufficient evidence of abjection. Pity for the poor, love for the humble, *misericordia,* could be found in the Prophets of Israel, and, with radiant definiteness, in the Gospel. But the evangelical spirit did not pass into secular literature. Pride and scorn remained the law.

Only at the very end of the seventeenth century do we hear a single prophetic cry. La Bruyère was moved to compassion by "those wild animals with the semblance of a human face: and indeed they are men." Under the Grand Monarch, two hundred years before Edwin Markham, he had discovered *The Man with the Hoe.* But the lone protest found no echo. The philosophers of the Enlightenment, generous as they were in their great fight against abuses and superstition, had no thought to spare for the common man. Early Romanticism was fiercely individualistic; it was reeking with pity, but it was self-pity. Faint notes were heard in Goldsmith (*The Deserted Village*), in Blake; but it is in the short early novels of Victor Hugo, *The Last Day of a Man Condemned to Death, Claude Gueux,* that we find the first clear indications of the new spirit. By the second half of the nineteenth century, the tide had fully set in, with Dickens, with Eugène Sue and his *Mysteries of Paris,* with *Les Misérables,* with the great Russians, Dostoevsky and Tolstoy. It was the flame of social consciousness that redeemed Zola from filth, and made *Germinal* the first full-grown proletarian epic. It gave its somber glow to Gerhart Hauptmann's *Weavers.* It took possession of the war novel with Barbusse's *Under Fire.* It serves as a much-needed justification for the propagandist literature of our own days, *In Dubious Battle* or *The Grapes of Wrath.*

A *Bible of Social Pity* would have unity of inspiration, no doubt: a unity borrowed from the Gospel itself. Although the fact might not be apparent at first, it would also have reasonable definiteness, an unmistakable atmosphere. The men we have mentioned belong together. There is in their voices an imperceptible tremor which is their peculiar accent. Some of the finest, most human works in the past, like *Tom Jones,* lack that dolorous and indignant note. Some men, with the noblest intentions, like Romain Rolland, strive to reproduce it and never quite succeed. As Pity need not be constantly tearful, we might have in such a Bible a great variety of tone, as well as an unlimited variety of scene. Tolstoy, in the latter stage of his career, would have endorsed such a Bible, not as one among five or six, but as the only one worthy to exist by the side of Holy Scripture. All else, including much of his own earlier work, he would ruthlessly have sacrificed, as mere "art for art's sake."

One practical difficulty, however, must be faced. Our evangelists of social pity are legion; most of them are abundant writers; they work on an epic scale: sonnets, short stories and brief excerpts would not convey the full force of their art. No Bible could include several of these massive masterpieces, and remain manageable.

There is another objection beside sheer bulk. Remember the

terms of our problem, or the rules of our game: we want a book which will provide a new Robinson Crusoe with adequate spiritual nutriment. But, on a desert island, what use would he have for "social pity"? This is not a mere jest. Every reader, at times, is imprisoned of his own free will upon his own desert island. He takes refuge there to commune with his own heart, and to face the eternal problems which torment the soul of man. He seeks to find himself, and God within himself, shutting out for the moment society, its pleasures and its evils. No reader, however unselfish and earnest, could live happily on undiluted "social literature."

Still we are reluctant to give up this latter-day Bible, these Fathers of the Humanitarian Church. Although the gospel of social pity does not seek beauty first of all and for its own sake, it achieves beauty of a singularly searching and impressive kind. Although it seems to forget or subordinate the individual, it quickens and ennobles him. When we have caught its fundamental note, we are aware of a lack even in the Olympian culture of Goethe, even in "myriad-souled Shakespeare," even in the harmonious discipline of the Greek mind. Its chaos is our chaos; its promise is our immediate hope.

Our device of a one-volume library for a modern Robinson Crusoe, although proposed and discussed half in jest, has a serious aspect. It is meant to emphasize the idea that, in "the pursuit of our total perfection," well-integrated reading is of far more importance than merely extensive reading. A man who should work his way through Sir John Lubbock's "Best Hundred Books" diligently, retentively, might yet remain a fool. A laborious fool, a plausible fool, an abundantly informed fool: all the more dangerous for the weapons thus placed in the hands of his foolishness. In this famous list, or in any other catalogue of World's Classics, there is no unifying principle that could serve as the indispensable nucleus of culture. Better one good book, if thought-provoking, than a hundred "best books," laden to the gunwale with dead facts. And all facts are dead, unless our living mind confers life upon them.

On the other hand, when the process of culture is fairly started, when we are able to turn "a stream of fresh and free thought upon our stock notions and habits," then abundant reading becomes a boon. Culture will not result automatically out of a prescribed course of study: it is an inward operation. But the growth in the soil is prepared and aided by assiduous tilling.

We can hardly separate, by lines as definite as national boundaries, the three aspects of reading: reading for information, reading for pleasure, reading for culture. Fortunately for us, two of these aspects are frequently blended, and not seldom all three. Culture is by far the most elusive. We know for certain when we acquire a new fact; we are able to tell whether or not we are amused; but how can we be sure that a book has "cultural value"? Because it figures on an approved list? No: because it gives us a sense of inner growth.

Advice about reading should therefore be an individual prescription, not a patent medicine. An obscure, half-forgotten book, a difficult book, a very light book, may be "the best" for us under definite circumstances. We cannot constantly be in the mood for Milton any more than for P. G. Wodehouse. But the most skillful doctors draw their remedies from a common store. There is no panacea for all men in all cases; there is, however, a Codex of products whose healing powers have been tested through extensive experience. A list of World Classics is such a pharmacopeia.

But we should never forget that a pharmacopeia does not exhaust the resources of nature, nor a list of classics the possibilities of literature. So far, we have proceeded in the conventional manner, and restricted our field without attempting to define it: if we are not overawed by arbitrary barriers, if we claim our right to explore at will, we shall soon discover that our realm extends far beyond the "best" hundred books, or thousand books, by whomsoever they be chosen. Perhaps, as we shall see in our next chapter, it extends beyond formal books themselves.

SUMMARY

A useful exercise, to sharpen our conception of World Literature, is to ask ourselves: "What books would I take with me, if I were to be out of touch with Western civilization?" Napoleon Bonaparte, Stanley, Theodore Roosevelt, starting for Africa, took traveling libraries with them. The only book that Stanley preserved throughout his arduous journey was the Bible.

Hence the tempting conception of a *Literary Bible:* a collection of manageable size, offering that spiritual unity which is the condition of depth, and so varied withal that a new Robinson Crusoe, with that single volume in his hands, would not be spiritually starved.

Professor Richard Moulton proposed a scheme of five such Bibles. We discuss his selection, and offer a few additional suggestions of our own.

The first two Bibles will no doubt secure unanimous endorsement: the Holy Bible, whose greatness as a literary document is still overlooked by many, and the Hellenic Bible of Epic, Drama, History and Philosophy.

More questionable is the grouping together, as a third Bible, of Dante's *Divine Comedy* and Milton's *Paradise Lost.* The unity is manifest, but there might be a lack of sufficient variety.

The works of Shakespeare are accepted without demur as a fourth Bible. The unity is that of the author's personality, mysterious but unmistakable; the variety is that of life itself.

As his fifth Bible, Professor Moulton suggested the Faust theme, as treated by various authors. We propose to retain *Faust* as the center, as it is one of the great philosophical myths in literature; and to include the principal works of Goethe, apostle of modern culture.

Are there other writings that could thus be grouped into *Bibles,* offering both unity and all-sufficient variety? Perhaps the *Cycle of Medieval Romance,* particularly the Arthurian and

Holy Grail stories? It forms a "country of the soul"; but it is overburdened with make-believe. So it needs, and has always needed, the corrective and complement of *Ironic Naturalism*, which brings us back to earth, mockingly and at times cynically. In this strain, the masterpiece is Cervantes's *Don Quixote*.

If we stress pity instead of irony as our chief source of inspiration, we have the *Bible of Social Pity:* Hugo, Dickens, Tolstoy, Dostoevsky, and many of our contemporaries. But it is too diffuse to be embodied into a compact Bible; and it minimizes individual problems.

The first aim of this discussion is to pass in review, informally, some of the greatest themes in world literature. Although it is not seriously suggested that a man's library might be reduced to a single volume, or to five, or even to eight, there might be a valid lesson in our apparent paradox: reading, in order to be profitable, should be well-integrated. Actually, a man could be more *cultivated* with a single essential book, a *Bible*, read intelligently, than with the Hundred Books proposed by Sir John Lubbock, read in a slavish or frivolous spirit.

CHAPTER V

FOLKLORE AND LITERATURE

"LITERATURE," said Fernand Baldensperger after Goethe, "is a fragment of fragments. Of all that ever was said and done, only an infinitesimal portion was written down; of all that ever was written down, only an infinitesimal portion is remembered."[1] To pursue this thought one step further: of all that is remembered, how much is, in the artistic sense of the term, genuine *literature?*

Literature can be defined from two points of view: technique and intention. Technically, literature is everything written. The driest information about the most matter-of-fact subject, scientific, administrative, legal, commercial, if it be consigned to writing, becomes part of the "literature" of that subject. The heading *Literature* in a professional publication means Bibliography or Book Review. To the student of letters, this all-inclusive definition will seem at the same time obvious and irrelevant. He knows that tables of logarithms, or a hardware catalogue, although printed, do not belong to his chosen domain. There are borderline cases; the research scholar often is a scientific investigator rather than a literary critic, and he may devote a lifetime of study to works without a particle of literary value. But on the whole, the distinction is fairly clear in our minds. It is evident that, in the enormous mass of writings, there are many which have no claim whatever to be called *literature.*

Literature, in the second sense, is not a technique for record-

---

[1] Fernand Baldensperger: *La Littérature, Création, Succès, Durée,* Paris, Flammarion, 1913.

ing facts, but an art. It is the art that uses language as its medium. Like all the arts, it implies conscious pleasure in the expression of personality.

With this as a test, we are able to dismiss the bulk of mere writing as not within the scope of our interest. On the other hand, our definition includes more than what is usually called literature and studied under that name. Everyone who reports news dramatically, who repeats a story with relish, who enjoys the sentimental or romantic aspects of a situation, and is able to convey his enjoyment, enters, were it for a moment, into the realm of *self-expression through words*, that is to say literature. And this gift is found among the primitive and the illiterate. A death scene which brings deep sorrow, but at the same time a sense of tragedy, has in it a secret element of pleasure; a quarrel worked up to a proper climax is a conscious work of art; chaffering, with its seasoning of indignation and banter, is a comedy which gives spice to a dull mercantile transaction. Animated gossip is literature in the raw: the basic intention is there, the right medium is used. Only the accident of recording separates such experiences from "literature" in the usual sense. Let the scene be witnessed by a Maupassant, and we shall have a "slice of life" in the best naturalistic vein. Stray jottings, scribbled diaries, hasty letters, informal chats, improvised speeches, are of the same stuff as conventional "works," and instinct with the same spirit. If they come from the right man, and fall into the right hands, they turn into literature of recognized value. But for Boswell, we might have missed the true Dr. Johnson. Luther's *Table Talk* appeals to modern readers more than his theological treatises, and Goethe's *Conversations with Eckermann* are more alive than several of his dramas.

Every man is an "author," then, whenever he strives to express himself. Every word acquires artistic value, if it is charged with a significance beyond its dictionary meaning. Common intercourse is the living, fluid, amorphous stuff out of which all literature is made.

"There is someone who is wittier than M. de Voltaire; and that is Mr. Everybody." But the epigrams of Mr. Everybody are evanescent; they elicit a smile, and are forgotten. How few of us ever say anything at all *momorable*, even in the literal and modest sense of the word! Some expressions, however, do not disappear with the utterance. They acquire consistency and collective significance, either because they strike many minds very much at the same time, or because they remain attached to some startling circumstance, or again because they possess a peculiar tang and power. These are vividly remembered for a while; then they pass into ever-widening and dimmer circles of acceptance. Here we have an intermediate stage between the evanescent enjoyment of direct experience and its definite, conscious recording. We might call it the semi-fluid or viscous stage. There is a coagulation of expression, but it has not yet reached the point of hardening into definite and permanent form. Opinions, types, themes, phrases, thus acquire an existence and a value beyond the moment and beyond the individual. Of such loose elements is composed the *Zeitgeist*, the spirit of the time. It may be called the *slang* of the hour, the words in fashion, and, negatively, those in disrepute, the peculiar connotation given to ancient terms, the current metaphors, the favorite jests. This spontaneous condition of speech has been called *Folksay*; it is the verbal translations of *Folkways*. Remember that, so far, it has not fully *set:* the slang of one circle is unintelligible or obnoxious in a different surrounding; the witticism of the evening may have lost salt and even sense by the dawn of the next day.

Some Folkways and Folksays, for obscure reasons, go beyond the ephemeral. They pass, not into slang merely, but into *language*, if by language we mean, not a code or a mail-order catalogue, but a set of symbols with powers of evocation, a mythology. Every change in collective mood gives a new meaning to the words of the tribe. Beyond the plain terms, we find the common feelings, the hoarded wisdom, the favorite themes of a generation and of several generations. When they have reached such a point of diffusion and fixity, when they have attained the status of *currency*, like the coin of the realm, then they are promoted from vogue to tradition, from *folksay* to *folklore*.

Folklore is not limited to fairy tales; and it is not found exclusively among primitive populations, out of touch with conscious culture—barbarians, pioneers, peasants in remote communities. It is not a crude substitute for organized thought, it is an inevitable phase in the organization of thought. Folklore continues to grow in our sophisticated age. There was a teeming mythology or folklore of the Great War: we are not alluding to the products of willful propaganda, but to themes and types that arose, it would seem, spontaneously, no one knew where or how. The Poilu and the Doughboy as popular heroes, the Boche and later the Bolshevist as bugaboos, acquired a weird intensity of life. In an educated nation, folklore need not be of the crudest kind. There is a "folklore of capitalism," a folklore of politics, even a folklore of science. When André Maurois spoke of the "Three American Ghosts, the Puritan, the Pioneer, the Robber Baron," he might have called them three leading characters in American folklore: no less real, no less vivid, than the knights, princes, ogres, giants and werewolves of olden times. National types—and not least among them our shrewd, kindly, humorous Uncle Sam with the absurd clothes—are creations of folklore. On a lower plane, quips, gags, wisecracks, anecdotes, flourish exceedingly in our rich American humus. No sphere is so dignified, and none so humble, that we cannot find in it this free, at times this riotous play of imagination upon facts and upon words.

All this is literature, in the deeper sense of the word; for it goes beyond the mere transmission of facts. But two elements are lacking, which we are accustomed to consider essential: this *literature* has no definite text, and it has no definite authorship. We remember the gist: we do not know who said it first, or exactly how it was said. In a lazy fashion, we are satisfied with the assurance that it "jest growed"; in more grandiloquent terms, that it arose of its own accord out of the people's soul. On closer scrutiny, the homely and the mystic expressions are equally absurd. They humorously or loftily take a miracle for granted. The biology of literature is reluctant to accept the hypothesis of spontaneous generation. The truth of the matter is perhaps not quite so mysterious. Except in our professional field, we are all apt to be careless reporters. We misquote without scruple, because we are not conscious that we are misquoting. This universal inaccuracy is to be regretted; yet it has two redeeming aspects. The first is a fine indifference to irrelevant details. If we are telling an Irish story, what does it matter whether the hero be called Pat or Mike? We are not sworn witnesses. The second—and this is essential in the literary process—is that we cannot repeat a thing with gusto and yet fail to add thereto something of our own personality. It may be an imperceptible twist, it may be an elusive shade: the story, if it gave something to us, takes something from us in return.

In opposition to folksay and folklore, we shall call *definite* literature those productions in which we are conscious of text and authorship. The text may be mutilated or corrupt, like that of Aristotle's *Poetics*, one of the most influential books in the world, and one of the worst mangled. It may be hard to decipher, like the shorthand of Pepys's *Diary*, or the "little language" of Swift's *Journal to Stella*. It may be jumbled, chaotic, full of cryptic indications, like Pascal's *Thoughts*—a heap of loose stones, some neatly cut and elaborately carved, others rough hewn, others broken, out of which a mighty defense of the Christian Religion was to be built. Such difficulties offer an unlimited field for textual critics and learned editors. Still, however imperfect the text may be, we never falter in our awareness of *a text*. In the same way, the authorship of the book may be unknown or in dispute; the work may have had a prototype now forgotten; obscure collaborators may have contributed to it; it may have been recast by a later hand; but, even though we do not know the actual facts, we know for a fact that the work originated with a certain person or persons. We had no doubt on that score before we knew (if indeed we know) that Thomas à Kempis wrote the *Imitation of Christ*, Guillaume Alexis the *Farce of Master Pathelin*, and Sir Philip Francis the *Letters of Junius*. It was not revealed in the writer's lifetime that the mysterious romantic lady Fiona Macleod was none other but the anthologist and biographer William Sharp; for generations, few people realized what a commanding share Auguste Maquet had had in the very best romances of Alexandre Dumas. We were ignorant or we were fooled; but no one thought for a moment that these dashing tales had simply sprung from the soil. A case of mistaken identity does not destroy the notion of definite identity.

It must be clearly borne in mind that the distinction between *folklore* (in our wide sense of the term) and *definite literature* is not a question of excellence or permanency. Every worthless book that sinks at once into the ooze of oblivion belonged, during its brief and inglorious life, to the body of definite literature. If a scholar cares to dig it out of the slime, as Robert Browning picked up Sibrandus Schafnaburgensis,[1] he will find it as dull, as trite, as confused, as vague as ever, yet definitely a book, with a text presupposing an author. Folktales may be far more valuable, as undoubtedly they are more enduring, than such "definite" literature.

For centuries, the accepted method for approaching masterpieces was to take *definite literature* alone into account. Books were treated as though they had sprung full grown into existence. The historian's task began with the printed word, or at most with the completed manuscript. If the ancestry of the work was sought, it was exclusively along the line of previous "definite" writings. Folksay and folklore were ignored altogether. In order to understand Pope, you might have to know Boileau, and, behind them both, Horace; but the talk of the

[1] Robert Browning: *Dramatic Lyrics*, Garden Fancies, II.

club house and the drawing room was left out of consideration. It was deemed as irrelevant in this field as it would be in mathematics.

This method still prevails, but it is no longer alone in the field. We have already alluded (p. 32) to the vast movement which, in the eighteenth century, led to the discovery, the appreciation, even the exaltation of the *folklike*, the primitive, the collective, the unconscious. We shall have to touch upon it again and again, for it is one of the major revolutions in the human mind. At the very moment when reason was attempting to bring thought, feeling, expression, to the utmost degree of clarity and consciousness, there was a rebellion against this alleged "Enlightenment." There was a deliberate striving after the spontaneous, a sedulous quest of the untutored; this of course verged on absurdity, but a revolt against reason could hardly be expected to be rational. But the claim of folklore to our respectful attention was thus established. Vico as early as 1725, Herder half a century later, sought the very souls of nations in those uncouth relics that reason affected to despise: myths, legends and songs. Vico even anticipated F. A. Wolf in the idea that our noblest "definite" literature is but the ultimate stage of folklore, that the Homeric stories existed before Homer, that Homer—if there ever was such a man— had only the merit of giving his name to a final version. This is exactly what the brothers Grimm, early in the nineteenth century, did in their beloved *Fairy Tales:* they placed their matchless scholarship, reverently, at the service of the naïve, the childlike, the folklike; they professed to give only a careful edition of a masterpiece drawn from the depths of the people's past.[1]

It was at that time that a confusion arose which has never been fully cleared up. The *folklike*, identified with the primi-

---

[1] For a similar process in America, cf. the Joel Chandler Harris versions of Uncle Remus; collections of Paul Bunyan stories; John A. Lomax: *Cowboy Songs and Other Frontier Ballads*; John A. and A. Lomax: *American Ballads and Folk-songs*; Louise Pound: *American Ballads and Songs*; Carl Sandburg: *The American Songbag*.

tive, was supposed to belong to the remote past. In our refined civilization, it survived as a fossil. It represented a vanished Golden Age. It was cherished because of its very antiquity, like the ruins of which the eighteenth century grew so fond. This was too modest a view. Folklore was not then, and is not now, a mere vestige; it has not lost its creative power. It does not belong to a particular era in history: it is a stage in the elaboration of thought and art. And, we repeat, it is not limited to the primitive in our midst, that is to say the uneducated. It is not plantation Negroes, cowboys and lumberjacks alone who have their folklore: there is a folklore of the Pullman smoker, the country club, the Stock Exchange and the Capitol. In like manner, there was a teeming and curiously naïve folklore in the sophisticated society that Rousseau denounced. The members of these refined circles were *folk* under their glitter. They believed in contradictory myths—"Progress" and the "Noble Savage"—in the same way as illiterate peasants might believe in elves and fairies. The eighteenth century wrote abundantly, but talked enormously more. It was the sociable age *par excellence*. The *Zeitgeist*, "Mr. Everybody," as we have seen, outshone even M. de Voltaire. The same wit, the same aspirations, the same unconscious prejudices, the same moods and fashions, were shared by the great, the near-great, the unknown. So the "definite" literature of that vital and fascinating age is in many cases but the muffled echo of a distant conversation, that is to say of folklore.

It is our contention, therefore, that the difference between *folklore* and *definite literature* is not a question of period—primitive vs. modern; and not a matter of education—the naïve vs. the sophisticated; the two are stages in the same creative process. But the relations between the two offer several puzzling problems. Broadly speaking, these relations may be examined under three different hypotheses.

The first is the *romantic-primitivist* theory. Literature originates spontaneously, collectively, anonymously. Great events, great heroes, great themes, force themselves upon folk consciousness; everybody talks about them, as we talk about the World War, the Russian Revolution or the mighty Dictators. Time winnows our talk. The flurry of the moment is soon forgotten; the hopes and dread that shook a people to its inmost depths remain. Ubiquitous talk turns to oral tradition; the survivors of the heroic period acquire authority; their versions of the events are transmitted to their disciples with the increasing dignity of years. These versions are gradually consolidated, and, if possible, harmonized; but, as a rule, many discrepancies survive. When that process of condensation and hardening has gone far enough, we realize that a work of *literature* has come into existence, although we could not tell exactly at what time. This work is finally written down. In a few outstanding cases, it is hailed as a masterpiece. Later ages, under the delusion that nothing so great and so definite could come to life without a definite author, will invent the man of genius who created the masterpiece. Every story that impresses the world is, like the characters in Pirandello's drama, "in search of an author," and usually the quest is rewarded. Posterity will even evolve (a true folklore process) a detailed biography of the mythical author. But the biography, to our chagrin, may refuse to set in a solid mold: we are told that seven cities claimed to be the birthplace of Homer.

Of this theory, the best illustration of course is the Homeric problem as presented in the *Prolegomena* of Friedrich August Wolf (1795). But the same method was applied in many other cases. Moses, for instance, ceased to be considered as the sole author of the *Pentateuch;* the attempt was made to trace through the pages of the sacred Books several traditional accounts, blending and at times conflicting. The Carolingian cycle of epic poetry was accounted for according to the same hypothesis. It was surmised that the mighty Emperor must have left an ineffaceable impression upon the popular mind. We know that there are many "romances" or ballads about the Spanish hero, El Cid; therefore, there must have been a similar crop of folksongs about Charlemagne and Roland. Obscurely, in the course of three centuries, these songs became fused and organized, and we have the *Song of Roland*. But it had no definite creator: the mysterious Turold whose name appears in the last line was not the author, only a singer, or perhaps a scribe.

One apparent weakness of this theory is that it applies only in the dimness of the past: it leaves "definite literature," individual, conscious creation, in sole possession of daylit periods, including our own. The objection disappears if our view be accepted that folklore is a living force at all times, today as well as a thousand or three thousand years ago. Then it can be shown that the most original works have their roots in the subconsciousness of the collectivity. No man could be less shadowy, more highly individualized, than Jean Jacques Rousseau; thanks to his *Confessions*, we know every blemish of his ailing body, every flaw in his ill-compacted soul. This man, Rousseau, spoke, challenged the world, and a great part of the world heeded his voice. This would seem to be the triumph of "definite literature." But is there no other explanation? Could we not say that "Rousseauism" had been afloat for decades before Rousseau himself became aware of it? That the very wording of the Prize Competition which gave Rousseau his opportunity proves that the problem was in the public mind? That Rousseau's sudden success, so outrageously out of proportion with the merits of his declamatory *Discourse*, is evidence that a vast portion of the public was Rousseauistic without knowing it? Rousseau is a portent, if you like; that implies that he is a symbol; like Homer, he might be called a "myth." Had there been no Jean Jacques, the world would have invented another one with a different name. Genius is but congruency with the unuttered aspirations of a people.

For two hundred years, this philosophy of the unconscious and the subconscious has been advanced, not in literature only, but in many other domains. Antiquity believed that Codes originated with lawgivers: Moses, Lycurgus, Solon, Numa

Pompilius. "Nonsense," says the apostle of the unconscious; "lawgivers are myths; laws are only customs slowly solidified." A written constitution is an absurdity; there is no actual English Constitution, but an amorphous mass of precedents. If the American Constitution seems to belie this theory, it is because it merely gave an eighteenth-century mask to the living American *mores*. Some of the political traditions to which we are most attached have no constitutional warrant; some very explicit articles in the sacred document are manifestly a dead letter; and when our admirable Constitution was adopted by other republics, it refused to work. You cannot "decree a city into existence," said Joseph de Maistre. Such is not the way of nature; a city must start by chance and grow unconsciously; the proposed capital to be named after Washington will never come to life. You cannot, by taking thought, manufacture a language: every Volapük or Esperanto is stillborn. And, in the same line of reasoning, you cannot, by your own individual effort, create a masterpiece. The masterpiece must pre-exist in the collective soul. The "author" is only the instrument that brings it to conscious life.

Against this romantic theory of obscure growth, the *Individualistic* conception has managed to hold its ground, and even to recapture some important positions. Homer remains part of "definite literature." There may have been two poets instead of one; there are minor discrepancies within each poem; and their text cannot claim the inerrancy of Holy Scripture. Still, the burden of proof is on the side of Wolf and his followers. Not because mankind has believed for so long in the existence of an individual genius named Homer; but because internal evidence, of a convincing nature, reveals a commanding artistic personality. To dissolve Homer into a myth or a committee, much stronger acid would be needed than the Wolfian school has been able to supply.

Although the theory of unconscious growth presents itself with a formidable apparatus of scholarship, it remains, in many cases, a product of the romantic imagination. The evidence it adduces is frequently not actual, but hypothetical. For instance the theory posits a wealth of popular ballads on Carolingian themes before the *Song of Roland;* but these ballads wickedly elude research, and perhaps they never existed at all. Between the Charlemagne of history and the Charlemagne of the epic, there is a gap of over two hundred years. The new Charlemagne, a French King, not a Frankish leader, is the embodiment of the spirit which was to be manifested in the first Crusade. Joseph Bédier takes it that the memory of Charlemagne was preserved, not in popular song, but by the clerics, chiefly in the form of Eginhard's *Vita Caroli.* This learned tradition *became* popular along the pilgrimage routes, particularly the one to Santiago de Compostella. Professor Hugh A. Smith makes a good case for considering the *Song of Roland* as a new departure, which started the vogue of the Carolingian theme. We do not claim that the memory of the great emperor had completely died out in the popular mind; we admit that there probably was a revival of interest in him before an unknown but definite author composed the *Song of Roland.* Still, the share of the individual remains overwhelming. In the same way, the Faust legend and the William Tell saga had survived humbly until the end of the eighteenth century. But it would be a mockery to assert that they automatically assumed definite shape, that they "got themselves written down," somehow, by scribes known as Goethe and Schiller.

The defenders of the Unconscious Growth theory have a tendency, not only to suppose evidence, but even to "fake" evidence. It has often been observed that in the splendid haze of the Romantic mind, there is but a shadowy frontier between the will to believe and the will to make-believe. The eighteenth century, which rediscovered the genuine ruins of Pompeii, was also fond of depicting imaginary ruins, and even of manufacturing them. In the same spirit, by the side of authentic *Reliques of Ancient Poetry* (Thomas Percy, 1765), there was a goodly crop of spurious "primitive" and "popular" poems. The vogue lasted for several generations, from Macpherson's

Ossian (1763 seq.), admired by Goethe and Napoleon, to Prosper Mérimée's *La Guzla* (1826), a treasure house of Slavonic folk poetry, and a priceless document—if it had not been a hoax. We might just as well take Heinrich Heine at his own word, and consider his *Lorelei* as "a fairy tale from remotest times."

A song by Béranger (*The Memories of the People*), a fine chapter in Balzac (*Story of Napoleon Told in a Barn*) are accepted as proofs that the Napoleonic saga grew spontaneously among the people. Both these documents, however, are not transcriptions of genuine folklore, but very clever creations of conscious literature. Napoleon as an epic theme was invented by the middle class, and taught by bourgeois poets to the masses; then and then only did retired old "grumblers" like Captain Coignet discover that they had been Napoleon-worshipers all the while. Even today, the Napoleonic cult is kept up by conservative bourgeois like Louis Madelin and Octave Aubry; among the common people, the legend is dead.

It is not denied that literature uses the same stuff as folklore; but it is claimed that folklore is turned into literature only through *an individual act of conscious organization*. A book is a piece of work, not an accident. There is a debatable border between the two: there are elements in folklore which are almost literature. In such cases, it is probable that we have to deal with conscious literature which has lost some of its definiteness, rather than with an amorphous mass vaguely struggling towards individuality.

To such a twilight zone belongs, for instance, "popular literature," that is to say, literature by men of the people for men of the people, not for the educated. It originates with definite men and in definite form: someone brought the sad story of *Frankie and Johnnie* into artistic life. But these modest ballad-mongers or storytellers did not belong to the world which carefully preserves all its documents, birth certificates, title deeds, original manuscripts. Their name was soon forgotten; their humble text treated in cavalier fashion: after all, the actual words of Shakespeare himself were at first recorded with great carelessness. So the outlines of man and work became blurred. Yet the starting point was a deliberate act of authorship.

At times, this half-effaced "popular literature" may not even be of popular origin at all. We have no way of telling to what extent alleged "folklore" is but the degradation of work that once was fully conscious and even sophisticated. In all cases, in the beginning was the Man—the individual author; it is the assertion of his uniqueness that creates, out of common talk, "literature." And at the end also is man, the individual reader. Collective genius, collective taste, provide a general atmosphere; but unless direct communication be established between author and reader, there can be no genuine literary experience. Literature is not a hubbub, but a dialogue.

The twilight zone mentioned above leads us naturally to the third theory, that of the *circulus*. Literature does not arise automatically out of folklore; on the other hand, the two are not separated by a chasm; between them there is a constant interchange. Every work of art uses as its material the stuff current at the time, even when it opposes its own time, denounces it, attempts to flee from it; classical critics, believers in "pure" literature, have woefully neglected that element. But the stuff, in order to become art, must be stamped with personality: this the folklorists underestimate. This imprint, added to folklore, transforms folklore. The origin of art is in consciousness, not in unconsciousness. At this second stage, the individualists are right.

But no sooner is art thus fixed through personality than it begins to dissolve. As we have already indicated, name and text gradually fade, until they are obliterated. Thus the contribution of an intensely individual man is added, anonymously, to the common hoard of folklore. This happens first with "popular" literature: the personal imprint was probably faint to begin with. But the same fate overtakes even the masterpieces which were thought to be indestructible. Still *definite* for the scholar, they are becoming *folklore* for the multitude. Hence the number of barely recognized literary words and allusions in our common speech: *to pander, hectoring, to curry favor,* a *benedick, quixotic,* a *boniface.* In French, *renard* (the fox) has completely supplanted *goupil; tartuffe* sounds more popular, more natural, than *hypocrite.* Rabelais offers a clear example of this *circulus* between definite literature and folklore. He borrowed his giants, Gargantua and Pantagruel, from medieval tradition, and from a cheap romance now completely forgotten. He transformed the worthless stuff into a book of incomparable charm and power: a hymn, coarse and merry, to kindly Mother Nature; a paean to Science, and the dauntless adventure of the enquiring mind. Everyone knows Rabelais— usually for the wrong reasons. Few people care to tackle his rank and monstrous text: the theme has gone back to folklore. "Gargantuan" and "Pantagruelic" denote joyous quaffing, and swilling on an epic scale. Curiously, the heroes have dragged the author with them into the vague region of folklore, and made him one of themselves. The encyclopedic knowledge, the robust philosophy, the marvelously colorful art of Rabelais, are forgotten; all that we remember is a third giant, a third glutton, a sort of ecclesiastical Falstaff, tun-bellied and uproarious. Goethe rescued Faust from oblivion, and turned the medieval puppet show into the most searching of philosophical dramas. But, except for an élite, the Goethean imprint is getting blurred. Faust, Gretchen with her blond tresses, Mephistopheles and his red cloak, are reverting to folklore. Don Juan, the Wandering Jew, would hardly survive as popular themes if they had not been adopted by conscious writers; but it is not as the Don Juan of Byron or the Wandering Jew of Eugène Sue that they are remembered.

We should constantly bear in mind, in our study of world masterpieces, both the connection between folklore and literature, and their essential difference. Perhaps, at the present moment, it is the difference that needs the greater emphasis. There is some danger of neglecting the individual contribution, and stressing the collective elements: this would turn the study of literature into a branch of sociology. We shall deal with this problem more fully in a later chapter, but its connection with the idea of folklore should be indicated at this stage. The old and constantly rejuvenated theory of "climates," the "economic interpretation" so dear to some modern critics, the "race" doctrine, which is the core of German ideology, are all attempts to explain the unique in terms of the mass. What they explain—to some extent—is folklore, not definite literature. They will describe the *Zeitgeist,* the common substratum: surely a field not to be neglected. They will give depth and precision to such concepts as "the Elizabethan mind" or "the Victorian code." They will not account for the rich variety of types among Elizabethans and Victorians; still less will they explain the miracle of one Elizabethan by the name of Shakespeare. Folkways, folksays, folklore, are part and parcel of anthropology, ethnology, sociology. They are the most fascinating elements in those respectable and somewhat austere sciences. They afford welcome relief from unmitigated statistics. They bring us, we have repeatedly admitted, to the very threshold of the literary domain; and, very properly, they stay without.

It must be taken for granted that both author and reader have their fund of folklore, use folklore liberally, commune through folklore. But it must be remembered also that both retain a certain leeway. Folklore is a storehouse, not a tyrant. There is no power that issues to us, as from an army magazine, rigidly identical equipments. To a very large extent, an author takes for granted the fundamental habits of thought of his time. Dante was not in any sense the average medieval man; but the unchallenged theology of the age was the very air he breathed. However, if we carried that ideal too far, it would lead to slavish, one-hundred-per-cent conformity; or, to use a still uglier term, totalitarianism, one hundred million minds with but a single set of thoughts. Some writers are great because they voice the subconscious mind of the multitude; some, because they are capable of "turning a stream of fresh and free thought upon our stock notions and habits." [1]

Neither is the reader in absolute bondage to folklore. He is able to enjoy literature with a folklore background different from his own: else ancient masterpieces would be absolutely dead, or they would assume a faint and precarious life only for those historical students who could recapture vanished time. The fact that there *is* a world literature is evidence of this liberty. There is an appeal of the universal, under whatever guise it may appear. After all, there is a human race; its widest differences are far less profound than its essential identity. It varies surprisingly little in space or time: in many thousand years, it has not been able to invent an eighth deadly sin. Folklore is the clothing, not the substance, of human thought. And we are able to change the clothing with a very slight effort, which is also a source of pleasure. We can reconstitute, for the time being, myths we no longer accept. Thus even the most severely trained scientist, unless he be thoroughly desiccated, can induce in himself a mood that will enable him to enjoy a fairy tale. We can attune ourselves to religious fervor in a faith which is not our own; we can thrill with an alien patriotism; we adopt, as a rule of the game, the strange codes of the medieval baron, the Indian tribesman, or even the gangster. This is due in part to the keen but childish pleasure of make-believe and dressing-up. It is due, far more, to the capacity of reaching the human substratum beneath the colorful surface. It is this that makes World Literature possible; conversely, it represents the highest service that World Literature can render.

Definite literature may be ephemeral; but its highest ambition is to achieve permanency. The bid for immortality is

---

[1] In Victorian England, said Hilaire Belloc, although the freedom of the press was officially unbounded, "a sort of cohesive public spirit glued and immobilized all individual expression. One could float imprisoned as in a stream of thick substance: one could not swim against it." Fortunately, this was not wholly true even of Victorian England; but this caricature of the *Zeitgeist* could well serve as a warning.

among the hoariest commonplaces in poetry. Innumerable variations have been rung on the words of Horace: "I shall not die altogether" and "I have raised unto myself a monument more lasting than bronze." The most acceptable definition of a classic is: a book that the world would not permit to die.

We have seen, however, that this hope is, for the vast majority of writers, an illusion. Out of several million books, those which have survived even for a few generations number at most a few thousands. Even among the Immortals, many are but tenuously alive. Some have only the kind of artificial existence that is conferred by scholarly study; others are slowly receding into the haze of folklore. If immortality were their sole incentive, writers would be sorry dupes. But another attitude is conceivable, and we believe that it is of increasing significance in the world of letters. It is not necessary that oblivion should be dreaded as identical with failure; *definite literature* may, without loss of pride, abandon the delusive hope of eternal fixity. Our work will die, we all know; most likely before us, perhaps a little after us, in rare cases long after us: but it will die. Let it die, then, and let the dead bury their dead. If we accomplish our task with the utmost care, as though we were laboring for posterity, if it gives us and others today a richer sense of life, "ephemeral" need not be a term of reproach.

The central chapter in Victor Hugo's romance, *Notre Dame of Paris,* is entitled: "This will destroy that": the printing press will supplant the edifice; man's soul will seek expression in the unceasing, turbulent, multitudinous stream of books, and no longer in the magnificent and immovable Bible of stone. Will not this thought apply to the written monument, the eternal classic, as well as to the unchanging monument of architecture?

Victor Hugo evokes a teeming activity shared by everyone in his degree; each at the same time a living man, with a purpose of his own, and a nameless soldier in the innumerable army. The individual is barely discerned, never remembered for long; the work goes on. This vision—for a vision it was rather than a doctrine—was offered to the world over a century ago. The evolution of mankind in those troublous hundred years has confirmed Victor Hugo's prophecy. Art is as *definite* as ever; it still has to raise itself, by a conscious effort, out of the indeterminate stream; but it is soon absorbed into the stream again. Giving a new twist to the ancient adage, we are tempted to say: *Ars brevis, vita longa.* Any work of art is but a fugitive apparition in the interminable life of the race.

Today, artists who are not inferior in dignity of purpose to the noblest in ages past frankly accept fugitivity as their condition. They work, not for posterity, but for the satisfaction of their own conscience, and for an audience of living men. If they deal with problems of the present in terms of the present, degradation does not necessarily follow. The very best service that we can perform for our children is to provide them with honest and intelligent parents. The "ephemeral" book can be great, if it gives an example of artistic integrity.

One step further: can we not envisage the possibility of the book itself being supplanted by the periodical, the daily press, the talking screen? Would it matter so much through what channel the stream is flowing? *Definite* literature is not identical with *fixed* literature. There is no *fixed* literature: nothing is perennial but the *flux* itself.

If it were so—and the hypothesis deserves our earnest attention—*literature,* in the perspective of time, would become harder to distinguish from *folklore* than it was yesterday: it would be diffused through the whole mass of the people instead of being differentiated and concentrated in a few firmly shaped and durable masterpieces.[1] We might have many thou-

---

[1] A similar change has come over science. Bertrand Russell says (*The Scientific Outlook*, p. 55): "It is typical of the modern attitude in science, as compared with that of Newton, or even Darwin, that Pavlov has not attempted a statuesque perfection in the presentation of his theories. 'The reason that I have not given a systematic exposition of our results during the last twenty years is the following. The field is an entirely new one, and the work has constantly advanced. How could I halt for any comprehensive conception, to

sands of able contributors to culture, whose work from day to day would be eagerly absorbed by an audience of millions. The individual effort would almost at once lose itself in the mass. Literary history as a series of clear-cut biographies would disappear; anonymous trends alone would remain.

Yet, although far more elusive to trace, the essential distinction between literature and folklore would not be abolished. The individual would soon be forgotten; but he would remain indispensable. Conscious effort, conscious enjoyment, are the keys of art. Definite art and folklore constantly mingle in the same stream, and it is difficult to distinguish them. But it is art alone that keeps the stream "fresh and free," and saves folklore from stagnation.

SUMMARY

Literature is not merely writing, but an art, the art of self-expression through words. This definition includes informal communication—talk, the spreading of news, storytelling, even gossip—if it be done with intention and relish. This element is present in the life of children, primitive tribes, illiterate people, as well as among the sophisticated. It is the living, fluid stuff out of which formal literature is made. In the mass, it is the translation into words of *Folkways*, the pervading "Spirit of the Time"; and for that reason it has been called *Folksay*. Certain portions of *Folksay* survive the immediate

systematize the results, when each day new experiments and observations brought us additional facts?' The rate of progress in science nowadays is much too great for such works as Newton's *Principia*, or Darwin's *Origin of Species*. Before such a book could be completed, it would be out of date. In many ways, this is regrettable, for the great books of the past possessed a certain beauty and magnificence, which is absent from the fugitive papers of our time, but it is an inevitable consequence of the rapid increase of knowledge, and must therefore be accepted philosophically."

Lewis Mumford, in *The Culture of the Cities*, applies the same idea to the art of fixity par excellence. Architecture, and prophesies "the passing of the Monument," just as Bertrand Russell noted the passing of the scientific "monument" or classic: "Generally, one may say that the classic civilizations of the world, up to our own, have been oriented toward death and fixity: the immobilization of life. . . . The aim of civilization was permanence: its highest achievement in cities was the grandeur of a Panthcon or a Temple."

occasion of utterance and acquire general currency. They thus harden into a set of expressions, thoughts, themes and myths, which may be transmitted from generation to generation. This is known as *Folklore*. Note that *folklore* still exists and is still being created in our own times: it is the common stock of ideas and phrases that everyone takes for granted. Although less fluid than *folksay*, it has no hard-and-fast, final form, and is not thought of as created by any single person.

In opposition to folksay and folklore, we call *definite literature* that which is attached in our minds to a particular text and a particular author, even when the text is imperfect and the author unknown. This definite literature may be inferior in quality and vitality to folklore, and it may be far less permanent. Every new book, however worthless, belongs to definite literature.

For centuries, the study of literature was limited to *definite* literature. Folklore was ignored or despised; the origin of definite works was sought exclusively in other definite works. In the eighteenth century, with Vico and Herder, folklore was rediscovered and rehabilitated. This worked in harmony with the teachings of Rousseau: rebellion against artificial civilization, return to primitive simplicity.

There are now three theories concerning the relations between folklore and definite literature.

1. Folklore is the source of all art; definite literature is artificial and superficial. A masterpiece like the *Iliad* is only the final form of an unconscious growth. Even today, no literature can be great unless it be the expression of folkways, the fixation of folklore.

2. The older theory of conscious creation still holds its ground. Art is always a definite personal act. Folklore is but the blurred shadow of definite literature, when it has lost its identity.

3. The *Circulus* theory. Between the two, there is constant interchange. Art demands conscious creation, but the material out of which the individual creates is the folklore of his time.

Almost as soon as it is created, definite literature dissolves into folklore again.

Permanency was long the ideal of definite literature: a classic is a book that survives. This ideal is fading. Science and literature are constantly in the making. We are beginning to accept change as the only permanent reality. The best work of the day may be ephemeral in its definite form. We are resigned to see it revert almost immediately to folklore. Let author and text be forgotten, if human thought lives and expands.

CHAPTER VI

THE BIOGRAPHY OF TASTE

OUR EXPLORATION, so far, has led us to question venerable certainties rather than to establish a firm body of truths. Ours seems to be "the spirit that ever denies." Today, there is no such thing as an independent national literature; but we had to confess that World Literature is still in the making. There is no invariable, authentic canon of the classics; there are no indispensable books. Literature draws its substance from the nebulous mass known as folklore and dissolves into folklore again. Permanency is a will-o'-the-wisp. Our only assured progress has been on the road of doubt.

Let us not be troubled: this is a well-traveled road, and probably the safest of all. It is the only path to honest thinking. The most reliable guide on such an intellectual venture remains old René Descartes. He did not invent the method, but he stripped it from pedantry and confusion. In his quest for truth, he began with systematic doubt. He rejected everything that rested on hearsay, convention, tradition. He doubted fearlessly; and—after three hundred years we can still feel it in his gray and sedate pages—he doubted joyously; for it is fear, not doubt itself, that engenders anguish and despair. He doubted honestly, until he could doubt no more; and not a moment longer, for doubt with him was a tool, and not a pose. The turning point was the consciousness of his own doubt. This, at any rate, he could not deny. It was a process of thought which implied a thinking instrument: "I doubt, therefore I think; I think, therefore I am."

At the core of this Cartesian philosophy, we find, not a dogma, but a fact of immediate experience: I am far less certain of the physical universe than I am of the Ego, by whom the universe is perceived. Our doubts and negations in literature lead us, through a similar process, to the same rock foundation: our inmost self. Folklore, writings of all kinds, classics, "the best which has been thought and said in the world," only provide nourishment for our spirit. If the spirit were dead, they would be but a dead heap of facts. This is what Matthew Arnold meant when he called culture, not the amassing of material knowledge, but an *inward experience*. In art as in religion, the kingdom is within you.

This was implicit in our provisional definition of art: conscious pleasure in the expression of personality. The instrument that apprehends, registers, defines that pleasure is *taste*. Taste is akin to the bodily senses, and borrows its name from one of them. It resembles the faculty to discriminate the true from the false, which, according to Descartes, is inherent in every man, and which he called "good sense." It resembles also the power of telling right from wrong, which we know as *conscience*. Like all these, it is not free from aberrations; it can be enriched; it can be trained; but it is not certain that it can be imparted.

The proper starting point for the study of world literature will be found, not in the indefinite accumulation of works, but in the solid, irrefutable center of personality, that is to say in the idea of Taste. It is obvious that the center, in the abstract, is but a mathematical point. Personality reveals itself through taste; but taste can be manifested only through the knowledge, selection, appreciation of works. Taste grows more enlightened, surer of its own power, better aware of its own flaws, more deft in its methods, through experience and exercise. But it must pre-exist, were it only in a rudimentary form. Shelves upon shelves of books will never create a soul; but a soul may find nourishment in books.

Literature is that which, out of the mass of mere writing, has been selected by taste: so, if you define taste, you also define literature. This is the essential problem; it is also the most confusing. The first difficulty is that *taste* frequently wears a supercilious mien; but whoever prides himself upon his taste, and seeks to impose it upon others, thereby commits an impardonable breach of taste. The second and far greater difficulty is that the word has many meanings. Between them, the differences are more than mere shades; some indeed seem irreconcilable. It might be well, for a start, to list the diverse and conflicting acceptations of the term; in the hope that we may discover the underlying thought that will bring it into harmony.

Taste then is first of all a bodily sense, whose organ is the palate, and whose function it is to distinguish savors. It is perhaps the most intimate, the most individual, of all. A sight, a smell, a sound, can be perceived at a distance, and by several people at once: a savor requires personal contact. It is therefore of all the senses the one hardest to measure by objective tests. We have units of light and sound; we can put down in figures the data of touch—texture, consistency, heat, weight. The findings of taste, on the contrary, are both definite and undefinable.[1]

This elusive quality of physical taste is transferred to the metaphorical use of the term. Taste means the capacity to like or dislike without reason: *"Non amo te"*: "I do not love thee,

---

[1] Two other senses, by the way, denote qualities closely similar to taste. The first is *flair*, a gift common among dogs, uncanny in man, for picking up a scent that eludes definition and scientific research. *Flair* is purely fact-finding; the detective, the collector, the *connoisseur* in the narrower sense, are credited with *flair*; but the critic should have taste. The second is *tact*: a subtle extension of *touch*, a capacity for feeling, as with invisible sensitive antennae, the possibility of unpleasant collisions, and thus avoiding them. Tact is the outer defense of taste. It discerns in advance the line between someone else's taste and your own, a line which cannot be crossed with comfort and safety. It should be allied with kindness, as the desire not to hurt. Frequently the two are irremediably divorced. There is a blustering benevolence that is tactless, and there is a tact that simply wards off contact. It enables us to "shrink while the shrinking is good." It respects the feelings of others only in order to preserve our own aloofness.

Dr. Fell":[1] what other justification is needed? I may reason out that things not to my taste are excellent in themselves, at any rate for other people; everyone has among his acquaintances at least one Dr. Fell who is a very worthy man. When I confess that I do not *like* a work of art, I am not presuming to criticize or to condemn it: reasoning does not directly affect our likes, dislikes and indifferences. As taste does not claim to be judicial, as it is personal, involuntary, irresponsible, it is, by common consent, beyond the sphere of argument: "Everyone to his taste." *Chacun son goût. De gustibus non est disputandum.*

By a further extension, we apply the word "taste" to *collective* likes and dislikes. A very dangerous but universal figure of speech endows the group with a *mind;* and mind here might be defined as a set of inclinations. In this sense, the term is practically synonymous with *fashion* or *style.* We speak of forms of art, all the way from architecture to clothing, as "in the modern taste," or "in the taste of the nineties." Strictly speaking, this collective taste is as irresponsible as individual taste. What right have we to sneer at our ancestors because they wore periwigs? It was the taste of their time. It is incongruous with our own habits, not with theirs.

Up to this point, we repeat, taste should neither judge, nor be judged. It merely registers a psychological fact. Yet we constantly speak of *good taste,* as though taste were amenable to a higher tribunal. That tribunal exists: it is Society. Taste, in this special sense, means conformity to social standards, the quest of harmony within the chosen group. A jarring note is a breach of discipline, and an evidence of bad taste. Taste, at this level, is closely related to politeness, and even more closely to etiquette. It consists in wearing the right clothes, uttering the right words, professing the right opinions. The

[1] Non amo te, Sabidi, nec possum dicere quare;
Hoc tantum possum dicere, non amo te.—Martial, *Epigrams,* Book I, 32

"I do not love thee, Dr. Fell—The reason why I cannot tell;
But this I know, and know full well:—I do not love thee, Dr. Fell."
—Thomas Brown

man of faultless taste is the one who submits in every detail and without apparent effort to this rule of taste. Thus our last conception of taste is in absolute contradiction with our initial one. We started with the assertion of individual independence; we end with the individual subjected to a bland but irresistible tyranny.

Let us now attempt to extract the elements common to all these conceptions: personal taste, collective taste, good taste. There is one that appears at once: taste is the sense, not of intrinsic excellence, but of *fitness*. A thing is not "to my taste" when it does not suit me; of this I am the only judge, for my palate is in my own mouth. A thing is not "in good taste" when it does not suit the company. Wearing a red tie with full dress, uttering a soldierly expletive, whistling a jazz tune, may be harmless in themselves, but become serious offenses in the ball room, the church or the council chamber.

A second general element is that of *consistency*. Taste implies, not a chance impression, but a constant predisposition or habit. Taste is part of our everyday personality: it does not deal with "acts of God." So it is with collective taste. It may be unaccountable in terms of clear reason; but, if it were wholly capricious, it would cease to exist as taste. Collective taste stands between *custom*, proud of its invincible inertia, and the vanguard of *fashion*, ever eager for change. "Freakishness" is invariably voted to be "in bad taste"; although in a surprisingly short time, the freakish may become the fashionable, and the fashionable turn into the tasteful; until the tasteful itself sinks into the commonplace.

Taste is therefore an instrument of self-realization and self-defense. It seeks to preserve, for the individual or for the group, that consistency without which there can be no personality. For personality, upon which we are founding our whole conception of taste and literature, is not purely an unquestioned birthright. It has to be achieved, and it has to be maintained. Man and society alike are in constant danger of dissolution.

They are able to remain themselves only by resisting the influences which might lead to disruption. "This way madness lies": frenzy and civil war are corresponding terms. Consciously or not, we pick out, by means of taste, "what is good for us." [1]

"What is good for us" is what contributes to the strengthening or expansion of our personality. The basis of our selection can be purely conservative: we accept willingly everything that agrees with our past experience. It may also be progressive: we are ready to take up that which enriches our experience, provided the acquisition does not entail a greater loss. This defines our tastes in the positive sense, the things we are ready to like. But Taste as a quality is mostly a method of rejection; it is a collection of distastes. We refuse admittance to anything that would weaken our personality, that would tend to make our experience worthless, that would divide us against ourselves. If we have acquired mastery in a game, we resent any change in the rules. If we have painfully learned to write academic English, the use of colloquial American will seem to us in very poor taste. It is the natural protection of our vested interests.

Society proceeds on the same principle. "Bad taste" means challenging the established hierarchies; "good taste" consists in keeping out every upstart and intruder. The dangers of this negative conception are apparent. A citadel that protects us too efficiently, and out of which we never dare to sally forth, is not very different from a prison. If taste prevents us from adopting the new, it soon hinders us from enjoying the old. Bent on rejecting, it finds more things to reject. A "delicate" taste turns into a "fastidious" taste. In Voltaire's *Candide*, Senator Pococurante, the epicure and connoisseur, could find no

---

[1] This, by the way, was the intended function of physical taste. The guardian of the gate, it rejects that which might be harmful to the organism. Unfortunately, the guardian has been bribed and can no longer be trusted: a poison may be palatable. It would be even less safe to believe that physical taste is infallibly wrong. The wholesomeness of a food—or of a doctrine—cannot be gauged by its unpleasantness.

pleasure in his exquisite possessions. He had become blind to quasi-perfection, and could see nothing but the imperceptible flaw. He was like the "sure-enough Princess" in the folk tale, who could not sleep because of the cherry pit under the thick downy bed. Thus there is eternal conflict between the *taste* that means zest, relish, gusto, and the *taste* which prides itself on squeamishness. Yet they are part of the same process: protection and expansion are both indispensable to life.

So far, we have considered individual taste and collective taste as parallel, and possibly antagonistic: Society attempts to impose conformity upon man, and man seeks to maintain his independence. But the two are normally found in friendly and fruitful association. For self-realization is most complete in contact with other personalities. What the individual needs is not solitude, but sympathy. Even conflict is better than loneliness. The rule of taste, as we have defined it above, applies to the selection of friends. It consists in drawing the line so as to exclude uncongenial people, and so as to include those with whom you desire to associate. Your social standard is but an extension of your personal ideal. You crave the company of gentlemen, because you want to be a gentleman.

This is fulfillment, not sacrifice; yet it cannot be achieved without a compromise. You have to fit yourself for the company you have chosen. You have to submit to a certain degree of formal, artificial conformity, for the sake of the deep-seated harmony which is your goal. You may have to give up some minor aspects of your personal taste; you may have to adopt, without any profound conviction, certain minor aspects of collective taste. All this is legitimate enough if, on the whole, you are more fully yourself within the group than you would be without.

If, on the contrary, the self is stifled by the group, then the loss may be disastrous. Acquiescence is no longer a willing and mutually advantageous compromise, it is a capitulation. In society, it leads to sheer snobbishness; man gives up his own worth and thinks only of rank and station; the "right" thing is the one which is done by the "right" class. In religion, it leads to pharisaical and ostentatious conformity. In art and literature, it leads to the adoption of artificial standards and stock judgments, whether they be those of academic tradition, or the shibboleths of the latest clique.

What we are studying in this book is the Constitution and By-laws of the World Literature Club. This Club should be an open association of free men. The sole basis for admission should be a taste *for* literature, not a prescribed taste *in* literature. It is, as we have attempted to show, a more natural Club for us to join than the national one. If we are to draw the line according to our taste, there are many writers in our own language with whom we have no desire to associate; and we should be extremely reluctant to debar ourselves from the company of Homer and Dante. There is no coincidence whatever between the circle of the things we like, and the sharp boundaries of our political or linguistic group.

To join such a Club, there is no creed to profess, there are no formulae to memorize. What binds us together is taste, not knowledge. However, a certain degree of culture in the narrower and more conventional sense of the term, that is to say some acquaintance with "the best which has been thought and said in the world," will be of great assistance. You will find intercourse easier if your words have, roughly, the same connotation as the words of your fellow members. People cannot even disagree unless they come within hailing distance. Without a few deep experiences in common, we can soliloquize and we can chatter, but we cannot converse. The incomparable value of the "classics" is that they provide such a meeting ground.

This Club idea, this necessary and profitable interaction between individual and collective taste, will make it easier for us to approach the problem: Can taste be improved, and, if it can, by what means? If we did cleave to the original meaning of the word, if taste were but a spontaneous, unaccountable, irresponsible reaction, if "I do not love thee, Doctor Fell" were the final argument, then any attempt at a literary education would be futile. If we tried to impose "good taste," it would be but the enforcement of hypocrisy.

Yet education may be justified, even on the basis of strictest individualism. Instead of stifling or warping our personal taste, it should provide for it a freer opportunity. The untutored man, for all his fine spontaneity, is the prisoner of his ignorance. Let us imagine a keen, sensitive spirit, with an inborn taste for literature. It happens that the only books within his reach are the cheap romantic novels of Ouida and Marie Corelli. He will take delight in them; to him, they will be "art" and "literature"—an escape from the humdrum, a widening of experience, a field for imagination. Even in their second-rate technique, he will find a fairly successful attempt to tell a connected, exciting story, to create characters, to use language with some effectiveness. These books, which we affect to despise, will come to him as a revelation of the magic land, with a force that even Shakespeare has lost for most of us. His misplaced enthusiasm would be proof of his taste for literature, since he could extract delight even out of such tawdry stuff. It would not be evidence of poor taste in literature, since, in our hypothesis, he had no access to anything better. In the same way, the first automobile brought into a backward country will be hailed as a wonder, however antiquated it may be. Be sure the purchaser will not cherish it *because* it is rattling and wheezy; he will overlook these blemishes, in the exhilaration of the added power and freedom that the new invention is bringing to him. In these cases, it is not taste that is deficient, but experience. Acquaintance with a few classics will correct this deficiency. A classic is by definition a standard. It is not a pattern to be reproduced: it gives you a sense of the values you have a right to demand. It does not limit, but enlightens, your choice.

Absolute spontaneity, manifesting itself through irresponsible taste, is a Romantic delusion. Rousseau imagined that man was "good" as he was shaped by the Creator of all things, and that through a return to "nature," he might recapture something of his pristine innocence. This doctrine, tempting as it may be, is not in great favor today. We are more inclined to agree with Pascal's dictum: "They say that habit is second nature. Who knows but Nature is only a first habit?" What we believe to be an inborn taste might well be an obscurely acquired prejudice. It would not be wise therefore to accept our dislike of Dr. Fell as final. We might be misinformed, and dislike in Dr. Fell mere externals which are not the real man at all. On better acquaintance, we might actually like him. We do not challenge the right of taste to be the ultimate judge; we want to be assured that we are dealing with genuine taste. The aim of education is not to supplant taste, but to purify it.

Taste is the manifestation of personality. But personality is not an abstract principle: no man is a walking theorem. Personality implies *unity in complexity*. The strongest individual is not the monomaniac, haunted by a single thought; it is the man who most efficiently keeps in order the multitude within. To every one of our recurring moods corresponds a shade of our taste. We cannot be constantly absorbed in solemn thought: *desipere in loco*, said Horace; [1] there is a proper time for cheerful nonsense. But how can we tell the proper time? Only according to a scheme that will establish a hierarchy among the various elements of our personality. Some must be kept under restraint, or they will weaken and even destroy us. Others may be allowed free play, but only at the right time and place. Others still are the natural rulers. If we accepted as equally valid all spontaneous manifestations of taste, this necessary subordination would be ruined. There are tastes to which we should not yield, because they would impair other tastes of a deeper and more permanent value. Thus our taste for danger should be held in check by our greater taste for life; an immoderate taste for drink should be tempered through a taste for health; our innocent taste for thrillers should be curbed by our taste for reason and truth. Perhaps we should call *taste* that power which keeps our various appetites within bounds.

[1] Horace, *Odes*, IV, 12-28.

To enlighten taste through wider knowledge; to purify taste by purging away mere prejudice; to organize taste by giving greater weight to the more permanent values: these are three methods of working upon our taste without denying its spontaneity or curtailing its autonomy. Our sole aim is to make taste a more delicate and more reliable instrument of our personality.

Now we have reached the time when these general ideas must be clothed with definite facts—the facts of the reader's own experience. Can *you* define your taste, and tell how it was formed?

For many years, I have been asking my students to give me, as their first essay, the *Biography of Their Literary Taste*. These papers, as a rule, provide delightful reading; for they are written with sincerity, knowledge and gusto. But easy pleasure is a minor consideration, except for the lazy man; the earnest and even the strenuous teacher also will find these papers invaluable. The teacher's task is not to pour the inert liquor of knowledge into empty and indifferent containers; he is dealing with living minds. In large classes, these minds do not spontaneously reveal themselves to him: he has to coax their confidences. He should attempt to know whom he is teaching, what misconceptions he has to correct, what foundations he can take for granted. For all these purposes, he will find these *Autobiographies* of commanding interest.

They have another field of usefulness. Teaching must go hand in hand with research; and research in literature should not be limited to the ascertaining of historical facts. It should be experimental as well as antiquarian; it should study the fundamental literary experiences, the processes of creation, communication and response. For the last of these at least, students are admirable guinea pigs; it is in the incipient stages, before conventions have hardened, before enthusiasm has faded, that esthetic response can most profitably be investigated. Discussions among scholars, controversies among critics, too often emphasize learning or theory at the expense of the basic facts.

If the teacher greatly profits by such a biography, the chief benefit goes, as it should, to the biographer himself. It is not necessary to be connected with a university: every reader should attempt to write the history of his own taste, even without any thought of submitting it to an adviser. Self-analysis, self-criticism, is the first step in sound criticism. It has been objected that it will make the young self-centered, egotistical, conceited: it is dangerous to tell a freshman that he is the sole judge of literature. I can only answer, as a good pragmatist: "Try the experiment, and note the results." I have found so far that my challenge, instead of fostering conceit, had a sobering effect. Conceit is most clearly manifested in those who repeat other people's opinions: the stock judgment cribbed from lecture or textbook, or, for the very daring, the latest formula of the ruling "Smart Set." Glib infallibility is invariably at secondhand. If you are compelled to pause and reflect, you realize that taste is not a matter of imitation and memory, that taste is not authority, whim or fashion, but a living development. A short case history—your own—reveals the fact that you have stumbled many times in your brief past, and that you have already outlived several crazes. There is no more effective lesson in humorous tolerance.

What such a challenge does bring out is a sense of responsibility. You are entering adult life: the State will expect you to give your decision upon all public affairs. Wisdom urges you not to do so without expert advice: still, you remain free to choose your advisers, and free not to adopt their opinion. The churches which most stringently insist upon authority teach also that, when you have reached a given age, you are accountable for your sins. To decide, in matters political as well as literary, without thought, without consultation, is dangerous foolishness. But "leaving it to one's betters" is not modesty: it is cowardice.

I have no intention of giving a composite picture of American youth. I am interested neither in the mass nor in the average, but in the individual. I do not propose, in this book at any rate, to tell about the one individual I ought to know, namely, myself: be sure, however, that I have not shirked the task that I imposed upon others. I shall merely note a few reflections, the fruit of a fairly long practice. I would not offer them if I thought they were totally worthless; but I must insist that the chief interest of the experiment lies beyond the reach of these general remarks, in the enriched experience of individual student and individual teacher.

The first point that these biographies bring out with great clearness is that the formation of literary taste is by no means purely a bookish affair. Taste, personality, life, cannot be severed. "Literature," even World Literature, as we said in our first chapter, begins in the nursery. It is not a matter of indifference what stories are told a child, and by whom they are told. Blessed is the baby who has the right kind of a grandmother! To be a mother is a very exacting business: to be a grandmother is an art. The nurses who could tell fairy tales and sing ballads with unfeigned delight are almost an extinct race; and with the old-fashioned nurses vanished the genuine nursery tale, created anew, out of immemorial themes, for the small entranced individual listener. We have to accept the fact that, in the pre-literate age, our children are largely fed on the comic sections. They command grown-ups to read the words that float ectoplastic out of the characters' mouths; they keep the Sabbath-day by hearing those stories over the radio. This, and not the tradition of Perrault and the Grimm Brothers, is now the basis of our American folklore. It is transmitted through the living voice and the picture long before the written word has opened its secret.

Visual influence, by the way, does not vanish with the nursery stage. In the first books we read, the illustrations count far more than the text. Gustave Doré has affected young imaginations more vividly than most poets. Somewhat to my surprise, I found that in America the Napoleonic Legend had remained visual rather than literary. Thousands of books have been written about the Corsican; but what we have in mind, when we read the prestigious name, is a series of dramatic scenes, famous paintings, monuments and statues. The cocked hat and the gray riding coat live in our memory much more definitely than Napoleon's Codes or even his strategy. When man becomes literate, he does not turn blind to everything but the printed word. The pure bookman is a monster: a literary education never is exclusively literary. Some classes had perhaps an orgy of print: the visual element is on the increase again. The illustrated periodicals, the moving pictures, television, are restoring, through the magic of modern technique, a condition which prevailed in the healthy childhood of the race.

It is also a matter of great moment whether the stories and characters of the Bible are made living to the young, whether the Book is read with perfunctory reverence, whether it is ignored altogether. A child may have his ears attuned to the grandest imagery and noblest rhythm in the language, or he may be bored and even repelled by what seems to him incomprehensible jargon.

The size of the family counts for a great deal. The lonely child enjoys privileges for which a crushing price has to be paid; the boisterousness of a large family group is a delight with very definite drawbacks. Health is a very important element: many a youngster acquired a taste for reading as the result of a long sickness; convalescence often leaves in the memory a lovely glow of returning strength and the ripening friendship of books.

Great also is the influence of individuals beyond the family circle: a grown-up who becomes a hero, a comrade whose taste alters our own, through the sole authority of affection. By all the rules of the game, love should be a determining factor. I must confess that my most outspoken students are strangely reticent on that subject. They are sufficiently grown up not to take their early experiences tragically; they are not mature enough, however, to view them with complete detachment. In this domain, the rights of scientific investigation expires.[1]

[1] A curious and plausible explanation for this divorce between adolescent love and literature was offered by one of my freshmen: "In the old days," he said, "you could write a sonnet and get away with it. Now you would be

The biography of taste is by no means a mere list of books; but the share of books in our formation is of course not to be denied. If we attempt to recapture our vanished past, it is sometimes the physical aspect of a book that will best revive our impression. Everyone remembers the very first volumes that counted in his life: the pictures, of course, the torn binding perhaps, the loose leaves, the very smell; no de luxe edition will ever rival the appeal of these tattered pages. And with these sensations is unconsciously linked a feeling that lingers in after life; the most dogmatic critic, if he searched his mind with sufficient care, would find at the basis of some arrogant theory the dim recollection of early childhood.

We should then have a place in our *History of Taste* for the personal companionship of books: those that were lying loose in the nursery, to be treated with comradely roughness; the more formal friends, with whom we had to be on our good behavior; the distant and respected acquaintances, taken out of grown-up shelves only under close supervision; perhaps an occasional raid on the dusty store in the attic; not to forget a chapter on the Forbidden Book, and how at last the ban was lifted—or circumvented. The deepest experience does not always come to those lucky children who have all the best books within easy reach. Happier still is the child with a very small hoard, for whom every addition to his treasure is an event and a delight: the book long desired, which at last appears as a present; or better still, the one for which he had patiently saved his pennies, until he could make it his very own. Such intimate factors, and not exclusively intrinsic worth, enter into our liking for a particular author. The reverse is conceivable: some work of literature can be made distasteful to us through unpleasant associations. This, as we shall see, frequently happens during adolescence; childhood is almost free from that curse. In that golden age, a book is considered as an opportunity for pleasure, not as a stern and strenuous means of self-improvement.

called a cheapskate: you have to take her out." The automobile and the ball room are dangerous rivals for lyric poetry.

The field of juvenile literature is enormous; with most of the reading of my students I am not acquainted, even at secondhand. The very old favorites are still alive, but some of them are growing feeble. I shall waste no sentiment on the passing away of the *Swiss Family Robinson;* but I cannot help regretting the decline of *Pilgrim's Progress.* It seems that with youthful readers, the *series* idea is largely prevalent: when once you have adopted a hero (preferably a pair of heroes), you want to see him (or them) roam through every continent, and range through every social condition. In this the very young public is not different from the mature or even the elderly: hence the success of interminable *series* like the *Forsyte Saga* or *Men of Good Will.* Of these juvenile series, the only one with which I am at all familiar is the *Oz Books.* Even a crabbed student of General and Comparative Literature is able to appreciate their directness, their easy humor, the masterly consistency of their weirdest characters.

It was Frank L. Baum's ambition to create an *American* folklore. Our children applauded him, but wisely refused to commit themselves to literary nationalism: in the last few years, I found A. A. Milne disputing first place with Frank Baum. There are widely different zones of taste among the very young. The most delicately lovely of children's books, those of Kenneth Grahame, are by no means a universal experience; but the chosen few love them with an almost fanatical passion. *Alice in Wonderland* and *Through the Looking-Glass* are among those indispensable books which, to their great loss, most young people manage to dispense with. Yet they were, and remain, genuine "juveniles," in spite of the rich vein of quotations, allusions and imitations they have started among grown-ups. It is now the fashion to consider Lewis Carroll as a forerunner of Einstein: his are profoundly *English* books—you laugh today, and you see the point twenty years later.

We find in childhood a form of literary appreciation which does not quite fade away in later years: the desire to act, indeed to live, your favorite fiction. Half in fun, half in earnest, children are romantic poets, and dwell happily on the borderland of make-believe. There are imperceptible degrees, for them as well as for us, between *Let's play* . . . *let's pretend* . . . *let's be.* Just as youthful explorers, pirates, Indian fighters, gangsters or G-men have to be returned by the police to their anxious families, we find adults seriously fancying themselves in the character, clothes and station of their chosen hero. French society, in the clear rational dawn of the Classical Age, attempted to copy the tone, manners, sentiments of Honoré d'Urfé's romance, *Astrée.* As far as Poland, there were Balzac Clubs, every member of which strove to be "Balzacian." Reality imitates art: there is no higher tribute. Of such an influence of reading upon life. there is of course no better example than *Don Quixote.*

The biography of literary taste, so far, has been a happy story. With adolescence, we enter upon a period of doubts and conflicts; at times of ludicrous contrasts, like the odd breaking of the voice. For a few, there is unchecked expansion; and indeed this ought to be the norm, for there is no lack of excellent books, substantial and artistic, accessible to boys and girls in their early teens. Yet, in many cases, the taste for reading almost disappears; in not a few, a genuine distaste for literature begins to be manifested. Of course, high school life brings with it greater interest in organized sports, social activities, and at least the adumbration of professional training: literature has to encounter vigorous rivals. Experience grows so suddenly richer that reading finds it hard to keep pace with it. Childish things are hastily put away; but the initiation into adult life is apt to be awkward, and at times painful.

It must be recognized therefore that the high school teachers of literature have to face an incredibly difficult task; it is not certain that they have always met it with adequate wisdom and sympathy. For years, many of my *Biographers of Taste* have complained that literature was utterly spoilt for them by pedantic methods. Masterpieces were forced upon unwilling palates; some were totally unsuitable to the age and preparation of the pupil; the very best were made insipid through mucilaginous pedagogy. Literature had been something to enjoy: it became something to be outlined, analyzed, commented upon, memorized—and dreaded. The boy who could not overcome or disguise his distaste was put down as dull. In certain years, the plaints were so unequivocal and so nearly unanimous that I was tempted to call these biographies "The Bitter Cry of the Children."

The chief cause of the trouble was the fallacy that "literature" consists in a shelf-full of standard works, to be piously, austerely transmitted; that any approved masterpiece was "good for you" under any circumstances. More ghastly than the failure of the teachers was their success: all too often, they managed to impress upon living young minds the deadening gospel of unreasoning conformity. I can honestly say that, within the last decade, the improvement in the teaching of literature has been startling. The approach to the humanities seems to have been made humane at last.

I do not believe that children should be left to the downward guidance of their cheapest taste. But, if the teacher is to lead them upward, she must consider their taste, and not a collection of classics, as the right point of departure. I am convinced that young people are very responsive to the challenge of difficulty; they like to take even their pleasures strenuously. But there is a profound difference between the difficulty that is a prowess and the difficulty that is merely a burden. It may be easier for the teacher to cram Milton down Johnny's throat than to take Johnny by the hand, shy, diffident, but secretly proud, into Milton's august presence. The result of the first method is an inveterate Miltonphobia: not a rare disease among college freshmen. The second brings an inestimable enrichment of life.

A biography of our taste, if it be honestly carried out, will bring a threefold benefit. In the first place, it compels us sharply to face our own responsibility. Literary orthodoxy, conventional *good taste*, the meek acceptance of a social standard: all these are but shelters for the timid soul. Let us hope that we shall find a large circle of congenial friends: to be alone is no sure sign of strength. But there is a fundamental integrity which should not be sacrificed to the desire for good company.

In the second place, it makes us realize that letters are not severed from life. Our likes and dislikes in reading are conditioned by our circumstances; in return, they define our personality and affect our career. Literature, thus woven into the substance of our thoughts and deeds, does bring pleasure, but a pleasure which is fraught with significance. This sense of life will correct the professional deformation, the pedantry, of the bookman—writer, critic, professor—who places literature in a realm apart; it will also correct the superciliousness of the practical man, for whom reading is a mere pastime.

In the third place, the sense of life is the sense of growth. Considered in the perspective of years, our taste will appear, not as a fixed entity, but as a sensitive struggling organism. It has had periods of happy development, and periods of stagnation. It has gone through a number of fevers and diseases, epidemic or individual. It has been renewed several times over, like the cells of our bodies, without losing its essential continuity. As it has changed, as it has grown, so it will change and grow in the years ahead. A blessèd assurance! No man needs to become a fossil except by his own consent.

A NOTE ON BAD TASTE

A negative definition is seldom safe. We are not likely to learn what taste is merely by listing all the things that taste is not. That is why the present reflections on bad taste are relegated to a postscript. However, if a positive definition be agreed upon, it will be made more precise by exploring its boundaries. I was told that Munich once established a *Museum of Kitsch* [1] This term, applied chiefly to painting, meant bad art; it was

---

[1] This was in the Pre-Nazi Era; I am not alluding to the parallel expositions of *Pure German Art* and *Decadent Art* which were later held in Munich under Nazi auspices.

hoped that a collection of the unmistakably bad would yield the secret of its badness. Bad art is essentially art in bad taste; crude and faulty art may be poor, it is not necessarily bad; and even conventional art may have its redeeming points.

Bad taste in art is not quite the same thing as bad taste in society. There it is synonymous with tactlessness, lack of consideration, hurting other people's feelings. The burlesque treatment of a sacred subject is, socially, in bad taste. Voltaire's dreary mock-heroic poem *La Pucelle* is rude and vulgar rather than wicked. But, if we made this social "good taste" the supreme test of art, we should be erecting a protective fence of taboos round our prejudices. There always will be well-bred people to whom "a stream of fresh and free thought" will seem in deplorable taste. There are moments when honesty compels us to give offense. All rebels in the name of conscience were "impolite."

The basic element in Kitsch is dishonesty, which may be allied with a very rich culture and a very clever technique. By dishonesty, I do not mean departing from literal truth: poets are not scientists, romancers are not historians. All art is pretense; but Kitsch is pretentiousness. It implies a desire to impress beyond the candid worth of the things presented. It is an attempt to steal pseudo-artistic effects through a non-artistic appeal.

The most evident form of Kitsch is vulgar display. Richness, *per se*, is a quality. It was no fault in the Parthenon to be built of marble and not of unbaked clay; and Pheidias himself worked in ivory and gold. Richness is the effort to secure the most adequate material: the finest in texture, the most pleasing to the eye and touch, the most durable. But, if richness be emphasized for its own sake, then we have the *gorgeous*, which is Kitsch. It is Kitsch even if the richness thus displayed be perfectly genuine; it is Kitsch in the second power if it be false, if we are offered tinsel for gold. Then we have the gaudy, the tawdry, the very essence of bad taste.

On this basis, we may write in parallel columns genuine qualities, and their equivalent in Kitsch. Here is a tentative list:

Rich	Tawdry, gaudy, gorgeous
Frank, outspoken	Indecent, obscene
Realistic	Vulgar, sordid
Attractive	Meretricious (alluring and seductive on borderline)
Touching, moving, pathetic	Sentimental
Eloquent	Bombastic, claptrap, ranting
Patriotic	Jingoistic
Great or grand	Colossal, grandiose
Pious	Sanctimonious
Courageous	Bragging, bullying, hectoring
Profound (or even honestly difficult)	Cryptic (esoteric on borderline)
Subtle, cultured, urbane	Sophisticated, smart

It will be noted that I am placing, unhesitatingly, in the Kitsch column three words at least which are frequently accepted as terms of praise: gorgeous, grandiose, and sophisticated. I admit they are capable of both interpretations. They are "bêtes noires" of mine which may be your "bêtes blanches."

It will readily be seen that Kitsch is not limited to popular, bourgeois or philistine art. Much "vanguard" literature betrays a desire to impress the public by aping the gestures of daring. "Épater le bourgeois"—to flabbergast George F. Babbitt, is a very authentic form of Kitsch. Edgar Allan Poe's *Ulalume* has been praised as a masterpiece of weird evocative power; to critics as different as Aldous Huxley and Yvor Winters, it is Kitsch. Every reader will find it profitable to draw up his own list, and supply definite illustrations.

SUMMARY

The pleasure that we find in self-expression is measured by an instrument, our *taste*. It is *taste* that discriminates between mere writing and literature, and therefore *defines* literature.

In its simplest meaning, taste is akin to the physical sense from which it takes its name. It is an immediate, personal reaction, unreasoning and irresponsible: "I do not love thee, Doctor Fell." This reaction is a plain fact, not open to argument.

Taste also means the collective likes and dislikes of a group or period—customs, styles, vogues, fashions. This also is a fact; the taste of the nineties is not our taste, but this should imply no condemnation.

Good taste means conformity to a social standard: adjusting our likes and dislikes to those of the people with whom we want to associate.

Two elements appear in all three conceptions. The first is *fitness:* taste condemns even a good thing, if it is not in its place. The second is *consistency:* capricious taste is no taste at all, for mere caprice is the denial of personality.

Individual and collective taste can be reconciled through the club idea: we are more completely ourselves in association with congenial minds. Compromise is justified, if we are more fully ourselves within the chosen circle than we would be without; otherwise, it is deadly.

Both for the individual and the group, taste is an instrument of defense; it rejects that which would harm our personality by destroying its unity. It accepts that which strengthens our identity, through confirmation or expansion. It is thus a method of *self-realization.*

Taste, for every man, is the final judge. But an automatic reaction is not the whole of taste: only its crudest form. Taste must be *enlightened,* through wider knowledge; *purified,* by purging away mere prejudice, which does not represent our true selves; *organized,* by giving greater weight to the more constructive and permanent element in our complex personalities.

Every reader should take stock of his own taste, historically, by noting under what influences it was formed: home, friends, teachers, books. This is what we call *The Autobiography of Our Literary Taste.* The present writer has read many hundreds of such Biographies, and offers a few reflections on his experience.

The benefit of this exercise is three-fold: (1) it compels us to face our responsibility; no one can judge for us; so we must train ourselves to be competent judges; (2) it makes us realize that literature is not severed from the life around us; (3) it makes us realize also that our taste, like our personality, is not a rigid set of dogmas, but a sensitive organism. It should grow with us, and never be allowed to become fossilized.

A Note on Bad Taste

Good taste is the sense of fitness; bad taste is unfitness. *Kitsch*, to borrow a convenient term from German slang, is *pretentiousness*, a discrepancy between professed intentions and means; particularly a dishonest attempt to achieve pseudo-artistic results through a non-artistic appeal. For instance, a vulgar display of wealth, strength, cleverness, virtue, meant to impress the naïve. We submit a tentative list of genuine qualities, with their translation into *Kitsch*.

CHAPTER VII

THE ESSENCE OF LITERA-
TURE

E HAVE attempted a preliminary and very rough survey of our domain. But we have been denied the satisfaction of driving stakes firmly into the ground, and exclaiming: "Within these limits, the field is mine!" What we called definite literature extends indefinitely beyond the ken even of the most learned. Everywhere it merges with the formless mass known as folklore. Out of this confusion, can we ever hope to extract an infallible, or dogmatic, definition of literature?

A definition is not merely a verbal game; it is an instrument. What do we expect of it? It may be either active or passive; that is to say, it may enable us to reproduce the thing described, or simply to recognize it. Geometry offers the model of active definitions: if we are told what a square is, it is easy for us to draw a square. In chemistry, at least in its simpler form, a formula is a recipe. In literature, there are sets of rules which amount to active definitions. Given the specifications for a sonnet, anyone can write a sonnet. But will this possibility extend beyond mere technique? Dramatic critics of the Classical Age, as late as Lessing, professed that, by obeying Aristotle's precepts, a docile pupil could write a tragedy without blemish. "Faults" could be detected and removed, in the same way as fallacies could be exposed in formal logic, and errors corrected in mathematical operations. You have only to follow instructions; the method is unerring, the result inevitable, and the addition, the syllogism, the tragedy, are bound to come out right.

We wonder if, in literature, there is a single dogmatist alive consistent enough to proclaim: "This that I am teaching you is the truth. Hold fast to this faith, and your work shall be perfect."

In general, we have to be satisfied with a passive definition. Such a definition applies admirably to matters of form. We may not be able to create a tragedy according to rule; but, when we see a play in five acts and in verse, with heroes of exalted rank who never crack a smile and who die before the final curtain, we are pretty safe in calling it a tragedy. But no definition of this kind will give us a key to values. A soulless and even a witless piece of work is likely to be, in externals, at least as "true to type" as a masterpiece: the word *standard* is capable of several interpretations. And it is a sense of value alone that can tell us whether a given page is mere writing, or literature.

We have sought to establish that this sense of value is what is called *taste*. But if we were asked to accept the infallibility of taste as a dogma, in the same way as Rousseau accepted the infallibility of conscience, we should have to demur. "I do not love thee, Doctor Fell" is no absolute criterion. For the *I* who claims to be the sovereign judge is itself a complex and changing entity. *We have to find ourselves before we can trust ourselves.* The individual mind is shaped, if not wholly determined, by the world in which it grows. Its choice is free only within the range that society affords. "We repair to the ballot box—and vote for Harding, or for Cox": such are the limits of our boasted political liberty. And so it goes with literature: too often, the things we like best are merely those we dislike least; and our taste is the measure, not of our inmost desires, but of our opportunities.

As for collective taste, it simply means acceptance by a group. But by what group? Not by the illiterate or barely literate majority; no one has thought of defining art in terms of universal suffrage. Even Tolstoy, when he advocated an art that would be intelligible to the masses and good for the masses, gave no assurance that the masses, of their own accord, would discover and adopt such an art. If we cannot trust the many, still less can we trust the few. The learned are desiccated by pedantry, the cliques are warped by a pose, the social élite is swayed irresponsibly by every vogue. The fate of literature lies in the hands of a fairly large and fairly well educated general public. How large, how well educated, cannot be stated with any precision.

But this "enlightened" public opinion seldom reaches unanimity; and, although it is not so easily stampeded as the cliques and the drawing rooms, it may veer with disconcerting suddenness. So we have to correct its very ambiguous and precarious verdict by the "test of time." Lincoln, it has often been remarked, was not completely right: you can fool all the people all the time, but not with the same thing. The aberrations and divagations of taste among the fathers are partly canceled by the aberrations and divagations in the taste of their children. The result is supposed to be tolerably safe. If we were to give a definition of literature on the basis of collective taste, we should arrive at such a formula as this: "Literature is that which is accepted as such by a sufficient number of people over a sufficient period of time."

This willful looseness may seem a mere caricature. What is the sense of a "definition" in which everything remains undefined? Yet it is good Empiricism: it simply faces the facts. Pick up any history of literature, be it popular or scholarly; you will find that many names are included, not in virtue of a dogmatic theory, not because of the author's personal liking, but on the basis of a fairly general and prolonged acceptance.

So we have the choice between three attitudes, the dogmatic, the individualistic and the empirical; and most of us decide to adopt all three, as each suits the mood of the moment, and without giving a thought to their radical incompatibility. We like to stand with the "right people," we take it for granted that their taste is *Taste*, and we attune our opinion, so far as we are able, to that of the "enlightened public." Few of us, however, are selfless enough to achieve perfect conformity; timidly or defiantly, our personal preferences reassert themselves. And, whether we are voicing our own taste, or public taste, we are tempted to speak as though we were expounding the eternal verities.

For such a blending of incongruous doctrines, the philosophers have devised the imposing term *syncretism;* the plain English name would be hodge-podge.[1] We may find some comfort in the thought that students of literature are not the only victims of such a confusion. Not one of our systems in any domain will fit at the same time our desire for logic, and the complexity of phenomena. In other words, reality is not wholly rational. We find the same syncretism in all realms of thought, and particularly in religion and in politics. A glance at these two fields may help us understand the difficulties that we have to face.

There are Christians for whom their religion is first of all a creed, a set of dogmas to be firmly believed. There are others for whom it is essentially a personal experience, the direct revelation of God's grace to the individual soul. And there are many who pay scant attention to theology, who never went through an intense crisis of conversion, who never had even a glimpse of the beatific vision, but who are unimpeachable members of their Church, as a congenial association of well-meaning men. The majority of us hold these three conceptions at the same time, trusting that, from day to day, life will adjust their contradictions. British-wise, we hope to "muddle through somehow" into the Kingdom of Heaven.

[1] Matthew Arnold's famous definition of culture could be given as a good example of such syncretism. *The pursuit of our total perfection:* this is an idealistic, absolutistic conception. "Be ye perfect as your Father in Heaven is perfect": perfection implies an eternal archetype, to which we should conform with absolute fidelity . . . *by means of getting to know, on all the matters which most concern us, the best which has been thought and said in the world:* a pragmatic conception—the body of works which have been admired by a sufficient number of people over a sufficient period of time. It leads to the usual conception of culture: knowing the right things, i.e., the things that the right people know; breaking into society, the society of the cultivated . . . *and through this knowledge, turning a stream of fresh and free thought upon our stock notions and habits . . . :* fresh and free, a reassertion of the individual.

There are men for whom the state is an Idea in the fullest sense of the term, an Absolute, a formidable, all-devouring deity, to the service of which we should devote the whole energy of our being, and which has the right to require the sacrifice of every personal inclination. Others are radical individualists, philosophical anarchists, for whom the state is but a necessary evil—far more definitely evil than it is necessary; this attitude of rugged independence is well expressed in the titles of Herbert Spencer's book, *Man vs. the State,* and of Albert Jay Nock's *Our Enemy the State.* Most of us are pragmatists. The state is a convenience, which we take for granted without any philosophical enquiry into its principles, simply because it has been accepted by the majority of sensible people over a long period of time. We serve it faithfully, but without any mystic glow. We feel free to point out its weaknesses and absurdities. When it hurts our personal interests, we grumble; if it were to antagonize our inmost convictions, we should rebel. We are absolutists, anarchists and empiricists according to circumstances.

Does this confusion impair our enjoyment of life? I doubt it. All through the nineteenth century, there were noble souls, sick with "the malady of the ideal," who bemoaned their Lost Absolute. I suspect they gave a metaphysical tinge to a melancholy which had far more earthly causes. The majority of men had a healthy unconscious belief in relativity long before Albert Einstein imparted a quasi-religious aura to that ancient term. Their attitude can be described in a homely parable. A passenger is pacing the deck at night, smoking a cigar. The problem is to plot the position of that little speck of ruddy light in Absolute Space. Absurd! The man is walking up and down, lurching perhaps if the night is rough; the ship is rolling and pitching, speeding toward her appointed port at twenty knots an hour; the earth is revolving on its axis and circling round the sun; the whole solar system is hurtling no one knows whither or at what appalling rate. We shall never be able to ascertain where that infinitesimal point of glowing red stands in the measureless universe. For the passenger, the problem is quite simple. The cigar is safe in his mouth, and he is enjoying it.

So in the welter of doctrines there is one inescapable fact: the experience of the individual self. We are driven back to it by the eternal and indecisive clash of all systems. *Driven back:* our inclination would be in favor of some lofty dogmatism that would bring us both prestige and comfort. Happy is he who, in literature, possesses a dogma that will confer authority upon him, and excuse him from further thought! With great reluctance, we are compelled to give up that hope. The essential element in art is not the service of an abstract idea, but self-expression.

This is the first test that will enable us to discern the *literary* element from mere language. Language transmits facts; literature conveys personal emotion. When an astronomer discovers a new star, he must feel intensely the solemn, the dramatic quality of the moment. As an astronomer, however, he will simply note down that at such a time a body of such a magnitude was seen in such a position. His awe and exultation are irrelevant. If he expresses them in a letter or in his diary, he goes beyond the realm of strict science, and becomes, for the nonce, a poet, the companion of Wordsworth and Keats.

Self-expression again explains the obvious fact that literature cannot be defined in terms of its subject matter. A mere trifle, an epigram, a love ditty, a bacchanalian song, may survive in literature; on the other hand, there is no theme that cannot be approached objectively, scientifically, to the complete elimination of art. There are formal treatises on beauty, passion, and God, which may be of surpassing value in esthetics, psychology and theology, but which have no standing in literature. There is material enough, of an obvious kind, in police records and in the case books of psychiatrists, to fill innumerable romances or dramas. But they have to await the transmuting touch.

And, for the same reason, literature cannot be defined in terms of form alone. A textbook, a scientific record, written with perfect adequacy, will yet remain outside the pale. The rules of composition, excellent as they may be, do not provide the magic password. On the other hand, there is no formal standard that a genuine artist is not allowed to break, if only the spirit is in him. The list of great writers who were accused of every fault is very impressive: in French, Rabelais, Molière, Saint-Simon, Balzac, Zola, Marcel Proust; in English, Robert Browning, Henry James, Theodore Dreiser, Gertrude Stein, James Joyce. They did everything that a teacher of composition must condemn. They were incorrect, laborious, fulsome, vulgar, halting, involved, obscure; they offended against grammar, taste and sense; they were the Legion of the Damned; and now professors are writing "faultless" books about them.

To make self-expression the very center of art raises a number of objections. The three most formidable are that two great literary schools, Classicism and Realism, claim to eliminate personality; that there is no correspondence, as there should be, between the greatness of a personality, and greatness as an artist; that in dramatic literature, the author is seeking to express, not himself, but others. We shall examine these objections, not with the set purpose of destroying them, but in the hope that we may learn from them.

According to the classicists, art consists in the expression, not of the unique self, but of universal truths. The obtrusion of the ego, in thought or form, is a blemish. "The ego is hateful," said Pascal; it was as a Christian moralist that he spoke; but his classical taste would have rendered the same verdict. Yet the classicists never achieved their boasted objectivity. Pascal in particular left us one of the most revealing, passionate, tragically personal, of all books. Much as they believed in the virtue of universal truth, the classicists knew that art presents truth in a unique, a novel, an individual way. They might start a book with the despairing admission: "Everything has been said"; but the book would nevertheless have a tang all its own, because ancient commonplaces had never been uttered just under *these* circumstances, and by *this* particular author. The law is written down in definite terms; yet a judge is not an automat, dealing out the proper article of the code, and the sentence attached thereto, as soon as the right levers are pressed. There are great judges, who read deeper and subtler meanings into the law. In the same way, the classicists recognized a hierarchy of poets; and the difference between them was not due to the mere impersonal knowledge of the rules. No doubt was entertained concerning the efficacy of those rules; but the sovereign rights of genius were also acknowledged. "That secret influence of heaven," as Boileau called it, through which "poets are born, not made," what is it but what we call more modestly *personality?* Among three men equally able to express general truths in correct language, one may be a pedant, the second a mere versifier, the third alone a poet. Did anyone ever suggest that Milton was greater than Abraham Cowley only because he observed the rules more meticulously, and succeeded better in suppressing his ego?

The aim of the realist is to be as objective, as dispassionate, as a scientist. He claims to see and reproduce "things as they actually are." "A novel," wrote Stendhal, "is a mirror that walks along the highway"; and Sologub used the same well-worn metaphor in defense of his curious story, *Little Demon:* "I have invented nothing; I have only polished a mirror with the utmost care; and I know that the mirror is true." The post-war period saw a revival of strictest Realism, a "new matter-of-factness" from which praise, blame, sympathy, were rigorously excluded. Irony and pity, the attitudes which best reveal an author's personality, excited derision. Words and gestures were transcribed with phonographic and photographic exactitude; not a word of comment; not a tremor of emotion.

The claims to scientific dispassionateness advanced by the realists and their followers the naturalists were mostly the delusions of very literary men. Granted that they offered mankind a true mirror, it was they, the individual writers, Stendhal or Sologub, who picked out the scenes and characters to be reflected. If they gave us "slices of life," there was art, that is to say intention, selection, skill, *personality*, in the cutting of the slice. They seemed cold, unresponsive, even cynical, because they declined to voice in the common terms the common forms of enthusiasm or indignation; but this refusal to be swayed by herd-psychology only made them more intensely personal. In a shrieking, gesticulating crowd, we might descry two rigid and obstinately silent figures: the one a dummy, the other a man, and the only free man among the slaves of collective passion. You may be sure that the man, conscious of his isolation, is inwardly burning with scorn, pity or despair; you may be sure also that the dummy, genuinely dispassionate, will never create art. Impassivity, if it were real, would be barren; but in art, it is only a mask to cover a tortured face, and at times more tragic in its frigidity than any living face could be. The two great waves of Realism, after 1850 and after 1920, were both the recoil of frustrated hope. It takes very little penetration to discover in Gustave Flaubert and in Ernest Hemingway two sensitive and tormented souls.

In technique, art is constantly swinging from the florid to the stark. Some realists—not all of them by any means—discovered the power of understatement. Tired of romantic clamor, they chose, in revealing their personality, to practice the most rigid economy of means. In this, they were harking back to Racine and the Greeks. But it is not the aloofness that impresses us; it is the emotion, which is enhanced by restraint.

The classicists, through Boileau, would say: "Art is Reason interpreted by *individual* genius"; and the realists, through Zola: "Art is Nature viewed through an *individual* temperament." In both cases, personality is the distinctive element, and our definition stands. But it has to face a totally different objection. If art were the expression of personality, should there not be a definite relation between the two—the greater the man, the greater the art? We know for certain that such is not the case. Men whom we believe to be great and good did not rise above mediocrity in their writings. On the other hand, although Literature is by no means a rogues' gallery, many poets whom the world cherishes seem to us foolish and pitiful creatures; not so much magnificently criminal as incompetent, mean and vain. There were better and stronger men in their days than Villon, Edgar Poe, Verlaine or Oscar Wilde. Rousseau, parading his turpitudes, challenged us: "I dare any man to say: I am better than this man!"; very few indeed would have to admit that they were much worse. Even when we meet a model of self-discipline, culture, sanity, like Goethe, we are not impressed by any genuine nobility of heart. There was pettiness in the Olympian Sage of Weimar, as there was meanness in Voltaire, the Patriarch of Ferney.

The issue is somewhat confused by the fact that men, irrespective of their personal worth, may possess very unequal instruments. A scamp may be glib, a saint tongue-tied. This affects immediate success, in journalism, in hackwriting, in politics, and even in the academic world. But not for long: the smooth humbug, the brilliant man who has nothing to say, will not indefinitely cumber the ground. There was more than insolent wit to Oscar Wilde, and perhaps even to Frank Harris; all that was superficial cleverness in them is fading, leaving but an unpleasant legend behind. Gifts of expression without adequate personality are but a temporary cause of error. The reverse—the absence of such gifts in good and strong men—is more serious. It would be a great comfort to believe that the earnest man is ultimately bound to compel attention, for all the uncouthness of his speech. There was clumsiness in St. Paul and in Lincoln, before they reached, respectively, the untrodden heights of the 13th Chapter in First Corinthians, and of the Gettysburg Address. It was not mere facility that gave them power. Yes, it would be a comfort; but this comfort is dubious. The success of St. Paul and Lincoln was a miracle. Many deserve to be heard who cannot speak.

This, however, does not go to the root of the matter. Among educated people, the majority can express themselves adequately, when they have anything to express. Everyone who is literate is also articulate. When genius is mute, it is for lack of an audience, rather than for lack of a voice. But, among people who are vocal, the stronger man is not invariably the greater artist; we cannot make our list of literary excellence tally with any list of personal merit. How can we account for such a discrepancy?

The first and easiest hypothesis—of great appeal to the literary mind—is that our "list of personal merit" is proved wrong by the very fact that it does not agree with the list of literary excellence. "That man *is* best who writes best"; what we need is a revaluation of all values, in terms of literary criticism.

This may seem an outrageous paradox. But it cannot be dismissed too lightly, for it has very frequently been defended, either outright or by implication. It fits well with Buffon's famous and ambiguous dictum: "Style is the very man": a *good* style implies a *good* man. "The list of personal merit" is certainly open to challenge. There lurks in every one of us a romanticist ready to rebel against the dull correctitudes. The New Testament is not reassuring for the men who are safely good according to the letter of the law. It would give us pleasure to find that the hard-working unprodigal son is a scoundrel at heart, and that every respectable citizen is but a whited sepulcher. *A man is to be measured by the intensity and sincerity of the spirit that is within him.* According to that standard, the poet outranks the banker (or "money changer"), the judge, and even the parson. The stock example, of course, is François Villon: there was more "virtue" in that common thief than in the Bishop who sent him to jail. George Bernard Shaw made this the theme of his very strong play, *Candida:* the sane, healthy, active, well-meaning Vicar, Morell, is found to be a weakling by the side of Marchbanks, outwardly a degenerate, inwardly a quivering mass of nerves, but first of all a poet.

A paradox it is, but with enough truth to save it from absurdity and to compel reflection. In literature as in life, there is indeed little merit in passive obedience to a literal code. "Virtue" means "power to save," not mere submissiveness. There is little doubt that more "virtue" lived in the grop ing and stumbling Shelley than in those friends of the Regent who managed to escape scandal; which does not mean that every blameless elder is at heart a rake, nor that every drunken bohemian has the soul of a Shelley.

It may be true, therefore, that the conformists are not invariably the good; "virtue," etymology tells us, is not meekness, but force, vigor, energy. Yet these qualities do not accurately translate themselves into literary value. If by "the good man" we mean "the strong man," he is not invariably the good writer. The man of energy, physically brave, mentally daring, the explorer, the pioneer, the promoter, the advocate of the strenuous life, the demagogue in the literal and favorable sense, that is to say the leader of a people, all, with their sharply defined, tautly knit, dynamic, colorful personalities, count for less in literature than the retiring spinsters Jane Austen, the Brontës, Emily Dickinson.

Is the literary test, "Style is the very man," proved wrong? Perhaps that test is more accurate in appraising personality than the enormous clanking machines of business, politics or warfare. There is surprisingly little "virtue" in bluster, and the lesson of the "still small voice" should be constantly in our minds. Napoleon had an admirable gift of eloquence; he was a master of the classical tradition, and transcended it; he could use daring contrasts with romantic effectiveness; he could achieve imperial brevity. Repeated efforts have been made to give him a prominent place in literature; somehow they invariably fail. Napoleon does not rank among the great writers, even of his own time. Strange irony: his own works are by no means the most popular in the immense field of Napoleonic lore. Is it not because the literary test reveals, behind his energy, his power, his splendor, a *personality* which was not genuinely great? Was not Napoleon, like his modern imitators, only vulgarity on an epic scale?

So far, in this discussion, we have favored the hypothesis that when the two scales, *literary excellence* and *personal merit*, were at variance, the literary scale was the more correct. A good man, a great man, who writes badly, cannot be quite so good and great as he is reputed to be. There is, however, another interpretation; just as favorable to *art*, not quite so flattering for *literature*. For if literature is an art, it is not the only art. We take it for granted that *personality* is best expressed through one particular artistic medium: universal geniuses like Michelangelo and Leonardo da Vinci are infinitely rare. We do not expect Shakespeare to be a great sculptor, and the world smiled at the painter Ingres because he was too proud of his modest talent on the violin. Now empire building is an art, too: coarse because it is gigantic, but undeniably effective. Perhaps our captains of industry have written the true epic of America. Perhaps Cecil Rhodes was no less a poet than if he had written a *Rhodesiad* instead of founding Rhodesia. Napoleon himself was aware of his artistry, and it is the artist in him that survives. His material achievements had crumbled away before his death; but he left a style, a legend, a character. Like the British Constitution, the Napoleonic Saga remains unwritten, although it has been so abundantly written about: Napoleon is both its subject and its author. It is not indifferent to create for the popular mind a theme of undying fascination. A military epic is not the kind of art that appeals to me; but, while I consider it as primitive and crude, I cannot deny that it is an artistic achievement; and it is exactly the expression of a personality.

We have honestly explored both aspects of the problem. We believe it is possible to accept the dictum *Style is the Man, Literature is Personality*, without committing ourselves to the proposition: *Style is the Whole Man*. The literary test does operate to a very large extent. It reveals the mediocrity of men who were apparently wise, good and strong, and who, in very truth, were merely successful. "Oh that my enemy had written a book!": statesmen immortalized in marble and bronze were actually as cheap as their rhetoric, as muddled in their thoughts as they were in their metaphors, as loose in their public ethics as they were in their syntax. The written words of famous "Leaders," judged by literary standards, form the basis of a damning indictment.

The converse is true: art brings out the genuine power concealed and indeed wasted, in apparent failure. Villon the great poet was great indeed, and greater than those who crushed him; not because of his sins, but because, with an intensity beyond their reach, he knew that he was a sinner.

Thus, in extreme cases, the literary test works well, and enables us to correct excessive admiration or unjust contempt. But, in the vast middle ground, its efficacy is far from certain. The better man may be handicapped by faulty technique; the lesser man may possess great imitative skill; so to appraise character in terms of style is an extremely delicate task. And even if the method were infallible, it would have to be practiced by the living critic, a very fallible man.

The third objection to the definition of art as self-expression is the very existence of dramatic literature. By this we mean, not exclusively the plays performed on a stage, but the presentation of characters wholly different from the author's. We are constantly tempted to seek the autobiographical element in a book, but we also resent the predominance of that element as a weakness. It is not to the credit of Lord Byron that we find in all his poems and dramas no living personage except Lord Byron himself in a bewildering variety of costumes. On the contrary, among the innumerable actors in the *Human Comedy*, there are scarcely a handful who bear a distinct resemblance to Balzac; and, in the even richer galaxy of Shakespeare's creations, there is not a single one of whom we might say with certainty: "This is Shakespeare himself!"

This objection simply condemns superficial egotism or vanity; it does not affect our essential principle. The author should refrain from strutting through his pages; but, unless he is there in spirit, his words are mere verbiage. We feel that, not indeed in every scene or in every chapter, but at the supreme moments, Shakespeare is unmistakably Shakespearian, and Balzac Balzacian. No definition of these terms is adequate; but the words themselves are heavy with meaning.

The difference between a great dramatist and a mediocre one is not that a Shakespeare is able to eliminate his personality, whereas a Bulwer-Lytton obtrudes his ego. It is that Shakespeare has a richer, deeper, more subtle self to express. Bulwer-Lytton can imagine himself as Richelieu, with the very obvious changes that the situation entails. He can put on the red robe and imitate the speech of his hero; but it remains at best a clever masquerade. Shakespeare carries the same process infinitely further. He feels all the delicate and profound modifications that would take place in Shakespeare's soul, if Shakespeare were Hamlet. But, at the core, Shakespeare *is* Hamlet, and Ophelia, and Polonius. That is why these characters are Shakespearian, while Lytton's Richelieu is merely Lyttonesque.

Art then is self-expression. But not all forms of self-expression can be accepted as art. Every gesture, every glance, every cry, reveals the personality. Yet it is not art: else a frightened or angry animal would have to be accounted an artist. The element of *consciousness* is indispensable. There is no unconscious art.

The phrase "unconscious art" is used, however, and does not sound absurd. But we do not take it literally. What we mean by it is simple, direct, elementary art, without intentional refinements in technique, without elaborate self-analysis. Still, the peasant who sings a popular ballad or takes part in a folk-dance knows, obscurely perhaps, that his activity is artistic. The common man who tells a story with effectiveness is as a rule well aware of the effect. We have previously expressed our belief that the sense of artistry exists among primitive and illiterate populations, as it does among children. Consciousness is not synonymous with sophistication.

Conscious, we must admit, frequently has unpleasant connotations. In common speech, "to be natural" is an element of charm; "to be self conscious" is to be awkward, embarrassed, and therefore inartistic. That is because we restrict the meaning of self-consciousness to the painful realization of our inadequacy. A performer who is afraid of his audience will almost inevitably betray his fear. He will thus be handicapped, even if the fear itself is groundless. He can sing when he is by himself, because he is aware of his powers, such as they may be. He is paralyzed before the public, because he is no longer "self-conscious," that is to say self-assured, but "public-conscious." The only way to be natural is to have self-confidence, that self-confidence which is the privilege of children, fools and geniuses.

No doubt an artistic effect may be produced by wholly unconscious means. There is nothing more richly picturesque than a market scene in a Moorish town; but the human actors are not playing their parts with esthetic intent, any more than the camels, the donkeys and the sheep. One step farther: a sunset is a masterpiece created by chance—unless we believe with John Ruskin that it was painted with deliberate and proud care by a Ruskinian God. But in these cases, the art element is contributed by the beholder. The market scene is not picturesque until it is contemplated by a man with a sense for the picturesque. A sunset is not beautiful if there is no eye to be aware of its beauty. It is the awareness that creates the appeal.

Our definition is not yet complete. A man who is pleading for his life draws upon all the resources of his personality; he is conscious of his efforts, conscious of the effect for which he is striving. But if his plight is desperate, he is not thinking in terms of art. Words, tones, gestures, are but weapons in his fight. He speaks only as he would wrestle with a wild beast, or scramble out of a precipice. Upon the detached listener, the impression may be artistic. A Nero, coolly adjusting his emerald monocle, might declare that the man is giving a very tolerable performance. For the performer himself, there is no art in a matter of life and death, because there is no inkling of *pleasure*.

Art implies *pleasure in conscious self-expression*. The element of pleasure is absolutely inseparable from the conception of art, either in its active or in its passive form. That man is no artist who finds no pleasure in what he is expressing; and the pleasure is none the less real if it be of a self-torturing kind. For the spectator also, pleasure is the test. If pleasure be totally absent, art disappears. If a Nero is able to seek art in the immediate reality of pain, it is because he is a Nero: a pervert and a degenerate. At the other extreme, a man simpleminded enough to forget the element of pleasure in a Shakespearian performance would find Iago's villainy or Lear's sufferings unbearable. What is purely and simply harrowing is not art. We must be able to "enjoy" a good shudder or a good cry.

These are facts of common experience. The inferences that can be drawn from them will not please those who believe too literally in the holiness of art. Conscious pleasure in expression is not incompatible with a high degree of earnestness: we are not impugning the spiritual veracity of Dante and Milton. But there are moments in life so deep and so intense that the thought of art should be banished from them. We may admire the conscious beauty of the Psalms, the Song of Solomon, the Book of Job; but we feel it would be sacrilegious to analyze the esthetic element in the Sermon on the Mount, the story of the Passion, or the grief of a mother over her dying child. It is only when grief has lost its immediacy, when it is recollected in tranquillity, when it has become part reality, part shadow, that the sense of beauty is allowed to enter.

Expression, in which feeling and technique are united, covers therefore a wide range. At one end of the scale, we find pure emotion, which transcends art. At the other end, we find pure technique, virtuosity, the consciousness of expression as an end in itself, the pleasure derived from the sheer display of skill. This is a low kind of art, for it reveals only a small part, and a superficial part, of man's nature. The prodigy who can perform marvelous tricks in music or in poetry is not a great musician or a great poet. Still, that low kind of art is undeniably art. Perhaps it is pure art, art for art's sake.

We are not concerned in this book with either of these extremes. The study of *pure* emotion, apart from the artistic value of its manifestation, belongs to psychology, and borders on ethics and religion. The study of *pure* technique fills many learned and useful treatises, particularly on prosody. Neither is properly *literature*. Literature covers the vast domain in which both elements are found. The proportion between the two varies, not merely with every author, but with every page. We may have a high degree of emotion with rudimentary powers of expression: this is frequently the case with popular art, and the result is at times admirable. We may have a very slender vein of genuine feeling worked out with consummate skill: this is sophistication, and, in its proper place, it has charm. Obviously, the greatest art is the one in which spiritual intensity is combined with masterly technique: which defines precisely the achievement of Dante and Milton.

We are aware that our definition can be interpreted in a very uncomplimentary manner. *Conscious pleasure in the expression of emotion* might denote art; but it might just as well stand for sentimentality. *Conscious pleasure in the expression of personality* is a pretty accurate description of conceit. There is nothing in this, however, to invalidate our definition; it merely points to the dangers which, manifestly, assail the literary mind.

If, in his unliterary hours, a man were to dwell upon his melancholy, the loneliness of his soul, his yearning for the beloved, as he does in his verse, he would be voted a sentimentalist. If in his sober moments, he were to assert his divine inspiration, his difference from other men, his claims to immortality, he would be derided as a monument of conceit. There are in each profession special dangers as well as special privileges. It is the scholar's business to be learned; but learning out of place is pedantry. It is the soldier's duty to be plain, direct, forcible; transposed from the battlefield or the drill ground to the drawing room, these virtues might turn to roughness. It is the minister's calling to be pious; but piety on the golf course would sound like sanctimoniousness. The poet's exquisite sensitivity, his power to voice his most intimate feelings, his noble confidence in his genius, are the glory and the peril of his craft. More than any other man, he is precariously poised between the sublime and the ridiculous.

The proposed definition, it must have been noticed, is so worded that it fits both aspects of literature, the active and the passive, the writer's and the reader's. Without committing ourselves to Benedetto Croce's paradox, "the identity of genius and taste," we may readily admit that the two processes, creation and appreciation, coincide to a very large extent. The reader enjoys the expression of personality on two and even three planes: the personality of the character, the personality of the author, and ultimately his own; through the exploration of Hamlet's soul and of Shakespeare's soul, John Smith comes to a fuller realization of himself. Whoever finds pleasure in a book is confronting it with his own experience, illuminating the written page with the living memory, rousing the slumbering unconscious with the borrowed light, re-creating the book in his own mind.

To the earnest reader, the word *pleasure* in our definition of art will be a stumbling block. It would seem that we are reducing literature to the level of entertainment. To this we might reply that good entertainment is well worth seeking, in a world which ceases to be drab only to become strenuous and tragic. But this would not affect the main issue: the vindication of literature. Pleasure is not mere relaxation, and it is certainly not identical with frivolousness. We do not claim that it is an infallible guide to right living: it is an elementary response, which tells us that some need in ourselves has found satisfaction. So there is pleasure in yielding to the lower appetites, and pleasure even in yielding to perversity; but no less surely there is deep pleasure in the quest of truth, and in the performance of duty. We cannot condemn literature because it brings pleasure. The problem is: What is the quality of the pleasure that it brings?

The pleasure we find in the expression of personality is none other than the affirmation of life. Whatever life may be on the chemical plane, for us, in our capacity as human beings, it means consciousness. A nation lives only when it is conscious of its own existence. The Congo Free State under Leopold II, with territory, sovereign, flag, and all the appurtenances of a country, never became a nation; Poland, partitioned for a hundred and twenty years, never ceased to be one. So it is with the individual. "Unconscious life," without thought, without action, without pleasure, without pain, is purely vegetative and deserves our scorn. This flickering consciousness is all the existence we know: our secret and constant dread is that it should be extinguished. Either we might altogether cease to be; or—a more immediate threat—we might be engulfed by the material, the mechanical, the lifeless. Under the guise of men, we might sink to the level of automata.

So we hurl the defiance of our consciousness at the soulless forces that would absorb us. On such a plane, self-affirmation is no mere strutting. The assertion of our personality is the very battleline of life. It is the "thinking reed" of Pascal, greater to the end than that which crushes him, because he knows he is being crushed; it is the "indomitable soul" of William Henley.

Pleasure then is not a cowardly shrinking from effort or from pain. Exertion, hardships, battling with the elements, actual combat with beast or man, in so far as they enhance our consciousness of life, can thus be turned into pleasure. Thus in literature: there is strenuous pleasure in scaling the crags of the Second *Faust*, in groping one's way through the intricate maze of *The Golden Bowl*, in plowing through the heavy mud of the last chapter in *Ulysses*.

Man craves for such a quickening, and art is one of the means that will bring it. It is neither the lowest, nor the highest. On the one hand, it is akin to physical enjoyment, to sport, to worldly ambition, and it may claim greater dignity than any of these. On the other hand, it merges with love and religion, which also bring us life, and bring it abundantly, and it must acknowledge the greater depth and intensity of their appeal. For there always is, even in the most sincere art, an element of make-believe. It deals with *safe* danger, with *remembered* sorrow, with *vicarious* experience. It leads us to the brink of suffering and death, but with the assurance that we are not immediately threatened. Its one point of excellence is its very directness: the promise is unequivocal, the fulfillment immediate. The rivals of art profess to have different ends; with them, the enhanced consciousness of life is only a by-product. But "Art comes to you proposing frankly to give nothing but the highest quality to your moments as they pass, and simply for those moments' sake." [1]

SUMMARY

There are three approaches to a definition of literature. The first path is *Dogmatism:* "This is the Truth, without which there is no salvation"; the second is *Individualism:* "I like what I like when I like it"; the third is *Empiricism* or *Pragmatism:* what is, or is not, literature, is determined by a "suffi-

---

[1] Walter Pater, *The Renaissance*, Conclusion. Pater was half afraid of this famous passage; it was withdrawn, then restored, in successive editions. In itself, it is singularly modest: it advances no extravagant claims for art, but rather sets its limits, and sets them narrowly. The objection lies in the over-emphasis of the "moment." Pater, it would seem, teaches that we should care for the isolated moment "as it passes"—*carpe diem, carpe horam*—without a thought for the morrow. This is dangerous doctrine, not only in economics and in ethics, but in esthetics. The "moment" is an abstraction: life, including the life of art, is a sequence of moments. No masterpiece can be generated without long travail; many "moments" have to be sacrificed to the ultimate purpose. And the "moment" of ecstasy—the joyful frenzy of murder, for instance—would be wholly inartistic, if it had to be followed by long years of remorse and expiation. Art exists, not in a flash, but in time. Of this, Walter Pater, in this passage, appears to be unaware. The "interval" which we should strive to expand, "the given time" into which we should be getting "as many pulsations as possible," is our whole lifetime, the duration of our "indefinite reprieve" from the death sentence.

cient consensus." Not only in art, but in religion and politics, we are tempted to confuse the three ways of approach. The result is called by philosophers *Syncretism;* in the vernacular, hodge-podge. Certainty is not within our reach. But if we frankly accept *Relativism,* we shall find that our enjoyment does not depend upon our exact place in the Absolute.

Neither subject matter nor form suffices to distinguish literature from mere writing. The essential character of literature is the expression of personality. To this statement three objections are offered:

1. Two great schools, Classicism and Realism, profess to eliminate personality; but they restore it under the names of "genius" and "temperament."

2. There is no correspondence between greatness of personality (virtue or power), and greatness in art. Perhaps it is our conception of greatness that is at fault. Greatness is not position, success, bluster, magnitude; neither is virtue mere conformity and submissiveness. On the other hand, art in the conventional sense (including literature) is not the only mode of self-expression. Constructive activities, empire-building, for instance, may be a form of art.

3. There is a *dramatic* element in literature, not merely on the stage, which aims at representing different characters, and not the author's own personality. Yet, if Shakespeare's plays are Shakespearian, is it not because of the unobtrusive omnipresence of Shakespeare?

The expression of personality must be *conscious;* a reflex action may betray the self, but is not art. There is no unconscious art. "Unconscious beauty," as in a landscape, is created by the beholder.

This conscious expression must be accompanied by *pleasure,* even though that pleasure be of an austere, strenuous, or self-torturing kind.

Consciousness of self is dangerously akin to *conceit;* and pleasure in the expression of emotion resembles *sentimentality.* It is not denied that these elements are present, at least on the boundaries of art; they are part of what may be called the professional deformation, or the professional license, or the professional danger, of the artistic life.

Pleasure often connotes frivolousness. But the pleasure sought by art need not be frivolous: it is the reaffirmation, the quickened sense, of life. Art in this respect is akin to sport, worldly ambition, love, and religion, which all enhance our consciousness. It is neither the lowest, nor the highest; it is the most direct method of securing that deepening, that intensification, of experience. In other material or spiritual activities, "the quickened sense of life" is only a by-product: but "Art comes to you proposing frankly to give nothing but the highest quality to your moments as they pass." Not, however, for the sake of the fleeting moment: it is life as a whole that should be made a work of art.

CHAPTER VIII

PROSE AND VERSE; DIS-COURSE AND POETRY

THERE is nothing so wearisome as to kill the dead; yet that unpleasant task is at times forced upon us. Molière's *Would-be Gentleman* was properly taught by his master of philosophy that "whatever is not verse is prose, and whatever is not prose is verse," and thus discovered with amazement that he had been talking prose all his life without knowing it. But, if this elementary distinction has long been perfectly clear, another truism seemed to be no less firmly established: to wit, that verse and poetry are by no means synonymous; and that the two, although they are frequently associated, may have a separate existence.

That *verse* is not *poetry* could be demonstrated by a wealth of ludicrous examples. We prefer to quote only two faultless lines by a faultless poet, Lord Tennyson:

> I waited for the train at Coventry [1]

and:

> Fifty years of ever-broadening Commerce! [2]

That prose can attain the loftiest summits of poetry is proved in no less palpable fashion by the English Bible, from the majesty of *Genesis* to the formidable imagery of the *Apocalypse*. Yet there are teachers and critics at the present time who still refuse to recognize poetry except in metrical form. This

---

[1] "Godiva."
[2] "On the Jubilee of Queen Victoria."

attitude gives them two distinct advantages. It enables them to concentrate on prosody, a very definite and indeed a quasi-scientific subject; and it excuses them from the necessity of pursuing the most elusive of all literary conceptions, the poetic principle. The desire to avoid vagueness is legitimate; but it is not legitimately satisfied when the definiteness we reach is merely a screen. Behind the tangible screen of verse, the mystery of poetry remains as baffling as ever.

To probe that mystery, many formal criteria have been offered. It has been maintained that certain *kinds* are, of their very essence, poetical, while others are the proper domain of prose; that the poetical quality is inherent in the *diction* adopted by the author; that it depends on the lavish and vivid use of *images;* that it results from a victory over *self-imposed difficulties;* that it can be measured by the intensity or better the *density* of the style, for poetry is concentrated power; and finally that it can be reduced to a kind of *musical technique.* We do not deny the interest and the importance of these elements; we doubt, however, whether any one of them singly, or all of them jointly, will afford us a clue to the true nature of poetry.

There was once a prejudice that certain *kinds* or *genres* of literature were poetical *per se,* and demanded the nobler vehicle of verse. Such was, for instance, the difference between high comedy and farce. Molière, for the slapstick humor of his *Doctor in Spite of Himself,* very properly made use of homeliest speech; but *The Misanthrope* deserved the dignity of rhymed couplets. It was deemed regrettable that his *Don Juan,* an ambitious, full-size play with an aristocratic hero, should be written in lowly prose; so Thomas Corneille hastened to translate it into the more fitting medium. According to that interpretation, there are castes among literary kinds: tragedy and the epic form an aristocracy, comedy and romance a middle class, farce and realistic tale a populace. Poetry is a quality that goes with rank, and verse is the badge of honor that it should wear.

History does not confirm such a theory. It shows that literature of every kind has been written under both forms. As a rule, verse was recorded before prose. This is natural enough, for tradition was long transmitted orally, and verse form is a great aid to memory. So everything "memorable," or worth preserving, was put into verse: proverbs, precepts, bits of weather wisdom, annals of the tribe, and even religious laws. It seems strange that handbooks of agriculture should once have been composed in meter: Hesiod's *Works and Days*, Vergil's *Georgics*, are the god-like brothers of such homely jingles as:

> Red in the morning
> Is the shepherd's warning;
> Red at night
> Is the shepherd's delight.

Fracastoro left us a famous medical treatise in elegant Latin verse: a method of exposition which would not have appealed to his distant successors Ehrlich and Wassermann. But the glorious tradition of the scientific-philosophical poem is not completely forgotten: there are remote echoes of Lucretius' *De Natura Rerum* in Robert Bridges' *Testament of Beauty*.

After some thirty centuries—such is the mad whirl of human progress—it was at last realized that writing had been invented, and we no longer use verse for mnemonic reasons. On the other hand, the revolution of the eighteenth century, literary, economic, social as well as political, has blurred if not absolutely destroyed class distinctions, among kinds of literature as well as among men. We easily accept high tragedy in prose as in Ibsen's *Ghosts* or Eugene O'Neill's *Mourning Becomes Electra*. We are not blind to the epic grandeur of Tolstoy's *War and Peace*, although it is not in the conventional medium of the epic. We do not believe that novels in verse like Mrs. Browning's *Aurora Leigh*, or *Lucile*, by Owen Meredith, are nobler achievements than Hardy's *Tess of the d'Urbervilles*. Verse may now be employed—very profitably—for journalism, and prose for the expression of the deepest feelings. Of this once universal prejudice, only one trace lingers: we are still reluctant to recognize as an ode a "thing" which is manifestly not in verse. Undiluted poetry still demands some kind of a formal badge.

The great change in society that we mentioned above disposed to a large extent of the problem of *diction*. The "noble" word went by the board with the "noble" kind. It is no longer an article of faith that an artificial vocabulary, coupled with a few tricks in syntax, will provide a safe test for poetry. In spite of some exaggeration in theory and practice, Wordsworth had won his battle: poetry *is* compatible with homely, common and even vulgar terms; and the choicest language, if the spirit be lacking, generates nothing but tedium. It is amusing to note what a fight had to be waged before the unpoetical word *mouchoir* (handkerchief) could be tolerated in a French translation of *Othello*. Finally, even conservative France had to capitulate to the Barbarians; Victor Hugo could boast that he had abolished all social inequalities among words, and, a verbal revolutionist, "clapped a Liberty cap on the old dictionary." In language as in the state, all feudal privileges ceased to be recognized. "Nobility was to be sought only in the hearts of men."

If we have given up the thought of a vocabulary intrinsically —and artificially—"noble," many still entertain the idea that certain words are intrinsically "beautiful," and that the heaping of beautiful words will determine poetry. A few simple facts should dispose of this fallacy. The words which are noblest in their associations, such as *Mother*, *Love*, and *God*, are among the plainest and most unassuming in sonority; trade terms and ugly diseases often have a more "poetical" ring. A symposium on "beautiful" words gave high rank to *cuspidor*. The name *Carmen*, which has a romantic appeal when it denotes the bewitching gypsy in Bizet's opera, loses all its glamor in the phrase: *Carmen strike for higher wages*.

Will *images* produce poetry? No: they may be charged with poetry, which is quite a different thing. A philosophical poetess, Madame Ackermann, persuaded that images are the very essence of poetry, always had one at hand: *l'esquif*, the ship. But, whatever happened to that eternal ship of hers, whether safe in port, battling, wrecked, triumphant, the verses through which she sailed were drearily unpoetical. The language of common intercourse is full of images: some of them blurred and forgotten, some trite and conventional, not a few, especially in slang, rough but vivid. When we say: "It dawned upon me that I was the goat," we have no idea that we are inditing poetry. For Gustave Flaubert, the duty of the artist is to be on his guard against the metaphors that come teeming to his mind. "I am devoured by them," he confessed, "as if by vermin, and spend my time crushing them." It is possible for prose, vulgar or artistic, to be a writhing mass of metaphors, and for poetry to rise stark above every figure of speech.

Does poetry consist in the taming of rebellious form, in the conquest of difficulty? Can we say that only that art is robust and will survive, which is the fruit of patient effort? This interpretation is tempting. It is a fact that some of the greatest poetry is difficult in every sense: strenuous for the writer, laborious for the reader. We cannot conceive Milton happily dashing off *Paradise Lost*. After all, any "Would-be Gentleman" can pour forth prose unaware.

Aye, but it will not be Milton's prose, nor Walter Pater's, nor Santayana's. On the other hand, with some training, our "Would-be Gentleman" might very well reel off smooth verse as abundantly as Martin Tupper himself. George Bernard Shaw avers that, after writing *The Admirable Bashville*, he gave up blank verse as too easy, and went back to the more exacting discipline of prose. The sonnet is conceded to be an arduous form to master: yet, in our own days, a young American Doctor has reached the point of thinking automatically in sonnets, and has let loose a spate of no less than a thousand all at once upon an astounded public.

If difficulty were in itself a merit, the prize would go to achievements which belong to acrobatics rather than to literature. Here are a few examples. We happen to know a number of sonnets in monosyllabic lines: a feat in which Wordsworth would most probably have failed. The acrostic, practiced by Edgar Allan Poe, would be a meritorious device; the double acrostic doubly meritorious; until we reach a happy blend of poetry and the crossword puzzle. There are lines which can be read starting from either end, on this pattern:

Able was I ere I saw Elba,

and Mr. Ripley assures us that a long poem was composed in this difficult medium. In French, there are alexandrine couplets in which the twelve syllables of the first line rhyme entirely with the twelve syllables of the second:

Galle, amant de la Reine, alla—tour magnanime!—
Galamment de l'Arène à la Tour Magne, à Nîme.[1]

We should like to believe that hard work is inevitably crowned with beauty, and that negligence is visited with worthlessness. Reality is not so edifying. It is not inconceivable, for instance, that Goethe's *Wanderer's Evensongs*, which are supremely simple, were written with utmost ease. Between difficulty and achievement, the relations are extremely complex. If we bear in mind that difficulty for the writer and difficulty for the reader do not necessarily coincide, we may arrive at such a classification as this:

1. Lines easy to write and easy to appreciate; and we believe that there are many such in the highest reaches of poetry.

2. Lines written with great pains, but smooth and perspicuous for the reader. Boileau boasted that he had taught Racine "how to write easy verse with difficulty." This is the lesson of the old adage: Art consists in concealing art.

3. At the other extreme, there are difficult lines composed with facility. Robert Browning was a very abundant writer. His obscurity is not invariably the result of profound cogitation

[1] Gallus, the Queen's lover, went—a magnanimous round!—
Courteously, from the Arena to the Magne Tower, at Nismes.

and prolonged effort: he wrote with ease, and left the worry to the Browning Societies. The huge metaphysical epics of Blake are infinitely more laborious for the commentator than they were for the poet; he seems to have moved without strain among his most intricate myths.

4. Finally, there are lines which demand severe exertion on the part of the reader, as they also did on the part of the author. Of this, Milton is the great example.

In not one of these cases is difficulty a key to poetic value. *Kubla Khan* does not lose standing because it was composed in a trance and is enjoyed in a trance-like mood; on the other hand, a poem would not be the better for being written on the Ouija board. We feel fully the perils of the obvious and the appeal of the cryptic; but a writer might spend ten years hermetically sealing his work against the danger of popular comprehension without thereby adding a particle to its poetic character. *Difficulty is no criterion.*

Can poetry be told from prose by its higher degree of condensation or concentration? If it were so, the divorce between *poetry* and *verse* would appear more flagrantly than ever. For the history of literature is filled with enormous poems, often of the highest merit, of which concentration is by no means the most eminent virtue. Homer started the fashion of majestically slow narrative, and epic poets after him have always indulged in episodes, digressions, descriptions, abundant speeches, and fully worked-out similes. Spenser is known as the poets' poet: the last thing we expect from him is terseness. What we enjoy in the *Faerie Queene* is the sense of infinite leisure, the unhurried, hypnotic pageantry of a magic land where, as in the island of the Lotos Eaters, it is always afternoon. Compare the interminable, river-like flowing of Byron's *Don Juan,* of Wordsworth's *The Prelude* and *The Excursion,* of Browning's *The Ring and the Book,* with the concentration of the French early psychological novels, *The Princess of Clèves* and *Manon Lescaut,*[1] or, in American literature, with the tenseness of *Ethan*

---

[1] By Madame de Lafayette and Abbé Prévost respectively.

Frome.[1] If brevity were the soul of poetry, the crown might go to Voltaire's *Candide,* which packs into a few pages an incredible wealth of incidents, a swarm of sharply drawn characters, a savage attack on all the absurdities of mankind, a disenchanted and courageous philosophy, and wit enough for several years' supply on Broadway. Personally, we should nominate La Rochefoucauld's *Maxims,* in which human experience is distilled to the highest degree of clarity and bitterness. In comparison with such "prose," most "poetry" is loose.

Finally, poetry is identified with a definite technique. This conception is foremost in the popular mind: a mere typographical arrangement will suffice to denote "poetry," and a "poet" is a writer who leaves uneven spaces on the right hand side of a page. But it exists also on a much higher level; few dare to call themselves poets, unless they wear some kind of poetic uniform.

In certain literatures, the essentials of poetic technique can be stated in fairly simple terms: in French, the rules of the game can be mastered by a child. In English, the situation is more complex. We have our choice between several systems, and the rules are both more elaborate and far less rigid than in French. When our survey extends beyond the confines of our own language, the variety of poetical devices becomes bewildering. Some of these we can understand, even though we do not consider them essential. Thanks to the Bible, we can feel to some extent the method of Hebrew poetry, based as it is on parallelism. In extreme cases, it amounts to repetition with slight changes, and Poe incorporated that device in his epitome of obvious poetical tricks, *Ulalume.* We have retained an ear for the alliteration of Anglo-Saxon poetry: a kind of inverted rhyme, in which the initial consonant, and not the final vowel sound, is the important element. Greatly modified, it reappeared in Swinburne with the virulence of a disease. We have been taught, not without a struggle, to understand *quantity* as the foundation of classical meter. Although we consider *accent* as the essence of our prosody, we are aware that much of our

[1] Mrs. Edith Wharton.

popular poetry—our religious hymns, for example—is almost as strictly syllabic as the French. All these are accessible enough to the willing mind; but the tricks of Chinese and Japanese poetry are beyond the comprehension of the average man. We feel that, in every case, there is a technique, more rigid, more conscious, than that of every-day prose. But what is the common element between these innumerable and widely different systems?

The one word that comes spontaneously to our minds is *Rhythm:* the following of a fairly regular and understandable pattern. For the greater part of poetry in the past, for popular poetry in the present, the importance of rhythm is manifest. Poetry has not completely severed its ancient connection with the ritual dance, the march, the procession, and their musical accompaniment. Rhythm is the time-keeper or *metronome* that guides collective action, as in the case of the sailors' chantey. This element survives in the song. A modern poet could cause a smile if he were to mention his harp or his lyre; but the drum, the ukulele, the banjo, the guitar, still hold their place; and poetry is still, in a very marked degree, "lyrical" in the original sense of the term.

But that literal sense is no longer predominant. In every great poet, there are many *songs,* which call for music, which are music in themselves. Even at this stage, the melody tends to follow a free and sinuous line of its own; it plays with the rhythm, it refuses to be imprisoned by the rhythm. But there are many passages, and among the greatest, which would actually suffer from any instrumental accompaniment. When that point is reached, the drum beat sounds primitive. The inner song will brook no metronome.

Thus we arrive at such prosodies as Walt Whitman's and Paul Claudel's: lines undefinable by any technical term, that swell freely into "verses" in the Biblical sense, with no limit but the reader's breath. It happens that these two poets are not among our favorites; but our objection is to the quality of their thought, not to the inadequacy of their medium. On the other hand, every "prose" that has artistic claims has its rhythm. But that rhythm is organic, not mechanical. It is not a repetitious pattern as in the dance. It is still less a string of detachable statements. It forms a living whole, in which each part reacts upon all the others, and is subordinated to the total effect. Flaubert read aloud everything that he wrote; it was for him the only way to test sonority and tempo. And Yvor Winters says: "The prose of *Moby Dick*, though mechanically it is prose and not verse, is by virtue of its elaborate rhythms and heightened rhetoric closer in its esthetic result to the poetry of *Paradise Lost* than to the prose of Mrs. Wharton. . . . On the whole, we may fairly regard the work as essentially a poetic performance." [1]

According to the foregoing discussion, we should have to define *verse* as "language with a more obvious and more mechanical rhythm than prose"; and this would seem to imply a condemnation. Nothing is farther from our thought. We do not believe that verse is essential to the highest poetry; neither do we maintain that it is incompatible with it. We are convinced that, on several levels, verse offers advantages which it would be senseless to forego.

On the popular level, the "lyric" in the stricter sense of the term, the song which calls for music or suggests music, is inconceivable in prose. It is true that such a "lyric" appeals with great directness to the unsophisticated; but not seldom the simple are proved right against the supercilious. It is true also that it is a hybrid of two arts, like the painting which tells a story; but this is a theoretical objection which has weight only with the pedant. The most common fault in the "pure" lyric is that it is not "pure" enough: it adds to its music melodrama, maudlin sentiment or bogus philosophy. It might be better if poems which sound well did not attempt to convey anything beyond their own musical loveliness. To the cheap sense of many lyrics, the absolute nonsense of Edward Lear is far to be

[1] Yvor Winters, *Maule's Curse*, p. 74.

preferred. There are few more delightful "lyrics" in the language than *The Jumblies* and *The Yonghy-Bonghy-Bo*.

On a higher plane, verse may be defended as a tradition. A tradition need not be merely a prejudice or a superstition: there is an element of strength and joy in the sense of continuity, an imaginative appeal in the deepening vistas of history. This is not the sole, nor even the first duty of art; but it is an essential service which art can perform admirably. If we want to preserve a sense of the past, it is not amiss to perform some of the gestures of the past, even those which would have no strict justification in the present. Our religion, our politics, are tinged with antiquarian feeling; this is legitimate, so long as the ritual of the past deepens and does not stifle the thought of today. On this basis, even pastiche may at times be an excellent form of art, for the same reason that there is still, in architecture, a field for the styles of former ages. One of Robert Bridges' most perfect poems, *Elegy on a Lady Whom Grief for the Death of Her Betrothed Killed*, has the remote and subdued charm of a seventeenth-century classic. A pastiche is but an extreme case. It is possible to remain in touch with tradition without any substantial sacrifice of originality. It is not indifferent, for author or reader, that a poem should have a Spenserian overtone, or a note which reminds us of Keats. A fourteen-line poem would not strike the same chords in us, if it were not a *sonnet*, evoking by its very form the distant and solemn voices of Wordsworth, Milton, Shakespeare and Petrarch.

The above is a defense of *conservative* verse writing. We believe that verse is justified for another and higher reason, which operates even though the form adopted be revolutionary. All that it needed is that it should be manifestly *verse*, that is to say that it should adopt a technique deliberately different from that of prose. The value of the form lies first of all in the very fact of that difference. For it is a declaration of purpose: "Be prepared! This is poetry!" It commits the author to a mood; it silences many inhibitions that would assail him if he were writing a realistic novel or an essay. If the reader be responsive at all, it re-creates the same mood in him. Verse, thus understood, is an *incantation:* it weaves a spell. A rare meaning given to a word, a twist of phrase, a technical device of any kind, provided it be manifest, may suffice to close and open the proper doors. Perhaps many pages of prose would be needed to reach that initial point. Verse is a short-cut to the magic land.

In admitting the validity of verse, we have come very little nearer to a clear understanding of the poetic principle. The difficulty is that two different issues keep blurring each other in our minds: the one pertains to the spirit, the other belongs to technique. The confusion is hard to dispel, for lack of an adequate vocabulary. A young friend of ours once started a *Glossary of Words Which Ought to Exist.* We shall attempt to contribute one item to this much-needed work of reference.

In the matter of form, we are tolerably safe: the master of philosophy, in Molière's *Would-be Gentleman,* established the classic distinction: "Whatever is not prose is verse, whatever is not verse is prose." [1] But we need a word which, in the sphere of thought and feeling, will bear the same relation to *poetry* as *prose* does to *verse.* At present, we use *prose* equivocally. The result of this confusion is to make the correlative terms,

[1] The distinction was good enough for M. Jourdain; in our days, the dividing line could not be quite so sharply drawn. There are devices, as we have seen, which cannot be classified under the rules of any prosody, and yet which consciously and definitely depart from the practices of plain prose. Such a medium is usually called "poetical prose"; but the phrase seldom connotes frank approval. There is a feeling that "poetical prose" tends to be ornate, florid, turgid, and, in certain cases, jeweled and perfumed beyond endurance. It is a dangerous instrument. Melville, who wielded it with such magnificent effectiveness in *Moby Dick,* failed almost ludicrously when he applied it in *Pierre.* Yet it has many splendid pages to its credit, by Thomas De Quincey, Edgar Poe, Oscar Wilde, Anatole France (*Thaïs*), Gabriele d'Annunzio (*The Virgins of the Rocks*), Valle Inclán (*Sonatas*). Its masterpieces are probably Renan's *Prayer on the Acropolis* (*Souvenirs d'Enfance et de Jeunesse*) and Walter Pater's interpretation of La Gioconda (*The Renaissance*): both a trifle too conscious of their rich and haunting beauty.

verse and *poetry*, roughly—and erroneously—synonymous. Even Benedetto Croce, among the sharpest of modern minds, did not attempt to clear up the ambiguity by coining an adequate word: he had to be satisfied with a negative: *Poesia e non Poesia.* But what he calls non-poetry is not simply poetry with something lopped off; as it possesses a definite existence, a field and a purpose, it is entitled to a name.

For this "something," we might propose the non-commital terms *language* or *speech.* But they are too general: prose, verse, poetry (in articulate form) are all manifestations of language. We cannot take the liberty of restricting their meaning arbitrarily to suit our purpose; they are in too general use for such cavalier treatment, and we cannot tamper with everybody's possession. Simply to clarify the argument, and without any illusion about the permanent fitness of the name, we shall adopt *discourse,* in the old-fashioned sense it had in philosophy and rhetoric: "the communication of mental states to other minds by means of language."

Now we have our two distinct pairs: prose and verse, on the one hand; on the other, discourse, or plain communication, and poetry. It is manifest that *discourse* can be translated into verse as well as into prose. For instance, the lucid and uninspiring declaration already quoted: "I waited for the train at Coventry" happens to be verse. It is perhaps a little less evident that *poetry* (still undefined) can be expressed into what is, technically, direct and unadorned prose. Yet there are few people who will not feel a shudder of awe at the words of Pascal: "The eternal silence of these infinite spaces frightens me." Their very simplicity is the essence of their strength. If the grand image: "Voyaging through strange seas of thought alone" [1] is, mechanically, a pentameter, the fact is irrelevant. The expression is in no way different from prose. The words

---

[1] The statue of Newton:

"The marble index of a mind forever
Voyaging through strange seas of thought alone."

—Wordsworth, *The Prelude,* Book Third, lines 62-63.

are commonplace, and without any rare sonority; the construction is simple; the rhythm unobtrusive. It is poetry which has no need to advertise itself. Compare it with a somewhat similar picture in Keats's *Ode to a Nightingale:*

> . . . magic casements, opening on the foam
> Of perilous seas, in faery lands forlorn.

Here the poetic quality, which is undeniable, is stressed, and perhaps over-stressed, by material means.

Now we are at least approaching a definition of poetry. At any rate, we have attempted to isolate the idea of poetry from other conceptions which are frequently blended and confused with it. Poetry, as a result of this analysis, appears as *discourse consciously charged with emotion.* We need hardly say that "emotion" is not identical with "emotionalism." Emotionalism revels in the externals of emotion, not seldom at the expense of its inner quality. Gushing does not invariably invalidate emotion; but it unquestionably weakens it. The emotion that poetry expresses is perfectly compatible with restraint; indeed it is enhanced by restraint. "Letting oneself go," giving a free rein to one's sentiments, is not an infallible recipe for poetry. The poetic emotion may be of an active, expansive kind; it may also be retractive. Pride, scorn, aloofness, the quest of solitude, the flight to the ivory tower, all these may be accompanied by emotion, and become the source of poetry.

We have an instrument, which enables us to detect this high potential of emotion: it is a tremor, a sympathetic vibration within ourselves. It is akin to the thrill of awe and wonder which attends sudden discovery or intense realization: the "wild surmise" as we stand "silent upon a peak in Darien."

Emotion is what is most individual, most intimate in man. Our definition of *poetry* is therefore identical with our definition of *literature:* the conscious expression of personality. We fully accept this identity: the literary principle and the poetic principle are one. All the difference is one of degree. If emotion and personality are totally absent, we have mere *discourse.*

As soon as they appear, we have *literature*. We reserve the word *poetry* for that literature in which the intensity of emotion is highest. The sole criterion to tell them apart is our inner response. But there is no objective scale, no accurate artistic thermometer, that will enable us to declare: "Exactly at this point, discourse turns into literature; this other point marks the beginning of poetry." The "tremor" mentioned above is valid for ourselves alone.

Yet between those myriads of instruments, the individual readers, there is such a remarkable degree of agreement, that we are able to tell, broadly, what is *discourse*, what is *literature*, what is *poetry*. This agreement is partly artificial: it results from convention, which blunts the sharpness of individual reactions. But it is also due to the oft-neglected fact that differences among men are far less important than resemblances. It must never be forgotten, however, that this consensus is a rough-and-ready affair. It is purely a matter of statistics, and does not compel the individual. Any man is free to dissent, not only about borderline cases, but even about extremes. There are excellent critics who find poetry of the highest order in Edgar Poe, and no less excellent critics who fail to see any poetry at all in Victor Hugo.

Finally, we must remember that there are "all sorts and conditions" in literature, and that, even if we supposed each one to be perfect within its own domain, there would still be a hierarchy. At every level, verse represents a higher degree of artistic consciousness, a greater striving toward artistic excellence, than the *corresponding* prose. An epigram in verse, like the jingle: "I do not love thee, Doctor Fell," has a little more permanent value than a chance witticism. A drinking song betrays an ambition not found in rambling convivial talk. But such *verse* is inferior to the *prose* of a higher kind, a serious novel or drama, for instance. There are degrees in emotion as well. The "tremor" created in us by a brass band, the "thrill" we experience at a football game, are genuine and legitimate enough, and therefore not without poetical quality. But such *poetry* is not on the same level as what might seem mere *discourse* concerning love or religion. Not form alone, not thought alone, not emotion alone, can be accepted as the sole test of high literature. At the summit, we expect to find the purest quality of *discourse,* lucid and cogent presentation of thought, combined with the most rigorously adequate technique, and charged with the most intense and noblest emotion. *The Yonghy-Bonghy-Bo* is no less perfect than the *Intimations of Immortality;* [1] but there are valid reasons why the *Intimations* outrank *The Yonghy-Bonghy-Bo.*

SUMMARY

It has long been obvious that poetry and verse were not synonymous; yet the confusion persists. It will persist so long as formal tests are proposed for the distinction between prose and poetry. A few of these tests are listed, and discussed:

1. Poetry is the medium used for exalted *genres,* such as the ode, the epic and the tragedy.

2. Poetry consists in elaborate *diction:* the choice of "noble" or "beautiful" words.

3. Poetry depends upon the use of *images.*

4. Poetry results from a victory over self-imposed difficulties.

5. Poetry offers a higher degree of *concentration* than prose.

6. Poetry is identified with a *musical technique;* the systems of prosody are many, but all have in common the element of *rhythm.* We attempt to show that in practice, all these tests fail. Even *rhythm* is found in good prose, but in a freer, less mechanical form than in verse.

The adoption of *verse* as a medium, however, is not a mere survival. It is justified in three cases: (1) in the pure lyric, when musical accompaniment demands an obvious rhythm; (2) as a tradition, to secure a wealth of overtones from the memories of familiar masterpieces. The effectiveness of the sonnet,

[1] Wordsworth: *Intimations of Immortality from Recollections of Early Childhood.*

for instance, is due to its long ancestry and rich heritage; (3) as a declaration of intention: the adoption of a technique manifestly different from prose commits the writer to a certain mood, and gives him certain privileges. It induces at once the same mood in the reader. Verse is an incantation, and a short cut to the magic land.

Still, *verse* is not identical with *poetry*, and poetry remains undefined. Our difficulty is the lack of one term. *Verse* and *prose* should refer exclusively to technique; *poetry* and *X* should refer to the spirit. For this X, we propose the term *discourse*, in the old-fashioned sense of mere communication.

On this basis, we define poetry as "discourse consciously charged with emotion." Between discourse and poetry, there is no formal difference; the presence of emotion can be detected only by a responsive tremor in the reader. Verse should act as a warning sign that the tremor is to be expected; but the sign by itself is neither necessary nor sufficient.

This definition is not radically different from that of literature itself. The literary principle and the poetic principle are one and the same: poetry only denotes a higher degree of intensity. We have thus three levels: plain *discourse*, or unimpassioned communication; *literature*, or discourse with a conscious element of personality; and, within literature, *poetry*, in which the personality is felt with greater directness and power.

Verse can be used even for discourse (mnemotechnic rhymes, etc.) and by itself, does not create poetry. But at each level, verse represents a greater striving toward artistic excellence than prose. Not form alone, not thought alone, not emotion alone, can be accepted as the sole test of high literature. At the summit, we expect to find the purest quality of discourse—lucid and cogent presentation of thought—combined with the most rigorously adequate technique, and charged with the most intense and noblest emotion.

PART TWO

MAIN DIVISIONS IN WORLD LITERATURE: TENDENCIES, GENRES AND PERIODS

CHAPTER IX

FUNDAMENTAL TENDENCIES

I. CLASSICISM AND ROMANTICISM

AFTER completing this preliminary survey of the literary field, we are now confronted with the grim giants of literary theory, Classicism, Romanticism, Realism, Symbolism. The convenient and comfortable policy is to affirm that these giants are mere shadows; that there is no profit in parleying with them; and that they may be ignored without scruple and without fear. In a very literal sense, this policy is in agreement with the facts. When we pick up a book, we need not concern ourselves in the slightest degree with the -*ism* with which critics might choose to label it. Our enjoyment is our sole guide. Theories have no objective existence; they do not enhance our pleasure; they afford no safe criterion of excellence. If we expected to find in those -*isms* a set of absolute verities, we might close our chapter at this point with a *Requiescant in Pace*.

However, there are other facts in literature which compel us to give these theories more than a passing glance. Delusive or not, they have played a great part in the history of thought. Authors have been definitely affected by them, or have used them to rationalize their own practices; and it would be rash to say that their power is exhausted today. There are creative writers and critics who are all too conscious of belonging to a school, and who, less consciously perhaps, allow the tenets of that school to deflect their impulses and to warp their judgments. Not a few novelists, for instance, allow their *Realism* to stand as a screen between their *real* selves and the *real* world without. In so far as ideas are forces, literary theories cannot be wholly neglected.

Even those who are most skeptical about the objective existence of these doctrines cannot keep the names out of their critical vocabulary. If we were to be duly careful in harmonizing our thought and our speech, we should have to make use of such complicated formulae as these: "*Marie Chapdelaine* may be considered as a perfect modern example of that nonexistent entity, Classicism"; or: "If there were such a thing as Romanticism (but of course we are aware there is not), William Butler Yeats would deserve to be called an incurable Romanticist." To avoid these cumbrous circumlocutions, let us once for all take it for granted that all *-isms* are mere figments of the critical imagination; but that, on the critical plane, this pale mythology of abstractions behaves *as if* it possessed some reality. We can enjoy a book without giving theory a thought; we cannot examine the problems of literature without facing the issues for which the *-isms* stand.

On closer view, we find that each one of these general words stands, not for a single issue, but for no less than four different things. Each represents a definite *doctrine,* taught by famous masters, embodied in various treatises, manifestoes and critical works. Each denotes also the *school* which professed that particular doctrine. Each designates the *period* during which the school was predominant. These three conceptions are closely linked; all three have a historical basis. The fourth is philosophical, not historical: it considers these entities as *universal and permanent tendencies*.

These four aspects are not incompatible, but they are not rigorously coextensive. There is more in literature than can be codified by any theorist; no writer ever quite conforms to the canons he accepts; no school is so completely in the ascendant that all others are absolutely eliminated; and there are far more than four tendencies in the human mind. We must repeat that no neat logical framework will ever fit the moving complexity of facts. But we should not believe that such confusion is peculiar to literature: we have seen that it also prevails in religion and in politics. In all fields, language, and the necessity of organizing for definite action, impose upon our minds a simplification which may be as artificial as it is ruthless. We must accept, gratefully, the service of words; but we should never allow ourselves to become their slaves or their dupes.

We shall deal, in a later chapter, with the long and at times tangled pageant of doctrines, schools and periods. It is with the fourth aspect of the question, the permanent tendencies in literature, that we are at present concerned. Between the *philosophy* of literature and the *history* of literature, there is, of course, a connection. Schools are historical accidents, but as a rule they are not willing to admit the fact. They often claim, not that they have invented a new truth, but that they have discovered a new approach to eternal truth. They proclaim the validity of their tenets, not only for all time to come, but also for all time past. So they strive to extend their sway upon the dead, and to annex, as forerunners, men who were unconscious of such allegiance. Thus Shakespeare is enrolled, willy-nilly, among the Romanticists, Daniel Defoe among the Realists, Homer among the Classicists. This process of retrospective conquest resembles the baptism of ancestors which, we understand, is practiced by the Church of the Latter-Day Saints. In this way, the notions of *doctrine* and of *tendency* are brought very close together; both escape the limitations of time, and refuse to be identified with a particular *period*. There are two differences, however. A doctrine is clearly formulated in intellectual terms, a tendency is not. A doctrine is an orthodoxy in its own eyes, to the exclusion of all rivals; whereas a tendency is frankly one of several similar elements.

In attempting to define the term *Classicism*, we have first to clear away many secondary meanings. Etymology tells us the word originated with Aulus Gellius, a Latin grammarian who lived under the Antonines. In his *Noctes Atticae*, he opposed *scriptor classicus* to *scriptor proletarius*; he thus transferred, like so many critics of today, notions and terms of sociology into the domain of literary criticism. *Classicus* could be translated by our colloquial expression "high class," and perhaps even more accurately by the unpleasant slang term "classy." A "classic" is a work that appeals to gentlemen, and that all gentlemen ought to know. If this were taken too literally, *Debrett's Peerage* would be the ideal of a classic, with the *Racing Calendar* as a good second.

Gentlemen were given a "classical" education, that is to say they were brought up in the tradition of their class. So, by a natural confusion, the word "classics" came to mean the works studied in classrooms, at such places as Eton or Oxford. In French, the confusion was even more complete, and this second sense usurped first place. *"Un livre classique"* is a school book, not necessarily a masterpiece of literature. In this sense, a thoroughly Romantic writer like Shelley turned into a "classic" when his works forced the gates of the colleges. Baudelaire, long under the ban, has recently achieved "classic" rank.

For centuries, of course, the only recognized classics were the writers of Greece and Rome. So the term remains attached in our minds primarily to antiquity, secondarily to those modern authors who borrowed inspiration, subject or form from antiquity. There are still "Schools of Classical Studies" and "Departments of Classical Languages," as well as "classical styles" in architecture.

Finally, the word is loosely applied to anything well-established or "standard": a yearly event in the domain of sport soon becomes a "classic." Through further degeneration, "classic" sank from an equivalent for "standard" to a humorous synonym for "stock," "well-worn," "trite": "He offered the classic alibi . . ." or "He played upon us the classic joke. . . ." We should not dismiss these popular developments as negligible; they might be the symptom of weaknesses and dangers inherent in the very conception of Classicism.

But what is "the very conception of Classicism"? None of the secondary meanings listed above offers us a definite answer.

Yet the answer is simple enough; this is one of the rare questions in literature upon which agreement is practically universal. *Classicism means Discipline.* It is on that ground that it is praised and attacked. Other words may be used instead of discipline: restraint, sense of law and order, conformity. But although the connotations are slightly different, the common elements between them are manifest. Discipline means submission to a rule; and the very idea of a rule implies that of authority. In order to understand Classicism, we shall therefore have to define the authority which it acknowledges; and this will compel us to take a brief excursion into elementary philosophy.

We get our impression of reality both directly and indirectly. The immediate apprehension of facts is of course primordial. Without some such basis, there could be no organized thought. "There is nothing in the intellect that was not originally provided by the senses." But we are all aware that this direct apprehension is constantly deceptive. My hand, held a few inches before my eyes, is larger than my neighbor's house. The rising moon is a flat disk not farther away than the hills which limit my horizon. A stick appears broken when half plunged into water. So we train ourselves, to a large extent unconsciously, not to accept uncritically the evidence of our senses, as, in another domain, we train ourselves not to follow blindly our impulses. We check our intuitions by comparing and reducing to a system the results of our experience. *System* here does not signify an elaborate construction of the mind; it is only the belief that things do not happen in a wholly capricious way, that there is a fair degree of consistency in the world.

Consistency is thus our test. A thing is accepted as true only when it fits in with the whole body of our previous knowledge. If a new fact refuses so to fit, we may adopt three attitudes. We may call it an accident; but this is a mere verbal evasion. An accident may be unforeseen; it never is causeless. When explained, it takes its place in the general scheme. We may deny the authenticity of the fact, call it a lie, the result of imperfect observation, a delusion. We may, more profitably, consider the new fact as a challenge which compels us to extend and recast our conception of experience. But, in all three cases, we retain our essential belief in a consistent universe, and we shape our conduct according to that belief. A burnt child dreads the fire, and, on the physical plane at any rate, we soon cease to reach for the moon.

In its most unassuming form, this belief, the substratum of our thought and action, is called common sense. As it grows definite and conscious, it assumes the status and dignity of "human reason." Organized into a doctrine, its name is Rationalism. *Reason is the authority which Classicism recognizes as its guide.* Boileau, the lawgiver of Parnassus, insisted that we should not merely obey, but also love reason; and that our writings should derive from that source alone their charm and their worth. Imagination is valid, passion is legitimate, only when submitted to the control of sovereign reason.

Unruly, lawless, are terms of unequivocal condemnation; but it must be noted that the classicists, while insisting on law, do not submit to arbitrary rule. The ultimate authority is reason itself, which the intermediate authorities, in Church, state or art, are bound to follow. The true classicists never preached the servile doctrine of obedience for obedience's sake. Even their religion was in accord with reason: *Fideism,* which denied the possibility of such an accord, has been condemned as a heretical tendency; and St. Thomas Aquinas was able to present the data of Revelation in the terms of human philosophy. If the Classical Age accepted the divine right of kings, it was as a reasonable hypothesis, not as a mystic intuition. And Aristotle's long dictatorship in literature was not founded on an unreasoning *Magister Dixit.* "I believe these rules to be true," said Corneille with great definiteness, "not because they are found in Aristotle, but because they are in agreement with human reason." It must be admitted that this sane and robust spirit, evident in the masters, is dimmed in the disciples and epigones. The constant danger of classicism is to over-emphasize authority at the expense of critical reason.

Classicism adopts consistency as the test of reality; but, at its point of perfection, it remained finely poised and hesitant between two interpretations of consistency. One, *inner consistency*, consisted in organizing thought into a flawless system, as closely knit, as inevitable as Euclid. The other, more pragmatic, sought *consistency* in conformity with common beliefs and with tradition: that alone is true which has been held *consistently*, that is to say at all times, everywhere, and by every-body: *quod semper, quod ubique, quod ab omnibus.* The Classicists were well aware that "excessive reasoning may drive reason away." Reason is but *common sense* raised to a higher degree of consciousness; the philosopher who believes that he can be right by himself, thanks to an infallible instrument in his own individual mind, departs from common sense no less than the visionary. The supreme test is consistency of experience among all men past and present. But then we escape the desert of abstract Logic only to fall into the morass of unreasoning conformity.

Historically, the Classicists eluded this dilemma by interpreting Reason as "reasonableness," and "the rule of reason" as the avoidance of extremes. The Classical spirit could thus be defined as a compromise rather than a doctrine; and a compromise is but a veil modestly thrown over the nakedness of inconsistency. But we are now dealing with a tendency, not with a formula. And the tendency of Classicism is plain: it could not define with irrefutable clearness the principles that it obeyed, but it stressed the virtue of discipline.

Discipline involves the sacrifice of whim and willfulness, not of personality. The classicists maintain that the individual is more fully himself in the well-regulated state than he would be in isolation or in the midst of anarchy: he is requested to give up only the liberty of harming himself as well as others. The block-system on a railroad is not meant to stop or slow down traffic; on the contrary, it is only because all the signals are rightly set that the train is free to proceed full speed ahead. There has been no dearth of great personalities under severe discipline, provided the discipline itself be in accord with reason. *"Non mi lascia più ir lo fren dell' arte,"* said Dante: [1] the curb of art lets me go no farther. And Milton's rugged integrity was not impaired by the strictness of his classical form.

The classical tendency at its best brings out qualities of inestimable value. Common sense assures Classicism of a solid foundation, upon which reason builds a well-balanced structure. Hand in hand with consistency go sanity and health, for disease, whether mental or physical, is only disorder. Intelligent restraint imparts to thought and form a quiet dignity. The supreme reward of classical discipline is harmony, a harmony consciously sought, kept within the simplest terms, and all the more impressive.

These merits are not limited to the field of art and literature. In religion, in morality, in politics, we may find a spirit that is truly classical: firmly orthodox, law-abiding, responsive to duty. The "good citizen," moderate, diligent, sober, is a classicist, and, even though he may be lacking in brilliancy, a "credit to the community"; the gentleman in the highest sense of the term is a masterpiece of the classical spirit.

On the other hand, it should be obvious that no tendency, by itself, can be coextensive with all virtue. Classicism is discipline, that is to say restraint: it presupposes something to be restrained. Man does not live by restraint alone; a system composed entirely of checks would be an absurdity. It would be an automobile with efficient brakes and no motor, a railroad all safety signals and without a locomotive. Whenever this negative attitude, wrongly identified with the whole of Classicism, has been made the sole rule of life, the result has been decay. In religion, it causes orthodoxy to degenerate into literalism, obedience into irresponsible servility, attachment to tradition into superstitious practices. In morality, it leads to pharisaical legalism: if you conform in externals, if you keep within

---

[1] *Purgatorio*, XXXIII, 141.

the law, you will be safe. In politics, it ends in the worship of a tyrannical and soulless bureaucracy. In art and in literature, this form of dry-rot is known as *pseudo-classicism:* the eternal and timorous imitation of imitation (for originality is sin), according to rules which grow ever more minute as they grow more formal; until the acme of inane correctness is reached in works which are faultless, but without a breath of life.

It is against this tedious conformity that the banner of Romanticism was raised: a rebellion against death, a reaffirmation of life. Here again, we must not allow ourselves to be misled by the superficial and almost fortuitous associations of the term. Romanticism is not necessarily connected with the Middle Ages, any more than Classicism is identified with antiquity. And a romantic work need not be filled with wild adventure. Goethe's short novel, *Werther,* and Vigny's drama, *Chatterton,* are among the most typical products of the romantic spirit. In both, the setting is drab enough, and the plot extremely simple. Both end with the suicide of the hero: but suicide had long been a commonplace of the classical stage.

The etymology of the term romantic is more tangled than that of classic. *Romance* first meant a corrupted form of Latin, after the disruption of the Empire: "the rustic Roman language," as it is called in an edict of Charlemagne. Out of decaying Latin arose, in the course of centuries, the modern vernaculars of Portugal, Spain, France, Italy, Roumania, still known as Romance languages. *Romance* was applied to the literature in the popular tongue, as opposed to the more learned literature in Latin. Then the term was restricted to long narrative works; but there was little enough in common between the *Romance of the Rose,* an allegory, the *Romance of Reynard the Fox,* a satire, and the various romances of chivalry. The latter remained in sole possession of the name; and they gave it a flavor which has never completely disappeared. They offered a blend of the heroic, the sentimental and the fantastic, which, like a potent philter, addled the brains of poor Don Quixote.

Nothing could be more averse to classical reasonableness than such extravagance; so, by the eighteenth century, the term "romantick" simply meant "absurd," just as "Gothick" meant "barbarous." But a reaction against the excessive tameness of the safe-and-sane was setting in. Even in the age of taste and reason, "romantick" assumed a less unfavorable meaning, and denoted the "picturesque." Wildness, not yet condoned in speech or conduct, first became attractive in the landscape. Crags, fells, torrents and precipices, came into vogue, by the side of formal gardens in the elaborate taste of France or Italy. Solitude ceased to be oppressive; and the charm of neatness and luxury, which so appealed to Voltaire, had to compete with the somber poetry of tombstones and ruins.[1]

Historically, Romanticism was a revolt: against arbitrary rules, against emasculated taste, against the weariness of copying forever the same impeccable models. Although there is in Romanticism a positive force, as an attitude it seems to represent the gospel of dissent. The first romanticist then was, not Rousseau, but Lucifer, who, in a Heaven of classical acquiescence, first dared to assert his indomitable personality and to declare: "I will not serve." So Lucifer, the eternal rebel, re-

---

[1] This tendency came very near bearing the name of Gothic instead of Romantic. The tale of mystery and terror became known as the Gothick novel. Walpole's Strawberry Hill and Beckford's Fonthill were egregious examples of the revival of interest in Gothic architecture. William Blake made a profound and epigrammatic comparison between the "Grecian," which we should call "classical" and the "Gothic," which corresponds to the romantic spirit. A generation later, in France, Victor Hugo's *Notre Dame* was both a masterpiece of Romantic fiction, and an impassioned defense of the Gothic style; among the young esthetes of those days, the highest term of praise was *ogival*. If the word "Gothic" had been adopted for the new trend, it would have been even more confusing than "Romantic." There was little in common, we must repeat, between medieval discipline and Romantic anarchy. Lord Byron would have been thoroughly out of place in the century of St. Thomas Aquinas. On the other hand, Keats and Shelley are undeniably romantic; yet many of their poems are of Greek inspiration.

mained a favorite hero of the romanticists, from Byron to Baudelaire. "The reason Milton wrote in fetters when he wrote of Angels and God, and at liberty when of Devils and Hell," said Blake, "is because he was a true Poet, and of the Devil's party without knowing it."[1]

For the upholder of the written law, of established values, of vested interests, this attitude is blasphemy, and Romanticism is the very essence of evil. "Romanticism is the Commune," said Adolphe Thiers, the first President of the present French Republic; and the Paris Commune of 1871, in his eyes, was nothing but an explosion of elemental ferocity, the wild beast in man straining against the salutary fetters of civilization. "Classicism is health, Romanticism disease," said Goethe, with the authority of one who had traversed and transcended both schools. If by *dis-ease* we understand the discomfort and the actual pains which attend maladjustment, Goethe was undeniably right. The Romanticists suffer, because they are at odds with themselves, and at odds with the world. If theirs is a mild case, if they are of a passive disposition, their brooding takes the form of gentle melancholy; if the suffering is more intense, if the sufferer is of a more aggressive temper, the Romantic malady is manifested in despair. But there is no lasting peace, no deep-seated serenity in Romanticism: the Romanticist always is a tormented soul.[2]

Again from the Classical point of view, Romanticism means *Egomania*. Instead of accepting the wisdom of the ages, the fruits of collective experience, the consensus of experts, the findings of dispassionate reason, the individual deifies his impulses and his dreams, that is to say himself. This worship of Self leads to the destruction of Self; for discipline alone can give consistency, without which there is no personality. Romanticism is *insane* pride; by its very rejection of "common

---

[1] W. Blake, *Marriage of Heaven and Hell.*

[2] This would make Pascal a romanticist, Wordsworth and Walter Scott classicists. There is no absurdity in that. Remember that we are dealing now, not with schools and periods, but with essential tendencies and attitudes.

sense," it is driven to the verge, or beyond the verge, of madness. The greatest single influence in the formation of Romantic consciousness was Jean Jacques Rousseau; and in Rousseau, passion, desire, imagination, revolt, melancholy, despair, egomania, insanity, are equally manifest. It is no mere coincidence that the most inspired prophet of Romanticism should be William Blake. There is more illumination in his few lightning flashes (*The Marriage of Heaven and Hell, The Laocoön Group, On Homer's Poetry and on Vergil*) than in many cogent and lucid treatises; but these flashes came from a darkened mind.

It is our constant endeavor, in this study, not to lose touch with undeniable facts. The romanticists may declare that Classicism is spiritual death, the classicists that Romanticism and insanity are one, the world refuses to give up cherished masterpieces of either kind. Blake urged us to reject "the Stolen and Perverted Writings of Homer and Ovid, of Plato and Cicero, which all men ought to contemn"; [1] but we smilingly decline to follow his iconoclastic zeal. On the other hand, according to Boileau's code, many passages in the Hebrew Prophets, in the Apocalypse, in Shakespeare, in Pascal, offend against the laws of good taste and good sense. Our verdict is: "So much the worse for the code of Boileau." Mutual condemnations do not quite cancel each other; they point out actual dangers in the things that are judged; but, more clearly still, they reveal flaws in the judge's own mind.

Yes, Romanticism is revolt; but only in its shallowest forms does it appear as sheer revolt. The true poet does not go out of his way to deny or to destroy; he wants to tear down only that which stands in his way. And what is his way? The one that is revealed to him by *direct intuition*. This is the path to the living truth; all rules, including those of mathematics and logic, are merely the organizing of what intuition has discovered, and alone could discover. By the aid of rules, we can neither invent nor explore, but only follow. In this organized

[1] William Blake, *Milton*, Preface.

world, neatly fenced in and parceled out by means of laws and regulations, the herd must be satisfied; and so must the poet himself, in his capacity as a gregarious or "political" animal. But the urge to go beyond the domain of the law is upon him. He is the seer, the prophet, the poet—*creator* or *shaper*—the Trouvère, or *finder*. If he is to voyage through strange seas of thought, it must be alone, and the seas must be uncharted.

For this fundamental conception, we could of course give chapter and verse from many poets labeled as romantic. We could also bring forth the testimony of Longinus, that mysterious Greek critic, who, in his treatise *On the Sublime*, so definitely proclaimed the rights of genius. We could appeal to Henri Bergson, whose philosophy of *Creative Evolution* is profoundly romantic. We prefer to quote a passage from Montaigne, because Montaigne was a skeptic, an apostle of moderation and common sense, steeped in the classic tradition, and writing two centuries before the romantic tendency was formally recognized: "At a certain low level, one may judge it [poetry] by rules and by art. But the true, supreme and divine poesy is above all rules and reason. Whoever discerns the beauty of it with assured and steady sight, he does not see it, any more than the splendor of a flash of lightning. It does not seduce our judgment; it ravishes and overwhelms it." [1]

By *poesy* we are free to understand here the essence of art in literature, that part which is furthest removed from mere discourse. It would seem that such a lofty conception is exceedingly aristocratic. Geniuses, daring to venture beyond the bourne of organized thought, must be infinitely rare. Montaigne is not so discouraging. He does not suggest that any man can bring forth "the true, supreme and divine poesy"; but he does imply that common man may be "transpierced and transported" by it; and that he can even infect others with his enthusiasm. "The frenzy that goads him who is able to penetrate into it also strikes a third person when he hears him talk

[1] Montaigne, *Essays*, Bk. I, Ch. XXXVII, Zeitlin Edition.

about it and recite it, like a loadstone that not only attracts the needle, but also infuses into it the virtue to attract others." The discovery of truth and beauty beyond the safe region of rules may be the privilege of a few, but the appreciation of that discovery is open to everyone.

Even to the simple; above all to the simple; for the knowledge of the rules is a hindrance, not a help. Between the true poet and the people stand in serried mass the learned, the formulators and keepers of the law. They claim the sole right to judge; yet discovery is the one thing they cannot judge, for their law is the very negation of discovery. Romanticism thus finds it necessary to break down the barrier of expert knowledge, which is closely akin to civilization itself. So the romantic tendency is democratic and even demagogic in character. It appeals to the primitive, for the primitive is unspoilt; and to the unenlightened, for the light of sophistication is darkness. Thus Rousseau declaimed against the arts and sciences, which had corrupted the native goodness of man; thus popular ballads and crude early epics were ranked above the exquisite elegance of Pope; thus Blake, fighting against the academicians and their artificial taste, asserted "that every man ought to be a judge of pictures, and every man is so who has not been connoisseured out of his senses." The connoisseur is the enemy.

But if the poet appeals directly to the masses, over the heads of the experts, and against the experts, he has no desire to submit to the verdict of the masses. His own voice is the voice of God—this is the meaning of "inspiration," a notion which is at the very center of Romanticism. If the people responds, that proves that the voice of the people is *also* the voice of God, and all is for the best. If the people fails to respond, it proves no less clearly that, deluded by experts and false prophets, it is not speaking with its own voice. Hence the curious alternation of aristocratic and democratic feelings among romanticists. At one time, the people is infallible, pure and holy; tomorrow, the people is merely the herd, the mob, the rabble, from whose stupid fury the poet must seek refuge in his ivory tower.

This intermittent "appeal to the people" is no doubt a dangerous procedure, and not always a very scrupulous one. Before we condemn it, we must ask ourselves whether it is radically different from that of all religious reformers; they too reject traditional and organized authority, and demand for all believers the right of interpreting freely the Sacred Book—provided of course that the "free" interpretation be the "right" one. And the initial steps of Descartes' famous method bear an unexpected resemblance to the romantic revolt. Descartes also swept aside the pretension of the learned to dictate his thought, and our thought. He descended alone into the unexplored abyss of his own doubt. He found there, by himself and within himself, the full assurance of truth, as an immediate personal experience. Then he returned to proclaim the new truth—to whom? Not to the professional philosophers, hampered by their scholastic erudition, but to the general public, that public which had no "preconceived idea," perhaps because it had no idea at all. So he embodied his method, not in a Latin treatise in syllogistic form, but in a small book in the vernacular, free from all technical apparatus, and made more readable by fragments of autobiography. And, even as Blake said that every man was a judge of pictures, so Descartes claimed that every man was a judge of philosophical issues, because, forsooth, "good sense" was a universal quality. This is pure democracy.

There is, however, a difference between the method of Descartes and that of Romanticism. Descartes sought certitude within himself, but he sought it critically, and by cautious steps. The Romanticist, on the other hand, is apt to be satisfied with the first flash of intuition, if only it be vivid enough. This, however, does not condemn Romanticism altogether; it enables us to discriminate between its shallower and its more profound manifestations. In all cases, the flash, the tremor, the thrill of wonder, is the starting point. But here shallow Romanticism stops; it does not go beyond an image or a chaos of images. The great romanticist works out the consequences of his initial vision. If they refuse to be worked out, he rejects the vision as useless, a mere fancy, a passing delusive gleam. Boileau could never have had the intense vision which inspired Dante; on the other hand, a host of madmen have glimpses of the other world even more torturingly real than that of the great Florentine; but they could not transmute their vision into art. It is therefore no fault in the romantic tendency that it should place inspiration first; it would be a damning fault if it placed inspiration "first, last and all the time."

To rely upon inspiration alone is thus the great danger that besets Romanticism. The gait of Classicism may be pedestrian at times, but it is steady; the flight of Romanticism is daring and uneven. Man's spirit cannot rise and soar forever. The poet who counts too heavily on inspiration is wholly lost when the "divine afflatus" fails him. Hence a well-marked form of romantic gloom: despair, not at "the giant sorrows of the world," but at the pathetic inadequacy of the human mind. Coleridge, who wrote *Kubla Khan* in a waking trance, was bound to feel "Dejection" when "the genial spirits" left him:

> A grief without a pang, void, dark and drear,
> A stifled, drowsy, unimpassioned grief,
> Which finds no natural outlet, no relief,
> In word, or sigh, or tear.

At times, as in Byron, in Musset, in Heine, even in medieval romance, the result is not so much dark despair as despairing irony—a sardonic, self-tormenting pleasure in the sudden inglorious tumbling of the poetic kite.

Classicism is restraint, Romanticism is urge; if these plain terms be accepted, it will be evident that the two tendencies are not parallel, independent, mutually exclusive; they are part of a single whole, they *must* co-exist in every work of art. Classicism has always recognized the need, and even the primacy, of the romantic element, under the names of "inspiration" or "genius." Romanticism fully accepts the necessity of discipline, in the form of careful, exacting, elaborate technique. Only at both extremes do we see the two elements almost completely divorced: in the bloodless artificiality of pseudo-Classicism, in the fury, frenzy and chaos of decadent Romanticism. There is no inspiration whatever in the poems of Henry James Pye; and there is no recognizable discipline in the lucubrations of the Dadaists. Fortunately the field is wide between the bleached fossils and the lunatic fringe.

Accustomed as we are to oppose the two terms, we may be tempted to believe that Romanticism and Classicism are antagonistic even though they are associated; that, in the same book, it is impossible to stress the one without sacrificing the other. This would imply that powerful inspiration must scorn discipline, and that great mastery of the instrument reduces almost to the vanishing point the need for inspiration. We know that this is not the case. A pianist or violinist, in order to be truly great, must have music in his soul, but also skill in his fingers. Victor Hugo, in Tennyson's apt and generous words, was a "Cloud-weaver of phantasmal hopes and fears"; but the "weird Titan" could manifest his power *because* he had trained himself to an incredible degree of virtuosity. No writer, therefore, is compelled to choose between the classic and the romantic paths; it should be his endeavor to be both classic and romantic to the utmost of his capacity.

SUMMARY

It is conceded that Classicism, Romanticism, Realism, Symbolism, the grim giants of literary theory, are abstractions, and do not contribute to our enjoyment of a masterpiece. But the terms cannot be lightly discarded, for they have greatly influenced critical thought. Each may stand for at least four different things: a doctrine, a school, a period, a permanent tendency. These four aspects are not incompatible, but they are not necessarily coextensive. It is with the *permanent tendencies* alone that we shall deal in this chapter and the next.

The word *classic* originally (in Aulus Gellius) referred to a *class* ideal: *scriptor classicus* as opposed to *scriptor proletarius.* A classic is a work which appeals to men of gentle breeding. By a natural extension: a book studied in the schools where gentlemen are trained; and pre-eminently the masterpieces of Greek and Latin literature.

Classicism means above all *discipline.* Discipline implies an authority. That authority, in Classicism, is not arbitrary: it is founded on human reason. The test of reality is consistency: whatever is incoherent is absurd. But there are two ways of attaining consistency, and Classicism has never frankly chosen between the two. The first is agreement with a system as closely knit as Euclid, the strict rationalistic ideal. The second is the consensus of all rational men, generation after generation. So reason and tradition are blended, and the compromise is veiled under the ambiguous names *common sense* and *reasonableness.*

Such discipline does not involve the sacrifice of personality, but ensures its fullest development. The reward of classical discipline is harmony. But if restraint be over-emphasized, Classicism turns into pseudo-classicism: the servile imitation of ancient models, the timorous acceptance of formal rules. The result is elegant frigidity, correct inanity, and spiritual decay.

It is against this slavish conformity that Romanticism rebels. It is a reaffirmation of life. Etymologically, romance applied first to the languages issued from Latin, then to the literature in these vernaculars, then to long poems, allegorical, narrative or satirical, finally to tales of chivalric adventure. The mixture of the heroic, the sentimental and the fantastic in these tales offended classic "reasonableness": so romantic, in the early eighteenth century, meant extravagant and absurd. It then assumed the more favorable sense of *picturesque.*

Romanticism is an attitude of dissent: to the upholders of the law, such rebellion must appear a blasphemy. So for the classicist, Romanticism means perversity, disease, insanity, egomania. It is true that the romanticist, at odds with the world, is as a rule a tormented soul. Rejecting external authority, he seems to deify himself; and the result is frequently isolation, melancholy and despair.

In rebelling against established authorities, Romanticism appeals to the unspoilt, the primitive, the unenlightened: so there is a democratic aspect to Romanticism. But the poet has no thought of submitting to the masses: his own inspiration is his only law. When that fails, all is darkness.

If we think of Classicism as *restraint*, of Romanticism as *urge*, it is evident that these tendencies are not mutually exclusive. On the contrary, they must co-exist in every work of art.

CHAPTER X

FUNDAMENTAL TENDENCIES

II. REALISM AND SYMBOLISM

DISCIPLINE and inspiration, the classical and the romantic, are tendencies in the human mind; the realistic and the symbolic tendencies are two ways of considering the material upon which the human mind is at work. *Realism* consists in dealing with the facts purely in and for themselves; *Symbolism* is interested only in what the facts signify.

Once more, we are compelled to be on our guard against associations of ideas which, although they have some historical justification, offer no philosophical validity. The temper of the realistic *school* and of the realistic *age* was, not dispassionate, but passionately harsh and cynical. In this, it was the reverse of scientific; but it succeeded in coloring even science with its own pessimism. This, of course, is not true of Realism as a permanent tendency. It is absurd to assume that only the sordid is real; a fragrance is no less real than a stench. Yet we find it almost impossible to dispel this confusion, now nearly a hundred years old. The policies we still call "realistic" are inspired by fanatical ideologies, like "race" or "empire," and lead to the ruthless sacrifice of obvious, practical, *real* values, such as wealth, comfort, liberty, and life itself. We are apt to call certain visionaries *realists* only because their dreams happen to be nightmares: to work for an organized world is far more *realistic* than to prophesy eternal and senseless conflict. Through a similar confusion, we believe that Symbolism is necessarily nebulous, because the school which adopted that name sedulously cultivated the vague. Surely, Dante, Milton,

Goethe in his *Faust,* were not describing mere objective facts, and only for the sake of the facts themselves; yet their works are marvels of definiteness, compared with those of many alleged realists.

Like Classicism and Romanticism, Realism and Symbolism are not mutually exclusive, or even antagonistic. They are two aspects of the same indissoluble whole. It is impossible for any work of art not to be both realistic and symbolical; and the greatest art is the one that is at the same time most realistic and most symbolical.

"Pure" Realism is a most unrealistic abstraction. Nothing is so stupid as a fact: a bare fact, *per se,* has no place either in literature or in science. Leopold von Ranke stated that his sole aim was to set forth "how it actually happened"; and it was thought he had given the perfect recipe for realistic history. But, among the innumerable events which all had happened, he had to choose those that were *significant;* significant with reference to himself, Leopold von Ranke, and to his more or less conscious philosophy. "My cat had kittens," said Herbert Spencer; "that is a fact, but it is not science." Untold apples fell unheeded, before the fact acquired significance in the mind of Newton. As with history and science, so with art; the fact that my janitor squints might be fitted into a literary masterpiece; by itself, it is not literature.

This explains why valid realism so easily, so inevitably, passes into symbolism. The delusion of the Spanish country squire Don Quixote would be a mere oddity for a psychiatrist to note in his case book; but Cervantes turned it into a symbol which, after three hundred years, shows no signs of exhaustion. The melancholy end of a certain Emma Bovary is fit for a brief coroner's report; but, thanks to Flaubert, we realize that we all have "Bovaryism" in our hearts, and we see ourselves dissected under the symbol of the village doctor's wife. Zola claimed to be a "Naturalist," by which he meant a "natural scientist." But who would care today for his more or less accurate reporting of a fictitious miners' strike under the Second

Empire? *Germinal* owes its rudimentary and vigorous life to Zola's power of giving us, through the symbol of a mere episode, an epic of social conflict. And the picture of abject poverty among the Silesian *Weavers* would have been purely depressing, if Gerhart Hauptmann had not compelled us to see, in their sordid lives, the eternal tragedy of the downtrodden, and the essential injustice of their fate.

There are naturally many kinds and degrees of realism, as there are many orders of reality; but the distinctions between them are fairly obvious. The various forms of symbolism, on the contrary, offer shades which are apt to be confusing. No one denies that language is in a sense symbolical; not only because certain sounds are made to stand for certain ideas, but because, except in the case of proper names, the general stands for the particular, and the particular for the general. When we say "the cat," we may mean, according to circumstances, all cats, or our own cherished Tommy. This elementary observation would soon lead us back to the source and origin of all classical symbolism, Plato's conception of the *Idea*. Every cat that purrs or scratches is but a shadowy symbol for the Ideal Cat, which alone possesses reality.

The first degree of symbolism, in the strictly literary domain, is the *comparison*. Condensed, it is known as the metaphor. When Wordsworth spoke of "strange seas of thought," he did not take the word *sea* realistically, that is to say literally. The sea is here a one-word symbol for magnitude, with overtones which suggest danger, and therefore daring. Even common speech is constantly metaphorical; the artistic metaphor stands out from the gray mass because it is unfamiliar, apposite and vivid. But the very best metaphor notes only a chance resemblance. It is strikingly true in the flash of the moment; it has no enduring validity. As a rule, our thought is not in the least like a sea.

Here is another metaphor: "scaling the crags of the Ideal." Expand it into thirty-six lines, and you have Longfellow's *Excelsior!* But, although the treatment is so conscientiously detailed, the poet is aware that, between the facts and the significance he chooses to give them, there is no necessary correspondence. For a few minutes, we are willing to play Longfellow's game; but we know, and he knows, that it is only a clever game. The plain interpretation of the youth's queer behavior would be not "Idealism" but "Lunacy"; and the obvious lesson: "Beware of strange devices."

We may expand a metaphor into thirty-six lines, as in *Excelsior!* We may expand it into more than twenty thousand, as in the *Romance of the Rose.* This is *Allegory,* a form of literature with a very long history, and a very wide appeal. *The Faerie Queene* is the masterpiece of poetic allegory; for generations, the book most widely read in the English language was *Pilgrim's Progress;* and Maurice Maeterlinck's *Blue Bird,* rather to the author's annoyance, eclipsed the fame of all his other works.

But Allegory is frankly conventional; it does not claim any objective reality for the relations that it establishes between two sets of phenomena. Even in its most exalted form, it remains a game: a pleasing, clever, compelling method of presentation, not a form of exploration. There is, however, a kind of symbolism which implies actual correspondence between the sign and the thing signified. What happens under our eyes on one plane also happens in very truth on another plane. This seems at first an absurd claim; and it may be advanced in an absurd fashion, when it is offered as a justification for magic. Magic belongs to the most ambitious kind of symbolism: its only fault is that it is spurious. If you know the proper *Abracadabra,* the right *Open Sesame,* matter will yield and spirits will do your bidding. If you stick red-hot pins into a wax figure of your enemy, the man will suffer and die. All spells and incantations are symbols in that sense.

If this should sound like primitive superstition, we must remember that the gestures of modern technique appear magical to the ignorant. Between turning a couple of knobs, and listening to music which originates a hundred miles away, there is no apparent connection; yet there is a secret and inevitable correspondence.

Science is symbolical in that deeper sense; and particularly Mathematics. Reduce reality to a set of signs, which bear no outward resemblance to that reality; work with those signs according to their own laws; then compare the result with the actual facts; and you will discover that Nature and the signs have followed rigorously the same course. The most impressive triumph of this symbolism was the discovery of the planet Neptune. Exclusively through the signs, that is to say through celestial mechanics, its existence and its position were determined. All that was necessary was to train the telescope upon a given area in the heavens: and lo! the actual Neptune was there.

The same symbolism is found at the core of religion. Two rites, outwardly very similar, with the same origin, using the same words and the same gestures, may be, the one allegorical, the other symbolical. In certain Protestant Churches, the ceremony of the Lord's Supper is but the traditional representation of a great spiritual truth, the communion in spirit between the Founder and his followers; it adds nothing essential to that truth, it creates no new fact. In the Catholic Church, the sacramental formulae actually call for a corresponding change on the spiritual plane. The presence of the Lord in the elements is not a figure of speech, but a reality. Most religious poetry is merely allegorical; but all theology is symbolical. It cannot explain the Divine in terms of the Divine, which is inaccessible to us: direct revelation is ineffable, and silence is the sole language of the pure mystic. But that which theology sets forth in human words, according to the methods of human reasoning, bears a definite relation to the ultimate and inscrutable Reality.[1]

It is this quality of Symbolism—magical, scientific and

---

[1] Kafka's book *The Castle* partakes of the nature of allegory and symbol. As allegory, it is tediously drawn out. But it contains a *theology* which could not be expressed except in symbolical terms.

mystic—that the highest kind of poetry seeks to capture. Poetry does not consist in tricking out discourse with pretty or impressive images; it is not solely the thrill that attends discovery; it is also discovery itself. Discourse, like Aristotelian logic, moves within a closed circle; poetry, by means of symbolism, strives to force the circle open. Nature, for the poet, is a treasure house, not of pleasing pictures, not of striking allegories, but of dark elusive truths, which can be approached only through the magic of "Correspondences":

> La Nature est un temple où de vivants piliers
> Laissent parfois sortir de confuses paroles;
> L'homme y passe à travers des forêts de symboles
> Qui l'observent avec des regards familiers.
>
> Comme de longs échos qui de loin se confondent
> Dans une ténébreuse et profonde unité,
> Vaste comme la nuit et comme la clarté,
> Les parfums, les couleurs et les sons se répondent.
>
> (A fane of living pillars, whence arise
> Whispers confused and rarely understood,
> Nature surrounds our pathway like a wood
> Of symbols gazing with familiar eyes.
>
> As trailing echoes blend within a bond
> Of harmony profound and tenebrous,
> Vast as the night, as fire luminous,
> Perfume and sound and color correspond.) [1]

Every work of art, therefore, even the most realistic, has a value beyond the factual, a significance beyond the literal. Dante recognized no less than four planes of meaning, the *literal*, the *allegorical*—"truth hidden under beauteous fiction" —the *moral*, the *anagogical*, which might be interpreted as spiritual or mystic symbolism, "signifying again some portion

---

[1] Charles Baudelaire: *Fleurs du Mal*, Correspondances; translation by Lewis Piaget Shanks, 1926.

of the supernal things of eternal glory."[1] The allegory can be explained, although, at its best, it should need no explaining; the symbol must be felt. If you reduce it to plain intelligible terms, you degrade it to the level of allegory, you close again the circle from which we were seeking to escape.

Poetry strikes a fundamental note, expressed in terms of sense; and this note has many harmonics, which ultimately dissolve into the infinite. All true poetry must have the quality that the Chinese seek in their "stop-short" stanza: the words stop, the meaning goes on. Observe that rich harmonics are more likely to accompany a strong, definite fundamental note than one that is blurred and faint. That is why the highest symbolism is so frequently the overtone of the most vigorous realism. Start from the vague, as some professed symbolists did, and the echoes will at once be engulfed in the inane. Begin, like Dante and Milton, with burning human passions, and a vision that is sharp and vivid, and the ultimate waves will reach the empyrean.

As an illustration of these harmonics, we beg leave to analyze briefly *The Eaglet* (*L'Aiglon*) by Edmond Rostand. We selected it, because Rostand was the model of a keen and clear mind, with very little philosophical depth, and no great intensity of feeling. When he did attempt "Symbolism," because Symbolism was in fashion, he produced *The Far-Away Princess*, which is allegory of the most obvious kind. In *L'Aiglon*, he gave us, first of all, an historical play: the hopes of Napoleon's son, the Duke of Reichstadt, to continue the work of the great emperor; his contest with Metternich, his struggle with disease, his defeat and his death. Back of these plain facts, we have a drama which is even more definitely historical, although it deals with collective sentiments rather than with actual men: from all parts, passionate love comes to the captive Eaglet, because he is the living emblem of the Napoleonic Legend, then raging throughout Europe. Napoleon himself had become a myth, the Prometheus of Democracy chained upon the rock,

---

[1] Dante, *Convivio*, 2nd Treatise, Ch. i.

and tortured by the relentless somber powers of reaction. In addition to this allegory, which keeps very close to the material and psychological facts, Rostand offers a spiritual interpretation of the story. Force, pride, violence, even though admirable, are excesses, and must be atoned for; the victims of Napoleon's glory need a Napoleonic victim, most acceptable because most innocent. It is through vicarious expiation that the King of Rome fulfills his father's destiny.

But there is another side to *L'Aiglon*. It was offered, quite consciously, as a Hamlet play, with the significance attaching to the Hamlet theme since Goethe and Coleridge. Sarah Bernhardt, for whom Rostand was writing, had presented first a French Hamlet, Musset's *Lorenzaccio*, then Shakespeare's tragedy itself. In the Duke of Reichstadt, reflection has numbed the power of action. Faced with a great duty—to avenge his father, to continue his father's work—he doubts whether he is equal to the task. The crucial moment is when Metternich compels the young man to look at himself in a mirror; what is there revealed is not a Bonaparte, but a Habsburg.

"It is not too far-fetched to seek in *L'Aiglon* the tragedy, not of the King of Rome alone, but of France at the end of the nineteenth century, that 'fin-de-siècle' France just emerging from a long fever of self-depreciation. The Duke of Reichstadt looks at himself in a mirror, and, shuddering, he detects in himself the Austrian taint. The destiny of which he is the heir is too great for him: he is sick, he is weary, the scion of a frivolous, worn-out race. Well might the patriots of 1900, after the orgy of 'Decadentism' in literature, the scandals of the Dreyfus Case, the humiliation of Fashoda, despair, for a moment, of their country. She was the heir of a unique tradition, but her mirror would reveal to her, in some features, the flabby selfishness of the *bourgeois*, the blasé cynicism of the Paris *Boulevardier*, the half-insane twitch of the anarchist. The France that had ruled Europe through the prestige of her culture, the generosity of her ideal, or the might of her armies, was in her grave: the new France was like the Eaglet, whose wings fluttered but for a moment, only to be bruised against the bars of fate, and folded silently in resignation and death.

"May we not see in this dramatic poem the symbol of Rostand's own career? He too had his Hamlet problem. The worldwide success of *Cyrano* had made him the young Napoleon of French literature. Yet Rostand was too keen a critic not to know that he was no Shakespeare *redivivus*, not even a Victor Hugo, but only miraculously clever. He was overawed by his own fame. When, in 1899, he looked at his mirror, he would inexorably feel, in his excessive delicacy and elegance, in the sparkle of his Southern eyes, what a fragile instrument he was for such a crushing destiny." [1]

And every one of us is, in his own sphere, a Rostand, an Eaglet, a Hamlet. The play is the mirror which is pitilessly held before our eyes: what do we read in the anxious features? Is it not, too often, a great trust betrayed, through weakness, through the damning and tragic weakness of self-doubt? The symbol, in Rostand's drama, is all the more poignant because it is unexpressed, and, in all probability, unconscious.

Is there any relation between our two pairs of tendencies, Classicism and Romanticism, Realism and Symbolism? A first glance would seem to reveal a close kinship between Classicism and Realism, a deep harmony between Romanticism and Symbolism. The classicist and the realist are both willing to subject their personality to discipline: the austere rule of reason, the even stricter restraint of facts. For both, the test of truth is *consistency;* the model of the classicist is logic, the model of the realist is science; and the goal of both is to formulate *laws,* that is to say uniformities. [2] Both, however, recognize the place that imagination must play in the activity of our thought.

---

[1] From the author's *Reflections on the Napoleonic Legend,* 248-249, abridged.

[2] Mathematics provides the meeting point or common ground for logic and science. Aristotle said in his *Metaphysics:* "The main elements of beauty are order, symmetry, definite limitation, and these are the chief properties that the mathematical sciences draw attention to."

Imagination is the "inspiration" before which classical rules are ready to bow; in science, it reveals itself as the power of originating a working hypothesis. But inspiration and hypothesis are not valid unless checked by exacting methods; they must be submitted to a double test, that of the critical intellect, and the close observation of facts. So great is the resemblance that, if we ignored "period" costumes, we should find it hard to tell whether Molière's *Miser* or his *Georges Dandin* should be called classical or realistic; or on which side of the conventional line we should place *Ethan Frome* or *Manon Lescaut*. On the other hand, the refusal to be confined by formal laws, the desire to escape from the closed circle of literal sense, are common elements between Romanticism and Symbolism.

A closer examination will lead us, not to deny these affinities, but to qualify them. Classicism, as we have already indicated, has also a symbolical quality. Classical action always takes place on two planes: back of the individuals, we descry or feel vast entities—the gods, who are themselves myths and symbols; kingdoms, races and faiths; and especially vices, virtues, passions. Of these entities, the hero is but the instrument, the representative, or the type. Molière's Harpagon is Harpagon and no one else: a realistic portrait of a Parisian bourgeois. But he is also the embodiment of Avarice; he is *the* Miser. In the same way, the characters in Corneille, Le Cid, Horace, Augustus (in *Cinna*), Polyeucte, are respectively Honor, Patriotism, Magnanimity and Faith.

This very symbolism led, in the seventeenth and eighteenth centuries, to a definite divorce between the classical and the realistic. The classicists insisted so strongly upon the *type* as alone worthy of our attention, that their works became almost as abstract as medieval moralities. Thomas Rymer objected to Shakespeare's Iago because the character was not in accordance with the conventional type of the soldier. Excessive respect for traditional forms, the fatigue of eternal imitation, the paralyzing restraint of fastidious taste, the artificialities of poetic diction, all contributed to blur the features and dim the color of late classical works. On the tragic stage, Greeks, Romans, Hindus, Chinamen, Peruvians, all moved with the same slow and stately steps, all spoke in the same lofty and eloquent couplets. At the very end of the period, under Napoleon, the censors prohibited a play on a Spanish subject; the author obediently shifted the scene from Renaissance Spain to semi-fabulous Nineveh. He could do so without difficulties, for in that twilight world of decadent Classicism, Spaniards and Ninevites were absolutely interchangeable.

Romanticism, we must remember, came to consciousness as the *picturesque*. In opposition to pseudo-Classicism, it attached the utmost importance to definite material details. For the romanticist, vividness, not consistency, is the test of truth; intense realization is its own warrant. There is a taint of unreality about the vague and the abstract. But even the wildest vision is valid and convincing, if it has the definiteness of the *Apocalypse*.

So there arose, for a time, a confusion between new-born Romanticism, and Realism, still unnamed. After the lapse of a hundred and fifty years, we find it hard to disentangle the two tendencies. A confusion it must be called: the wildly Romantic imaginations of Blake are most unrealistic, and the Realism of George Crabbe, or, in many cases, of William Wordsworth, is not genuinely romantic. Of this almost inevitable confusion, we shall offer, as examples, two commonplaces of literary history, which we believe to be as fallacious as they are commonplace.

The first is that Romanticism implies a deeper appreciation of nature, in the physical sense, than does Classicism. This assertion would make Vergil's *Georgics* a romantic poem; it does ignore the long tradition of bucolic and pastoral poetry, not all of it artificial. It would turn James Thomson, for his *Seasons*, and even Thomas Gray, for his *Elegy*, into romanticists. It would see in Rev. Gilbert White's *Natural History of Selborne*, so fragrant and dewy with a love for the English countryside, a manifestation of Romanticism. On the other hand, we must repeat that there is no touch of "nature" in the most typical poems of Blake, as there is none in *Kubla Khan*. In French literature, Vigny, with the courage of a stoic soul, dared to avow his indifference to an indifferent nature: "Not a word of love shall you receive from me"; [1] and Baudelaire, a late but manifest romanticist, confessed: "I am incapable of becoming sentimental over vegetation." [2] Romanticism *per se* is not closer to nature than Classicism; what is undeniable is that in the eighteenth century, there was a rebellion against a vague abstract style, and a striving for a more direct, graphic, *realistic* presentation. The eighteenth-century revolt was then both romantic and realistic; but, as so frequently happens in history, the allies of the moment were not permanent friends.

The second fallacy is to consider Sir Walter Scott and the whole historical school of poetry and fiction as essentially romantic because they were historical. There was nothing romantic in the gentle, sunny, equable temper of Sir Walter, or in the slow, even-flowing course of his novels. His medieval scenes are not prestigious, fantastic evocations: they are careful, painstaking descriptions of reality. We should like to submit as evidence a passage from Scott's *Ivanhoe*, and compare it with one from Balzac's *Modeste Mignon:*

His garment was of the simplest form imaginable, being a close jacket with sleeves, composed of the tanned skin of some animal, on which the hair had originally been left, but which had been worn off in so many places, that it would have been difficult to distinguish, from the patches that remained, to what creature the fur had belonged. . . . Sandals, bound with thongs of boar's hide, protected the feet, and a roll of thin leather was twined round the legs, and ascending above the calf, left the knees bare, like those of a Scottish Highlander.

As everything, in this interview, depended upon the first impression, he put on a black pair of trousers, high shoes shined with particular care, a sulphur-colored vest, low-necked enough to reveal a shirt of softest linen, with opal buttons; a black stock, a short blue frock-coat

[1] Alfred de Vigny: *La Maison du Berger.*
[2] To Fernand Desnoyers, 1855.

adorned with the *rosette* (of the Legion of Honor), so close-fitting that it seemed glued, by some newly invented process, to the waist and to the back.

In both cases, we had to cut the description short; for Sir Walter and Balzac alike revel in the accumulation of details. The method is scrupulously the same. Sir Walter was as conscientious as Balzac about the accuracy of his picture; Balzac was as anxious as Sir Walter to produce a vivid, definite image. At present, the dress of an early nineteenth-century *dandy* seems almost as remote as that of a late twelfth-century swineherd; and, we may add, not a whit less preposterous.

To sum up: the *schools* are historical phenomena, and, like all collective movements in history, they are at the same time concrete and confused. We can date the birth certificate of English Romanticism 1798, with the publication of the *Lyrical Ballads*, by Wordsworth and Coleridge; or that of French Romanticism 1820, with Lamartine's *Méditations;* but it is not so easy to tell what was that Romanticism so definitely set down in time. It was a temporary coalition which drove Classicism from exclusive authority, but broke down as soon as it had achieved power. On the other hand, the *tendencies* are the results of a philosophical analysis. They are timeless. In comparison with the schools, they are mere abstractions; in compensation, they are far more definite, consistent and permanent.

The chief difference is that the schools, like religious sects or political parties, are or believe themselves to be mutually exclusive; everyone must enroll under one or the other of the four banners. The tendencies are co-operative, not inimical; no work of art is complete unless it offers both discipline and inspiration; unless it keeps in close touch with the facts, and sees more in the facts than their crude materiality. So we must repeat and extend the formula with which we closed our preceding chapter: "It should be a writer's endeavor to be at the same time classical and romantic, realistic and symbolical, to the utmost of his capacity."

SUMMARY

Realism consists in dealing with facts purely in and for themselves; symbolism is interested only in what the facts signify. These general tendencies should be kept distinct from the historical schools which adopted these names. The sordid is not the only reality, and symbolism need not be nebulous.

Pure Realism is an unrealistic abstraction; a bare fact has no standing in literature or science; it is worth recording only because of its significance, i.e., because of its symbolical value. Thus realism passes inevitably into symbolism.

The distinction between the various orders of reality are fairly clear; the various forms of symbolism are not so obvious. As a starting point, we find the comparison: in abridged form, the metaphor; expanded, the allegory. But metaphor and allegory are merely illustrations, and frankly arbitrary. True symbolism implies an actual correspondence between the sign and the thing signified. Magic is a spurious form of symbolism; science, and especially mathematics, is highly symbolical; the highest forms of ritual and theology are pure symbol. It is this quality of symbolism—magical, scientific or mystic—that poetry seeks to capture. Every work of art has a value beyond the factual, a significance beyond the literal. Poetry strikes a fundamental note: its power of suggestion lies chiefly in the harmonics. As an illustration, Rostand's *L'Aiglon* is analyzed; it tells a very definite story, but in addition, five or six interpretations, allegorical and symbolical, can be offered.

What is the relationship between the two pairs of tendencies? Usually, Classicism and Realism are thought to have much in common, Romanticism and Symbolism offer strong resemblances. Both classicist and realist subject their personality to discipline, and accept as their authority human reason in agreement with ascertained facts. For both, the test of truth is consistency. If both recognize the role of imagination, they accept its findings only when they are checked by the critical intellect and by observation. On the other hand, both romanticism and symbolism refuse to be confined by formal law.

1. Classicism has a symbolical quality; the classic hero exemplifies the *type;* to such an extent that the works of the late, or pseudo-classical, period became extremely abstract. The *particular* was offered only for the sake of the *general.*

2. In rebellion against this abstract, colorless character, Romanticism insisted on vividness as the test of truth, and therefore was, in externals at any rate, far more realistic than classicism.

There are two misconceptions arising from this confusion between Realism and Romanticism. The first is that Romanticism implies a deeper appreciation of nature than Classicism. This is by no means certain. All that is established is that Romanticism offered a more vivid, picturesque, *realistic* presentation of nature. The second is to consider Sir Walter Scott and all historical fiction as romantic because of the picturesque elements. Sir Walter's descriptions were accurate, painstaking, *realistic;* his method is not different from that of Balzac.

These four fundamental *tendencies,* the result of a philosophical analysis, are abstract compared with the *schools.* On the other hand, they are more consistent and permanent. The schools believe themselves to be mutually exclusive; the tendencies are co-operative. It should be the writer's endeavor to be at the same time classical and romantic, realistic and symbolical, to the utmost of his capacity.

CHAPTER XI

THE THEORY OF GENRES

"Tous les genres sont bons, hors le genre
ennuyeux."—*Voltaire.*

ONLY a trembling line separates literature from mere communication. At any moment, in the course of ordinary talk, in a commonplace letter, in a business or scientific report, there may appear that note of conscious pleasure in self-expression which is the essential characteristic of art. At any moment also, in the midst of plain discourse, that note may attain the degree of intensity, the fundamental unity, the richness in harmonics, which are the signs of poetry. This impossibility to trace a sharp and permanent line round our field does not imply that literature is non-existent, or even that it is undefinable. It proves only that creations of the mind cannot be surveyed by the same methods as real estate. While holding fast to the principle of literature, we must be ready constantly to readjust the boundaries of its application.

What is true of the frontiers of literature is true also of the divisions within literature. They seem at the same time very real and very shadowy; the truth of the matter is that they are the reverse of rigid. Their *reality* can be denied only by the most dogmatic of theorists. Whoever starts from the plain facts and not from a haughty doctrine knows that, in any bookstore or public library, the volumes are not heaped up haphazard. There always is a rough attempt at classification. Some of the arrangements may be frankly non-literary: "Latest Books," "Cheap Reprints," "De Luxe Editions," publishers' Series, are grouped together irrespective of their true nature. But, as a rule, even under the most commercial circumstances, a few categories appear very plainly: poetry, drama, classics, juveniles, fiction, history and biography, travel, public affairs, arts and belles-lettres, etc. All abstract denials fade away before that undeniable condition.

This material arrangement in store and library is not purely an arbitrary device, like the alphabetical order in dictionary, index or catalogue. It corresponds to categories which exist in the public mind. If we find it convenient to display detective fiction on a particular shelf or counter, it is because we know that a certain number of people will request, not "a book" irrespective of kind, but a good thrilling murder story. Even the most hidebound critic will recognize that an epigram by Matthew Prior, a nonsense rhyme by Edward Lear, a fugitive poem by Austin Dobson, an "ode" by Ogden Nash, may be good "of their kind," which is manifestly not the Miltonic. In their recognition of such differences, the booksellers and the scholars are in substantial agreement.

We should blush to insist upon such truisms, if they had not been challenged by critics of such standing as Benedetto Croce, and his American disciple, J. E. Spingarn. The great Italian polygrapher oddly combines a paradoxical turn of mind with an autocratic temper, so that he lays down "the Laws of Anarchy" with a rigor that brooks no discussion.[1] It is a frequent phenomenon, in the history of thought, that a legitimate rebellion against some form of dogmatism leads to a counter-dogmatism even less in accord with the facts. "We have done," says J. E. Spingarn,[2] "with the *genres* or literary kinds. . . . The lyric, the pastoral, the epic, are abstractions without concrete reality in the world of art. Poets do not really write epics, pastorals, lyrics, *however much they may be deceived by these false abstractions* [italics ours]; they express themselves, and this expression is their only form. There are not, therefore,

---

[1] Benedetto Croce, *Æsthetics*, Pt. II, Ch. XIX, 2.

[2] J. E. Spingarn: "The New Criticism," in *Creative Criticism*, 1917; first as a Columbia lecture, 1910.

only three, or ten, or a hundred literary kinds; there are as many kinds as there are individual poets."

Yet Mr. Spingarn, when penning these brave words, must have been thoroughly "deceived by that false abstraction," criticism; he did write a contribution to the non-existent *genre* wrongly called criticism; but, as publishers, reviewers, booksellers, librarians and reading public were all guilty of exactly the same error, this "confusion"—*felix culpa!*—resulted in increased clarity and more definite enjoyment. No one is so Crocean as to have any hesitation about the various *genres*—history, philosophy, criticism—so ably cultivated by Benedetto Croce.[1]

We may take for granted, then, that there are actual divisions and subdivisions in literature. The problem is: "To what do they correspond?" For a classification may stand for a set of conventions, or it may represent natural laws. The distinction is of capital importance, in every domain of thought; unfortunately, it is by no means easy to establish. Most of our ills

[1] J. E. Spingarn, with a number of literary historians and critics, uses the French word *genre*, because the English words *kind* or *type* seem so woefully vague. Every adjective applied to a work of art suffices to denote a *kind*: good, bad, popular, learned, religious, amusing and even nondescript and indefinite: "Would you call *Finnegans Wake* a novel?"—"Well: a *kind* of a novel." The word *type* refers chiefly to a clear-cut example of a *kind*: *Pilgrim's Progress* may be called the type of the allegory. It may also refer to differences within the same kind: *The Faerie Queene* and *Pilgrim's Progress* are both allegories, but of a different type; the tragedies of Æschylus and those of Shakespeare belong to the same kind, but not to the same type, of dramatic literature. Historically, the use of the word *genre* is a trace of the authority long enjoyed by the French theorists. Perhaps it was adopted in the hope of finding definiteness in a language which prides itself on its logic and precision. But *genre* in its general acceptation is fully as vague as our own *kind*. It may mean, more particularly, *manner, type, style*: "C'est un type dans le genre de Victor Hugo": a fellow of Victor Hugo's type. "Dans le genre canaille, c'est assez réussi": it is a good sample of the cynical style. "Elle a mauvais genre": she looks like a wrong 'un. In painting, *tableau de genre* indicates an anecdotic subject from common life: it is thus narrowed down to one *genre* among many: allegorical, historical, religious, landscape, portrait, interior, still life, etc. Perhaps we should have gone farther back, and sought safety in the Latin term, *genus, genera*.

would be on a fair way to healing, if we could tell, among all the rules which claim to guide and frequently bewilder us, which are *conventions* and which are genuine *laws*.

Shall we say that a convention simply meets the needs of a given situation, whereas a law is in profound harmony with the permanent facts? Yes, but how many conventions honestly believe themselves to be laws! And how difficult it is to disprove their claims, when the facts have long been selected and adjusted so as to fit the conventions! If for several centuries, only red-headed people had been allowed to write, we should accept it as a law of nature that there is a pre-established harmony between red hair and literary gifts. Tradition is collective habit, and habit becomes second nature.

Shall we say that a convention is frankly *arbitrary*, like the alphabetical order, drawing by lot, driving on the right side rather than on the left, or using red as the stop sign; whereas a law can be proved to be *rational?* But it is far easier to "rationalize" conventions than it is to give a "reasonable" account of manifest but mysterious laws. The defenders of vested interests can demonstrate, like Burke, the profound wisdom of prejudice; but many phenomena, in physics and biology, have to be accepted without a satisfactory explanation.

Shall we say—this, no doubt, would be a very practical test—that a convention can be altered at will, but that "you cannot repeal the law of gravitation"? In literary terms, you can smash the pedantic rules of the Italian dogmatists, Vida, Scaliger, Castelvetro, but you cannot throw human nature into the discard. But when our desires for freedom dash themselves in vain against the iron bars of a rule, who is to tell us whether the obstacle is an infrangible law, or merely a convention too strong for our despairing efforts?

The true question remains, not: "Are there *genres* in Literature?" but: "Are the *genres* founded on convention, or on law?" According to neo-classical theory, best expressed perhaps by the formidable Julius Caesar Scaliger (*Poetics*, 1561), there is but a small number of very definite *genres*, each regulated by a set of inflexible laws. To infringe these laws means disaster; and the highest of all the laws is that the *genres* should be kept rigorously pure. This doctrine was transmitted from pedant to pedant until the very end of the Classical Age; let it be noted, however, that it never was made the center of literary theory by those men who rose above the level of mere pedantry. France was, of all countries, the one most definitely committed to Classicism; and, for fully a century, the doctrine of *genres* was accepted without question. But Boileau, as we have seen, placed genius first, then reason, both in close touch with nature, that is to say with observable fact; strict obedience to formal rules plays only a small part in the teachings of his *Art Poétique*. Molière uttered the liberating words: "As if the great rule of all rules were not to please!" In *Don Juan*, he offered a "monstrous" play which respected neither the three unities, nor the sharp distinction between the *genres*. Voltaire was, in criticism, the faithful and at times surprisingly timid disciple of Boileau: no less sensible than his master, he averred that "all kinds are good, except the tedious kind." The question of *genres* was thus subordinated to the far more vital problem of taste.

The *genres* were not a burning issue at the best moment of the Classical Era; writers and public were ready for a tolerant interpretation. Unfortunately, we cannot rely upon "the inevitability of gradualness." In literature as in politics, the ancient regime stiffened in its old age; and the last classicists were as trenchant in their affirmations and condemnations as Julius Caesar Scaliger himself. On the Continent, the purists, we might even say the puritans, of literature heroically resisted the sinful temptation of admiring Shakespeare. He had power, but he did not observe the rules; he blended the *genres* in barbaric fashion. The question of the *genres*, hitherto a minor one, thus became one of the chief issues of the romantic revolt. The ultimate defenders of classical orthodoxy, true to their faith, died, but never surrendered. As late as 1843, they were still putting up a stiff fight. The "regular" tragedy had an aftermath of favor, and a "mixed" drama by Victor Hugo met with signal failure.[1]

Croce's attack on the *genres* is therefore not an original paradox: the "new criticism," in this respect, offers but an echo of the great conflict between classicists and romanticists, which had raged nearly a hundred years before. It was a belated skirmish among the stragglers of two armies, once mighty, but long disbanded and half-forgotten. It should be said in Croce's defense that if he was battling over antiquated issues, he was not fighting mere phantoms. At the time when he published his *Estetica* (1900-1901), Ferdinand Brunetière was still a power in the literary world; and, in the preceding decade, Brunetière had attempted to rejuvenate the old doctrine of *genres* by clothing it in pseudo-Darwinian or Spencerian garb. Considering *genres* as akin to Darwinian species, he had tried to trace their *evolution:* their differentiation, their stability, their inner growth, their modifications under external influences, or adaptation to environment, their struggle for life, the survival of the fittest among them, and their increasing complexity. The whole may seem to us an ingenious metaphor elaborated into a long and minute allegory; but Brunetière's guides in this field, Darwin, Spencer and Taine, were impressive names; Brunetière himself enjoyed an authority thoroughly justified by his erudition, his laborious lucidity, his industry, his courage. Under these circumstances, we can easily understand why Brunetière's dogmatic affirmations should have called forth Croce's emphatic denials.

But a mere negation will not dispose of the problem: we have *not* done with the literary kinds or *genres*. Between the extreme positions of Scaliger and Croce, there is ample room for realistic enquiry. Any conclusion concerning the validity of

---

[1] The "regular" tragedy triumphed with *Lucrèce*, by François Ponsard, champion of common sense; and with Rachel's brilliant revivals of Corneille and Racine; Hugo's play was *Les Burgraves*, a splendid medley of epic, lyric and melodramatic elements; without counting the comic, which, in this case, was unconscious.

genres might profitably be postponed until the completion of such a survey.

In examining the question, we shall have to take into account its logical as well as its historical aspects. For every term we use is an attempt to impose upon a loose mass of memories the unity of an ideal. When we say *tragedy*, our thought is influenced by all the tragedies that we happen to know, and by our conception of what a tragedy should be. Seldom are the two tendencies in perfect harmony; still, if the composite picture of past tragedies did not roughly coincide with our *idea* of tragedy, we should be compelled to select another term.

A genre is a commonly accepted grouping of literary works which offer among themselves significant resemblances in form as well as in spirit. We must insist that both spirit and form are indispensable. The *tragic* alone, if we had defined it, would not be sufficient to determine a *tragedy* in the technical sense of the term. For the *tragic* exists in real life, and not exclusively in art; among literary works, it may be found in history, in the epic, in the novel, even in lyric poetry: there is a *tragic* note in Coleridge's ode, *Dejection*. The tragedy, as a kind, must be a play. But it is even more evident that dramatic form, by itself, will not enable us to recognize a tragedy. Take *The Two Gentlemen of Verona* and *Romeo and Juliet*: both are plays, both in verse with a few passages in prose, both have the same Italian setting. If you read the list of *dramatis personae* in Molière's *Amphitryon*, all gods and heroes of antiquity, you might expect a classical tragedy. Here it is the spirit, not the form, that creates a difference.

It would be possible to draw up a sort of literary multiplication table: so many "spirits" in a vertical column, so many "forms" on a horizontal line; each square thus determined would represent a *genre*, actual or potential. Each *genre* in its turn might be subdivided according to the time and place of the action, to the social standing of the characters, to the style or tone adopted by the author. Thus we might become the Linnaeus of literary history; failing that glory, we should at any rate have all the elements of an ingenious parlor game.[1]

There are two very simple and time-honored forms of classification which seem to us of no great significance. The first is the distinction between verse and prose; the second, that between fiction and non-fiction.

We have already expressed our belief that the technical difference between verse and prose is far less important than the spiritual difference between discourse and poetry; and we have mentioned the fact that every kind of literature can be written, and has been written, in metrical as well as in non-metrical form. There are famous scientific and technical treatises in verse, and Baudelaire left a collection of delicate *Poems in Prose*. Homer, Vergil, Dante, have been translated both into verse and into prose; as a rule, the prose versions are preferred, because they are more faithful. The loss involved by the change of medium is undeniable, but it is not sufficient to obliterate the nature of the original: Dante in good English prose remains Dante, and remains poetry. At most, the use of verse determines a subkind; in some cases, a very minor one, like the *novel in verse*.[2] Tradition, however, plays a greater part than logic in these matters, and will not be denied. We have to recognize the fact that the pure lyric is *usually* in verse; and we are compelled to put together under protest works which have practically nothing in common, like a drinking song and *The Testament of Beauty*, because both of them offer themselves as "poems."

It will seem paradoxical to question, not indeed the validity, but the importance, of the distinction between *fiction* and *non-fiction*. This distinction is one of the sharpest in the minds of most readers, and it has played a great part in the history of literature. *Fiction*, in the most obvious sense, is a deviation from truth; in plain words, a lie. So, logically enough, rigid

[1] A classification of this kind will be found under the novel: it seemed the most expedient way of clearing a few paths through that jungle.

[2] Cf. Pushkin: *Eugene Onegin*; Lamartine: *Jocelyn*; Mrs. Browning: *Aurora Leigh*; "Owen Meredith" (2nd Lord Lytton): *Lucile*.

moralists have frowned upon the perversity, or at least the
frivolousness, of those who could seek pleasure in untruth.
Religion, science, the State, business, all, in their several degrees, deal with realities and deserve the attention of a
righteous and sober mind. But lies, however pleasing, are unworthy. The Puritans frowned upon romances as well as upon
plays; and the tradition they established is not completely lost
even today; we have met worthy persons proud of the fact
that they had never read a work of fiction. The Jansenists,
those Puritans within the Catholic Church, rebuked young
Racine for reading such a dangerous work as *Theagenes and
Charicles*, a Greek romance of the third century.[1] Curiously
enough, this prohibition seldom included Vergil's *Æneid*, which
has so many elements of romance. Jean Jacques Rousseau
affected to consider fiction as a deadly peril to innocence: "No
pure girl," he wrote in the Preface of his *New Heloise*, "has
ever read a novel. . . . A girl who, in spite of my warning,
should read a single line of this book, must be considered as
ruined. . . ."[2] It would be wise not to take the solemn ranting
of Jean Jacques too tragically; still, he was only adding a touch
of absurd exaggeration to the Calvinistic severity of Geneva,
his birthplace.

But, if there is an aura of wickedness about fiction, there is
also a very high, perhaps an excessive, degree of prestige. Not
only do works of fiction, as a rule, outsell all others, but they
alone are considered truly creative. A fictionist is a genuine author; a critic is at best a dignified parasite. A young man, for a
book of promising but crude short stories, or for a turgid, chaotic, vociferous novel, will reach a position in the literary world
that historians and philosophers seldom achieve in a lifetime.
The Last Puritan brought to George Santayana all the obvious
rewards that thirty volumes of delicately nebulous philosophy

[1] By Heliodorus; also known as *Æthiopica*; a very curious work.

[2] He pursues, with semi-conscious humor: "But let her not blame the book
for her ruin; the harm had been done already. So, if she starts, she might
as well go through with it: she no longer has anything to lose."

had failed to secure. If sales, popular fame and social success were reliable criteria, it would seem that it does not pay to tell the truth.

This would be demoralizing indeed; fortunately, the discrimination against truth-telling shows signs of passing away. The brilliant success of biography in our own days has proved that the public wanted, not necessarily lies, but above all life. Pardonably enough, the average reader shuns boredom: after all, the one aim of literature as of all the arts is to bring delight. But he prefers lively truth to dull fiction; he is apt to call dull anything that is not easy, and he will pick up Ludwig or Maurois rather than Henry James. He wants swift moving, colorful life; he is not trained to recognize life in abstractions, in the growth of ideas, in collective trends, in age-long anonymous processes. He wants heroes of flesh and blood; if they are offered to him, he will not insist that they be fictitious.

From the artistic point of view, the difference between fiction and non-fiction becomes attenuated to the vanishing point. Realism has schooled us to find pleasure in the accurate presentation of the commonplace, and to be shocked rather than entertained by the incredible. Fairy tales still have their place in adult literature, but it is a minor one; it takes sophistication to enjoy a fantasy. At present, the spirit of romance, abandoning fiction, is seeking refuge in science and history. We like history, not primarily because it is true, but because it is exciting; events and characters that fiction would reject as unbelievable acquire validity because they happen to be authentic. No romancer would dare to concoct such an impossible tale as the career of Napoleon.

Autobiography is a favorite *genre: fiction* or *non-fiction?* Does it lose its character when it is proved that the author has taken liberties with the truth? Few writers are considered reliable authorities about their own lives. All achieve a certain consciousness of their personality: this means that, in drawing their own likeness, they compose their own personage. Facts are—innocently perhaps—selected, reconstructed, arranged, and at times altered, so as to bring out the essential truth, so as to contribute to the artistic whole, the portrait of the auhor as he sees himself, as he wants us to see him. Rousseau, who practically created autobiography as a major *genre*, admitted with commendable honesty that, when his memory failed, he felt free to use his imagination. Goethe, wisest of men, called the story of his own life *Dichtung und Wahrheit;* which may be translated as Poesy and Realism; but also, and more plainly, Fiction and Truth.

A historian loses standing as a scholar if he accepts uncritically facts which are demonstrably false. But the literary quality of his work is not affected thereby; and that quality is essentially the power to create or re-create life, which is the virtue of dramatist and novelist. The first books of Livy are full of very definite stories which were piously reproduced by all historians for nearly eighteen hundred years, and which we now consider to be mythical. In this, Livy was honestly deluded, or half-deluded; but he must have known beyond peradventure that he had no authority for all the fine speeches which he ascribed to his heroes. He "reported" them, because they fitted the scene as he conceived it, and especially because he was a master of eloquence. Lamartine, in this a true disciple of Livy, related in detail a last supper of the Girondists for which there is no evidence, but which has almost the quality of a Platonic dialogue. To pay off his huge debts, he concocted a series of popular biographies, and published, one year a *Columbus* (1862), the next a *William Tell* (1863). Now, William Tell happens to be a myth; but that would not have invalidated Lamartine's story any more than it disposes of Schiller's tragedy; the book is weak, not because it is fictitious, but because it is hackwork. Carlyle, in his *French Revolution,* described with the vividness of an eye-witness the sinking of the *Vengeur.* He found out afterwards that, with the rest of Europe, he had been fooled by the brazen prevarications of Barère. His lurid version of the episode thus passed from straight history into historical fiction;

but the transfer affected neither its qualities nor its faults, which remained as Carlylean as before.

Conversely, a book does not change its character if the facts it relates are discovered to be true. Research scholars are constantly unearthing the realities that underlie fiction: there were actual cases back of Stendhal's *Red and Black* and back of Flaubert's *Madame Bovary*. Our enjoyment of these masterpieces, while not appreciably deepened, should not be lessened by such knowledge. The uninitiated might consider George Meredith's novel *The Tragic Comedians* (1880) as fiction of a particularly audacious kind; it is on the contrary a very searching attempt to explain psychologically the events which led to the dramatic death of the German Socialist, Ferdinand Lassalle.

This is true in other fields than history. Early reviewers, and most readers after them, could not make up their minds whether Melville's *Omoo* and *Typee* were straight narratives, exotic romances, Utopian idyls, or a blend of all three. If, after a sensational vogue, Joan Lowell's *Cradle of the Deep* was so soon forgotten, it was not because it was a hoax, but because it was not a masterly hoax. We are ready to enjoy *Mutiny on the Bounty, Two Years Before the Mast, Moby Dick* and *The Rime of the Ancient Mariner:* any yarn of the sea will do, provided it be well told. This is not indifference to truth: it is the admission that factual truth and artistic merit have no common measure. Literature and science must be judged each according to its own standards. In literature, the distinction between fiction and non-fiction is irrelevant.

We must be on our guard against two fallacies, of very unequal significance. The first is: "This is true, *therefore* it cannot be interesting." This prejudice, once very common, but now waning, was matched by the scholarly prejudice: "This is true, therefore it should not be made interesting." Such a misconception only curtails our pleasure, but does not warp our judgment. Far more dangerous is the second fallacy: "This is consistent, vivid, pathetic: *therefore* it must be literally true." Esthetic per-

fection is no warranty; in the realm of facts, a clumsy police report outweighs the gods of Homer.

The division of literature into three fundamental kinds, *lyric,*
epic, drama, is so commonly accepted that it seems inevitable. It
is curious to note that it never was clearly formulated by the
ancients, or even by the earlier theorists of the Renaissance.
Scaliger, for instance, distinguishes two modes: simple narration, "as in the poems of Lucretius," and conversation (or
drama); the epic he considers as a mixed form.[1] Boileau, in the
second canto of his *Art Poétique,* passes in review a number of
minor kinds, the "elegant" idyl, the "plaintive" elegy, the
"dazzling and energetic" ode, the exacting sonnet, the Gallic-
born rondel, the old-fashioned ballade, the "noble and tender"
madrigal, the satire, the merry mocking song (*vaudeville*):
surely a motley collection, which only by courtesy could be labeled *lyrical.* In the third canto, he takes up the major kinds,
which, in his opinion, are tragedy, the epic, and comedy. Paradoxically, it was with Romanticism, at the very moment when
poets were rebelling against artificial distinctions, that the three-
fold division appeared most clearly. It is found in Friedrich
Schelling; and Victor Hugo made it the basis of his famous
manifesto, the *Preface* to his drama *Cromwell.* Most textbooks
take this classification for granted, like the three "Faculties of
the Soul" and the three "Powers in the State." At times, a
fourth kind is suggested: the didactic—a catch-all for scientific
writing, philosophy, criticism, and that delightful literary Pro-
teus, born of Protean Montaigne, the essay.

But, ancient or modern, this standard division affords at least
a convenient framework, and we may preserve it without committing ourselves to its absolute and eternal validity. The most
respectful readers of Locke and Montesquieu do not believe any
more that there are only three powers in the state, or that it
has ever been found feasible to keep them strictly separate. We
know that all Presidents attempt to initiate and force legislation,

[1] J. C. Scaliger: *Poetics,* Book I, Ch. 3.

and that all Congresses strive to control executive policies. Yet, the old theory has proved useful as a norm, and the excessive confusion of the three powers in other states leads us to cherish it more than ever. In the same way, although the distinction between lyric, epic and drama threatens to break down at every point, still, with many dents and bulges, with many leaks and patches, it retains its clumsy efficiency.

The most obvious, and the crudest, difference between the fundamental *genres* is a typographical one. We put the label *lyric* on all short poems, *drama* on all dialogue, *epic* (or narrative) on long continuous pieces in prose or verse. In most cases, this rough test works well enough; so well that it will be sufficient to note a few manifest exceptions.

The dialogue form, in particular, may be delusive. It is possible to have works written entirely in dialogue, which are not meant to be considered as dramas. *La Celestina* is on the borderline. This odd and fascinating Spanish masterpiece appeared as *La Comedia de Calisto y Melibea* (1499) in *sixteen* acts; it grew to twenty-one, perhaps to twenty-two. Needless to say that it never was performed as it stands; it is far too long for the stage; and the story, although full of exciting incidents, is too diffuse for dramatic interest. It is purely and simply a novel; and, to make confusion more unfathomable, it is a double hybrid, for it offers a most curious blend of the romantic and the realistic. The novel in dialogue has not disappeared: the best treatment of the Dreyfus crisis that has come to our notice, *Jean Barois*, by the Nobel Prize winner Roger Martin du Gard, is in that unusual form.

Thanks to Plato, the philosophical dialogue is well established as a genre; it is found in all literatures, and, only yesterday, Salvador de Madariaga used it to discuss contemporary problems.[1] It hovers on the uncertain boundaries of the drama: it is not essentially dramatic. An attempt was made to extract out of Plato a tragedy on the death of Socrates: but it was not a

[1] Salvador de Madariaga: *Elysian Fields*, 1938.

tragedy. In this case, however, to trace an assured line would be a very delicate task. Ernest Renan wrote *Philosophical Dialogues* and also *Philosophical Dramas:* there is a difference. One at least of these dramas, *The Abbess of Jouarre*, proved to be a good acting play; another, *Caliban*, is not unworthy of its model, *The Tempest*. It may be asserted that the second part of Goethe's *Faust*, and Thomas Hardy's epic of the Napoleonic era, *The Dynasts*, do not offer themselves as plays, but as philosophical poems.

On the other hand, Scaliger was right in noting that the epic seldom is pure narration, but usually contains elements of dialogue. At times, the proportion of conversation is so overwhelming that the work might be called a *crypto-drama*, or drama concealed under narrative form. The most striking example of this is the *Book of Job*. Although it has the framework of a narrative, its essential parts are pure conversations. It has been successfully presented as a tragedy; it is undoubtedly far more dramatic, in every sense of the term, than *Samson Agonistes*. A sudden flight across the centuries will bring us to *The Egoist*, by George Meredith. This is a novel which the author very properly called a comedy; each chapter is a conversation, as in the *Book of Job;* and it would not be difficult to reduce the non-dialogue parts to mere stage indications.[1]

Our chief difficulty, however, is not the existence of hybrids: it is our familiar trouble, the ambiguity of words. Lyric, epic, drama, have at least two meanings: one applies to the spirit, the other to the form. The lyric, the epic, the dramatic spirits, severally, can be clothed in lyric, epic and dramatic form. In order to take all these elements into account, we shall have therefore to establish a ninefold division: this would satisfy our master Julius Caesar Scaliger, for, in agreement with many medieval and Renaissance thinkers, he considered nine as the perfect number. Such a classification was proposed by Eduard von

---

[1] Cf. also, in lighter vein: Anthony Hope: *The Dolly Dialogues;* E. F. Benson: *Dodo;* John Erskine: *The Private Life of Helen of Troy*, etc.

Hartmann; [1] it is from him that we borrow it, with modifications.

According to the "fearful symmetry" of this scheme, we should find first, under the lyric, the *lyrical lyric*. An auspicious start: the genre does exist, under the simpler name of pure lyric. But a pure lyric cannot be long sustained without danger to its purity: the only safe examples will be brief poems, like Goethe's *Evensongs*. The *Anthology of Pure Poetry* compiled by George Moore may be accepted as a collection of lyrical lyrics. Next comes the *epic (narrative) lyric*: the best type of this is probably the ballad, like "the grand old Ballad of Sir Patrick Spence," which tells a story, but in lyric form. Finally, we have the *dramatic lyric*: here Robert Browning comes to our assistance, for this was the name that he gave to the best known of his poems.

Under the epic, our classification would offer, first, the *lyrical epic*, a term which fits very well *The Faerie Queene*, and also a number of romantic narratives such as Byron's *Don Juan*. The *epic narrative*, or pure epic, causes no difficulty: we are safe in considering Homer as its authorized exponent. The *dramatic epic* would be exemplified by the innumerable romances and novels which offer a dramatic problem, a dramatic conflict of characters, or a series of dramatic incidents. *Notre Dame de*

---

[1] In his *Philosophie des Schönen,* and in *Grundriss der Aesthetik,* pp. 235-259. Die Kunst des Phantasieschein oder die Poesie.

I. Die Vortragspoesie:

    A. die Epik: a. die plastische Epik, oder die rein epische Epik
                       b. die malerische Epik, oder die lyrische Epik
    B. die Lyrik: a. die epische Lyrik
                       b. die rein lyrische Lyrik
                       c. die dramatische Lyrik
    C. die Dramatik: a. die lyrische Dramatik
                       b. die epische Dramatik
                       c. die rein dramatische Dramatik

II. Die Lesepoesie

We are not here concerned with Hartmann's distinction, which does not seem to us to be vital, between "Poetry meant to be recited in public" (representation, Vortrag) and "Poetry meant to be privately read" (Lesepoesie).

Paris and *A Tale of Two Cities* are extreme instances of the type; but the term would not be a misnomer for Dante's *Inferno*.

Under the drama, we find first the *lyrical drama*. In a literal sense, all operas, comic operas and musical comedies deserve the name; and with the works of Richard Wagner, especially with *Tristan and Isolde,* this genre attains a very high level as literature. The term could be extended to denote the poetical play, such as *Midsummer Night's Dream* and *The Tempest.* This kind, in reaction against excesses of realism, had a curious vogue at the end of the nineteenth century, with long echoes into the twentieth. As examples, we may quote Gerhart Hauptmann's *The Sunken Bell,* Oscar Wilde's *Salome,* Rostand's *The Far-Away Princess,* and most of the plays of Maurice Maeterlinck and Gabriele d'Annunzio.

The *epic drama,* which we expect next, is a recognized kind, of which Æschylus was the first master and remains the best exponent. Shelley's *Prometheus Unbound,* and Paul Claudel's cryptic but magnificent *Tête d'Or,* quite consciously follow the tradition of Æschylus. *The Burgraves,* by Victor Hugo, is a fine epic evocation of medieval Germany, with the superhuman and legendary figure of Barbarossa as its center. Its proper place is, not with the author's dramatic works, but with his epic collection, *La Légende des Siècles* (*The Legend of the Centuries*). Apart from the lyrical element, Wagner's *Tetralogy* is epic in theme and spirit. Hardy's *The Dynasts* is an epic in dramatic form, which could be condensed into an epic drama.

Last of all, our table calls for the *Dramatic Drama,* or pure drama. This formula would satisfy those critics who, like Francisque Sarcey, consider the drama as an art *per se,* to be judged exclusively according to its own laws. "Never ask: is it true? is it good? is it beautiful? but: is it effective on the stage?" When Professor George Baker took his class to see *Abie's Irish Rose,* he was seeking to emphasize the point that the thing was a good acting play; it was a *dramatic drama,* if it was little else. The *genre* includes therefore all stagey productions, the melodrama, the farce; but also the "well-made play" of Scribe, Sardou, Dumas Fils, against which our fathers rebelled, and which we regret at times. If we were tempted to despise the *genre* as unliterary, we should remember that, at all times, prominent actor-playwrights had a sense of the stage which led them to compose *effective* plays; in that goodly company we should count Noel Coward, Sacha Guitry, David Belasco, Dion Boucicault, Molière and Shakespeare. The virtues of the stage play, or *dramatic drama*, are best brought out by comparison with its scholarly and often lifeless opposite, the *closet drama*.

Our ninefold classification, therefore, is not in absolute contradiction with the facts. But it does not cover all the important facts, and when we pass in review, in our next chapter, the kinds generally recognized, we shall take them up, pragmatically, in the historical order of their appearance. History should be in agreement with logic, and seldom is. Even Schelling admitted the discrepancy between the two orders of knowledge, when he confessed that, *historically*, the epic should be given precedence, although, *logically*, the first place belongs to the lyric.

Other theorists were less cautious than Schelling; there is a widespread tendency to assert that the lyric is the most primitive of the *genre*. Saintsbury, who, as a rule, is extremely skeptical about general laws, is inclined to endorse that opinion. The most definite statement about the historical succession and genealogy of the *genres* was offered by Victor Hugo, in that capital document of Romantic doctrine, the Preface to *Cromwell* (1827).

Hugo divides history into three periods, primitive times, antiquity, the modern age. To these periods correspond the lyric, the epic, the drama. Of the first, the model is the Bible; of the second, Homer; of the third, Shakespeare.

Hugo was a prestigious juggler with facts and ideas, as well as with words. He could make a good case for considering Shakespeare as the perfect symbol of the modern spirit: a Hamlet civilization, tormented by self-doubt, so complex that it could find expression only in the drama, which is the presentation of conflict. He did not tell us, however, that the novel, even more complex than the drama, had already become the leading *genre* in literature.

His contention that all antiquity is summed up in Homer is open to challenge: philosophy, history, eloquence, tragedy, comedy, deserve more consideration. Still, he could argue that there was an epic quality about the Greek tragedies, that they might indeed be considered as Homeric fragments, bathed in pure Homeric light; and that the supremacy of Homer was never questioned. But when it comes to the Bible, the theory breaks down. The Bible is a whole literature, parts of which are not so "primitive" as Homer. The earliest element, which, according to Hugo, should have been lyrical, is *Genesis,* and *Genesis* is undoubtedly epic in character.

We should like to dwell a while longer on this genealogy of the kinds, not for its intrinsic worth, but as a problem in method. The desire to reduce human evolution to simple laws is eternal: the prudence of the scientific age has not stifled it. Three generations after the Preface to *Cromwell,* there appeared an able little book: *Lyrisme, Epopée, Drame: Une Loi de l'Histoire Littéraire expliquée par l'Evolution Générale.* A law of literary history explained in terms of general evolution! Surely a very ambitious program. The author, Ernest Bovet, following Victor Hugo, recognizes three steps in the development of mankind: an age of enthusiastic faith, which is lyrical; an age of realization and action, which expresses itself in the epic; an age of doubt and conflict, which can be voiced only through the drama. With the ingenuity of an Oswald Spengler, Bovet applies his system, not only like Victor Hugo to history as a whole, but to the divisions and subdivisions of the great periods, down to a single century. In the nineteenth, for instance, we find first a lyrical moment: in England, Wordsworth, Coleridge, Byron, Shelley, Keats; in France, a little later, Lamartine, Vigny, Hugo, Musset. This is followed by a moment when the novel (epic) asserts its predominance, with Balzac, Dumas, George Sand in France, with Dickens and Thackeray in England. Here the facts begin to offer some resistance; but with a firm hand, we can keep them in order. In the third period, we should see the triumph of the drama, and we do not. Ibsen undoubtedly became one of the masters of European literature; but not more so than Tolstoy, Dostoevsky and Nietzsche. It remains to be proved that Augier, Dumas Fils, Sardou, in France, that Pinero, Henry Arthur Jones, even George Bernard Shaw in England, outranked the novelists, their contemporaries, Flaubert, Zola, Daudet, Maupassant, Meredith, Thomas Hardy. Hauptmann and Sudermann gave new prestige to the German stage; but they were successful as novelists also; and in the drama, they never reached the height of the earlier masters, Kleist early in the century, Hebbel in its middle decades.[1]

In order to establish a law in literature, the only safe method is that advocated by Jean Jacques Rousseau: "First of all, let us brush aside the facts." If we hesitate before such a radical measure, our next line of defense is the good old maxim: "The exception proves the rule." Finally, we can take refuge in the notion of *pseudomorphism*, which, being interpreted, means that things are not what they seem. We were once taught an infallible means of telling mushrooms from toadstools. The ones (we have forgotten which) have a ring which is not found in the others. Only, this ring may be so faint as to be totally invisible; while the other kind occasionally offers a spurious ring hard to detect from a true one. With such dialectical instruments at our disposal, we should find it easy to prove that, in spite of appearances, *Genesis* is lyrical, that Plato is epic, while *Paradise Lost* is manifestly a drama. Our own conclusion is that,

[1] This law has many sponsors beside Schelling, Hugo and Bovet. A. W. Ward (art. Drama, *Encyclopaedia Britannica*, 11th edition) says: "Their [the Hindus'] dramatic poetry arose later than their epos, whose great works, the *Mahabharata* and the *Ramayana*, had themselves been long preceded by the hymnody of the *Vedas*—just as the Greek drama followed upon the Homeric poems, and these had been preceded by the early hymns."

in the literary field, *laws* are entertaining, but futile. *Quod non erat demonstrandum.*[1]

What conclusions can we draw from this rapid review?

Our minds are constantly torn between two tendencies, the legalistic and the anarchistic. The first leads us to harden resemblances into identities, statistics into logic, customs and conventions into laws. The rule must be definite and inflexible: as soon as it is proclaimed, conformity is the highest merit, dissent the unforgivable sin. The other tendency would have us reject every form of organization and discipline, because not one of them can be proved to possess absolute validity. Every manifestation of life is unique, unpredictable, irrepeatable. No two minds, and no two poems, can ever be identical. Where there is no common measure, there is no possibility of law.

These modes of reasoning, or of unreasoning, have been carried into other fields. Molière railed bitterly at the doctors, who killed their patients with a clear conscience, because they did so according to the principles of Hippocrates and Galen. On the opposite side, we have the declaration: "There are no sicknesses, there are only sick people." Each case is an individual problem. It is foolish to talk of fever and pneumonia, as though they were goddesses of evil, with an existence of their own, swooping down upon unfortunate mortals. Men do not have fever, any more than poets write epics, "however much they may be deceived by these false abstractions; they express themselves, and this expression is their only form."

We are not seeking a compromise between these two extremes. We stand resolutely against both, *because they are one and the same.* They are two manifestations of a single spirit,

---

[1] It seems that the earliest kinds were, first, *wisdom literature* (gnomic): proverbs, maxims, precepts, popular saws; and second the *commemorative ritual,* a combination of pageant, dance, song and drama. The full consciousness of individual selfhood, voiced in the pure lyric, is the conquest of an advanced civilization. Perhaps a sign of decadence: Adolf Hitler and Jules Romains would have us return to *Unanimism:* the supremacy of the collective mind.

which is absolutism. Croce is no whit less arrogant and dogmatic than Scaliger.

A relativist must recognize the existence of *genros* in literature, as he must also recognize their looseness. They exist in the same way as races and nations exist. There is no universally admitted criterion of race, there is no agreement as to race classification, and the best races are highly complex, undefinable hybrids. Yet when we see a Scandinavian, a Negro, a Chinaman, side by side, we know for certain that the physical differences between them are not purely individual. We are aware that nations are recent and highly artificial products; that race, language, traditions, economic interests, political rule, natural boundaries, hardly ever coincide. But we cannot dispose of the torturing national problem simply by denying its existence. "However much men may be deceived by these false abstractions," to quote J. E. Spingarn again, their delusion remains a formidable fact. Like a nation, a *genre* is partly natural and partly artificial. It is hard to tell, in each case, to what extent its existence is due to essential psychological factors, to obscure or explicit traditions, or to a convention hardened into a doctrine.

Genres are at any rate a convenience. How can we establish contact between soul and soul? We must find some meeting point: a common language, common memories, common experiences, a few essential categories of thought. Without these, we should be imprisoned in our uniqueness, blind and deaf to the world of other men. The more extensive our common ground, the more resemblances we are able to take for granted, the freer we shall be to reveal what is specifically our own in our personality.

But in art personality must remain paramount. We shall condemn the *genres* if they hamper self-expression, we shall approve of them if they help the individual to be more freely himself. From this point of view, we may distinguish three aspects to the question. *The genre may be thought of as a machine.* Select your genre; press down a number of keys—situation, setting, types of character, etc.—turn the handle, and pull out your masterpiece. This is obviously a mere caricature; no classical, neo-classical, post-classical or pseudo-classical pedant ever put forth such a claim; the critic who came nearest that absurdity, was a very intelligent man and a great defender of Shakespeare, Lessing.[1] *The genre may be considered as a game:* the game allows free scope for the skill, the inventiveness of the player; but once he has started, he has no right to disregard the rules, arbitrary as they may be; that is called cheating. *The genre may be considered as the keynote of a mood.* The author informs us, by means of a few agreed signs, that his thoughts have an idyllic, an elegiac, a tragic or a merry cast. Thus warned, we may either close the book at once, or attune ourselves to the writer's temper.

In all three cases, the *genre* stands for a promise of consistency, a consistency which is purely mechanical at one extreme, and organic at the other. A breach of that consistency need not be a "fault": it certainly is a danger. "Inconsistent," "incongruous," are still terms of reproach. To a large extent, we are still unconsciously guided by the old warning against "mixing the kinds."

Let us accept this warning then, but with at least three qualifications. The first is that the list of *genres* should not be unduly simplified. The ancients knew but four elements; we recognize about a hundred. The complex formulae of organic chemistry would stagger Boyle and Lavoisier. Every generation discovers some new and subtler shade, and no *genre* ever dies if it deserved to live at all.

---

[1] "I do not hesitate to confess (even if in these enlightened times I am to be laughed out of countenance for it) that I hold the *Poetics* to be as infallible as the elements of Euclid. Its principles are just as true and as certain, only not so simple, and therefore more exposed to misrepresentation. . . . There is no play of the great Corneille which I could not improve upon . . . and ought not to think much of myself for doing so. I should have done nothing but what anyone could do whose faith in Aristotle is as firm as mine." (Truly a faith that moves mountains!) Lessing, *Hamburgische Dramaturgie*, II.

The second proviso is that we should admit the validity of hybrids. The finest breed of horses, the English racer, was the result of a successful crossing. The delightful architecture of the early French Renaissance offers a daring, yet finely measured compounding of elements: the silhouette of Chambord, Chenonceaux, the old Paris Town Hall, is still purely Gothic; the details of ornamentation are Italianate. To seek comedy among the gods, and tragedy among the humble, implies the adoption of intermediate *genres* which rigorous doctrinaires might condemn. Balzac evolved a new kind when, in *Melmoth Reconciled*, he blended the Gothic romance of mystery and terror with the most extreme realism in setting and treatment. Most daring of all was Pascal who, in his *Provincial Letters*, discussed with intense earnestness the highest problems of theology, but in a tone of well-bred irony. Once established, a composite *genre* evolves its own laws, and must conform to them. A mock-heroic poem like *The Rape of the Lock* is manifestly a mixed kind. But Pope would have been open to censure if, in his sedate fantasy, he had allowed himself to grow either too flippant or too solemn.

Finally, our respect for consistency should not lead us to ignore the effectiveness of contrast. If harmony is the secret of beauty, contrast is not seldom the key to power. This was well understood by Longinus, who could see, not merely in simplicity, but even in vulgarity, a possible element of the sublime. There are many passages in Shakespeare without a jarring note; but his most Shakespearian effects are obtained by means of dramatic opposition. The grave diggers are necessary, not to relieve, but to deepen, the tragic tension in the last act of *Hamlet*.

The right to use such contrasts was Victor Hugo's chief demand in his Romantic manifesto, the Preface to *Cromwell*. He did not want to abolish the *genres;* he did not even want to "mix the kinds"; he wanted to secure recognition for a drama in which terror and pity would be heightened by the contrast and fusion of tragedy and comedy. In his theory, he may have over-emphasized this point; in his practice, he may have carried it to the verge of the absurd. But it would be wrong to consider it merely as a melodramatic device. We may yearn for classic simplicity and harmony: we know that they do not prevail in our haggard world. It would be well for us if we could choose between ennobling sorrow and pure laughter; but the ludicrous has its pathetic aspects, and the tragic may be linked with the sordid. The spiritual universe of St. John, of Dante, even of Luther, was not bathed in serene splendor; it was a vision in which grotesque shapes writhed horribly against the eternal light.

SUMMARY

Literary kinds, or *genres,* are a practical fact, denied only by dogmatists like Croce and Spingarn. The problem is not whether they exist, but to what do they correspond: to mere *conventions* or to natural *laws?*

The theory of *genres* belongs chiefly to Renaissance criticism. It implied that the *genres* were few, unchangeable, subject to strict rules, and that they should be kept pure. The great classicists were far less assertive. But the late classicists insisted on a rigorous interpretation of the doctrine of *genres.* It became one of the issues in the romantic rebellion. Late in the nineteenth century, Brunetière revived the idea in Darwinian garb: this explains to some extent Croce's radical denial.

Definition: A *genre* is a commonly accepted grouping of works which offer significant resemblances in spirit and in form. It must be noted that the combination of spirit and form is necessary to define a genre.

Two popular modes of classification are discussed and dismissed as irrelevant: (a) verse and prose (all kinds can be treated in either form); (b) fiction and non-fiction. This distinction seems important from the moral and from the practical points of view; but it lacks reality. There are elements of fiction, i.e., imaginative reconstruction of reality, in biography and history; and elements of fact, at times predominant, in so-called fiction.

The three fundamental kinds are the lyric, the epic (or narrative) and the drama. This standard division is comparatively recent. It corresponds roughly to typographical differences: brief poems, continuous narrative in verse or prose, dialogue. But there are many exceptions, and many hybrid forms.

As the terms lyric, epic, drama apply both to spirit and form, it is possible to establish (after von Hartmann) a ninefold division: lyrical lyric, epic lyric, dramatic lyric; lyrical epic, epic epic, dramatic epic; lyrical drama, epic drama, dramatic drama (the lyrical lyric, the epic epic, the dramatic drama, may be called *pure* lyric, epic, drama). Although we are suspicious of such ingenious symmetry, this division is not in flagrant contradiction with the facts, and examples of the nine subdivisions are offered.

Genealogy of the Kinds. A theory widely accepted, and most brilliantly expounded by Victor Hugo, considers the lyric as the most primitive kind, then the epic, and finally the drama. Hugo accepts the Bible as representative of primitive lyricism, Homer as the incarnation of antiquity, Shakespeare as the symbol of the modern age. The contradictions and dangers of such generalizations are pointed out.

A *genre* may be considered as a *machine*; as a *game* with conventional rules; as the *keynote of a mood*. In all cases, it implies a certain consistency. We are inclined to accept the *genres* at least as a convenience, with three provisos: (1) the list should not be unduly simplified; (2) we should admit the validity of hybrids; (3) respect for consistency should not lead us to ignore the effectiveness of contrast.

CHAPTER XII

SURVEY OF THE GENRES

I. THE LYRIC

HOMER is always represented with his lyre, and King David with his harp. Like the Greek ἀοιδός and the Psalmist of Israel, scop, skald, bard, minstrel, troubadour, all were singers who accompanied themselves on a string instrument. If the harp and the lute are somewhat antiquated, the guitar, the banjo and the ukulele are still heard in the land. Such then is the elementary meaning of *lyric:* a song. The ditties which adorn a musical comedy are properly called *lyrics,* even when they are most inane.

The song in the simplest sense of the term is perhaps the most universal of the *genres.* It is found among all races and among all classes. Even in our own complex civilization, the sailor's chantey, the soldier's marching tune, the cowboy song, the Negro spirituals, count among the most authentic forms of folklore. Professor Louise Pound, Messrs. Lomax and Carl Sandburg have been doing invaluable work in preserving these unsophisticated creations. It would be easy to exaggerate their significance; we know of none that is truly great, and we should be most reluctant to have them used as the measure of the national soul. But there are moments when the complications and clevernesses of artificial literature drive us back to the popular, even though the popular be crude. This feeling is admirably expressed in a scene of Molière's *Misanthrope.* Disgusted with the pretentious vapidity of a fashionable sonnet, the hero, Alceste, quotes and praises a folk song of the most rudimentary kind:

great as a collection of lyrics. There is no saving grace in poor verse.

The *folk ballad*, primitive or modern, is also a true lyric in the literal sense of the term. It is a *song*, with a tune and a musical accompaniment. The name, which comes to us from the Provençal, implies that the ballad was connected with the dance, most probably with communal dancing. Between the song and the ballad, no definite line can be drawn. The song as a rule is shorter, but there are interminable songs and brief ballads. Perhaps the chief difference is that the song expresses a feeling or a mood, whereas the ballad tells a story. The *art ballad*, a deliberate imitation of the popular form, retains the simple and vigorous rhythm, the repetitions, and frequently the refrain, which suggest and even seem to demand a tune.

The folk ballad, long forgotten, ignored or despised by the *literati*, came into its own again in the second half of the eighteenth century. Its rediscovery was part of the romantic revolt against excessive sophistication, a revolt of which Rousseau was the major prophet. The Age of Reason, all exquisite refinement, urbanity, luxury, yearned pathetically for the primitive. Molière's Alceste, the enemy of polite convention, had his way after nearly a hundred years, and his fondness for *"J'aime mieux ma mie, ô gué!"* no longer appeared as an outrageous paradox. *The Reliques of Ancient English Poetry*, published by Thomas Percy in 1765, satisfied that craving. The revival of the folk ballad brought with it the flowering of the art ballad, so that the two could hardly be separated. Bürger's *Lenore* (1774), in Germany, was literally epoch-making. Soon Herder was to edit a collection of *Volkslieder* (1778-9) which greatly influenced Goethe and Schiller; their example was followed in the nineteenth century by Heine and Uhland. It was from Bürger, not directly from Percy, that Walter Scott and Coleridge caught their enthusiasm for medieval minstrelsy. Thus the lowly ballad became, in one generation, the favorite of learned and very conscious poets. France, belatedly, followed the lead of the Northern countries; after a few classical Odes, young Victor Hugo published a number of all-too-brilliant Ballads.

Doctrinaires will tell us that this is all wrong. The romantic ballad was purely an antiquarian pastiche. It did not reflect the conditions of an age which was already scientific and industrial; therefore it should have been lifeless and barren. But it would be wise not to be guided by theoretical scruples: as a matter of fact, the revived ballad had a glorious career. It survived the first generation of Romanticism: there are good ballads in Browning (*Hervé Riel*) and in Tennyson (*The Revenge*). Nor did the ballad show any sign of exhaustion in the third and fourth generations: Rudyard Kipling and G. K. Chesterton had the true ballad spirit. There may be a surprising vigor of life in *genres* which are artificially revived. Racine's Greek tragedies are at the same time respectful imitations, and profoundly original creations. The Gothic revival in architecture was somewhat akin to the favor enjoyed by the ballad in literature: it produced many atrocities, but also a few monuments like the Houses of Parliament in London, which we condemn in theory, and secretly admire.[1] Keats had no business to sing *La Belle Dame sans Merci:* he should have sought inspiration in the cotton mills. Perhaps; but is there any reason why we should conform in every respect to the conditions of our own age, and take, for instance, an "industrial" view of religion because we happen to live in an industrial era? Some aspects of the thirteenth century might very well be more congenial to us than the corresponding aspects of the twentieth. The modern ballad is make-believe, if you please: but all art, we must repeat, is make-believe. And the ballad spirit of wonder, heroism, reckless adventure, appeals eternally to the eternal barbarian, or the eternal boy, that lurks in our hearts.

If the ballad is technically a lyric, that is to say a song, it is

[1] There are under construction at present, in Liverpool and in New York, two Gothic Cathedrals which challenge comparison with the vast majority of medieval churches.

as a rule narrative in subject. It has often been considered as a miniature epic, or as an epic fragment. A theory, accepted without challenge for several generations, claimed that all great epics had been prepared by an abundant production of ballads, that they were indeed but a compilation and co-ordination of ballad episodes. If the ballad is usually epic in character, it may also be dramatic in spirit and even in form. Several folk ballads, and among the most impressive, *Edward, Lord Randal*, are in dialogue. Goethe's famous *Erlkönig*, which sings in our memory with the tempestuous accompaniment of Schubert's music, is a scene with three voices.

In modern usage, the term Ballad has become extremely vague. Oscar Wilde's *Ballad of Reading Gaol* is reflective rather than narrative; the word "ballad" however may be justified by the tragic background, by the simple and strongly marked rhythm, and by a certain affectation of folklike simplicity.

There is a point where our capacity for make-believe breaks down; then romantic intensity calls for its corrective, romantic irony. Even in the Middle Ages, the tragic ballad spontaneously generated its counterpart, the *mock-heroic ballad*. This is a minor, but a fertile and delightful *genre* in English literature. Its masterpiece is probably Barham's *Ingoldsby Legends*. But *The Ride of John Gilpin* may be considered as a ballad-parody, Browning's *Pied Piper of Hamelin* as a humorous ballad; Tom Hood, Praed, Thackeray, Edward Lear, Lewis Carroll, run the gamut from half-earnest satire to irrepressible nonsense. After the sternly patriotic nautical ballads of Tennyson, Newbolt and Kipling, we find peculiar relish in Anthony Deane's rollicking *Ballad of the "Billicock."*

The *ode* is defined by Sir Edmund Gosse as "a form of stately and elaborate lyrical verse. As its name shows, the original signification of an ode was a chant, a poem arranged to be sung to an instrumental accompaniment." In this the ode resembles the ballad; the chief difference is that the ballad is of medieval origin, and seeks to retain a popular flavor; the ode is of Greco-Roman ancestry, and its appeal is to the learned.[1]

But with the Ode, we are able to study the change from the literal meaning of the word *lyric* to the deeper sense it has assumed in the modern mind. The history of the *genre* is confusing. Pindar was constantly worshiped from afar, and very imperfectly understood. In the full Greek Ode, a threefold division corresponded to motions of the chorus, perhaps symbolical of the inner development of the poem. The singers moved to one side during the *strophe*, to the other side for the *antistrophe*, and stood still during the *epode*. This division, although nominally preserved by imitators of the Greeks, has long lost any particle of significance. In his *Ode to Naples*, Shelley uses a strange arrangement of two epodes, followed by two strophes, four antistrophes, and finally two more epodes.

It seems that even in Greek times, the ode had ceased to be a choral performance, and that it no longer required even the accompaniment of the flute. The musical origin of the ode survives mainly in a set of conventions. Of these, Thomas Gray's *Progress of Poesy* offers good examples:

> Awake, Æolian lyre, awake,
> And give to rapture all thy trembling strings. . . .
> Hark, his hands the lyre explore!

Ronsard, in the middle of the sixteenth century, was the first modern poet to revive the ode. He has been accused of intro-

---

[1] On the musical character of the ode: Dryden's perfect *Song for St. Cecilia's Day* (1687), is an ode in spirit and form. Tennyson's *Ode for the Opening of the Exposition* was to be sung, and might be called a commercial-industrial Cantata.

On the kinship between ode and ballad: *The Bard*, by Thomas Gray, is a curious hybrid, the product of a transitional age. The subject is medieval, and fit for a ballad; the form is that of a conventional Pindaric ode, and the diction classical; but there is a ballad quality in verses like the following:

> "Edward, lo! To sudden fate
> (Weave we the woof. The thread is spun)
> Half of thy heart we consecrate.
> (The web is wove. The work is done.)"

ducing pedantic and antiquarian forms into French poetry, thus hampering its free development. A few of his attempts deserve this stricture. But most of the poems he called by that classical name have little in common with the Pindaric tradition. They are truly French and truly modern, and offer the greatest variety of subjects and forms, including the long discourse in rhymed couplets.

From the days of Ronsard, the modern Ode has been a spirit vainly seeking for a definite body. In France, the success of Malherbe almost imposed a ten-line strophe as a standard; not only the pedestrian lyricists of the Classical Age, from Boileau to Lebrun-Pindare, adopted that stanza, but the great Romanticists, Lamartine, Hugo, used it with masterly effect. The English ode remained completely free. The modern poet can use whatever stanza he favors; he is not even compelled to abide by his own choice and keep the same stanzaic form throughout. Some of the very finest Odes in the language, Coleridge's *Dejection*, Wordsworth's *Intimations of Immortality*, are thoroughly irregular. No one questioned the right of Paul Claudel to designate as odes admirable compositions in his own medium —a verse ruled by its own inner law, measured solely by the poet's breath, reminiscent at times of Walt Whitman, at times of the Hebrew Prophets. The sole implication of the word ode is a certain loftiness of purpose.

With the nominal tradition of instrumental music went a second tradition, which in some cases had ludicrous results: the convention of the "fine frenzy." It was so difficult to follow the intricate flight of Pindar's song, that the Pindaric Ode was supposed to be "governed by utter lawlessness." As the Greeks could do no wrong, this disorder was voted the highest triumph of art. Abraham Cowley, whose Pindaric Odes appeared in 1656, is held responsible for this conception, which held sway for two centuries. To quote Sir Edmund Gosse again, the Ode according to Cowley was "a lofty and tempestuous piece of indefinite poetry, conducted without sail or oar in whatever direction the enthusiasm of the poet chose to take it." [1] This view was confirmed by Boileau in his *Art Poétique;* the sage Lawgiver of Parnassus went the length of composing an *Ode on the Taking of Namur,* in which he feigned, laboriously, the "holy intoxication" required by the *genre.* But, to save his dignity, he insisted that the intoxication be "learned" as well as "holy": *docte et sainte ivresse.*

This convention, however, is not due merely to a misreading of Pindar. It is rooted in ancient Greek tradition. Scaliger tells us: "The poets invoke the Muses, that the divine madness may imbue them to do their work. Of these divinely possessed ones, two classes are to be recognized. The one class are those to whom the divine power comes from above. . . . The other class is aroused by the fumes of unmixed wine. . . . Horace said that Ennius was such a poet, and such we consider Horace himself." [2] The ode, therefore, implies a license to rave. In more respectful terms, we may say that the poet is not the thrall of facts or sense: he is his own law. In theory at least, the ode remained an inviolate fastness of Romanticism in the well-ordered and fruitful classical plain.

Already the Greeks had recognized a distinction between the choric song, which expressed collective sentiments, and the lyric proper, which was the personal utterance of the poet. Both were to develop into the ode. From the time of Ronsard to the present day, the modern ode bears the mark of this double origin. The odes which Tennyson wrote in his capacity as Poet Laureate, the *Ode on the Death of the Duke of Wellington,* the *Ode Sung at the Opening of the International Exposition,* are decidedly choric in character. It is not the sensitive artist Tennyson who speaks in his own name; it is sturdy Victorian England. The Wellington Ode is but an exalted obituary notice,

---

[1] This has left a trace in our common speech: we use the word *lyrical*—at times with humorous intent—to denote wild enthusiasm: "He grew quite lyrical about his new car."

[2] J. C. Scaliger: *Poetics,* I, 2; tr. Padelford.

and the Exposition Ode a *Manchester Guardian* leading article in praise of free trade. The sole difference lies in the sober and solemn music of the language; the Laureate is only an incomparable choirmaster. In Wordsworth's *Ode to Duty*, the choric element is still very strong: the poet is thinking in general terms, but with definite application to himself. In the *Intimations of Immortality*—one of the austere and magnificent summits in world poetry—the proportion is reversed. Wordsworth is seeking to establish a universal truth, but on the basis of intense personal experiences. Coleridge's *Dejection* is pure lyric in the deeper sense; it is a chapter in the poet's biography, the frankest, the most intimate of confessions, the despairing cry of a soul engulfed in "a grief without a pang, void, dark and drear." [1]

As the result of this discussion, the following definition may be submitted: The Ode is a poem of medium length; of no fixed form; bearing traces of its musical origin; meditative, not narrative; characterized by solemnity of thought and diction; capable of expressing collective and individual feelings.

This definition fails to apply to the *Anacreontic Ode*, which blithely sings of "wine, love and the Muses." It seems a pity that the noble term Ode should be accorded to these light compositions, insufferable when they fail to be exquisite. But the tradition is an ancient one. It was strengthened and made "more perennial than bronze" by the example of Horace. For, if this wise and witty man of the world could sound, officially, the heroic trumpet, or descant solemnly on pallid Death, he did not despise the erotic and bacchanalian strain. It was Horace rather than Pindar that Ronsard imitated most successfully, and, for

[1] The same distinction can be made among the Psalms, which are odes of a religious nature. Most of them, particularly the Psalms of Praise, are choric; they express collective sentiments, those of universal man, or those of Israel as a nation. But, even to these, the intense conviction of the poet imparts a personal accent. Others, particularly the Penitential Psalms, are the cries, not of man, not of Israel, but of a wounded individual soul.

over three centuries, we have been taught by the Anacreontics to "enjoy the day" and "gather rosebuds."[1]

The song, the ballad and the ode are true lyrics, because, in their origin at least, they were set to music. It has been noted that not one of the three is bound to a definite and invariable form. There is a "common meter" for hymn tunes; but many of our favorites, like *Ein festes Burg* or *Lead, Kindly Light*, do not conform to it. There is a ballad stanza, the one used in *Sir Patrick Spence*; but neither popular nor romantic ballads limit themselves to that single arrangement. And the ode reached its greatest heights when it was freest from technical trammels.

We shall now pass in review a series of poems which, on the contrary, are defined not by their spirit or by their musical quality, but by a fixed form. Of these, a great number are of French origin and go back to the Middle Ages: a vestige of the supremacy long enjoyed by medieval French culture, not merely in England, but over a great part of Europe. Some of them, like the elaborate and indeed torturing *sestina* came to Northern France from the Provençal. The *pantoum* is of Malay origin. Among these French forms may be mentioned the neatly tripping *triolet*, the *rondeau* with its brood, the *rondel*, Swinburne's *roundel*, and the *roundelay*, the *villanelle*, the *virelay*, the *ballade*, and the *chant royal*.

It is not within the scope of this book to discuss their technical aspects; we shall simply note that, as a rule, they are used only for fugitive poetry or society verse—a compliment, an epigram, a passing fancy. They are excellent vehicles for the anacreontic muse; easy morality is corrected, to some slight extent, by strict

[1] Théodore de Banville evolved a minor form of this minor *genre* in his *Odelettes* and *Odes Funambulesques* (literally tight-rope walking odes). Lighter than even the airiest fantasies of Robert Herrick, these trifles, beside their matchless technical skill, have a genuine lyrical quality; their delightful acrobatics are the self-expression of a proud and delicate soul. As the Tumbler of Notre Dame served the Virgin by turning somersault before her altar, so did the merry clown Banville worthily honor his god Apollo. Swinburne loved him, and his example contributed to the revival of anacreontic and fugitive poetry in modern English, with such masters in miniature as Andrew Lang and Austin Dobson.

discipline in the weaving of rhymes. Austin Dobson has proved himself the laureate of such light and formal verse, and only a surly pedant could refuse to enjoy *At the Sign of the Lyre*.

These tricky baubles, however, may be more than frail *jeux d'esprit*. Leconte de Lisle gave to the *pantoum* his own somber cast of thought, and included among his aptly named *Poèmes Tragiques* a very impressive philosophical *villanelle* (*Le Temps, l'Etendue et le Nombre*). There is in Baudelaire a *pantoum* of such serene and melancholy beauty that we forget the excessive elaborateness of the form.[1]

The *ballade* was a very fruitful *genre* in the French Middle Ages; our Chaucer practiced it, not however in strict accordance with Gallic rules.[2] It survived in full force, with the dainty Court songster Clément Marot, until the dawn of the Renaissance. Then it suddenly lost caste; the haughty poets of the *Pléiade* scorned it as rude and Gothic. It preserved an underground, despised existence during the Classical Age: Molière and Boileau made a contemptuous allusion to the *ballade*, as vapid, capricious and antiquated. It was Théodore de Banville who revived the *ballade* in the middle of the nineteenth century, and the English *ballade* writers such as Swinburne were his disciples. Swinburne dedicated a beautiful *ballade* to his dead master; his own *Ballade of Dreamland*, with the refrain *Only the song of a secret bird*, does full justice to the musical possibilities of the *genre*, with a Swinburnian touch of excess.[3]

But the long history of the *ballade* can be summed up in a single name, François Villon. It is the undying prestige of that tragic vagabond that makes the *ballade* deathless. In three at

---

[1] Ch. Baudelaire, *Fleurs du Mal, Harmonie du Soir*.

[2] He dropped the envoy at times; in other cases, he used a seven line stanza, instead of eight or ten, as in the two standard types of the French *ballade*.

[3] Two forms of the *ballade*: octosyllabic, three stanzas of eight lines, rhymed alike *ababbcbc*; an envoy—which should begin with the word Prince, rhymed *bcbc*; the eighth line of the three stanzas and the 4th of the envoy are the same and form the refrain. Decasyllabic, 3 stanzas of 10 lines, rhyming alike *ababbccdcd*; envoy of 5, 6 or 7 lines, on *c* and *d* rhymes. Refrain as above.

least of his *ballades,* he has treated essential themes with that
directness which abolishes all barriers between subject, author
and reader: Villon is an immediate experience. Yet the *Ballade
to the Virgin Mary,* written at his mother's request, is far from
simple. It is a romantic blend of sincere piety and conscious
esthetic enjoyment. Villon shares the unquestioning religion of
the old woman; but he is also detached enough to relish the
artistic charm of that very naïveté. The poem is a masterpiece
of half-conscious sophistication—belief enhanced by make-believe. It has been called "a stained glass window glowing with
the splendor of a setting faith."

The *Ballade of the Gibbet* reveals its full poignancy when
we realize that Villon himself and his companions expected
shortly to be hanged. Never were the physical sense of death,
the grotesque horror of bodily dissolution, conveyed with such
shuddering power; and this gives full force to the refrain: *Pray
God pardon us out of His grace.* Finally, the supreme *ballade,
The Fair Ladies of Olden Times:* a round dozen of romances
and tragedies, fleeting visions of loveliness and doom, evoked
at times by a mere musical name, at times by a phrase as inevitable as a scientific formula:

> And Joan, the good Lorrainer
> Whom Englishmen burned at Rouen. . . .

In the refrain: But where are the snows of yesteryear? an extraordinary complexity of feelings, without a trace of mawkish-
ness, is condensed into the absolute purity of a single note. It is
the very essence of lyric poetry.[1]

The destiny of the *sonnet* admirably illustrates the power of
tradition. Between the Petrarchan sonnet, the Shakespearean,
and Shelley's superb *Ozymandias,* there is nothing in common

---

[1] The first two *ballades* are in the longer form, ten-line stanzas of ten-
syllable lines; the last in the briefer and more familiar form, eight-line
stanzas of eight-syllable lines. The poems of Villon have been translated by
Andrew Lang, Arthur Symons, W. E. Henley, A. C. Swinburne, and particularly D. G. Rossetti; they still remain the torment of translators.

but the number of lines;[1] and it would take a very bold dogmatist to assert that there is a mystic virtue in the figure fourteen. A lyric by William Butler Yeats, "When you are old," manifestly inspired by Ronsard's famous *Sonnet to Hélène*, has all the qualities that we demand of a sonnet: the solemn mood, the concentration, the definiteness, the unity, the stately, rhythmic ascent to a noble climax. But it is composed of twelve lines only. Technically, the sonnet, even the stricter Petrarchan kind, is less difficult than the *ballade*. What makes it exacting is its heavy heritage of glory. Six centuries have poured beauty into that severely disciplined form, and permeated it with beauty; whoso attempts a sonnet measures himself against the masters. The result is, as Boileau rather reluctantly admitted, that "a faultless sonnet is worth a long poem."

As the *ballade* is Villon, so the sonnet is Petrarch. Neither invented the *genre* he practiced with such mastery: he only made it immortal. With great differences, however. Villon's is the more solitary achievement, and for that reason the more impressive. No one has ever challenged, in his own field, the lyric gangster of medieval Paris; but there have been greater sonneteers than the one who so gloriously opened the way. On the other hand, the destiny of the *ballade* was modest compared with that of the sonnet. The *ballade* today is an archaic and half-humorous exercise. The sonnet, in six hundred years, has suffered no total eclipse, and shows no signs of exhaustion.

It is generally admitted that the sonnet is of Italian origin; but it was in Provence, in or about the Papal city of Avignon,

---

[1] The Petrarchan sonnet is divided into an *octave*, 8 lines rhyming abbaabba, and a *sestet*, six lines with two or three rhymes, variously arranged. It is the standard form in French as well as in Italian, and was adopted by many of the great English sonneteers. But for Shakespeare's example, it would be the only one recognized as legitimate. The Shakespearean sonnet has three quatrains, each with its own rhyme scheme, and concludes with a couplet. The arrangement of rhymes in *Ozymandias* is absolutely free. Baudelaire frequently departed from the Petrarchan by using two double sets of rhymes instead of one in the octave: abbacddc. The French sonnet is usually printed in four divisions: two quatrains, two *tercets*. This makes its structure more apparent, and, for that reason, a little too rigid.

that Petrarch established the tradition of the *genre;* and his *Canzoniere,* or *Rhymes on the Life and Death of His Lady, Laura,* is quite in the spirit of Provençal love poetry. Thus the delicate culture of the South, brutally suppressed by the Northern Barbarians, is still bearing exquisite fruit under alien skies.

It is from Petrarch that we derive, not only the sonnet, but the *sonnet sequence,* the kind which was to yield such works as Sir Philip Sydney's *Astrophel and Stella,* Daniel's *Delia,* Spenser's *Amoretti,* Shakespeare's long cycle, "the key" wherewith he "unlocked his heart" [1] to the utter bewilderment of posterity; Mrs. Browning's *Sonnets from the Portuguese,* and, to reach our own days, William Ellery Leonard's *Two Lives,* and Edna St. Vincent Millay's *Fatal Interview.*

It was in the sixteenth century that the sonnet spread from Petrarch's Italy to the Northern lands, with Joachim Du Bellay and Ronsard in France, with Wyatt and Surrey in England. It must be noted that already with Du Bellay, the sonnet had transcended the conventionalities of courtly love. In several of his sonnets on *The Antiquities of Rome,* he achieved an effect of majesty and noble melancholy which would seem to require a much vaster frame. It seems incredible that fourteen lines could open such an awe-inspiring vista across the centuries. This great tradition, fortunately, was never broken. In Milton's *On the Late Massacre in Piedmont,* in Wordsworth's *Composed on Westminster Bridge,* in Keats's *On First Looking into Chapman's Homer,* in Shelley's *Ozymandias,* "the Thing" can "become a trumpet" [2] or the peal of a mighty organ, or the tolling of solemn bells.

This high seriousness of the sonnet is not intrinsic in the form. The sonnet can be the vehicle of the comic spirit. We do

---

[1] Sequence: a series or cycle of sonnets on the same theme or in the same mood. As a rule, they do not tell a connected story, and the component sonnets may be understood and enjoyed individually. But some sequences may be considered as single works, with an organic unity. Shakespeare's sonnets have been so interpreted.

[2] This phrase (and also "With such a key," above) is from Wordsworth's *Scorn not the sonnet,* a fine defense, imitated by Sainte-Beuve.

not mean merely in the way of parody: the most earnest of *genres*, even the tragedy and the epic, are thus teasingly followed by their irreverent counterparts. Lope de Vega, who could do all things well, turned out very deft playful sonnets; Molière wrote one, on imposed rhymes (*bouts-rimés*); one of the very few sonnets by Victor Hugo is of a light nature. The comical possibilities of the sonnet have been proved by Leigh Hunt, in a delightful triad, *The Fish, the Man, and the Spirit*. The sonnet as a rule demands the noblest line in the language, such as the iambic pentameter in English, the Alexandrine in French. But there are serious sonnets in shorter measures; as a technical feat, we should mention the sonnet in lines of one syllable, of which there are good examples in French and in English.

It is strange that the greatest French romanticists, Lamartine, Hugo, Vigny, should have written few sonnets or none at all. The *genre*, however, was to have its vindication in the latter half of the nineteenth century, with Baudelaire, with Mallarmé, and especially with José Maria de Heredia. Heredia was the sonneteer par excellence, the sonneteer in almost absolute purity. He departed but a few times from his chosen form; fully realizing its exacting nature, he spurned the least capitulation to mediocrity. He spent a laborious lifetime filing away every trace of effort from a very slender volume, *The Trophies*. His unswerving ambition and conscientiousness had their reward: not a poet of abundant gifts, he yet created masterpieces of tantalizing perfection. They are not elaborate gems merely, "Enamels and Cameos," according to the advice of Théophile Gautier; a few times at least, he rivals the masters in the epic grandeur of his flawless miniatures. The fourteen lines of his *Antony and Cleopatra* stand, uncrushed and undimmed, by the glowing mass of Shakespeare's drama. A kinsman of the *Conquistadores*, he distilled into a supreme sonnet their "heroic and brutal dream." There are no less than four translations of *The Trophies* in America: unique tribute to a great minor poet, indifferent to the market place and the squabbles of the day.[1]

If a fixed form sufficed to determine a *genre*, we should logically include in our survey all rhyme schemes and stanzaic patterns, such as Dante's *terza rima* and the Spenserian stanza. There is no radical difference: if most of the fixed forms are of definite length, some, like the *virelay* and the *pantoum*, are not; and a sonnet sequence, in certain cases, might be considered as a single poem divided into fourteen-line stanzas. But we are by this time familiar with the thought that logic does not rule literary classifications. Not only do stanzaic forms fail to establish a *genre*, but they are themselves frequently without a name. Let us be grateful for this injustice, which simplifies our task.

We have so far considered the lyric in its original meaning, that is to say as a song; and the lyric as embodied in a strict conventional pattern, like the *ballade* and the sonnet. We shall now examine the lyric from a third point of view: as determined by its subject matter. This new classification, like the other two, is neither all-inclusive, nor properly symmetrical. Blind chance, the prestige of a few masters, the dogmatism of a few pedants, have combined to give us a nomenclature remarkably incomplete as well as perverse. Thus, there are warlike songs, hymns, odes, ballads, sonnets: but there is no *genre* that is characterized exclusively by the martial spirit; whereas, thanks to Theocritus and Vergil, the pastoral life—or the sophisticated pastoral convention—inspired the eclogue, the bucolics, and to some extent the idyl. The idyl usually connotes a tale of innocent love, with a setting rural or sylvan: but the poem of fierce passion, which is no less real than the idyl, is not recognized as a distinct *genre*. To deepen our bewilder-

[1] The best of these translations as well as the most complete is the one by John Myers O'Hara and John Hervey. The French Heredia dedicated three fine sonnets in Spanish to his kinsman and namesake, long dead, greatest of Cuban poets.

choric, the second properly *lyric*. The choric, unduly emphasized, might lead to mere sonorous platitudes: "Nature is beautiful; all men must die." The lyric, if it voiced only individual aspirations and sufferings, would seem insufferably egotistical. The full dignity and power of lyric poetry is attained only when the poet's heart and the universal soul throb in unison.[1]

SUMMARY

The original meaning of the word lyric is a song, with a musical accompaniment. Greek poet, psalmist, bard, scop, skald, minstrel, troubadour, all were singers. The *song* is the most universal of genres; the most spontaneous and popular, it has also been practiced by the greatest, like Shakespeare and Goethe. It has found its noblest form in religious literature, with the psalm and the hymn.

The folk *ballad* is also a true lyric, for it is meant to be sung. But it is usually narrative—a rudimentary or miniature epic—or even dramatic. The rediscovery of the folk ballad in the eighteenth century was part of the romantic revolt against sophistication; the old ballads were imitated with brilliant success (Bürger, Scott, Coleridge, Goethe); and the *genre* is still active today.

The *ode* likewise is a song; originally it was a choral performance; but already in Greek times the musical element had become a mere tradition. The modern ode, revived particularly by Ronsard, is absolutely free to adopt any verse form: the sole implication of the word is a certain loftiness of spirit.

A second tradition is attached to the ode: that of the "fine frenzy." The poet is supposed to sing in rapture, or in holy

---

[1] We must mention in passing two *genres* which, if they are poetical at all, must be so on account of some lyrical quality: the *descriptive* and the *philosophical*. The descriptive is best illustrated by James Thomson's *Seasons*, the influence of which was enormous, and which is still a delight. Of the philosophical, *De Natura Rerum*, by Lucretius, remains the incomparable and gloomy masterpiece. The unexpected success of the *Testament of Beauty*, by Robert Bridges, proved that there was an eager public for a *genre* that all doctors had long pronounced dead.

intoxication. This convention goes back to the religious origin of the ode: the poet is literally "inspired": a spirit speaks through him. It was also due in part to the intrinsic difficulty of Pindar's poems, which seemed to defy timid common sense.

The Greeks made a distinction between the choric song, which expressed collective sentiments, and the lyric proper, the personal utterance of the poet. The ode bears the marks of this double origin. Although the ode is as a rule a meditative poem characterized by solemnity of thought and diction, there is an ancient and very active tradition in lighter vein, the anacreontic.

Song, ballad and ode are true lyrics because of their musical origin; but they have no fixed form. The word lyric is also applied to poems which on the contrary are defined by their technical arrangement. Several of these are of Provençal and French origin, and are now mere *jeux d'esprit*, used for fugitive poetry and society verse. Two fixed forms are singled out, as of greater significance: the *ballade*, of which François Villon gave the supreme examples, and the *sonnet*. Petrarch, if he did not invent the form, created the sonnet tradition. But the sonnet is not limited to the expression of love: within the narrow limits of fourteen lines, it can attain an effect of epic majesty. It has produced masterpieces in many literatures. The great master of the modern sonnet was José Maria de Heredia.

Classical and neo-classical times recognized *genres* determined by their subject matter: the pastoral life inspired the *eclogue*, the *bucolic*, the *idyl* (a song of innocent love in rural or sylvan setting). The *elegy* is a plaintive poem, generally a meditation on death. The bridal poem or *epithalamion* is best exemplified by the *Song of Solomon* and Spenser's work. The *epistle* and the *satire* once were well established *genres;* they are now obsolete. The *descriptive* and the *philosophical* poems are justified only when they offer a lyrical quality.

The lyric remains fundamentally a song; as a rule, it implies earnestness, although the light lyric is not to be despised. In the highest lyric, two elements are blended: general reflections

on the problems of man's destiny, and a personal confession—
the *choric* and the *lyric* proper. The full dignity and power of
the lyric are attained when those two elements are inseparably
united, when the poet's heart and the universal soul throb in
unison.

CHAPTER XIII

SURVEY OF THE GENRES

II. THE EPIC OR NARRATIVE

A. TRUE EPIC AND ROMANCE

EPIC in Greek simply means a story; and German theorists are justified in using "epic" to denote any kind of narrative. However, the connotations of a word are not to be disregarded; if we applied the word "epic" to the compositions of Ring Lardner or P. G. Wodehouse, it would certainly be with humorous intent. The epic, in our minds, is inseparable from the idea of grandeur. The poem itself must have magnitude: it is the miracle of the sonnet that it can produce an epic impression in the brief compass of fourteen lines. Even in material facts, we excuse in the epic, we almost expect, an exaggeration which, in any other *genre*, would be ludicrous: this is particularly well marked in the enormous Hindu epic, the *Mahabharata*. But the gigantic is not invariably the great; and when we think of events or characters as "of epic scale," we have in mind something very different from sheer massiveness.

Of epic deeds, war is the most obvious example; and Voltaire was not wholly wrong when he described the epic as "a narrative in verse of warlike adventures." The majority of the epics in all literatures are tales of fighting. Fortunately, we are able to recognize greatness under other forms than slaughter. When James Truslow Adams called his history *The Epic of America*, he implied that the taming of a continent, the growth of democracy, the giant strides of science and industry, have a

231

nobility not inferior to ruthless massacre. The epic quality is manifest in certain religious poems, in Dante's *Commedia*, in Milton's *Paradise Regained* (we do not mention *Paradise Lost*, because the battle element is an impressive part of the narrative), in Klopstock's *Messiah*. However, our minds are still confused on this point. We are apt to think of Napoleon's Russian campaign as an "epic," although it was a masterpiece of futility and mismanagement, simply because of its martial nature, and of the very immensity of the disaster.

From this fundamental quality of *grandeur*, the first inference that may be drawn is that no man, purely as an individual, is the proper subject for a true epic. A hero does not tower very high above the average human stature: he becomes "epic" only when he represents something greater than himself—a nation, a race, a faith. In all true epics, the central interest is collective and symbolical, not purely biographical. The *Iliad* does not sing only the wrath of Achilles; it evokes the whole Trojan War, which, in the Homeric world, was an event of unique magnitude. The *Æneid* tells more than the wanderings of a pious exile: it opens an impressive prospect upon the destinies of imperial Rome. The *Song of Roland* is not the story of a rearguard skirmish, in which a willful commander paid the price for his pride and obstinacy: it is filled with crusading zeal, Christendom against Islam. This again is the essential subject of Tasso's *Jerusalem Delivered*. In the strictly religious epic, Dante's, Milton's, Klopstock's, the stake is nothing less than the eternal fate of the human soul.

Although this conception of epic grandeur is a commonplace, it leads to consequences which are not all in accord with literary tradition. The first is that the *Odyssey*, which we can hardly separate in our minds from the *Iliad*, is not a true epic. Ulysses does not stand for anything but his subtle, cunning, indomitable self. Very similar in externals to the sister poem, the *Odyssey* is a great romance of adventure. Between the true epic and the romance, the line should not be drawn with too heavy a hand. Many medieval poems hover between the two; and Tasso's *Jerusalem Delivered*, epic in structure, is full of romantic episodes, better remembered perhaps than the main theme.[1]

The second corollary is that history, and certain historical novels like Tolstoy's *War and Peace*, are unmistakably epic in character. The chief difference between history and the epic in the commonly accepted sense of the term lies in the form. The epic adopts certain devices established by the Homeric tradition, such as the use of verse, of invocations, of amply developed similes. But it is impossible to read certain passages from Thucydides, Livy, Bossuet, Gibbon, without being impressed by their truly epic majesty.

From this same conception of collective greatness, we may also conclude that it is legitimate to recognize the epic spirit in modern, even in realistic fiction, whenever more is at stake than the fate of the individual heroes. There is something truly epic about *Les Misérables*, quite apart from the sheer mass of that monumental narrative; there is a conflict of ideals, charity under both its Christian and its humanitarian forms at war against pharisaical heartlessness; and that conflict sways the destinies of innumerable men. Zola was a true epic poet, in *Germinal* for instance, one of the earliest and still one of the greatest of the proletarian novels; we forget the protagonists; we think of the miners as a class, and of all those who toil in squalor and despair.

It was one of the tenets of the neo-classic creed that the epic needed the supernatural; it was part of its "machinery," as

---

[1] The same reason explains why Napoleon has proved so disappointing as an epic theme. The events of his career are on an epic scale; his personality was not, because he never was fully identified with any cause greater than himself. He led the French, but he never was "France"; for he was not a Frenchman, and he loved his own glory better than the welfare of the country he ruled. He posed, after his downfall, as the champion of the Revolution—Democracy with a crown and a sword; but, so long as his power was expanding, he appealed to the conservatives as the man who had conquered Revolutionary nonsense and anarchy. The best epics on Napoleonic themes are those in which the Emperor's figure is dwarfed by the events—Tolstoy's *War and Peace*, Hardy's *The Dynasts*.

the French critics ingenuously put it. This "mechanical" belief, which at times led to ludicrous results, was founded to a large extent on the example of Homer and Vergil. Since they had used gods and goddesses, no genuine epic was conceivable without them; a narrative of great events, without supernatural intervention, could only be a slightly inferior *genre* called the *heroic poem*. But there is more in this idea than superstitious reverence for ancient models. A cause "greater than any individual man" easily assumes a superhuman character. Any ideal for which we are willing to fight and die becomes a god (and conversely, any god for whose sake we are not ready to suffer martyrdom is a mere name). All nations, as objects of worship, are in truth tribal deities, and the patriotic poem is a religious epic. There are other idols beside the nations: classes, parties, régimes, have assumed a place in our militant Valhalla. Nineteenth-century Frenchmen, shrewd and stodgy, could yet see with the eyes of faith the spirit of the Marseillaise hovering over the hosts of the Revolution; and the figure of Germania looms, barbaric and formidable, in the minds of learned and gentle Teutons. The people have not lost their power of creating myths; or, if you prefer, they have not outgrown their weakness for bowing to idols. Every collective conflict is in sooth a war of the gods; and all true epics sing heroes who are, not of the flesh, but of the spirit. The only difference between the proper and the artificial use of the supernatural lies in the intensity of the poet's own belief.

It would seem easy enough to separate the sheep from the goats: the genuine poet, for whom the supernatural world he describes is real, more real than the merely material, from the sophisticated epic-monger, who borrows or makes up a mythology, simply as a conventional device. But the distinction is not quite so obvious. The epic is a work of art, and in all art, we must repeat, there is an element of make-believe. The sincerity of Homer and Vergil remains a fascinating problem. We take it for granted that these poets were pious, in their own fashion; we can detect in them no Voltairian note of irony; yet the liberties that Homer took with the Olympians verge on irreverence; and Vergil's faith in his own mythology can scarcely have been literal. Dante, Milton, even the unknown author of the *Song of Roland*, earnest Christians though they were, could not help knowing that they were using their poetic imagination in sacred subjects, that they were relating with great solemnity things for which they had no scriptural warrant.

It was as a good Christian, not as a slavish follower of classic tradition, that Boileau refused to blend "the awful mysteries of our faith" with "pleasantly adorned fiction." We can easily guess what he would have thought of Camoens, who, in his *Lusiads*, had the gods and goddesses of Olympus guide or thwart the course of a modern Christian discoverer; who had Tethys describe the apostolate of St. Thomas in India; and who further complicated matters by introducing Adamastor, neither a legitimate Pagan, nor a Catholic in good standing. This *baroque* confusion is delightful, but thoroughly unconvincing. And Tasso is hardly less absurd.

Fairy lore, which does not command serious belief, is supernatural, but not epic; Edmund Spenser is the master of allegorical romance, a quasi-epic kind; he is not the companion of Dante and Milton.

Of all forms of the supernatural, the most dismal, no doubt, is a mythology of willful abstractions. Voltaire wanted to write an epic according to the approved recipe. He had sense enough not to drag in Mars and Venus to preside over the destiny of the shrewd and cheerful Gascon Henry of Navarre; he had taste enough, as an obedient disciple of Boileau, not to press the Trinity, the Virgin, the angels and the saints into active service. So he had to create such pale and tenuous characters as Truth, Discord, Politics, Fanaticism. Voltaire failed, and deserved to fail. Yet in our own century, Thomas Hardy introduced in his "Epic-Drama" *The Dynasts* a number of "Phantom Intelligences," the Ancient Spirit of the Years, the Spirit of the Pities, the Spirits Sinister and Ironic, the Spirit of Rumor, the Shade of the Earth, which are not more substantial than Voltaire's creations. But these ghostly presences have a weird and compelling life, and do not elicit a skeptical smile. Great as Voltaire was, his common sense and wit seldom attained the level of poetic inspiration; Hardy, a lesser man, possessed the miraculous power.

One last point about the definition of the epic: it must be a *poem*. To this we do not demur, provided it be remembered that verse and poetry are not synonymous. As we have noted, the great foreign epics, translated into English prose, do not lose their majesty; a novel in verse—the *genre* is still intermittently alive—does not *ipso facto* become an epic. We set little store by the French epics in poetical prose, a highly artificial product: Fénelon's pedagogical romance in the guise of a Vergilian pastiche, *Telemachus*, or Chateaubriand's vast, elaborate and indigestible *Martyrs*. But emotion and solemnity of thought are capable of raising prose above the level of mere discourse. There is a wingéd prose, as there is pedestrian verse. Even Zola could soar with heavy but powerful flight; the climax of *Germinal* has a somber impressiveness which can justly be defined as epic.

The epic appears in all major literatures; in most of them, it is among the earliest forms on record. In most of them also, those poems, even when they are crude, have retained singular vitality, and are accounted among the world's masterpieces: let it suffice to mention, by the side of the *Iliad* and the *Odyssey*, the Sanskrit *Ramayana* and *Mahabharata*, the *Nibelungenlied*, the *Song of Roland*, and *El Poema de Mio Cid*.

The early epic thus appears in an incomparable morning light; but its pre-history is exceedingly obscure. The very magnitude and the poetic value of these ancient works prove that they cannot be absolutely primitive. But the legends, tales, ballads which preceded them have vanished. In that obscurity, only guesses are permissible; but there is a strong temptation to turn a hypothesis into a doctrine, and a doctrine into an established fact.

We find in many critical and historical books such affirmations as the following: "The first epics took shape from the scattered work of various unknown poets. Through accretion these early episodes were gradually molded into a unified whole and an ordered sequence." This takes for granted the theory of "unconscious growth," which we already had the opportunity to challenge. We admit easily enough that no epic ever sprang full-armed from the brains of a single poet, with its whole universe of heroes, events, mythology and traditions. Homer did not create the Homeric world *ex nihilo*. Every work of art has its roots in the deep humus of reality. But this does not prove that, at the crucial moment, an act of deliberate artistic creation was not indispensable.

We may some day have a definitive masterpiece about Lincoln—whether it be called epic, history or biographical romance is not relevant to our present argument. This supreme Lincoln will have been prepared by innumerable half-successful works, interwoven with Lincoln folklore; but it will certainly not be an automatic agglutination of sayings, anecdotes, detached poems, chapters from earlier historians. A Lincoln hodge-podge will never turn of its own accord into a Lincoln saga. In the same way, no process of accretion could account for the grand unity of theme, development, character, spirit and style which we find in Homer. We might as well imagine that the Parthenon results from the chance conglomeration of rude cabins in the course of centuries.

The hypothesis of "gradual molding" may apply to the rank and truly jungle-like Hindu epic, the *Mahabharata*, in the huge and loose mass of which incongruous fragments may easily be discerned. It fails to apply to the *Iliad*, to the *Odyssey*, to the *Song of Roland*, to the *Poema de Mio Cid*, in which conscious artistic unity is manifest. In other cases, *Genesis*, the *Ramayana*, the *Nibelungenlied*, even *Beowulf*, several interpretations are possible. There are discrepancies and even contradictions which prove that, in their present form, these epics are not the finished and unified product of a single author. But they are far removed from chaos. They give the impression, not of spontaneous growth, but of definite *and mixed* authorship. To resume our comparison: they are not, like an old-world village, a mere conglomeration of huts; they are not, like the Parthenon, or St. Paul's in London, the working out of a single design, definite in structure, refined in every detail with the utmost degree of consciousness; they resemble rather a palace like the château of Blois, or like the Louvre, a church like St. John the Divine in New York, revealing the hand of successive architects. We have the literary equivalent of this in the medieval allegory, the *Romance of the Rose*, begun by Guillaume of Lorris, completed by Jean Clopinel, of Meung; or in the Holy Grail story, *Perceval*, which Chrétien of Troyes left unfinished, and which was continued by three other poets. These composite monuments in stone or words grew indeed; they never reached the point of complete subordination to a single, final plan; but at no moment was the growth unconscious.[1]

If we refuse to accept in all its rigor the "accretion and molding" theory, we shall have to question the time-honored distinction between the *folk-epic* and the *art-epic*. This distinction is really a fossil of romantic, or late eighteenth-century, criticism. We believe that the *Iliad* and the *Song of Roland* belong definitely to the art-epic. We surmise—but without proof—that even looser works such as the *Mahabharata* show the degradation and confusion of earlier art epics, rather than a mere collection of folk tales.

We are fully conscious that there is a great difference between the *Iliad* and the *Æneid*, and also between the *Æneid* and Voltaire's *Henriad*. But all three are "art" epic. To define this difference, we propose the term *original* epic and *deriva-*

---

[1] This process does not always imply the existence of several different artists. There are works by single authors which have never been fully integrated. This is the case with the first four books of Rabelais (the fifth is almost certainly not wholly his), with the two parts of Goethe's *Faust*, with Samuel Butler's *Erewhon*, in which various layers can easily be detected (*Erewhon Revisited* has much more unity), with Proust's *Remembrance of Things Past*.

tive, or *imitative*, epic. Both these terms require qualification. When we say that the *Iliad* is original, we do not mean that the Trojan War had not been sung before; there may even have existed epics on the subject, closely resembling Homer's. In the same way, we know for certain that Dante did not invent the theme, or even the framework, of his *Comedy*; visions of the other world existed in medieval as well as in classical literatures. What we mean is that, so far as we are aware, Homer and Dante were not consciously attempting to pastiche or rival an earlier poet, whereas such was the declared intention of Vergil and Voltaire. On the other hand, the words *derivative* and *imitative* should not be taken in a derogatory sense. Vergil's debt to Homer does not detract from his greatness as a poet. In style, at any rate, Milton's epic is "imitative." But if it be a pastiche, it is such an inspired pastiche that it fears no comparison with the greatest of original works. True originality lies neither in form nor in theme, but in the soul of the writer.

If there is a curse upon certain "artificial" epics, it is not because they are derivative, but because they are lifeless. This is best illustrated in classical French literature. For three centuries, the poets who aspired to be its official leaders formed the noble purpose of giving their country a national epic: Ronsard with his *Franciade*, Chapelain with his *Pucelle* (Maid of Orleans), Voltaire with his *Henriade*. Chapelain was a smooth and shrewd nonentity, but Ronsard was a genuine poet, and Voltaire the cleverest man of his time. All three failed utterly. The cause of their failure was that, imitating an imitator—for their model was Vergil rather than Homer—they borrowed the conventions, but not the spirit, of the *genre*. Nothing could expose the vanity of mere technique better than Voltaire's *Henriade*. Not one of the approved devices has been neglected. We have the invocation, the beginning *in medias res* (the earlier events being related afterwards by the hero himself), the use of the supernatural, the profuse description of combats, the prophetic vision of an illustrious line. The result was greatly admired by connoisseurs.

After three centuries of such resounding failures, the critics were forced to the conclusion that "the French had no head for the epic"; one of those decisive and delusive formulae which are a convenient substitute for thought. The nineteenth century proved them wrong. The epic revived, as soon as it was freed from the trammels of Greco-Roman convention. But it is hard to reverse critical momentum. Even today, we keep repeating that the age of the epic is over. Many Frenchmen, and the English-reading public almost to a man, still fail to realize that Victor Hugo is an epic writer of matchless originality and power. No philosopher in the technical sense of the term, he had a gift of apocalyptic vision which made him the companion of the Hebrew prophets. He could believe so intensely in the myths of his own creation that, for a moment, our own skepticism is stifled. His great trilogy, *The End of Satan, the Legend of the Centuries, God* [1] borrows from all civilizations and all mythologies, but resembles nothing hitherto attempted. It is not an anthology of pastiches: it is Hugolian throughout, and possesses a singleness of inspiration which turns the huge mass of fragments into a monstrous and living whole. The *genre*, which within the same generation [2] has produced *The Legend of the Centuries* and *The Dynasts*, is not the shadow of a shadow. The epic is rare today—rare as it has always been. But it still is a force and a promise.

The secret of epic grandeur lies in earnestness: solemnity without conviction is not impressive. So the genuine epic must be based on truth, historical and religious; and, from this point of view, the authentic stories of nations and great movements, as well as the sacred books of mankind, are the most legitimate forms of the epic. But the ideal of pure truth is seldom attained; the popular mind is uncritical; poets, in their fine frenzy, easily mistake for truth their more brilliant imaginings.

[1] *La Fin de Satan, La Légende des Siècles, Dieu.*
[2] *Legend of the Centuries*, I, 1859; II, 1877; III, 1883; *End of Satan, God*, 1886; *The Dynasts*, 1905.

An epic is not scientific history: it is history reconstructed so as to be most edifying or most effective. This subordination of "mere" fact to artistic law leads to what is known as the *legend*: a blend of myth and reality, which incorrigible romanticists tell us is more profoundly true than sober history. At any rate, the legend is far better known and far more persistent. The renown of Napoleon's invincibility survives the paltry fact that he lost six wars out of twelve; and we wonder whether anything will be remembered of General Pershing, except the famous words he did not utter: "Lafayette, we are here!"

So no epic is wholly true; probably not one was meant to be wholly true, and not one was accepted by all listeners as literal truth. There is in the minds of children, nations and even sophisticated readers a twilight zone, where fact and fiction are allowed to dwell side by side, in friendly and fascinating interplay.

However, in the true epic, which deals with vast collective movements, there is a massive core of historical reality, which the poet is not at liberty to alter at will. When the hero is an individual, not a tribe, a race or a religion, then the poet is not under the same restraint, and the result is *Romance*. This does not mean that, in particular cases, a romance may not be more authentic than an epic. But, in a general way, the aim of the epic is to present truth, even though embellished; the aim of romance is to offer pleasing fiction. Between the two extremes hover allegories and symbols, myths and legends.

It is obviously a very delicate task to disentagle these various elements. Scholars still dispute whether the Nordic poems, culminating in the *Nibelungenlied*, are to be interpreted as tragic fairy tales, that is to say as pure romance; as mythological narratives, confused statements of a dimly remembered faith; or as blurred and distorted versions of a great historical catastrophe—the downfall of the Burgundian kingdom. In the *Mahabharata*, it seems that those elements also commingle. We know for certain that the same people, at the same time, on the same theme, can evolve both history and fiction. If the *Song of Roland* is "straight" history (straight in spirit, although amplified and elaborated according to the rules of popular imagination), *The Pilgrimage of Charlemagne to Constantinople*, which is as early, is riotous and irreverent fancy.

In the Arthurian Cycle, there is no doubt that the element of romance predominates. It is a moot point whether Arthur, King of the Britons, ever existed as a historical character. Even if he did live in the flesh, nothing but his name had survived by the time the Breton stories arose. In his legend, the genuine epic element, the living memory of a national or religious hero, is negligible. What we are offered is a picture of individual prowess and individual passion, in a setting as fantastic as the events themselves. And the supernatural element in the Arthurian stories is not religious: as in the Oriental tales, as in folklore, it is founded on magic, not on spiritual faith; it is a mythology of fairies and enchanters, with their spells, their talismans, their potent philters. When this cycle reached definiteness with Chrétien of Troyes, it had no national and no religious significance; it was "pure sophistication," if we dare to couple these clashing words. It was only after Chrétien, with Robert of Boron and others, that the Breton cycle was linked, through the Holy Grail motive, with a religious ideal. This association came too late to become fully convincing. On all Grail stories, medieval as well as modern, rests the suspicion of insincerity. No one ever believed in them. The poet makes them up; he is *romancing*.

The romance, in its most ambitious form, closely resembles the epic in all externals. It is a long and dignified poem; it tells of kings, great lords and noble ladies; it loves to dwell on heroic combats; it is not averse to exaggeration; it makes liberal use of the supernatural. But it is only a quasi—or pseudo—epic: for it is willful make-believe.

It would seem then that the romance is a degenerate epic, delightful perhaps, but frivolous. We might compare it with the glamorous and futile pageant of chivalry, at the very close of the Middle Ages; while the epic reminds us of the ardent and stern crusading spirit of the eleventh century: *Deus vult!* This would not be strictly fair. The romance, by its very nature, is capable of reaching depths which are alien to the epic. In the true epic, love can hardly be more than an episode. The fate of races should not be swayed by personal sentiment. The man who, like Mark Antony, abandons his post for the woman he loves, forfeits his standing in history, and loses caste as an epic hero. Although the Trojan War was fought for the sake of a woman, we surmise that Helen was a mere pretext. In the *Iliad*, it was the wounded pride of Achilles, not thwarted passion, that sent him sulking under his tent. In the *Roland*, the insignificance of love in the grave contest for Christendom and empire is brought out starkly: fair Aude, Roland's bride, appears but a moment and dies. But, in the life of the individual, love is the great adventure, and Romance thus assumes its familiar meaning as a tale of passion. Already in the *Odyssey*, less purely epic than the *Iliad*, the Calypso episode is given greater importance than would be possible in the companion poem. In the *Æneid*, romance appears in the character of Dido —only to be defeated by the epic spirit which urges Æneas on to his appointed task. In Tasso's *Jerusalem Delivered*, an epic-romance hybrid, the part of Calypso and Dido is played by the enchantress Armida.

The greatest of "romances" is that of Tristan and Isolde. Not that antiquity had ignored fatal passion altogether: Sappho and the Elegiac poets cannot be accused of frigidity, and the tragic figures of Phaedra and Dido were not to be forgotten by the Western world. But never before had the theme of all-conquering love been treated with such directness. It was in a sense a discovery, comparable with the most revolutionary advances in science. The miracle is that the story established its supremacy without the assistance of a supreme poet. Thomas and Beroul, who wrote the earliest versions that survive, have no claim to genius; and the work of Gottfried of Strasbourg (ca. 1210) already has a decadent aura.[1]

The essence of the epic is *awe:* the awe that is inspired in us by the magnitude of an enterprise or of a catastrophe. The essence of romance is *wonder:* the delighted surprise at the discovery of strange lands, the unrolling of marvelous happenings, the miracle of love. Both are ancient, and both are eternal: for if mankind has always striven to preserve the memory of heroic deeds, it has no less constantly reveled in fairy lore.

As early as the twelfth century, with Chrétien of Troyes, the romance was already an urbane form of entertainment; it appealed to high society, and particularly to the ladies. These stories, as we have noted, still resembled the epic in form; but soon, either in meter, or turned into prose, they became frankly *romances of chivalry*. It was they which, two centuries later, were to fill the idle brains of Don Quixote with gorgeous and gigantic dreams. The romances of chivalry lost caste during the Classical Age; it was replaced by the conventional story of pastoral life, or by interminable pseudo-antique narratives; but it survived among the common people, often in barely recognizable form.[2]

---

[1] Among the innumerable Tristans that we now possess, we believe that Joseph Bédier's deserves first place, as the truest to the medieval origins of the tale. In spite of its composite character, the narrative offers perfect continuity and transparency: it is a masterpiece of inspired scholarship. Wagner's lyrical drama, for obvious reasons, stands apart.

[2] Before we abandon the epic and the romance of chivalry, mention should be made of their transposition into the comic key. Three main forms of this may be noted. Lowest of all is the *parody* (travesty or burlesque) in which a great theme is deliberately debased. If in some *genres*, the parody is a legitimate brand of criticism, and ridicules most effectively absurdities, pretensions and tricks of style, in the epic it is little short of sacrilegious, and its appeal is of a vulgar nature (e.g., Scarron: *L'Enéide Travestie*). There is of course an element of parody in the early epic, *The Pilgrimage of Charlemagne to Constantinople*, in Chaucer's *Sir Thopas*, in *Don Quixote*, in Samuel Butler's *Hudibras*, and in Voltaire's *Pucelle*.

In the *mock-heroic poem*, a trifling subject is treated with epic majesty: Homer was long credited with the *Batrachomyomachy*, or Combat of the Frogs and the Mice; Tassoni's *Stolen Bucket*, Boileau's *Lectern*, Pope's *Rape*

The romance was destined to enjoy a new and very active life, by blending with the rival *genre*, which we shall consider later, the novel. Historical fiction has almost invariably a romantic appeal; even when the facts it relates are scrupulously true, remoteness in time lends them a magic which they do not possess in themselves. A "knight-at-arms" represents a cruder and more prosaic stage of the killing business than an aviator, but we love the far-away sound of the name. Thus the painstaking Carthaginian scholarship of Gustave Flaubert in *Salammbo* is voted "romantic" simply because the subject is unfamiliar; and the sober narratives of Walter Scott acquire a glamor which lies neither in the characters nor in the style.

The spirit of romance even invades the chosen field of the novel, the description of contemporary every-day life. In a drab setting, amid commonplace happenings, we become aware of a strange glow which is emphatically not "realism," and probably not reality. When skillfully done, this mixing of kinds may be extremely pleasing. Examples are innumerable: we shall quote only two, because they are very well-known and widely different. One is *All Sorts and Conditions of Men*, by Walter Besant: a particularly wholesome tale of the London slums, with a practical purpose which the writer did achieve— the creation, in sodden and squalid Whitechapel, of a People's Palace. But with the realism and the sociology, we are offered

of the Lock, are the acknowledged masterpieces of this pleasing, but frankly minor kind.

Far more important is the *gay romance*. There heroes and themes are not degraded; but their humorous possibilities are exploited by a mocking yet poetic imagination. In its rich fancy, blithe spirit and artistic perfection, the gay romance expressed admirably certain aspects of the Italian Renaissance: the pagan joy of living in a world of freedom and beauty. Thus, in the hands of Pulci, Boiardo, and especially Ariosto (*Orlando Furioso*), the stern Roland saga became a delightful medley of fantastic adventures. Spenser's art owes not a little to Ariosto, although *The Faerie Queene* lacks, and perhaps eschews, the sprightliness and irresponsibility of the Italian poem. The atmosphere of Shakespeare's romantic comedies reminds us of Ariosto; and Byron had him in mind when he wrote his *Don Juan*. But *Don Juan*, with its labored archness and sedulous wickedness, is pedestrian by the side of *Orlando Furioso*.

a thin and pretty "romance," which we accept with a smile. The other is *Le Grand Meaulnes*, by Alain Fournier, a story of adolescence, with a haunting dreamlike quality.

But romance need not conceal itself under the cloak of the novel. It has continued an independent existence, which is still very vigorous today. Early in the eighteenth century, when the extravagant romances of a previous age were derided, and when, with De Foe and Lesage, realism was dawning in fiction, new paths of romance were being opened. One of these was the *Oriental*. In this, the translation of the *Arabian Nights* by Antoine Galland had a great influence. Oddly enough, in the atmosphere of the Enlightenment, the Oriental tale became philosophical. Eastern romance tinges, faintly, Montesquieu's satire, *The Persian Letters*, and Voltaire's string of apologues, *Zadig*. It tempted even Dr. Johnson, with *Rasselas*; it achieved an effect of horror with Beckford's *Vathek* (originally in French); it was to take lyrical as well as narrative form with the Romantic poets; and it was finally distilled, a perfect quintessence, into Coleridge's fragment of a vision, *Kubla Khan*.

But the East was not the only land of romance. The horizon widened so as to include the full magic of the exotic. There is exoticism already in Mrs. Afra Behn; and it was a rich vein of romance that Daniel De Foe, the master of minute realism, opened in his *Robinson Crusoe*. For what children seek in *Robinson Crusoe* is the same glamor of "Otherwhere" that gave excessive prestige to Bernardin de Saint-Pierre's *Paul and Virginia*, and to Chateaubriand's *Atala*. The *exotic romance* is in truth a magic casement, opening on the foam of perilous seas in faery lands forlorn. It is a genre of unexampled range. It appeals to the boyish mind, with Captain Mayne Reid,[1] Gustave Aymard, Jules Verne, "Ballantyne the Bold," Rider Haggard, Robert Louis Stevenson. It is elegiac with Pierre

---

[1] Fenimore Cooper, for us a historical novelist, the American Walter Scott, had in Europe the appeal of the exotic: a more sedate Mayne Reid. Cf. in German literature Charles Sealsfield.

Loti, imperially tough with Rudyard Kipling, somberly, oppressively subtle with Joseph Conrad, delightfully marketable (this implies no slur) with Somerset Maugham and Pierre Benoit. In Herman Melville's *Moby Dick*, the exotic appeal is heightened by spiritual significance and a diction which is not afraid of Elizabethan splendor; so that this unique book, which contains a very substantial and instructive report on the whaling industry, also ranks among the noblest of romances.

Another eighteenth-century contribution to romance was the *Gothic tale*. Its rise corresponded with the revived interest in medieval ballads and feudal ruins. Reveling in mystery and terror, with dark hints of the supernatural, it started as the thinnest of make-believe. *The Castle of Otranto*, by that ultrasophisticated wit and fop Horace Walpole, had almost a touch of conscious self-parody. The genre never acquired seriousness; its best representatives, Walpole himself, Mrs. Ann Radcliffe with her *Mysteries of Udolpho*, "Monk" Lewis, Maturin with his *Melmoth the Wanderer*, occupy but a modest place in literature; and their distant successors at the end of the nineteenth century frankly appealed—and with sensational success—to the most naïve of readers. At any rate, Miss Marie Corelli, in her *Sorrows of Satan*, worked on a grand, a truly cosmogonic scale; and Bram Stoker, in *Dracula*, extracted every possible thrill and shudder from the gruesome vampire theme.

But if the Gothic tale as a separate kind remained a very minor achievement, its influence upon kindred forms was surprisingly great. It deserves credit, indirectly, for inspiring delightful satires: the puzzling and spirited fantasies of Thomas Love Peacock, and, in milder vein, Jane Austen's *Northanger Abbey*. The Gothic tale may be considered as an early and rather crude form of the historical novel, and Sir Walter Scott generously acknowledged his indebtedness to Ann Radcliffe. There is a "Gothic" element in *Jane Eyre*, and especially in *Wuthering Heights*. The "Gothic" appears in the guise of grotesque and formidable monsters in several of Victor Hugo's novels and plays; the background of his very impressive epic drama, *The Burgraves*, is worthy of Ann Radcliffe herself. Balzac borrowed from Maturin his mysterious Melmoth, and daringly brought him into the realistic atmosphere of the Paris financial world.

In continental Romanticism, the tale of terror and the supernatural enjoyed an incredible vogue with the works of Amadeus Hoffmann—a fame now tarnished, but not altogether forgotten. With Edgar Poe, it forced its way at last into the artistic regions of literature. Poe has become the classic of that *genre*; and the adjective Poesque has frequently displaced both Hoffmannesque and Gothic in the critic's glossary. Baudelaire translated Poe, and there is a "Gothic" aspect to some of his *Flowers of Evil*. Oscar Wilde's *Picture of Dorian Gray* ends on a Gothic note. These are names which cannot be shrugged away. Yet, even if we made the list much more extensive, the reader would be justified in refusing to be impressed. After all, it is difficult to give high rank to a *genre* the sole purpose of which is to make our flesh creep. Under favorable circumstances, we may be willing to play the game, and pretend to take the Gothic tale tragically; but we firmly refuse to take it seriously.

In Mrs. Shelley's *Frankenstein*, the "supernatural" element of terror is of a pseudo-scientific nature: the creation by man of a soulless, yet pathetic, fiend. In the medieval mind, there was little difference between black magic and science: whoever sought to probe the mysteries of nature was suspected of having made a pact with the Devil. Traces of this superstition can still be detected; and so the scientific tale of mystery and horror has proved an attractive field, in a century whose mind lagged so far behind its material achievements. Poe's gruesome tale, *The Case of Mr. Valdemar*, is pseudo-science at its most horrific. Villiers de l'Isle-Adam, one of the forerunners of the symbolist school, used the formula in *Tribulat Bonhommet*. H. G. Wells, in the earlier stages of his career, was the acknowledged master of the "Scientific Gothic," not merely in a number of short stories, but in fairly long tales such as *The Invisible Man* and *The Island of Dr. Moreau.*

Of these pseudo-scientific nightmares, some are mere thrillers, like *Mr. Valdemar* and *The Invisible Man;* others, like *Frankenstein, Tribulat Bonhommet* and *The Island of Dr. Moreau,* have philosophical pretensions. For, like the Oriental tale in the eighteenth century, the scientific allegory may be used as a vehicle for thought. The danger of romance is frivolous make-believe; the curse of pure science is to be dry as dust; philosophy is venturesome, but laborious and austere. Combine the three, and the result, albeit absurd, may not be lacking in piquancy.

The *Philosophical Romance* is therefore a *genre* which, although exceptional, is well-recognized, and, although indefensible in theory, may in practice provide entertainment while promoting thought. It is probably the best method of introducing an unfamiliar truth, or paradox; and particularly those elaborate, systematic paradoxes which we call Utopias. This element is found in Plato, and it would be safer to consider his references to the Lost Atlantis as an adumbration of the scientific romance rather than as the objective reporting of a tradition.

The philosophical romance may be associated with the historical, the Oriental, the scientific; it blends particularly well with the exotic in the form of the Fantastic Voyage. It thus makes use of a desire immemorial in the human mind, and which inspired both the *Odyssey* and the *Oz* books: the dreams of strange countries beyond our horizon. This folklore theme received a new impetus, at the time of the Renaissance, from the epic of discovery: back of the solid lands ransacked by the Conquistadores shimmered fabulous hopes, the Fountain of Youth, El Dorado. To this "wild surmise," we owe, in part, Rabelais' *Pantagruel,* More's *Utopia,* Bacon's *New Atlantis,* Swift's *Gulliver,* Voltaire's *Candide,* Melville's *Mardi,* Butler's *Erewhon.* To the fantastic voyage in space was added the fantastic voyage in time: retrospective or prospective "Uchronias"—for William

Morris' *News from Nowhere* is in fact *News from Nowhen*; Bellamy's *Looking Backward*; the all-too-rich collection of Wells's satires and prophecies, the most artistic of which remains, in our opinion, one of the earliest, *The Time-Machine*; Anatole France's *On the White Stone* and *Penguin Island*; and Aldous Huxley's corrosive anticipation, *Brave New World*.

It will readily be seen that the fantastic philosophical romance, whether Utopian or Uchronian, is not invariably optimistic. It works out a hypothesis: not seldom the result is a satire and a warning. The optimistic Utopias, like Sir Thomas More's and Bellamy's, which have unduly monopolized the name, are apt to be a trifle insipid. Some at least of the satirical Utopias have the bitter tang of wisdom, made more palatable with an effervescence of wit and fancy.[1]

From the *Iliad* and the *Mahabharata* to H. G. Wells and Aldous Huxley, the range seems measureless. But in these narratives from all ages and climes, we find one element in common: a definite departure from everyday reality. The *epic* is based on truth; but upon exceptional truth, great and rare events of a collective nature; and in the clash of nations and faiths, it enrolls gods and spirits under warring banners. The *romance* is a tale of wonders: adventure, discovery, heroes and monsters, mysterious and overwhelming passion, the supernatural. It is now time to come back to earth, and pass in review those *genres* which elect for their domain "the humble truth." [2]

[1] *The Sleeper Awakes*, by H. G. Wells, for instance, is a dire prophecy of what would happen to the world, if capitalism and the Salvation Army were allowed to develop unhampered.

[2] An inverted form of the fantastic voyage is the Visit from Otherwhere: the contradictions and hypocrisies of our civilization, so familiar that we are not aware of their absurdities, exposed, with apparent naïveté, by a guest from a presumably saner world: from Persia, in Montesquieu's *Persian Letters*; from America, in Voltaire's *L'Ingénu* (*The Huron*); from Saturn and Sirius, in his *Micromegas*; from Altruria, as in the unassuming and very shrewd satires by William Dean Howells.

The mystery and detective stories, which have elements of Gothic romance, claim to be realistic, and will be treated under the novel.

SUMMARY

Although the word Epic has been applied to narrative in general, it is inseparable in our minds from the idea of *grandeur*. An epic deals with events on a large scale; and that is why most epics treat of war. But there are other epic subjects, particularly religion. An individual as such is no proper subject for the true epic; the interest must be collective: the fate of a race, a nation, a faith. The individual himself is but a symbol of the larger issue. According to this conception, the *Odyssey* is a romance of adventure rather than a true epic; the epic spirit is found in historical writing, and even in realistic fiction, when more is at stake than the personal fate of the heroes.

Classical tradition, after the models of Homer and Vergil, demanded the use of the supernatural. This was degraded into a mere convention, which turned the Gods into literary devices, or inspired the creation of lifeless allegorical figures; but the Supernatural, as the symbol of collective and spiritual issues, can still be effective, if the poet has faith in the myths he creates. Fairy lore, which is not seriously believed in, is not truly epic.

The epic is one of the earliest and grandest forms in all literatures. We refuse to accept the conventional distinction between *folk* epic and *art* epic: the *Iliad* and the *Song of Roland* are the products of conscious art. More real is the difference between *original* epics and *imitative* or *derivative* epics. The latter may have high merits, like the *Æneid*. But the imitation of imitations is likely to prove lifeless. Hence the failure of the French neo-classical epic for three centuries (Ronsard, Chapelain, Voltaire). Freed from artificial conventions, the epic revived: Hugo wrote a great epic in the second half of the nineteenth century, and Thomas Hardy in the twentieth (*The Dynasts*).

The aim of the epic is to present truth, even though truth be amplified or reconstructed so as to be most effective; the aim of the romance is to offer pleasing fiction; so, while the essence of the epic is *awe,* the very spirit of romance is *wonder.* In externals, the romance closely resembles the epic: a long, dignified poem, singing of great personages and heroic combats, and making liberal use of the supernatural. But it is only a pseudo-epic: the deep earnestness of the true epic is lacking.

In one respect, the romance is able to go deeper than the epic: it deals with love as the supreme adventure, whereas in the true epic, love plays only an episodic part. The greatest of romances is *Tristan and Isolde.*

The excesses of the romance spirit bring about an ironical reaction under three forms: the *parody,* the *mock-heroic poem,* the *gay romance* (Ariosto's *Orlando Furioso*).

The spirit of romance survives in historical and exotic fiction. It is found also in the *oriental tale,* often philosophical, a great favorite in the eighteenth century; in the *gothic* story of mystery and terror; in the *scientific* (or pseudo-scientific) *gothic,* from Mrs. Shelley's *Frankenstein* to the early works of H. G. Wells; in the various forms of *utopias.*

In both epic and romance, there is a deliberate departure from commonplace reality: the truth of the epic is exceptional, the romance is a tale of wonder, and both are freely mingled with supernatural elements.

CHAPTER XIV

SURVEY OF THE GENRES

II. THE EPIC OR NARRATIVE
(continued)

B. REALISTIC NARRATIVE: HISTORY AND THE NOVEL

OR SEVERAL generations, historians have repeated with aggressive humility the watchword of Leopold von Ranke: "to present things as they actually happened." Through some irony of fate, these words enjoining strict accuracy are quoted in a great variety of versions. The word *"eigentlich"*—*actually*—is the only one that occurs in all.[1] This word is the essence of *Realism* as we have defined it. Poetry spurns and transcends the actual. The epic magnifies and embellishes the truth; at times, soaring far beyond modest truth, it turns its themes into myths and legends. The romance tells of the exceptional, is not afraid of the fantastic, and rejoices in make-believe. History and the novel, on the contrary, strive to limit themselves, strictly, to the field of reality.

It may seem perverse to bracket together two genres apparently so antagonistic: the one devoted to the undeviating pursuit of factual truth, the other free to create at will characters and events. It sounds paradoxical only because, under the name of history, we understand at least three different things: the *field* of history, the *study* of history, the *writing* of history. The first is the sum total of past events, recorded or not. This,

---

[1] "Man hat der Historie das Amt, die Vergangenheit zu richten, die Mitwelt zum Nutzen zukunftiger Jahre zu belehren, beigemessen; so hoher Aemter unterwindet sich gegenwärtiger Versuch nicht: er will blos zeigen, wie es eigentlich gewesen." Ranke, *Geschichten der romanischen und germanischen Völker von 1494 bis 1514*, Vorrede (First edition, 1824).

of course, no man has any power to alter. What has been has been, irrevocably; it is the universal storehouse of experience from which historians and novelists alike have to draw. It is all-embracing, unselective, unwritten. It bears the same relation to history in the narrower sense as the earth in its fullness does to our geographies.

The second meaning is the process whereby facts, belonging to a pre-selected class, are gathered and tested. This is the task of the auxiliary sciences, epigraphy, paleography, numismatics, and all other methods of research. This is the *study* of history, or, if we might coin the term, *historiology*. It brings together a wealth of ascertained data; there its activity ends.

It belongs to history in the third sense to arrange these facts into an intelligible pattern. History is an effort to understand. So long as pure chaos prevails, so long as no rational sequence can be traced, we do not know "what actually happened"; we have merely a loose heap of documents, but no "history." This attempt at organization is historical *writing*. It does not exist until it is *composed*. It is this last kind of history alone that is a literary *genre:* Clio, the full-grown Muse. The others are but her material or her handmaidens.

Now the facts selected by the novelist are, as a rule, more accessible than those assembled by the historian. They might be found in the police records, in the newspapers, in current gossip, in the writer's own experience. But the novelist also will have to arrange his facts in such a way that they appear credible. Or he may reverse the process; he may start with a given character or situation; then he will have to deduce or evolve the facts that character or situation demand. In either case, his aim will be to establish a connection between factual reality and psychological reality; in homely language, to relate happenings so that they will make sense. And this describes exactly the task of the historian.

In defining history as an intelligible narrative, we are not limiting ourselves to the older type, which was purely biographical and dramatic. Just as a novel is the better for depicting a *milieu* in its complexity, so is history the richer for embracing more than political and military events. History should not ignore the earth trodden by its characters, the air they breathed, the food they ate, the dreams they nursed. There may be schematic history as there may be schematic fiction, reduced to a few essential lines; but it is possible also to strive for "integral" history, for "integral" fiction: the total reconstitution of life. Even that history which is exclusively concerned with anonymous trends, like the Industrial Revolution, or the rise of the proletariat, if it be history at all, dynamic and not static, is a *narrative*, and presents events in organic sequence.

History gathers, selects and interprets, but is not allowed to invent; the novel may seem the freer, and therefore the easier, game. This is by no means certain. Both history and fiction are at liberty to violate their own laws, but it is at their own peril: the laws are inexorable in both cases. A novel in which the author capriciously alters the terms of the problem is as faulty as a history which makes use of an uncertain fact or an unproved hypothesis. Yet there is nothing rigidly deterministic about history any more than there is about the novel: both are debarred from such absolute certainty, and freed from such thraldom, by the infinite complexity of events and motives. We shall never know beyond a doubt why Anna Karenina or the Emperor Justinian acted as they did on a particular occasion; we can only express our conviction that Tolstoy, or Gibbon, have offered so far the most plausible version of the events. That is why history can be, and must be, constantly rewritten; that is why the greater masterpieces of fiction can be, and must be, constantly reinterpreted. We have no absolute criterion of truth; we have to be satisfied with the semblance of truth, verisimilitude. The plain facts being granted, both history and fiction rank highest when they are most convincing. If history has to relate "incredible" facts—and there are careers in our own days far stranger than wild romance—it must be with the support of such overwhelming evidence that our doubt will be silenced. If the novel chooses to present an "incredible" character or an "incredible" situation, it must compel the reader to admit: "Impossible as it seems, yet it might be true." Epic and romance demand what Coleridge called "the unwilling suspension of disbelief": in order to enjoy *The Ancient Mariner*, we must be ready to play the poet's game. History and the novel, on the contrary, call for the full exercise of the critical spirit.

If, without departing from sober truth, history and the novel succeed in attaining the grandeur of the epic or the glamor of romance, we have no right to complain. We must remember that the real is not inevitably the mean, the dull, the trite, the trivial. Heroism, saintliness, passionate love, madness, are facts also, quite as authentic, although not quite so common, as selfish mediocrity. We firmly believe, for instance, that the glow of enthusiasm at the time of the French Revolution and at certain moments of the World War, was a psychological factor of the utmost importance. No sorry tale of brutality, deceit and greed will suffice to account for those great waves of hope, nor for the troughs of disenchantment that followed. But grandeur and glamor must appear of their own accord, as the inevitable splendor of truth. If they are sought for their own sake, without regard for factual reality, they are blemishes, and destroy the very condition of sound history and valid realistic fiction.

It is not our purpose to follow the course of historical writing through the centuries. We are only attempting to define its place in literature, and its paradoxical, but very close, affinities with the novel. In antiquity, the realistic narrative was represented chiefly by history. The ancients have left us epics and a few romances, but practically no novel. When we read the great historians of Greece and Rome as literature, the nature and the quality of our pleasure are the same as if we were reading fiction of the highest order. Much of it, we must confess, *is* fiction, and half-conscious of its fictional character. Herodotus, the delightful garrulous Father of History, openly enjoyed strange tales because of their very strangeness; and he hinted broadly enough that they were good stories, even if, perhaps, they were

not quite true. Livy, less ingenuous, told the mythical origins of Rome with consummate diplomacy: he neither exposed them as mere legends, nor committed himself fully to their authenticity; and we have seen that the orations with which his *Decades* are so liberally adorned are deliberate works of art. Thucydides and Tacitus, on the other hand, are uncompromising realists. They may distort the truth, for they are partisans; but they believe that the events they relate actually occurred, and that the interpretations they offer are reasonable.

The novelistic interest is even more evident among the minor historians. Xenophon's *Anabasis*, the record of a desperate adventure, is all the more thrilling for the extreme directness of the style: it rings true. Sallust was a "realist" in the narrower sense of the term: he enjoyed stories of turbid ambition, "damaged souls," corruption in high places: his Catiline is a Balzacian hero. Suetonius, in his *Lives of the Twelve Caesars*, tranquilly revels in atrocious scandal. So did Procopius, whose *Secret History* offers such a shameful contrast with his official writings. It would take very little editing to turn "history" of this type into a particularly lurid brand of "novel."

These indications must suffice. We could show, through innumerable examples, that historical works survive as literature only when they offer the qualities of a good novel: not a jumble of unrelated episodes, not a loose mob of indistinct figures flitting aimlessly across the stage, but living characters, a definite setting, events which progress with apparent inevitability, and, above all, some kind of perspective that will order the scene into an artistic whole. We do not mean that the historian and the novelist should attempt to explain everything, and that they should present life as exclusively the clear-cut conflict of definite thoughts and definite wills. Reality includes the vague and the chaotic. Historian and novelist must recognize the enormous part played in human destiny by such irrational elements as blind chance, blind passion, blind confusion. But pure chaos offers no picture, no story, no history. The drama of human destiny, collective or individual, is the struggle of some purpose against the forces of unreason. What we call the character of a man, the culture of a race, is their affirmation of existence, their organization against chaos. Man or race may be crushed in the contest with the blind powers, and remain greater in defeat than that which crushes them.

The literary nature of historical writing is best proved by the fact that, while scientists pursue their autonomous course, historians are swayed by the same fashions as artists, poets and fictionists. History was rational, lucid, urbane, ironical, with Voltaire and Gibbon, in the age of Enlightenment. It was glowing, picturesque, prophetic, with Carlyle and Michelet, in the romantic era. It became economic-minded, materialistic, harshly "positivist," with Buckle and Taine, when Realism was in the ascendant. In most cases, the change of spirit affected literature before it influenced history. Voltaire's great *Essay on Manners* was frankly an attempt to bring history, the laggard, into line with the thought of the time. The interest in the picturesque past manifested itself first in poetry and the arts, with Percy's *Reliques* and the Gothic revival. People began to enjoy the past before they had any accurate knowledge of the past: it was the moment of faked ruins and faked ancient poems, like Chatterton's and Macpherson's. Chateaubriand and Walter Scott had to precede Augustin Thierry, Michelet, Carlyle. Balzac gave an economic interpretation of society which paved the way for the Marxian economic interpretation of history. Zola wrote a great labor novel before France had a good history of the labor movement. William Blake discovered the Industrial Revolution and its "dark Satanic mills" many decades before the historians Arnold Toynbee and Paul Mantoux.

It is easy to understand why the novel should be the pathfinder for history. The novel is hypothetical history; it is, as Zola put it, "experimental." It is free, not to depart from the facts of life, but to arrange those facts into a new pattern. If the pattern is artistically successful, that is to say convincing, history will test it, and ultimately adopt it. Be sure that when we have a great school of fiction based, for instance, on abnormal psychology, we shall have soon after a school of "scientific history" exactly on the same lines.

There are many kinds of historical writings. The most complex is the *history of civilization*, which might be called historical sociology, and which claims to be all-embracing. Voltaire, in his *Century of Louis XIV*, included not only the story of the king and of the Court, not only wars and treaties, but religion, the arts, the sciences, the crafts, and—this was two hundred years ago—even economic conditions. A splendid attempt and a great achievement; yet it cannot be pronounced an unqualified success. Its shortcomings from the artistic and from the scientific standpoints are due to the same cause: the innumerable activities described by Voltaire are not fully integrated in his own mind. When we lose sight of the king's imperious figure, the various chapters have a tendency to fall apart, like unrelated articles in an Encyclopedia. This is a difficulty which the history of civilization has never been able to overcome, even when it is limited, as in this case, to a single country and the lifetime of a single ruler.

The remedy for this looseness is provided by *philosophical history*, which reduces the evolution of mankind to the development of one central idea: providence, liberty, nationalism, economic interests, or race. Bossuet, Hegel, Karl Marx, Houston Stuart Chamberlain, are among the masters of this very impressive *genre*. It has the appeal of intellectual unity, and it marshals the events with epic grandeur. The *Discourse on Universal History*, by Bossuet, has the sovereign majesty that arises from the certitude of unveiling the plans of God Himself. The danger of this kind of history is that it orders the march of mankind a little too autocratically: mankind in its painful and erratic course has never shown any evidence of being guided by a definite principle. Swarms of objections will rise in the realistic and critical mind while Bossuet or his modern rivals expound their magnificent schemes.

In the standard kind of history, pure *narrative* predominates: the swift or slow-moving march of events, accompanied perhaps, but not hampered, by descriptions and reflections. The drawback, in this case, is that events capable of being related in clear and telling sequence, almost inevitably mean *dramatic* events. Narrative history is tempted, and perhaps compelled, to neglect age-long, unobvious, almost imperceptible changes. It must deal with striking personalities, great crises, decisive contests. We need hardly say that, the more dramatic the narrative, the greater its popular appeal. Not merely in books, but in actual politics, we love to be entertained by colorful and exciting scenes. The wisest and most efficient régime is doomed, if it allows the country to be bored; the most reckless adventurer will have his chance, if he knows how to dramatize himself and the people whom he leads. In the deeper sense of the term, we need far more "realism" than we have at present in our historical thinking; more of the humble truth, less of dazzling make-believe.

Narrative history, with its tendency to the dramatic, is associated with the *biographical;* as a rule, events are never so striking as when they are focused in the career of individuals. The French Revolution, enormously greater than any of its protagonists, hero or victim, has been for that reason something of a puzzle and a scandal. We are constantly attempting to reinterpret it in terms of outstanding personalities: Mirabeau, Lafayette, Danton, Marat, Robespierre, and even Marie Antoinette: all frail vessels tossed for a moment on the angry flood. According to that view, ideas are but shadows, common men are lost anonymously in the herd: the born king of men is God's chosen instrument. This is a theory as ancient as history itself, although it was most clearly expressed in the nineteenth century, by Carlyle in *Heroes and Hero-Worship,* by Napoleon III in the famous Preface to his *Life of Caesar.* On the other side stands Tolstoy, who, in *War and Peace,* denies that Napoleon's will could in any way deflect the course of history. For very different reasons, the sociological historians agree with the Russian apostle. The essential realities, in their opinion, are collective and anonymous; every apparent leader is but a symptom or a symbol.

Between history on a biographical basis, and pure *biography,* the only difference is a slight shift of emphasis: in the hero, we seek the man. The result is not seldom disappointing. Between career, station, prestige, on the one hand, and the limitations, the pettinesses, the frailties, the ailments of the individual on the other, there may be a cruel contrast. No man is a hero to his valet. That is why so many "intimate" biographies have an ironical touch, which was not invented by Lytton Strachey. It will be felt—a barely perceptible tang—even in Joinville's *Life of St. Louis,* which is a piece of hagiography, a detached chapter of the Golden Legend. Saint-Simon's portrait of Louis XIV is damaging; and, in spite of his whole-souled devotion to his hero, Boswell frequently presents Dr. Johnson in a ludicrous light.

This greatest of English biographies is devoted to a man who belongs to the annals of literature, not of politics. Still, it must be considered as a masterly contribution to historical writing. Any truthful reconstitution of the past is history. Much *literary criticism* is primarily biographical. We first seek to explain the works in terms of the author's life; then the interest shifts, the growth and struggles of a human being become the chief subject, and his books are mentioned merely as milestones in the author's progress. This was definitely the case with Sainte-Beuve, who is acknowledged as the prince of critics, and who is, far more evidently, a psychological biographer; he gave us, for instance, a searching portrait of Stendhal the man, and failed to realize the greatness of Stendhal the novelist. Many of his essays are devoted to men who were not prominent as writers. The complementary works of Van Wyck Brooks and Bernard de Voto on Mark Twain may be labeled "criticism," for they have a definite bearing on literary interpretation; but they are first of all attempts to understand the man Samuel Clemens, and, through him, his America.

The biographical *genre* obviously included the *autobiograph-*

ical; and with it, all the contributions that a man may offer to the history of his time, in the form of memoirs, souvenirs, diaries, notebooks and correspondence. All these are not formal history; but they are, unmistakably, historical documents. With them we pass, by imperceptible degrees, from history proper to something much more obviously akin to the novel. History is supposed to deal with vast entities—nations, races, classes, parties—and with individuals only when they are the spokesmen of a group—the larger the group, the more "historical." But there are so many doubtful cases that the very definition becomes doubtful. When a Caesar writes his *Commentaries,* it is of course history of the most approved kind. The *Memoirs* of Chateaubriand, on the other hand, will be placed on the literary shelves. The man was no mere witness, but a prominent actor in many events of national and European importance; yet, even when he was restoring in France the altar and the throne, or when he was reconquering Spain for her king (he earnestly believed he had achieved all these things), he remained René, the incurable dreamer, the arch egotist, the romantic poet. The *Confessions* of Rousseau relate the life of a man who never filled even the humblest of official functions; his love affairs, his petty quarrels, his ailments and turpitudes, seem to have little to do with the fate of empires. But the thought of that man is supposed to have shaken society to its foundations; and the boldest, the most paradoxical, of his doctrines—the innate goodness of the natural man—can best be discussed in terms of his own experience. In the world of the spirit, the issue whether Jean Jacques Rousseau was an inspired prophet or an addle-pated bohemian is of commanding significance; and the proper battleground to fight it out is Rousseau's *Confessions.* The melancholy of Amiel's *Journal* is not the wearisome sighing of a middle-aged Genevan professor; it is a document on one of the great revolutions in human thought, the advent of a scientific spirit too tough for his gentle culture. Every personal document is at least a potential footnote to history.

This is true also of private correspondences. The letters of

Cicero and Voltaire obviously throw a sharper light on their times than many a learned tome. Madame de Sévigné, Lord Chesterfield, Horace Walpole, were not aggressive leaders in politics or philosophy, like Cicero or Voltaire; but they were excellent representatives of their class, and shrewd observers of aristocratic life. The letters of the Paston family are a veritable treasure for the student of English life in the fifteenth century. If the aim of History is "merely to show how it actually happened," this unquestionably belongs to history.

Another genre verges on the historical, because of its autobiographical elements: the personal, self-revelatory *essay* created by Montaigne. His *Essays* are fragmentary memoirs. They give us the portrait of a shrewd and sturdy character, breathing, chatting, smiling before us, with a triple background of extraordinary vividness: first of all, the ease and sober elegance of his household; then, a rich library of ancient wisdom; and beyond, seldom mentioned but never forgotten, the fury of fanaticism, bloodshed, destruction and raging hate, in the name of goodness and truth. Montaigne is a living voice, and perhaps the one that we most need to hear.[1]

By a *novel*, we understand a narrative which does not, like history, claim to embody literal truth, but which seeks to

[1] All *scientific writing* that has any claim to be called literature, anything that is not an impersonal string of facts and formulae, has in it a narrative, and frequently a biographical element. If certain *philosophers* like Pascal, Schopenhauer and Nietzsche count in literature, while others, at least as great, like Spinoza and Hegel, do not, it is not on account of mere tricks of style; it is because the former convey to the reader the drama of their quest, and give him a spiritual self-portrait on a background of doctrines.

It is plain that *journalism* is—or should be—historical writing. Reporting is realistic narrative, convincing and factually true. Victor Hugo's *Choses Vues* (*Things I have seen*) is a masterpiece of journalistic style, terse, vivid, unadorned, easily rising to the level of history. Political journalism should be a judgment upon contemporary issues, and therefore a contribution to history. Burke's *Reflections on the French Revolution* may be considered as an interminable leading article against radicalism.

Impressionistic Criticism, as practiced by Anatole France, is an extension of the personal essay. For him, criticism was "the adventures of a sensitive soul amid masterpieces," that is to say, a form of spiritual biography.

produce the impression, the complete illusion, of reality. In this respect, it differs from the other form of fiction, the romance; even when the facts used by the romancer happen to be authentic, the aim of the artist is to create in us a sense of wonder. The novelist, on the contrary, does not expect his reader to exclaim: "How marvelous!" but "How true!"

The novel is at present, and has been for generations, the leading *genre* in Western literature. It outsells both romance and biography, its closest competitors. This success is not of a purely financial and popular nature. In all countries, novelists will be mentioned among the greatest of literary men, in no way inferior to poets and dramatists. In nineteenth-century Russia, Gogol, Dostoevsky, Turgenev, Tolstoy, outranked all other writers. In France, Balzac, Flaubert, Zola, yielded to none of their contemporaries. So complete is this supremacy of the novel that some effort is needed to realize that it is extremely recent. In a literary tradition of some twenty-five centuries, the prestige now enjoyed by the novel goes back barely two hundred years. In the seventeenth century, the novel as a major kind could hardly be said to exist. In the first half of the eighteenth, it suddenly achieved greatness in England, but not yet full recognition. We doubt whether many of the best judges would have prophesied, by 1750, that De Foe, Richardson, Fielding, would be counted among the greatest writers of their age.

This late development, however, can easily be explained. The novel, which seems to us the most natural, the most accessible of all the *genres*, is in fact the most paradoxical. "Realistic fiction" is a contradiction in terms. If we want to know and preserve the truth, let it be the truth. If we want to give our imagination a feast, if we yearn to escape from the commonplaceness of our daily life, let it be through a bold flight into the land of Faerie. Even today, this objection is valid, at least against certain thorough-going forms of realistic fiction. Why should we care to meet, in the pages of a book, those very people whom, in real life, we find so insufferably tedious? It is the most absurd kind of a busman's holiday.

The origin of realistic fiction, we believe, is to be found in a reaction against the excesses of romance; and in a parallel reaction against the prestige of a class whose tastes and mode of life were associated with romance. In other words, realistic fiction is the product of the *bourgeois* spirit, as opposed both to the aristocratic and to the popular mind. It had its vigorous beginning in that period of the Middle Ages when the bourgeoisie was rising. It suffered an eclipse when, for two centuries, literature became learned and aristocratic. The prestige it now enjoys began with the accession to power of the commercial class in England. If there is any substance in this hypothesis, the manifest decline of the bourgeois class may involve the decadence of this eminently bourgeois art. Neither the élites nor the masses rejoice in realistic fiction.

The realism of the Middle Ages had in it an element of parody and satire. It was the revenge of common sense against the absurd pretensions of heroes, saints and lovers. Long before Pascal, it adopted as a guiding principle: "Whoever tries to play the angel makes an ass of himself." So the stock characters in the mocking tales or *Fabliaux* are the bragging and stupid fighter, the lecherous monk, the unfaithful wife; and the favorite is the clever rogue, a human Reynard the Fox. We have already noted that this element of parody was found as early as the *Song of Roland*, in the *Pilgrimage of Charlemagne to Constantinople*; and we have indicated that at times there was an abrupt change in the trend of the work: the second part of the *Romance of the Rose* is as "realistic" in spirit as the first was daintily allegorical; *Le Petit Johan de Saintré* begins as a refined tale of courtly love, and ends in merry cynicism; Chaucer tags an ironical Envoy to his sentimental tale of Griselda's patience.

But this cynical strain is not the only element in medieval realism. A totally different one is found in those very romances of chivalry which seem to be poles asunder from anything so vulgar as reality. It is a strain of accurate and subtle psychology, especially in the discussion of love. The heroes of the old epic were rough-hewn: Chrétien of Troyes was writing for delicate ladies, who were curiously expert in matters of the heart. Fantastic as the setting and the adventures might be, the sentiments of the heroes were analyzed with surprising precision; and Chrétien was called a Paul Bourget (we might say a Henry James) of the twelfth century.

The two strains are combined in Boccaccio, a hybrid in many senses, a Parisian and a Florentine, a bourgeois and a humanist. In his *Decameron,* we find the fundamental cynicism of the medieval *fabliaux:* a laxity which is a reaction against the exalted conception of love symbolized by Dante's Beatrice and Petrarch's Laura. Many of his hundred tales are the broadest kind of *fabliaux* in more artistic form: it is this element that gives the *Decameron* its equivocal renown. But Boccaccio was very different from a medieval bourgeois. The scene, the tone, the style, of his tales are aristocratic. The free enjoyment of life is not purely a rebellion against Christian asceticism or chivalric purity: it goes beyond them and ignores their very existence. It is already tinged with the rich glow of Renaissance paganism. Boccaccio is one of the fountainheads of European art; far from pure, we must concede, but perennial. A study of his themes and forms through the centuries, from Chaucer to Anatole France and James Branch Cabell, would be a very long chapter in comparative literature.

With the Renaissance, a more purely aristocratic art prevailed; the revival of learning created an abyss between the poets and the masses; and the great Courts attained a degree of magnificence and sophistication which the commoners could not match. Then the sonnet sequence, the artificial pastoral, the Arcadian romance, the long allegory, held sway. But if the bourgeois spirit receded, it did not altogether disappear. It survived in Rabelais: a strange medley of folklore and humanism, his work shows many traces of the old *fabliaux.* But there is no sardonic leer in Rabelais: his laughter rings with the joy that goes with immense hope. His obscenities are not meant to humiliate human nature: they only signify the full acceptance of life. So Rabelais is the representative of a realism all his own, more earnest than the medieval, more serene than the modern. Rabelais was read through the Classical Age, even by those who affected to despise in him "the delight of the *canaille.*" Thanks to him, the realistic tradition suffered no complete interruption. It was partly through Rabelais, partly through the popular farces and tales, that the spirit of bourgeois realism was transmitted to Molière.

There were a few realistic novels in seventeenth-century France, Scarron's *Roman Comique,* Sorel's *Francion;* they are still readable, but they count for very little. At that time, it was through the drama, not through prose fiction, that the growing spirit of the bourgeoisie reasserted itself. So Molière, who never wrote a novel, is a necessary link in the development which, a few decades after his death, was to produce the modern novel. With the support of Louis XIV himself, Molière made fun of aristocratic coxcombs and denounced aristocratic sharpers; he attacked all forms of sophistication and hypocrisy, in religion, culture and love. The ladies who so elaborately mapped out "the country of Tenderness" were laughed at for their absurd refinement; the once honored term *Précieuses* remained branded with ridicule. Molière is the master of gaiety; but he faced, without flinching, characters and situations that were no laughing matter. If you could imagine *The Miser, The Would-be Gentleman,* parts of *Don Juan, Georges Dandin, The Imaginary Invalid,* in narrative form, the result would resemble the work of Balzac.

Realistic fiction is woven of many strands. We have followed, up to the close of the seventeenth century, the French tradition of bourgeois satire. We must now return, and pick up the Spanish thread; for it was in Spain that long realistic fiction found its earliest and most vigorous development. It took a form which, even more frankly than in France, was the parody of romance; perhaps because nowhere else had the romantic virtues been more ardently extolled, or the romantic stories, such as *Amadis of Gaul*, reached a higher degree of favor and extravagance. For the "quest" of the Arthurian Knight was substituted the highway adventures of the *picaro*, or rogue; for the lady of exalted renown, the easy wench and the bawd; for the baronial keep, the inn which is also a thieves' den. So the story rambled on, still half-romance in the profusion and high color of its episodes, but suffering an earth-change into the mock-heroic, the cynical and the sordid. It is curious to note how the same reaction against high-flown romance brought about, within the same half-century, such radically different works as the poetic *Orlando Furioso* in Italy, the coarse, merry and humanistic *Gargantua* and *Pantagruel* in France, and *Lazarillo de Tormes* in Spain.

Already *La Celestina*, that strange novel in dramatic form, had presented many of the characteristics of the picaresque; but *Lazarillo* became the standard of the *genre*; *Guzman de Alfarache*, by Alemán, one of its most successful products; and finally, the Spanish picaresque attained one of the summits of literature with *Don Quixote*. Cervantes had given brief masterpieces of realistic fiction in his *Novelas Ejemplares*; with *Don Quixote*, he worked on the epic scale. Here the element of parody and satire, which we consider as the main origin of realism, is manifest; it is the romance to end all romances, or, as La Bruyère rather unjustly put it, "the one good book the Spaniards have, showing up the absurdity of all the rest." It marked the end of extravagance; but also the passing of a magnificent dream. The glamor of the chivalric Middle Ages was over, and the first splendor of the Renaissance had waned. The epic of the reconquest, the epic of discovery, had ended; the knight-errantry of Spain, as crusader, missionary, sword of the Catholic Church, was finished, to be followed by two centuries of slow decay. Just at the moment when Don Quixote was waking up to soberness and death, Prospero was abjuring his magic, breaking his staff, drowning his book—not without a sigh.

The influence of the picaresque was immense and prolonged. It gave its form to the first masterpiece of pure realistic fiction in France, Lesage's *Gil Blas*. Lesage offered in his comedy *Turcaret* a cruel and strikingly modern picture of the rising financial power; he might therefore have been expected to depict contemporary life in strictly contemporary terms. But the picaresque tradition was too strong; and this masterpiece of direct observation, which still affords delightful reading, appeared in the guise of a Spanish novel. So successful was the pastiche that, for generations, scholars ransacked Spanish literature in the hope of finding Lesage's original. Certain it is that, translated by Padre Isla, *Gil Blas* became at once a Spanish classic. A striking confirmation of the European, as opposed to the purely national, conception of literature: when human nature is accurately described, *"il n'y a plus de Pyrénées,"* the Pyrenees cease to divide.

De Foe's *Moll Flanders* is most decidedly a tale of roguery, with a female of the species as the central character. Smollett translated *Gil Blas*, acknowledged his indebtedness to Lesage, and followed in his own works the picaresque pattern. But the highest claim of the picaresque is to have affected Fielding himself. *The Life of Mr. Jonathan Wild the Great* is the perfection of the mock-heroic; the high deeds of a jailbird are told with a sustained irony worthy of Swift; it is a "Newgate epic" in the same way as Gay's famous *Beggar's Opera* is a "Newgate pastoral." In *Joseph Andrews*, the starting point, as is so often the case with realistic fiction, was a parody: a satire on Richardson's *Pamela*; and the work professed to be written "in imitation of the manner of Cervantes." *Tom Jones* itself retains a strong element of the picaresque; rogues are not lacking in that great gallery of characters; many of the adventures take place on the road. But Fielding, like Cervantes, transcends the picaresque; he has freed himself from the tyranny of cynicism; there is in his work a large and warm naturalness which reminds us, not of *Lazarillo*, but of *Pantagruel*.

It may be said that, in spite of its fantastic elements, Voltaire's *Candide* is a picaresque novel in miniature. In the nineteenth century, Gogol's *Dead Souls*, belying its somber title, is in fact a model of the picaresque: a swindler as the hero, a constantly shifting scene, and a satirical purpose. But, in most writers, these three elements became dissociated. *The Pickwick Papers* and J. B. Priestley's *Good Companions* have been called picaresque because they were stories of the road; but they are the reverse of cynical. The pure novel of roguery, told with ironical seriousness, did not disappear: Thackeray's *Barry Lyndon* is a good model of the kind. O. Henry might have turned into a great picaresque novelist, if he had not been swallowed up by his journalistic success as a writer of clever, slangy, trickily twisted stories. Prostitutes, thieves and criminals appear abundantly in modern fiction; but they are seldom treated with the light cynicism which is characteristic of the true picaresque.

Although the picaresque produced masterpieces, it was not destined—fortunately—to remain the principal form of realistic fiction. Three other elements had to be added, or at least developed to their fullest capacity, before the novel could become the leading form in modern literature.

The first of these was *psychological depth*. Not that character study was absent from the best of the picaresque stories, and particularly *Don Quixote*. But it was too frequently subordinated to the teeming incidents; many of the personages were as conventional as in medieval farce or Italian comedy; and the traditional tone of cynical humor stifled any subtle study of motive. A sneer, which so many still consider as the badge of "realism," denotes a failure to understand. The novel, still crude, had to go to school under those great investigators of human conduct, the French "Moralistes," La Rochefoucauld, Pascal, La Bruyère, and their peers in the drama, Molière and Racine. The age of Louis XIV was qualified to write great "realistic" novels; it was debarred from that achievement because the artificial romance still held the field, and because "realism," in the form of the picaresque, was too low for the dignified taste of that periwigged society. What French classicism might have yielded is indicated by a miraculous little book, *La Princesse de Clèves*, by Madame de Lafayette. The scene is laid in aristocratic circles, not for the sake of glamor, but because such a *milieu* was perfectly familiar to the authoress. The action takes place a hundred years before the time of writing; but there is no attempt at romantic picturesqueness. The sentiments are lofty, but never unnatural. We are not overwhelmed: we seek to understand. It is realism in its purest form, not only credible, but convincing.

Marivaux, as a playwright, was a master of sophisticated analysis. He "weighed airy nothings on gossamer scales"; as the psychologist of love, he was called a Racine in Dresden china. In this he continued an immemorial tradition, that of Chrétien of Troyes and of the Précieuses; but every element of improbable romance had been purged away. The setting of Marivaux's plays may be fanciful, and even fantastic: there is, in some of his comedies, a poetic atmosphere that reminds us, distantly, of *Midsummer Night's Dream* and of *The Tempest;* but even in that land of unreality, the sentiments are true to life, and their delineation extremely accurate. Now Marivaux turned his subtlety to account in his long novel *Marianne* (1731-41). It has repeatedly been asserted that Marianne inspired Richardson's *Pamela* (1740-42); at any rate, there are between the two striking resemblances in theme and treatment. Both France and England were ready at the same time for heroines of flesh and blood, neither absurdly ethereal, nor farcically gross.

A man whose life was a picaresque romance, Abbé Prévost, Jesuit, soldier, Benedictine, hackwriter and exile, left a huge mass of undistinguished fiction, original or translated, and one little work of inestimable price, *Manon Lescaut*. This very brief novel has still more than a touch of the picaresque, but simplified and toned down so as to convey the impression of immediate reality. The glory of *Manon Lescaut*, however, is not the subdued realism of plot and style: it is the picture, pathetic and pitiless, of irresistible love. In this short tale of a prostitute and a weakling, we feel the same formidable presence as in *Tristan* or as in Racine's *Phèdre*.

This leads us to the second of the new elements in realistic fiction: the element of *earnestness*. Hitherto, born of parody and satire, the novel had retained a strong tinge of the comic. Chaucer, Boccaccio, Rabelais, Cervantes, Lesage, De Foe, are among those writers whose first aim is to amuse; and this was to remain true of Smollett and even of Fielding. When they have a serious purpose, it comes in almost surreptitiously. *Manon Lescaut*, on the contrary, is frankly a tragedy. It opens a long line of psychological narrative without a trace of frivolousness: the fictionist is a medical observer or a confessor rather than a jester. This is the kind that was illustrated by Benjamin Constant in his *Adolphe*, by Stendhal in *The Red and the Black*, by Tolstoy in *The Kreutzer Sonata*. It was to lead to Paul Bourget, André Gide and Marcel Proust: Swann's passion for Odette is as irresistible and as tragic as the love of Des Grieux for Manon.

This elimination of the comic from realistic fiction was aided by a vast social change: the rise of the bourgeoisie to conscious predominance. In the eighteenth century, for the first time, the middle class insisted upon being taken *seriously*. Hitherto, the dignity of tragedy had been reserved for the well-born. In Molière—a bourgeois himself, and proud of his class—the bourgeois could only be funny: even when he cursed a rebellious son, even when his death was eagerly awaited by his wife, and most of all when he was betrayed. Before the reign of Louis XIV was over, the futility of the aristocracy had been made manifest, and economic realities, concentrated in the form of money power, had begun to assert themselves: the financier Samuel Bernard had compelled the king to honor him, in front of the silently raging courtiers. In the same way, the bourgeoisie compelled literature to recognize that a human being who was not a parasite could have passions, and suffer deeply. This revolution was more sharply marked on the stage, but it was more profoundly felt in the novel. Marianne and Pamela are heroines of the new type: neither fanciful Clelias, nor abandoned Moll Flanders. They are poor, virtuous and shrewd; they play their cards well enough to save their innocence and win their reward; they are perfect little bourgeoises. From that moment, class privilege was abolished in literature. There have been aristocratic heroines in the fiction of the last two centuries: we do not grudge Henry James his fondness for Mayfair. But in art, a title is no longer an advantage. We are fully as interested in the fate of Emma Bovary as in that of Madame de Guermantes. This breaking down of conventional barriers was one of the conditions of genuine realism.

The greater seriousness of the novel was accompanied by a new earnestness in moral tone; this also, particularly in England, was the contribution of the bourgeoisie. The picaresque had been the reverse of edifying: on the contrary, Richardson was a professor of virtue. His fiction is pervaded by a moral sense which we may find a trifle ambiguous in Pamela, insufferably artificial in Sir Charles Grandison, but not without power in Clarissa. It was the fame of Richardson that induced Rousseau to write his *Julie, or the New Heloise,* in the clumsy epistolary form that the English printer had made popular. Rousseau still asserted, theoretically, that the novel was an instrument of perdition; in practice, he turned it into a very effective vehicle for religious and moral propaganda. Now this may be the reverse of *realism:* but it marked the final ascent of the novel to supremacy. It is probable that Richardson was a better novelist than Rousseau; but Rousseau was the greater artist; and, especially, he had already achieved fame as a moralist, a reformer, a prophet, before he wrote *Julie.* Henceforth, no serious writer need feel ashamed for writing prose fiction; the last stigma of moral inferiority, as compared with the epic or with tragedy, had been removed from the *genre.* Rousseau heralded that blend of realism and social purpose that we find in Dickens, George Eliot, Tolstoy, Hugo, Zola, Hemingway, Steinbeck. Without it, the novel would lack a supreme touch of dignity.

The third element that was needed to complete our conception of realistic fiction is extreme *definiteness and accuracy in material details*. The French classical tragedy too often had for its setting "a hall in a palace": such vagueness will no longer do. We want the atmosphere of the place, even if, as in Balzac's *Father Goriot*, it involves an analysis of "the boarding-house odor." Definiteness and accuracy were not absent from the picaresque; but, like character analysis, they had not been emphasized. They were not prominent either in the best psychological novels, such as *La Princesse de Clèves* and *Manon Lescaut*. They existed, minute and faultless, in that incomparable reporter Daniel De Foe: but the importance of his contribution was not fully realized for many generations. Rousseau, here again, is a forerunner. His descriptions of nature are not sheer "romanticism," if by romanticism we mean sentimentality and make-believe: they are realistic. He had a glowing soul, but he had also eyes that could see the external world, and a pen that could describe it.

External realism reached realistic fiction chiefly in a roundabout way: through the romantic love of the picturesque. After a generation that reveled vaguely in the glamor of the past, came a generation that inventoried that glamor into concrete terms. Sir Walter Scott's local and historical coloring is essentially realistic. He is not satisfied, like his younger contemporary Keats, magically to evoke a knight-at-arms, alone and palely loitering: he must describe, with the precision of an expert, the various parts of his armor. As in the case of Richardson and in the case of Rousseau, the enormous popularity of one man caused—or, more accurately, indicated—a revolution in public taste. No doubt there was a great deal of sheer antiquarianism in Scott and his imitators—the *Wardour Street*, or, as we should say in America, the *Antique Shoppe* taint in art and literature; but there was also, and predominantly, a desire to reconstitute reality. That desire, and the method whereby it was carried out, were consciously borrowed by Balzac from Walter Scott and transferred to the contemporary scene. As we have already shown, the picture of a swineherd in *Ivanhoe* and that of a dandy in *Modeste Mignon* follow scrupulously the same technique.

With Balzac, the realistic novel reached, not its perfection, but its completeness. After a hundred years, *Father Goriot* and *Eugénie Grandet* are still our contemporaries, and many works are successful today which are old-fashioned compared with *Lost Illusions* or *Cousin Betty*. Flaubert's *Madame Bovary* is frequently mentioned as the first novel that was realistic in the strictly modern sense of the term. But, when it appeared, everyone recognized in it the faithful application of the Balzacian formula, and Flaubert himself did not demur. Zola consciously attempted to do for the Second Empire what Balzac had done for the bourgeois monarchy. His Naturalism, with its somber delectation in the sordid, and with its pseudo-scientific insistence on physiology, is but the exaggeration of certain aspects in Balzac. Zola differs from Balzac only when he draws closer to Victor Hugo. His *Rougon-Macquart* series never is more realistic than *The Human Comedy*; but it reflects at times something of the epic and humanitarian spirit found in *Les Misérables*.

Balzac's realism did not consist primarily in the microscopic study of details; he continued the great tradition of Rabelais, Cervantes, Fielding, and took a soaring view of mankind as a whole. He could report the silly jokes of Gaudissart, the commercial traveler; but his monument is aptly called *The Human Comedy*, and challenges comparison with Dante's. The cyclic novels which are such a feature of our "hurried" age, *Jean-Christophe*, *The Forsyte Saga*, *Remembrance of Things Past*, *Men of Good Will*, are Balzacian in spirit and in scope.

The novel has thus enjoyed a full century of glorious development, nearly a century of unquestioned supremacy: few *genres* can boast of so absolute and so prolonged a reign. Established powers always believe their rule to be eternal: the novel might be thought to be the ultimate form of our literature, so long, at any rate, as our present stage of civilization endures. It would be prudent, however, to discount this prophecy as well as any other kind of prophecy.

The novel, as we have pointed out, is based on an antinomy: "realistic fiction." It would be natural for its components to break apart: on the one hand, frank fiction, or romance; on the other, the scrupulous, unaltered reproduction of reality, in the form of history, biography, sociological reports, psychological studies. But experience does not bow to logic. Indefensible compromises have endured for centuries in religion, politics, society; a hybrid like the novel may endure indefinitely in the domain of art.

If Realism were reduced to its "realistic" elements, we believe it would disappear as art. In painting or sculpture, unmitigated realism leads to what the French call *trompe-l'œil:* the art that actually fools our senses, and scores its greatest triumph in the famed waxworks of Madame Tussaud's. Realism can survive only when it blends with its opposite, imagination. For this blend, which is the very definition of the novel, we can see at least three fields of usefulness.

In the first place, Realism may serve as a springboard for imagination. It is extraordinarily difficult to enjoy, and even to conceive, undiluted romance. Nursery audiences will insist on realistic touches, to make fairy tales more impressive. Fantastic stories, like *Dr. Jekyll and Mr. Hyde,* or *The Invisible Man,* are impressive only because they have a matter-of-fact background. In this case, romance is the goal, realism is but a means. But the proportion between the two may vary *ad libitum.*

The second justification for "realistic fiction" is satire. In this, the novel has remained true to its medieval origin: *The Human Comedy, Vanity Fair, Buddenbrooks, Remembrance of Things Past, The Forsyte Saga, The Sun Also Rises, The Grapes of Wrath,* are huge satires on classes, systems and ideals. Satire implies a departure from pure realism in two ways. It does not represent the whole of reality; it must isolate and emphasize the object of its criticism; its portraits always have a touch of caricature. And the selection of what it condemns is determined by what it would uphold. If Balzac, for instance, gave such a powerful picture of the profit motive, it was undoubtedly because that motive was strong within him: *realism*. But it was also because he was able to transcend the profit motive, to judge it from without, as an artist, as a monarchist, as a Catholic: *idealism*. Every satire implies an unformulated Utopia, and is indeed an inverted Utopia. But what the writer does select as the object of his satire must be absolutely real: nothing could be so futile as a criticism of imaginary vices.

The third field for realistic fiction is *experiment*. The most realistic of material projects have to go through the blue print stage. The bridge that we are planning is still a "fiction," the dream of our prophetic imagination; but such a dream must be based on the most realistic data—the known resistance of materials, the nature of the soil for the foundations. In the same way, every realistic novel is a hypothesis, a set of blue prints, a design for living. The facts being given, what motivation can we find for them? Or, conversely, the characters being given, what events will result from their interaction? If the solution we work out is artistically convincing, it confirms our hypothesis, and it can be transferred to real life. It enables us to understand motives which are unconfessed, and which hitherto had remained mysterious to us; it is a guide for our own conduct. Every novel that is worth reading presents a problem, and, as the solution of that problem, a thesis. Some novelists do it forcibly, clumsily, by means of over-simplification, like Paul Bourget; others subtly, unobtrusively, almost unconsciously, like Thomas Mann. But, in order to be convincing as an argument, the novel must use exclusively data which are in accordance with reality. A faked experiment is a trick. It may delude us, it may amuse us: not for long. When it comes to serious thought, we do not enjoy being fooled.

It is therefore unlikely that "realistic fiction" will disappear. It may, and we trust it will, cease to be too closely associated with a pessimistic conception of life. It is probable also that we shall lose patience with irrelevant elements of fiction in the presentation of facts and ideas. Certain problems which belong essentially to bourgeois civilization—class conflicts, ambition reduced to financial terms, marriage as a business contract—will lose something of their importance if that civilization suffers radical changes. But the method of exploration offered by the novel will remain valid under new circumstances; and we shall continue to enjoy its paradoxical mixture of realism and imagination.

Note on Detective Fiction

The mystery and detective story undoubtedly has many elements of romance. The events it relates are unusual and exciting. Among Poe's masterpieces, *The Gold Bug*, for instance, has a "faked" supernatural element; and *The Murders in the Rue Morgue* has a touch of "Gothic" grotesqueness and horror; but the treatment must be realistic: Sherlock Holmes in Faerie Land would cease to be interesting. Detective fiction is the delight of scholars: partly as an escape from their humdrum and sedentary occupation, partly because their own craft involves the solving of mysteries and the use of elusive clues: the mental equipment of Sherlock Holmes, if it could have been turned to the field of philology, would have made him a great investigator. Detective fiction reached a high level as a form of art with Edgar Poe (Dupin stories), with Dickens (*Mystery of Edwin Drood*), and above all with Dostoevsky (*Crime and Punishment, The Brothers Karamazov*); there is a detective element in Balzac as well as in *Les Misérables*. It may range from the "Gothic" (gruesome with a touch of the supernatural) to the rough-and-tough realistic (Dashiell Hammet).

The subdivisions of the Novel are so numerous that no complete survey could be attempted in this chapter. Various standard classifications, with examples, will be found in the Appendix, pages 478-482.

SUMMARY

Both history and the novel are forms of realistic narrative; their aim is to reproduce actual truth, or to give the illusion of truth. Both seek to be credible and convincing. This is attained in both cases by presenting events in intelligible sequence, by establishing an acceptable connection between factual reality and psychological reality.

Ancient historians were conscious artists; they retain their place in literature for qualities which are those of the best novelists. In modern times, historians (unlike scientists) have been swayed by exactly the same fashions as artists, poets and fictionists; historical writing takes on the color of the period, classical, Enlightenment, romantic, realistic, like the other forms of literature.

The most complex kind of historical writing is the history of civilization, or *historical sociology; philosophical history* is guided by some dominant idea: providence, nation, race, liberty, etc. The standard kind is purely *narrative history*, which emphasizes, and probably over-emphasizes, the exceptional, dramatic element, and the careers of exceptional, colorful individuals. Between such history and *biography*, the sole difference is that, in biography, the central character is studied as a man, and not exclusively as the symbol or leader of a movement. Autobiographical literature includes formal *autobiographies* (memoirs, confessions), diaries, notes, conversations and correspondences. In the essay, in impressionistic criticism, in those scientific and philosophical writings which clearly belong to literature, the autobiographical element is manifest.

Realistic fiction, which, like history, seeks to create the impression of reality, was at first a reaction against romance. In the Middle Ages, it embodied the practical, mocking spirit of the bourgeoisie. That spirit, subordinated at the time of the Renaissance to learned, aristocratic and poetic elements, revived first in the comedy, chiefly with Molière. With the rise of the middle class in the eighteenth century, realistic fiction assumed predominance.

A more intense form of that anti-romantic reaction was the *picaresque* novel of Spain: a cynical parody of romance, adventures of roguery substituted for adventures of chivalry. The genre, which culminated in *Don Quixote*, had immense and prolonged influence. In the eighteenth century, new essential elements were added to realistic fiction: psychological depth, learned from the dramatists and moralists; a higher degree of earnestness: the bourgeoisie, well on its way to power, insisted on being taken seriously; and finally, through the revived interest in the picturesque past, more vividness and accuracy in material detail: Sir Walter Scott was the master of Balzac, with whom the novel reaches completeness.

The novel has been for a century at least the leading form in literature: the most popular, the richest, and, purely as art, inferior to none. Yet "realistic fiction" is based on an antinomy, and might break up into its component parts: pure imagination, or romance; pure realism, the unadulterated presentation of facts, in the form of history, sociology, psychology. Still, "realistic fiction" may be justified: (1) as a springboard for imagination; (2) as satire; (3) as experiment: a novel is a workable hypothesis, a set of blue prints, a design for living.

CHAPTER XV

SURVEY OF THE GENRES

III. THE DRAMA

TYMOLOGY is a fascinating and a whimsical guide. It tells us that *drama* in Greek means *action:* this is plain and illuminating. It tells us that *comedy* means a *song of revelry*. This is at least a valid indication, for we feel that the term "tearful comedy," coined in the eighteenth century, is something of an absurdity. But it tells us also that *tragedy* means *goat song:* a piece of information that is both picturesque and puzzling. We are informed that this refers to some aspect in the cult of Dionysus; either because the goat was the sacrificial animal, or because there figured in those Dionysian mysteries a chorus of goat-legged satyrs.

Behind this dim and cryptic allusion lies a fact which seems to be of widespread, if not of universal, experience; the origin of the drama is to be sought in religious worship. This is admitted to be the case with the drama of India; more clearly still with that of Greece, which is the direct ancestor of our own; and the same evolution was to be manifest again in the Christian Middle Ages.

It would be unsafe, however, to interpret the drama as an offshoot of religion. If the two were once associated, it is even more evident that they have repeatedly been in very sharp conflict. The ritual dance, with the accompaniment of vocal and instrumental music, existed in ancient Israel, and we are told by the Psalmist to praise the Lord "with the timbrel and the dance." But even in those days, the combination of worship and choregraphy was apt to give offense. Michal, Saul's daughter, when she saw King David leaping and dancing before the Ark, "despised him in her heart." Michal was rebuked; yet no sacred drama was to evolve out of the Jewish ritual.

The tragedies of Æschylus bear unmistakable traces of ritual origin. Indeed, in their hieratic solemnity, they resemble a religious service far more than a wordly entertainment. We cannot tell to what extent the gods, in the mind of Æschylus, were myths and symbols, to what extent they were dogmatic realities. But the plays are profoundly religious, because they imply that the fate of men and nations lies in the hands of powers unseen. They are religious in a still deeper sense: they are, like many of the Psalms, like the *Book of Job*, meditations upon human destiny. Passive acceptance might be superstitious: true religion comes with questioning. We possess only one part of the *Prometheus* Trilogy; and we may not be justified when we read into that noble myth the rebellion of man's intelligence against a capricious tyranny; but at any rate, *Prometheus Bound* is capable of such an interpretation. In the catastrophe that overwhelms the chained Titan, we are sustained by Pascal's thought: he who knows for what cause he suffers is greater than that which crushes him. Our very uncertainty about that monumental fragment is a tribute to the genius of Æschylus. If his dramas are religious, his religion is *dramatic*. The poet sets forth a conflict greater than humanity, but upon which the fate of humanity depends; and when the second part of the trilogy closes, we cannot forecast the ending. This is *suspense* on the cosmic plane.

The emancipation of the stage from its liturgical origins proceeded with startling rapidity, and was practically complete within the span of a single lifetime. Euripides was full grown when Aeschylus died; yet it looked as though ages had elapsed between them. Religion is still the background of Sophocles' tragedies, but it remains in the background; the plays themselves are the presentation of human experiences. This was rightly felt by Aristotle when he said in his *Poetics:* "Within the action, there must be nothing irrational. If the irrational cannot be excluded, it should be outside the scope of the tragedy. Such is the irrational element in the *Œdipus* of Sophocles." For Euripides, only a few years younger than Sophocles, it was hard to retain absolute faith in the old legends. He did not quite know what to do with his gods. When they intervene, they produce the effect of a clumsy trick—the *deus ex machina* that was to be condemned by Horace after Aristotle. No wonder the arch-reactionary Aristophanes, passionately attached to the good old ways, revered Æschylus, and pursued Euripides with untiring and ferocious satire.

Greek tragedy may be considered as the perfect example of a formal *genre*. For, having reached and maintained for a brief period a miraculous degree of excellence, it was analyzed, defined, reduced to principles, by the most authoritative of all critics, Aristotle himself. With such models and with such a guide, it seemed that the path to perfection was clearly traced. For three centuries, from the Italian critics of the Renaissance to Victor Hugo's Preface to *Cromwell*, the Neo-Classical Age clutched that unconquerable hope; and once at least, with Racine, its faith appeared justified: after two thousand years, masterpieces were created by following scrupulously the example and the precepts of ancient genius.

If we take up the *Poetics* in a respectful but critical spirit, we are astounded at the quasi-divine authority that this little book once enjoyed. It is the work of a mind both powerful and shrewd; but it has reached us in very imperfect condition; it is fragmentary; it contains some irrelevant matter; and it offers at times the character of rough jottings. Above all, it is not a dogmatic treatise: it is a pragmatic study of the Greek stage, by a man whose turn of mind and whose training were not purely literary, but scientific.

We can say without paradox that it is the very incompleteness of this little book that made it so pregnant. If Aristotle had told us in unmistakable terms what he meant by *mimesis*, or "imitation," by *catharsis*, or "purgation," we should have missed the vast critical literature that arose out of their ambiguity. It is the privilege of a master to stimulate even when he fails to enlighten. One thing we do take for granted: when Aristotle, a great philosopher, used a word like "imitation," he could not possibly have had in mind anything so crude as "imitation." This simple assumption opens an unlimited and fruitful field for speculation.

Into this field we cannot be tempted. It would take us far beyond the limits of this brief survey. We must be satisfied with the essential points of Aristotle's discussion. Tragedy he defines as an *action* reproduced ("imitated") directly, not in the form of a narrative. This action must have gravity, completeness and grandeur; its language must be adorned with rhythm, harmony and song; and, through pity and fear, it must accomplish the proper purification (*catharsis*) of these emotions.

Aristotle insists upon *action* as the essence of drama; for him, the plot is the thing, the depiction of character is subsidiary. A character study without sufficient action, he tells us, would fail on the stage; and in fact, although Molière is a master of his craft, his *Misanthrope* is admired, but coldly received. Not only does the critic want a plot, with a beginning, a middle and an end; but he avows his preference for a plot with elements of surprise: a *peripeteia*, or reversal of intention; recognition scenes, in which long-lost brothers, lovers, children, are found again. In all this, Aristotle shows himself a good pragmatist. He is describing, not perhaps the highest type of tragedy, that of Æschylus, but the most effective. He stands for the "well-made play" against the closet drama. Plays may be enjoyed by the reader, but they are meant to be acted, and performance is the test.

A tragic action presents the change from good to bad fortune. But not all such changes are equally tragic. The undeserved suffering of a good man is harrowing and revolting; the just retribution of a bad man's crimes inspires in us neither fear nor pity. Our sympathy is stirred when a man suffers as we might suffer ourselves: not through irremediable depravity, but through some error, some flaw (*hamartia*); most of all perhaps when the flaw is but the exaggeration of some trait which, in itself, is not base. Thus Roland fell through excess of pride, Napoleon through excess of ambition. There lurks in this conception a trace of ancient fear: the jealous gods smite the mortal who dares to rise above the common level. But it remains valid in terms of modern psychology.

At no time does Aristotle lay down an abstract and absolute law. He recognizes that Euripides is "faulty," and at the same time that he is acknowledged as the most tragic of Greek poets. He notes that *many*—not all—of his plays end unhappily: "the best proof that this kind of ending is right is that on the stage and in dramatic competition, such plays are the most tragic in effect." He advocates a single, definite action: a tragedy depicting the whole Trojan War, the whole life of a man, a chronicle or biographical play, would in his opinion lack effectiveness. But we surmise that, if he had seen good plays of this type, he would not have been blind to their merits. Nowhere does it formulate the Law of the Three Unities with the rigidity of a Castelvetro.

Thanks to his philosophical acumen and to his experimental temper, Aristotle was infinitely less dogmatic than the Aristotelians. That is why, in his *Hamburgische Dramaturgie*, Lessing was able, without glaring absurdity, to condemn Corneille and extoll Shakespeare in the name of Aristotle. There are few tragedies worthy of the term that depart markedly from the precepts of the *Poetics*. One of them is *Alcestis*, by Euripides. It offers a singular blend of the mythological and the realistic. The quarrel between father and son has a tinge of cynical humor. The muscular and thick-witted hero, Heracles, who gets riotously drunk in the house of mourning, is a farcical character in the guise of a demi-god. And all ends well: death gives up his prey. Yet the noble sacrifice of Alcestis is sufficient to make this unique play a tragedy, and a great tragedy. A lesser example of the non-Aristotelian is Corneille's *Nicomède*. Although we can vouch that it is extremely effective on the stage, it rouses neither terror nor pity. It appeals solely to our admiration. It is written in a tone of lofty irony, of heroic banter; timorous old King Prusias and his scheming second wife are a comic pair; and, when the curtain falls, no one is slain. Yet it would be a misnomer to call this play a "hilaro-tragedy" (that absurd term does exist, a fit counterpart for "tearful comedy") or even a tragi-comedy. For it evokes magnificently the cruel drama of conquest, the insidious and inexorable advance of Roman power. But the extreme rarity of these exceptions is the best tribute to the perennial validity of Aristotle's *Poetics*.

Comedy, like tragedy, had its origin in the cult of Dionysus. It reached its summit almost at the same time—barely a few decades later; a summit which is not humbled by the triumphs of the graver muse. Here the resemblance ends. Greek tragedy achieved a form so definite and so harmonious that it can serve as a pattern even today; Greek comedy is a magnificent monster, which must remain unique in the history of literature. Of the "middle" and "new" comedy, we possess only fragments, and Roman imitations; of Aristophanes, master of the "old" comedy, we have some eleven plays, and they defy all classification. A poetic fancy freer, more lyrical, than Shakespeare's in *Midsummer Night's Dream*; political journalism of the most virulent, most scurrilous type; philosophical controversy and literary criticism; and withal—intermittently —a scenic gift, a comic verve not unworthy of Molière: such are a few of the discordant elements thrown together in the glorious Aristophanesque medley. He could attack viciously the teachings of Socrates, the art of Euripides, demagogy, the fondness of the Athenians for litigation; he could plead for peace, regret the glories of the Persian wars, build his Nephelococcygia in "Cloud-cuckoo-land," swoop down to bedroom farce in *Lysistrata*; and, in the clouds or in the gutter, he remained a splendid poet and a furious reactionary. When we are told that the Greek genius is all lucidity, harmony, measure and taste, we must think of Aristophanes, and smile.

Beside the two fundamental kinds, permanent contributions to world literature, the Greek stage offered minor varieties which have not survived. Of the *satyr drama*, only one example has been preserved: *The Cyclops* (Polyphemus), by Euripides. The satyr drama was probably intended as comic relief for the sustained and somber sublimity of the tragic trilogy. The *mimes* were brief spirited sketches of common life, not seldom coarse in language and cynical in tone. Out of this unpretentious and ephemeral form of entertainment, a poet of the Alexandrian period, Herondas, evolved little masterpieces of singular vivacity and charm. These scenes are as modern and as elegant in style as Tanagra statuettes, but with greater liveliness. They prove that our boasted realism and sophistication had their counterparts in Hellenic society in the third century before Christ. The mimes were part of what would now be called vaudeville shows; they continued until they were frowned upon by the Church. The name reappeared in the Middle Ages, and the spirit in the farces and interludes. But there is no evidence of a continuous tradition. No period needs to learn from another how to mock and jeer: that tendency is as ubiquitous, as permanent, as irrepressible, as the foibles it derides.

The Latin drama was confessedly inferior to the Greek. Yet its influence upon modern literature has been more direct and more obvious. We still read and admire Æschylus, Sophocles, Euripides, and not Seneca; but it was from Seneca that the Neo-Classical tragedy received its form, its tone, many of its themes, and most of its conventions. Among these are the division into five acts, the foreboding dream, the specter, the confidant, the long narrative speeches substituted for the direct presentation of events. These are purely formal, and, while not harmless, they are not radically incompatible with artistic sincerity. Far more pervasive and dangerous is the stiff, tense, artificial sublimity in attitude and tone. Seneca, who perhaps did not write for the stage, is theatrical in the worst sense of the term. He loves tales of horror, and sensational scenes (after

all, Sophocles had shown a dangerous example with his
(*Œdipus*). His heroes and villains strut and mouth mightily,
displaying their unmitigated virtues and vices with histrionic
immodesty. He is chiefly remembered for his turgid eloquence,
adorned with sonorous and quotable maxims. The worst of it is
that he has culture, skill, power; his art offers the same kind
of appeal as the grandiose, the ornate, the gorgeous in architecture: an elaborate, sophisticated vulgarity which is fundamentally false, but undeniably impressive.

Nothing is so obvious, and therefore so easy to pastiche, as
the Senecan tragedy; that is why, when tragedy was revived by
the Italian Renaissance, it sought its pattern in Seneca, not in
Sophocles. England did not fall completely under his sway:
there are popular elements in the Elizabethan drama which are
free from the Roman bane. Yet, in Marlowe and even in
Shakespeare, echoes of Senecan bombast are heard. In France,
the Senecan tradition triumphed with Corneille: a more genuine artist than Seneca, but addicted to conventional heroism
and pompous eloquence. Corneille, in his turn, strengthened
the regrettable Senecan element in Dryden. Even Racine who,
rare among his contemporaries, had a direct and thorough
knowledge of Greek tragedy, was not altogether immune. This
tradition continued interminably, not only in the stiff pseudo-
classical tragedies of the eighteenth century, but even in the
lesser romantic dramas of the nineteenth.

Latin comedy was no less influential than Latin tragedy. It
had a freer field: Aristophanes could not serve as a model, and
Menander had perished. So classical comedy, although purely
Greek in origin, is for us that of Plautus and Terence. It provided also a number of conventions: the identical twins; the
confidential servant, indispensable and tricky; the pretty slave
with whom the rich young man falls in love; the resulting conflict between father and son; and finally, a comic transcription
of the recognition scenes recommended by Aristotle: everybody
is recognized to be somebody else, stolen years ago by the
pirates; this somehow removes every obstacle, and all ends

well. But we owe to the Romans more than a few tricks and a set of stock situations. The plays of Plautus, although not over-subtle, are well organized: situation, character, language, co-operate in creating amusement. Terence—probably the shadow of Menander—made comedy respectable: decent in manners, elegant in style. Faint praise, it would seem, now that we are inclined to place vitality far above correctness and restraint. But this modest quality helped Terence survive through the long centuries of Church censure. Manuscripts of his plays were preserved in many monasteries; and the nun Hrosvitha consciously imitated the form of his comedies in her modest dramas of martyrdom and miraculous conversion.

Between the downfall of Pagan culture and the first clear manifestations of modern literature, there is a chasm of five hundred years. When the medieval drama came into existence, it was not as a continuation of the Greco-Roman; but, like the Greek itself, it evolved out of religious festivals. It was an extension, an illustration of the liturgy, the symbolism of which was not accessible to the popular mind. The fact that the language of Church services had ceased to be generally understood made tableaux and pageants all the more welcome as an instrument of religious instruction.

It has long been customary to divide the plays of Christian inspiration into three groups, *mysteries, miracles* and *moralities*. The last, which are allegories, stand clearly apart. But the distinction between the other two is somewhat dubious. The mysteries are supposed to be founded entirely on Holy Scripture, the miracles on the lives of the Virgin and of the Saints. Unfortunately, the word "mystery" is equivocal. There are dramas called mysteries, which yet are not scriptural. The origin of the word itself is uncertain: it might come from *ministerium* (trade or craft), rather than from *mysterium*. Mystery in that sense was not used in medieval England; it was introduced from the French in the eighteenth century only; finally, it might lead to an absurd confusion with the modern mystery play, a popular kind of melodrama.

But if the terms are ambiguous, the distinction is very real, and not without importance. The Scriptural plays are the more solemn and the more elaborate; at the very end of the Middle Ages, they were still enjoying immense popularity. Yet, when we consider the grandeur of the theme, the magnificence of the original language, the ardent faith of the spectators, the medieval mysteries are profoundly disappointing. Although fragments of the Nativity plays are occasionally performed, rather for the quaint realism of the interludes than for their sacred character, and although Passion plays have survived here and there, as at Oberammergau, believers do not turn to them for edification, nor artists for esthetic pleasure. This is not because the medieval mind was unequal to such a task. We have not improved upon the Gothic cathedrals, the philosophy of St. Thomas Aquinas, or the poetry of Dante. There is no theoretical reason why the immense Passion Play of Arnoul Greban, for instance, revised by Jean Michel in the second half of the fifteenth century, should not have been a major masterpiece; but it is utterly mediocre. We must accept this disappointment as a fact.

But even if Christianity had found its Æschylus, it is doubtful whether the mysteries could have remained a fruitful branch of dramatic art. The invention of the poets was restricted to the episodes; and these could not be developed beyond a certain point without the risk of sacrilege. This was felt in the sixteenth century. What killed the mysteries was not so much the revival of the pagan spirit in aristocratic literature: it was the growth of a more sensitive, a more anxious faith, which came with the Reformation. It was feared that these spectacles, harmless in a less critical age, might become blocks of stumbling. In France, they were suppressed by royal edict in 1548.[1]

---

[1] The Brotherhood of the Passion kept the privilege of performing "other mysteries, profane and licit"; it remained in existence until 1670.

Green Pastures may be considered as a modern mystery of the Old Testa-

The miracles afforded much greater freedom; but they also fell far below the achievements of their times in lyric or epic poetry. Yet the *genre*, which did not produce any great work in the ages of unquestioning faith, had a long, uneven and very interesting career. We are not alluding to classical or modern plays with a saint for their hero: *Polyeucte* or *Murder in the Cathedral* are not "miracles" any more than *Samson Agonistes* or *Athaliah* are "mysteries." We are not thinking either of clever pastiches, like Anatole France's *Tumbler of Notre Dame* and Maeterlinck's *Sister Beatrice:* both very appropriately belong to the operatic stage, for both are the products of willful make-believe. But the miracles, as *Comedias de Santos,* continued in Spain throughout the *Siglo de Oro,* the Golden Century, which closed with the death of Calderón (1681). In that paradoxical country, the medieval spirit survived at the height of the classical age. Lope de Vega, Calderón and their innumerable fellow dramatists did not revel romantically in picturesque legends; the Virgin was not for them a convenient and unconvincing *dea ex machina*. A drama such as *La Devoción de la Cruz* offers no psychological conflict. It embodies a truth which, to Calderón, is the very essence of spiritual life: the grace of God can cause the most hardened sinner to repent, and through penitence, to enter suddenly into saintliness. This, for the believer, is the eternal miracle; the suspension of natural laws is but its visible sign.

A "miracle" theme is found at the basis of the mightiest of philosophical dramas, *Faust*. In the thirteenth century, Rutebeuf wrote his *Miracle of Theophilus:* a monk sells his soul to the Devil, repents, and is saved through the intercession of the Virgin. In the sixteenth century, Christopher Marlowe gave his *Dr. Faustus;* in the sevententh, Calderón brought out his *Mágico Prodigioso:* a young pagan strikes the same bargain,

ment. The task of the author was extraordinarily delicate: nothing less than the harmonious blending of irony, sympathy and reverence. The spectator must at the same time smile at the naïve faith of the Negroes, and never forget that this faith is also his own. So far as we know, the play did not give offense; but it was bound to remain unique.

in the hope of conquering a Christian maiden; but she is saved from him through faith, and he from the Devil through her; he is converted, and both suffer glorious martyrdom. The pact with the Devil is a ubiquitous medieval motive, and no filiation can be traced between Rutebeuf, Calderón and Goethe. But it is an oddity of literature that the most profound of dramas and the most popular of operas, *Faust*, should be a "miracle" born out of due time.

The morality is an allegorical drama, in which the characters are abstractions: principles, virtues, vices, classes and conditions of men. This simple definition covers a wide range of varieties, from the theological to the journalistic. The theological is best represented by the *Autos Sacramentales* of Spain, of which Calderón is the supreme master. These brief dramas, presented on the day of Corpus Christi, have for their theme the mystery of the Eucharist, the dogma of Transsubstantiation; and for their characters such symbolical figures as Faith, Idolatry, Sin, Grace, Nature, Necessity. There is something of that element in the last scene of the second *Faust*. On a less exalted plane, still religious, but from the human point of view, are the plays which have for their subject the salvation of man's soul; not of one particular man, as in the miracle, but of every man. And *Everyman*, which has been revived, imitated and abundantly parodied, may be considered as the purest type of the morality. From the religious, the descent is easy into the merely moral, as in Skelton's *Magnificence;* and from the moral to the political—for are not our opponents the embodiment of all vices? Skelton may have written at the behest of Henry VIII; his contemporary Pierre Gringoire, in his moralities, was a propagandist for King Louis XII, and attacked, allegorically, but plainly enough, the policy of the Pope himself. The Pierre Gringoire or Gringore of history, by the way, is but a dim figure compared with the delightful and pathetic Gringoire created by Victor Hugo in *Notre Dame de Paris*. By that time, the morality had almost merged with the *Sotie,* a satirical play acted by the clerks of the Paris Law Courts, and with the farce.[1]

The morality in its pure form has practically disappeared, although allegorical dramas such as Kennedy's *The Servant in the House*, Sutton Vane's *Outward Bound*, or Karel Capek's *R.U.R.*, might be considered as modern "moralities." It survives, in shadowy fashion, as a limit and as a warning. The comedy of character and the problem play, if too general and too abstract, tend to turn into "moralities." If the type or class are emphasized at the expense of the living individual, if we are offered a picture of *the* miser, *the* Jew, *the* capitalist, *the* proletarian, instead of complex personalities, puzzling and bewildered, the work is in danger of reverting to the stiff and bloodless abstractions of the late Middle Ages. The type proves nothing, because it has no life; the individual proves nothing, because he is unique. A neat dilemma: but Molière and Ibsen have managed to elude its horns.

Etymology plays upon us one of its neatest tricks with the word *farce*. The term passed from the kitchen to the stage by way of the Church. Originally, it meant *stuffing*, and still does in French cooking. Then those additions "stuffed" into the liturgy or the sermon received the name; then it denoted the interludes, the extemporaneous jokes, the patter and gags added to the regular plays; at last, the "stuffing" became a dish by itself; the rough comic elements formed the substance of independent plays, briefer, more popular, less elaborate than formal comedies.

The farce is therefore a frank attempt to raise a laugh. The most direct method is the surest and best. If tumbling about, slapping faces, or throwing pies, will do it, they are not to be despised: the roar of laughter is the sole aim and the sole test. Unashamed buffoonery is eternal; there was a farcical element

---

[1] Sotie: so called because the association of merrymakers called themselves *Sots* (fools); cf. popularity of the Ship of Fools theme at that time, and the election of a Pope of Fools. For some recondite reason, André Gide has elected to call some of his works *soties*.

to Aristophanes as well as to Plautus; the Hellenic *Mimes* were akin to farces, and so were the Roman *Atellanae*. But the medieval farce need not borrow dignity by claiming Greco-Roman ancestry: it arose spontaneously from the spirit of satire and fun. In this, it closely resembles those of the *Fabliaux* that are, first of all, merry and mocking tales. Molière's most typical farce, *The Doctor in Spite of Himself*, is but the stage version of a medieval story.

The chief character of the farce, therefore, is its unpretentious simplicity. As the best tricks are the oldest, the farce frankly relies upon stock characters and stock situations. This being admitted, it does not result that the farce is bound to be coarse, or even crude. It simplifies, it exaggerates, as does the caricature; but like the caricature, it may be based on sound observation; when it seizes upon essential traits, it turns into a valid, and even a profound satire.

Two examples will suffice to give the spirit of the medieval farce. The first is the *Farce of the Vat* (*Cuvier*). A man is henpecked by both wife and mother-in-law; he rebels mildly, and wants at least to know what his duties are. On the dictation of the two women, he enters them into a little book; and a very long, very miscellaneous list it is. Now he feels that he enjoys constitutional guarantees. The mother-in-law falls into a vat; the man whips out his little book, reads it attentively, and finds no article compelling him to rescue her. In despair, she promises him to let him henceforth have his own way. He pulls her out, and he will now be the master in his own house—until she is thoroughly dry.

The other, and better known, is that of *Master Pierre Pathelin*, a rascally lawyer duped in the end by an innocent-looking, but even more rascally shepherd. This little play has enriched the French language with a common term: *patelin* means a smooth humbug, and with an expression: "Let us get back to our sheep": *Mais revenons à nos moutons*.

Of all the medieval *genres*, the modest farce is the only one that has survived without change. *Pathelin* is still acted. A very faithful pastiche by Anatole France, *The Farce of a Man Who Married a Dumb Wife*, has proved extremely effective. *The Merry Wives of Windsor* is frankly nothing but farce, and *The Taming of the Shrew* is at least a farcical comedy. Nearly one half of Molière's plays are farces; and Eugène Labiche entered the French Academy on the strength of shrewd, wholesome farces. The tricks and gags that tickled our ancestors five hundred years ago are in constant use in our comic strips and our comic films. Sophistication has its brief day: broad laughter is eternal.

In masterly hands, bold simplification is a merit. Strong emphasis on purpose, economy of means, result in the quality that we now praise as "functionalism." Nothing could be more frankly farcical than Molière's *Les Précieuses Ridicules:* it is a mere practical joke, which ends with a Punch-and-Judy drubbing. Yet it marked the historic rebellion of classical and bourgeois common sense against absurd affectation in manners, sentiments and speech; and tradition has it that an old man in the pit cried out at the end: "Courage, Molière! This is real comedy." In *Georges Dandin*, we have a farce which is also a social satire, and in which laughter has a background of bitterness. Jules Romains boldly uses farce technique to present paradoxical ideas. In the *Le Trouhadec* series of plays, particularly in *Donogoo Tonka*, he expounds his curious theory of "creative mystification": error as well as truth may serve as a starting point for useful action; the original lie disappears, imbedded in the valuable reality that has crystallized round it. *Knock or The Triumph of Medicine* is not merely a vigorous satire on medical fakers; it touches upon the psychological basis of disease. "Every well man," proclaims Knock, "is but an invalid unaware that he is sick." It is the Doctor's duty—if he knows his business—to make him conscious of his trouble. To invent, to discover, to create, are frequently one and the same. Bernard Shaw is not in the least afraid of the farcical, even of the most elementary kind. It is not impossible that Oscar Wilde's trifle, *The Importance of Being Earnest*, will survive his florid and sultry *Picture of Dorian Gray*. Let us finally mention the fact that Henry James, whose labyrinthine subtlety is the exact reverse of the farcical spirit, yet attempted the *genre*, not disastrously.

With the Renaissance, the two great classical kinds were formally revived, the tragedy with Seneca as its model, the comedy patterned after Plautus and Terence. But the Renaissance was a learned and aristocratic movement: the stage must have some popular appeal; so the victory of pastiche and pedantic rule was not immediate, and was far from complete. For generations, neo-classical plays were successful only in colleges or in very limited circles. The dramas of England and Spain remained almost completely free; the histories or chronicle plays, found in both countries, were thoroughly un-Aristotelian. Even in France, the famous "Rules" did not triumph until the "Quarrel of *Le Cid*" in 1637; they did not prevent Molière from producing his *Don Juan*, a romantic medley of the miracle, the melodrama, the comedy of manners, and the farce.

Of the various national schools, the greatest by common consent is that of Elizabethan England; but, until the eighteenth century, it had no influence on the Continent. Italy provided the first models, and sharpened the rules, of the neo-classical drama. But her special contribution, the one that retained an unmistakable Italian flavor, was of a more modest nature. It was a comedy of gay and irresponsible trickery, more intricate and more brilliant than anything of the kind in Plautus. It might be called a transposition of the Machiavellian spirit on the farcical plane: in real life, the great adventurer Mazarin was a supreme diplomat with a touch of Italian comedy. Usually, the characters were conventional, wore traditional costumes, like those of Harlequin and Columbine, and spoke the dialect of some particular city. It was a brilliant puppet show for adults; it produced a kind of farce more poetical, more artistic, than the robust realism of Gallic tradition; and, thanks to Italian verve, it left long and delightful traces in literature. In France, for instance, Molière, Lesage, Marivaux, Musset, Rostand, among others, borrowed the names, the costumes, the tricks of the Italian buffoons.[1]

Spain, for many years, exported dramas of extravagant adventure, which were finally defeated by the more severe neoclassical tragedy. The "cloak-and-sword comedy," full of plots and counterplots, disguises, elopements, duels, long remained a favorite. The Spanish dramas of Victor Hugo, *Hernani* and *Ruy Blas*, and Rostand's *Cyrano de Bergerac*, retain something of that flavor.

The French brought the Senecan tragedy to perfection with Corneille; with Racine, they created a form extraordinarily complex in its apparent simplicity: a drama which is Greek rather than Latin, but most of all French and modern; Pagan in themes, Christian in spirit; for the unwary, a mere pastiche; yet as intense, as passionate as Shakespeare's under its veil of severe restraint. Thanks to its intrinsic virtues, and to the prestige of French society, this neo-classical tragedy remained the recognized pattern of the serious drama for several generations: even in England, with Addison's *Cato* and Samuel Johnson's *Irene*. Dislodged from its supremacy by the powerful attacks of Lessing, the Shakespearian revival, and the triumph of Romanticism, it continued to bear fruit. It is seldom realized that tragedies of a severely classical character, and of very high artistic merit, were produced late in the eighteenth century, and throughout the first half of the nineteenth. It will be sufficient to mention the works of the Italian Alfieri; some of the noblest plays of Goethe, Schiller and Kleist; the antique dramas of Grillparzer, far too little known and appreciated by English readers; and those of Hebbel, intensely modern in spirit, purely classical in technique.

But the greatest contribution of the French to the develop-

---

[1] In the *Commedia dell' Arte*, only the scenario was indicated; the players acted "in character," according to their costumes, and improvised their lines; a kind of entertainment still used in charades and masked balls.

ment of the drama was the many-sided activity of Molière. Borrowing on all hands, with the same sovereign indifference as Shakespeare, from Rome, Italy, Spain and medieval France, he covered the whole range of the comic *genres*—poetically burlesquing Olympus in *Amphitryon*, keeping close to popular farce in *Monsieur de Pourceaugnac*, carelessly romantic in *Don Juan*. In all this, he was but a glorious epitome of all traditions; in two fields, he was an initiator and remains a master. There had been "types" and "humors" on the stage before, particularly with Ben Jonson; but it was Molière who created the "comedy of character," the searching psychological and moral study of some universal trait in some individual man: thus avarice and misanthropy, not in the abstract, but in the living persons of Harpagon and Alceste; thus hypocrisy, not the "False Semblance" of medieval morality, but with the bloated, florid, disquieting, unforgettable figure of Tartuffe. Perhaps Molière attempted the impossible: the stage does not lend itself to psychological subtlety, and Aristotle was probably right in placing action above character. But, impossible as it was, he achieved it, as no one achieved it again. Compared with Molière's flesh and blood creations, the heroes of Ibsen's dramas are premises in a syllogism.

His second contribution was the "comedy of manners." He can depict a *milieu*, the conflict and transformation of classes, as in *The Would-be Gentleman*, *Georges Dandin*, *The Miser*. In this respect, the greatest of his disciples was not a dramatist, but Balzac. Molière can also present and discuss, in concrete, dramatic terms, a social or moral problem, as in *The School for Wives*, *The Learned Ladies*, *The Misanthrope*, *Tartuffe*. These plays are not classics because they belong to the past: they are classics because they are alive today. Like Shakespeare's *Hamlet*, they can be performed in modern clothes; like *Hamlet*, they are still the center of endless argument.[1]

---

[1] Among the secondary genres of the late Renaissance and Neo-Classic period was the *masque*. It was an elaborate aristocratic entertainment, in which pageantry, dancing, stage machinery, combined with high literature to pro-

With Shakespeare, Racine, Molière, the modern drama was fully formed. The eighteenth century achieved much, but created nothing essential. Its most brilliant playwrights, Goldoni, Beaumarchais, Goldsmith, Sheridan, added very little to the technique of Molière. The most evident change was social rather than artistic. As we have noted in discussing the novel, the rising bourgeoisie insisted on being taken seriously: hence the growth of "intermediate *genres* for intermediate classes," the tearful comedy, the domestic tragedy. Of the latter, Lillo, with his *George Barnwell*, was the pioneer, and the encyclopedist Diderot the theorist. Lessing himself cultivated the kind; and so did, with lamentable results, the sprightly Beaumarchais.

As an indication of further social change, we find, at the end of the century, the *melodrama* attaining definiteness, if not respectability; a *genre* as frankly popular in its appeal as the medieval farce, or as the novels of Eugène Sue. The confessed melodrama never reached full literary stature, although writers as different as Balzac, Henry Arthur Jones, Oscar Wilde, and William Vaughan Moody tried their hands at it. But it greatly influenced the *romantic drama*, which in many cases is but the despised melodrama in more flamboyant clothes. The romantic drama itself, which began with Goethe's *Goetz von Berlichingen*, and Schiller's *The Brigands*, may embody a new spirit

duce an effect of artistic sumptuosity. The *genre* reached its peak in England with Ben Jonson, assisted by the great architect Inigo Jones. Of the literary or closet masque, the best example is Milton's *Comus:* a stately mythological fantasy, to be enjoyed for sheer beauty rather than for moral significance or dramatic power. Robert Bridges revived the *genre*. The French equivalent was at first the ballet, in which young King Louis XIV loved to take part. This could be combined with the lyrical and spectacular tragedy (*Psyche*), with comedy (*The Would-be Gentleman*), and even with farce (*Love as a Doctor*). The spectacular tragedy easily changed into the opera; with the librettist Quinault and the composer Lulli, it became the favorite form of Court entertainment. The opera was thus from the beginning a quasi-literary *genre; Psyche* is a near-masterpiece, and Quinault almost a great writer. In the eighteenth century, Metastasio, Imperial Court poet, was highly esteemed for the lyric charm and dramatic skill of his libretti. In the nineteenth century, Richard Wagner made the opera again a respected *genre* in literature.

of revolt, but it is not a new form: only a return to the freedom enjoyed by the Elizabethans and by the Spanish writers of the Golden Age.

It is frequently taken for granted that the *problem play* is a creation of our own age, and that it sprang full-armed from the Nordic brains of Henrik Ibsen. The history of the *genre* is much longer, and its evolution far more gradual. There are problem plays in the strictest sense of the term among the works of Molière: *The School for Wives* could be matched against *A Doll's House*, and *The Misanthrope* against *An Enemy of the People*. The eighteenth century was perhaps the most intelligent in the history of mankind, if by intelligence we mean the eager discussion of ideas; its chief fault, from the point of view of dramatic art, was that it could not keep *problems* off the stage. The propagandist ("philosophical") tragedies of Voltaire, the "tearful comedies" of Nivelle de la Chaussée, the domestic dramas of Diderot and Sedaine, the coruscating satires of Beaumarchais, all discussed social, political, moral theses with a zest that Bernard Shaw himself would find it hard to rival.

The general spirit of revolt, which inspired the early romantic drama, turned into definite attacks against prejudices and conventions, in a spirit which might be called Ibsenian. *Antony*, by Alexandre Dumas Père, is the problem of the illegitimate child at war with society, which refuses him a fair chance. *Chatterton*, by Alfred de Vigny, is the problem of the idealist, stifling in a world ruled by the profit motive. *Marion Delorme*, by Victor Hugo, *The Lady of the Camellias* (*Camille*), by Alexandre Dumas Fils, treat the eternal Mary-Magdalene problem: can genuine love efface a transgression against the social code? That theme had been a commonplace of Romantic literature, before it was taken up, realistically, by Emile Augier in *Olympia's Marriage*, by Arthur Wing Pinero in *The Second Mrs. Tanqueray*, by Schnitzler in *The Fairy Tale* (*Das Märchen*).

Realistically: what we usually understand by the problem play is the discussion of a modern question through realistic technique. This is what Ibsen, who started as a very conventional romanticist and ended as a very nebulous symbolist, achieved gloriously in the middle part of his career. He led a welcome reaction against the Parisian conventions of Dumas Fils and especially of Victorien Sardou: the clever plot, or "well-made play," and the pyrotechnic dialogue. But this reaction brought nothing new: Ibsen never was simpler or more direct than Vigny or Molière. This is said in no spirit of depreciation against a sturdy, conscientious, humorless playwright, no less respectable in his craft than his contemporary Herbert Spencer was in philosophy. We are not passing judgment on individuals, but attempting to define *genres* and their subdivisions. And our conclusion is simply that the problem play is much older and much wider a phenomenon than Ibsenism.

The most original development in our times is not the realistic play, which existed full-grown in Molière and Lesage, but the *fantasy* with a philosophical background, such as we find in J. M. Barrie and Karel Capek. Here again, originality must not be taken too literally; we are in presence, not of an invention, but of a revival. Certain plays of Marivaux offer such a character; and, more obviously still, Shakespeare's *The Tempest*. The modern fantasy with serious psychological purport is an attractive kind: we have it most clearly represented perhaps in Pirandello's *Six Characters in Search of an Author*. If we wanted to pass in review "all *genres* knowable and a few others beside," it would be sufficient to list the productions of Eugene O'Neill. They range from ancient Cathay to the Caribbean, and from Æschylean tragedy (*Mourning Becomes Electra*) to sentimental "period" comedy (*Ah, Wilderness!*). Before such appalling variety of techniques, we are tempted to believe at times that the dramatist is more interested in the new trick than in the substance of the play; and the art of Eugene O'Neill has been likened to those magnificent pipe organs on which indifferent music was played, because the very profusion of keys, registers and stops distracted the attention of performer and audience alike. Scribe and Sardou had only five or six patterns of the "well-made play"; O'Neill has twenty. The student of the drama should be deeply thankful for such a fascinating museum.[1]

Oratory should be classed among the kinds of dramatic literature; for it is a spoken form of expression, in which the presence, the voice, the gesture, the infectious emotion of the performer, are of supreme importance. If Antony had actually given the speech that Shakespeare ascribed to him, it would be, in real life as well as on the stage, a model of splendid oratory as well as of effective drama. There is nothing "theatrical" about the Gettysburg Address: but the occasion, the scene, the personality of the speaker, imparted to those few simple lines a *dramatic* power which no narrative and no essay could hope to attain.

Eloquence is meant to be heard, and its immediate effectiveness is our first criterion. It may later be enjoyed by the reader: but this is also the case with the drama. And there is a "closet" or bookish eloquence as there is a "closet" drama. Victor Hugo wrote magnificent speeches, full of the most approved rhetorical devices; he delivered them well, and yet they failed to move his audience; he lacked the gift of the genuine orator, just as some great novelists and poets, such as Balzac and Tennyson, lacked the gift of the genuine dramatist.

Demosthenes and Cicero remain the accepted masters of forensic eloquence; it would be a little harder to agree on the best representative of sacred oratory. It was thought that the printing press would reduce the importance of the spoken word; modern technique has altered conditions again, and now, through the amplifier and the radio, the living voice has recovered much of its ancient power. The curious delusion about "strong, silent men" is disproved by all history, and most of all by contemporary experience. Men who achieved

---

[1] An almost equal fertility of invention, in themes if not in forms, is found in another Nobel Prize winner, Jacinto Benavente.

mighty deeds in the past, Pericles, Caesar, St. Paul, St. Bernard, Napoleon, Lincoln, Bismarck, were also great orators. Today, a whole nation is a single agora. This is obviously a danger, for the very reason that eloquence is a dramatic art, and that the drama appeals to elementary passions rather than to cool and lucid reason. Through a severe course in literary criticism, a man can train himself to appreciate tragedy and reject melodrama; in the same way, a people must be trained, while communing in mighty emotions, to detect, resent and resist the least trace of bathos.

SUMMARY

It is usually admitted that the origin of the drama is to be found in religious worship. The tragedies of Æschylus still resemble a solemn liturgy more than a secular entertainment. But already with Euripides, the drama has become purely human, and the gods are reduced to the position of stage devices.

Greek tragedy, with Æschylus, Sophocles and Euripides, is one of the supreme achievements in literature, and it was studied by the most authoritative of critics, Aristotle. Tragedy he defines as an action "imitated" directly, not in the form of narrative. This action must have gravity, completeness and grandeur . . . and, through pity and fear, it must accomplish the proper purification (*catharsis*) of these emotions. The doctrine of Aristotle is partly veiled in uncertainty, for the *Poetics* reached us in very imperfect form. But many of his observations are still valid; and, an open-minded investigator, he did not lay down abstract and absolute laws.

The "old" comedy is represented by Aristophanes, who offers an extraordinary medley of poetry, journalistic virulence and comic verve. The "new" comedy (Menander) has perished; but its indirect influence was great through its Latin imitators, Plautus and Terence.

Between the downfall of Pagan culture and the first clear manifestations of modern literature, five hundred years elapsed.

The medieval drama was not a continuation of the Greco-Roman, but evolved out of religious festivals.

The dramas founded on Holy Scripture (often called *mysteries*) proved disappointing, and lost vitality at the time of the Reformation. Those which had as their subjects the *miracles* of the Virgin and the Saints had a freer field: they survived in Spain in the "golden century," the seventeenth. There is an element of the medieval *miracle* in Goethe's *Faust*. The *moralities* were allegories in which the characters were abstractions. *Everyman* is the best known of the moralities. The medieval *farce* arose, like the mocking tale, from the spirit of fun and satire. It is a rudimentary and vigorous *genre*, practiced by Shakespeare and Molière, and very much alive today.

With the Renaissance, the classical *genres*, tragedy and comedy, were revived, and the influence of Seneca was great, chiefly in Italy and France. But the national schools of England and Spain retained their independence. The English stage, incomparably the greatest under Elizabeth, was little known abroad for a full century. From Italy came a brilliant comedy of rascality, and the *commedia dell' arte*, with its conventional characters and costumes: from Spain, dramas of extravagant adventure, and the cloak-and-sword comedy. France brought the Senecan tragedy to perfection with Corneille and transcended it with Racine. But the chief contribution of France was the many-sided activity of Molière: classical, medieval and Italian farce, Spanish drama (*Don Juan*), and especially comedy of manners and comedy of character.

With Shakespeare, Racine, Molière, the modern drama was fully formed. The eighteenth century created nothing essential. The most evident change was social rather than literary: intermediate kinds were created for the intermediate classes, the "tearful" comedy, the domestic tragedy, etc. The *melodrama* appealed frankly to the populace. The *romantic drama* was in part a return to the Elizabethan, with a touch of melodrama, and a new spirit of revolt.

The *problem play* is not the creation of Ibsen, or even of the nineteenth century. Molière, Voltaire, Diderot, Beaumarchais, had discussed social, political and moral theses on the stage; many romantic dramas had a "problem" element. The problem play as we understand it is the presentation of a contemporary question through *realistic* technique—a reaction against the excesses of technical skill and purely theatrical wit indulged in by certain Parisian dramatists. Perhaps the most original development in the twentieth century is the *Fantasy* with a philosophical background: J. M. Barrie, G. B. Shaw, L. Pirandello, K. Capek. Eugene O'Neill offers a veritable museum of all possible kinds and techniques.

Oratory, as a spoken form of expression, should be classed among the varieties of drama.

CHAPTER XVI

PERIODS IN LITERATURE

I. THEORY OF THE PERIODS

WITH the study of periods, we encounter for the third time the same fundamental difficulty: periods, like tendencies and *genres*, are abstractions and conventions. All boundaries that we may attempt to trace are misty; all definitions that we may propose are elusive. Would it not be clear gain to discard this obsolete mythology, which simply throws a pedantic veil over the only concrete reality, the individual works?

This criticism has undeniable validity. History is not a series of separate tableaux, each perfectly still and perfectly consistent, called Periods, with unpleasant intervals of noisy and confused scene shifting, which we call "moments of transition." If we were to believe that the Elizabethan Age began with the accession of the Virgin Queen and ended with her death; that all Elizabethans dressed, thought, felt and wrote alike; that in every respect they were different from their predecessors and their successors; then we should have a clear-cut conception of a period, and it would be grotesquely at odds with the facts. Presumably we belong to a period; the things we most heartily despise in the contemporary scene will be "period" pieces some day; but it would be an amusing game to tag a name on this "period" of ours. Even if we could agree upon a dominant tendency or a dominant personality, there is no certainty that posterity would ratify our choice. There is, in some of our textbooks, an "Age of Johnson." The autocrat himself was magnificently assured in his own classical faith.

There, it would seem, we have the proper elements for a well-defined period: the man and the doctrine. But the age of Johnson was also the age of "Ossian" Macpherson, of "Gothic" Walpole, of sentimental Mackenzie, of antiquarian Percy, and of the Rev. Laurence Sterne, a law unto himself.

A rigid conception of a period may be called "chronological totalitarianism": it implies that all men living at the same time are identical, or at least that they inevitably have some profound elements in common. Perhaps an image will help us realize why this is a fallacy. The heavens are our cosmic clock: we keep time by the sun and the stars. Yet our heavens, at any moment, do not offer a scene in which all the elements are contemporary: they represent a deep historical perspective. The light that reaches us may be a few minutes old, a few years or a few centuries. Some of our luminaries have long been dead. Some stars may exist now, which only our remote descendants will be able to see.

In like manner, men who live side by side, converse and fight as contemporaries, do not necessarily belong to the same "period." Men remain to a large extent what they were in their formative years. Many a writer active at sixty is a living fossil of his twenties. Note that "living fossil" is here used with no touch of scorn. If there are "models" in minds, it is not proved that the latest are the best, as in the case of automobiles. Shaw at eighty was more agile than solemn youngsters one fourth his age. With the years, most men grow old; some grow up; a few simply grow: the ripeness of a genius is a richer, deeper, timeless adolescence. When Thomas Mann addressed American audiences in 1938 on *The Coming Victory of Democracy*, he was younger in spirit than most of his hearers, less cynical, less disenchanted, more resilient. But his voice was that of cultured pre-war Germany. Its notes were deepened by twenty years of questioning and sorrow: but its fundamental ring was unaltered.

There is also the lag due to the difference in opportunities. Jean Jacques Rousseau, brought up haphazard in remote

Geneva, still belonged to the seventeenth century, read romances which had long been obsolete in Paris, never mastered the sharp analytical wit, the searching irony, which had become universal in the salons of the French capital. Out of touch with his own era, he was a reactionary whom chance turned into a prophet.

Most of all, there are inborn differences, which may be enhanced or checked, but never quite overcome, by the "spirit of the period," or atmosphere of the time. In any assembly of soberly dressed, sensible men of our own days, there are some who belong, mind and soul, to the great thirteenth century; some to the seventeenth; not a few to the primeval jungle; and others to the mysterious millennia ahead. This is true, not merely of any group of men, but of any individual man. We are never fully "contemporary with ourselves." There were ruling fashions in 1900; but there was no single personality that was solidly "1900." Every one of us exists on several chronological planes, like society itself, and like the stars above. There is truth in the odd saying that there are but three classes of minds: the historical museum, the Antique Shoppe, and the junk yard. Our religious thought may be coeval with Isaiah, St. Paul, St. Francis or Calvin. Our scientific thought may not have moved an inch beyond Galileo, Bacon and Newton. Our philosophy may be as old as Plato or Kant. Our politics may hark back to Louis XIV, William Pitt or George Washington; our economy to Colbert, Adam Smith or Karl Marx. We are all at the same time fossils, heirs, experimenters and dreamers.

This historical complexity is most evident in terms of literature. Some people refuse to look at any book more than three years old. But even they have been exposed to a few classics in their youth; they cannot quite obliterate the influence of what they read ten years before; they too live, not in the *moment* only, but in *time*. Most of us consciously move up and down the centuries: today, Job, Ecclesiastes or King David may be our companions, far closer to us than our next door neighbor; tomorrow, it may be Shakespeare, Cervantes or Voltaire.

To isolate "our times," or any "times," from the rest of time is therefore a delusion. But it is an almost irresistible one. It is not found exclusively among the naïve and the uneducated. That masterly and most stimulating essay by J. E. Spingarn, "The New Criticism," offers a perfect example of the "period" fallacy. The author uses as his refrain the trenchant phrase: "We have done with . . ." He proceeds to enumerate no less than eleven things that "we" have discarded; and he offers, as a substitute, "the only possible method," the "New Criticism." [1] This is the notion of a New Era with a vengeance: as it is said in the *International:* "The world must change its basis; we were nothing, let us be everything." But, in the first place, who are the *we* who have done with all the conventions and paraphernalia of the "old" criticism? The literary world in a solid body? No; only Benedetto Croce and a handful of disciples. What is the "new" and "only possible" method? One which had been better expressed by Goethe a hundred years, by Alexander Pope two hundred years before.[2] What has become of the eleven principles or doctrines that *we* have tossed upon the junk pile? Every one of them is still used by some reputable critic. The "new" criticism takes its place as an eddy in the long and complex evolution of the *genre;* the Age of Croce is a myth, like the Age of Johnson; the epoch-making manifesto failed to make an epoch.

Shall we say then: "We have done with periods, epochs, centuries, ages, eras; with all artificial groupings of men who merely happened to be contemporaries; with all arbitrary sectioning of ever-flowing time"? Yes, if the idea of period, a

---

[1] "When Criticism first propounded as its real concern the oft-repeated question: 'What has the poet tried to express, and how has he expressed it?', Criticism prescribed for itself the only possible method." J. E. Spingarn, "The New Criticism," in *Creative Criticism.*

[2] "A perfect judge will read each work of wit
With the same spirit that its author writ"
—A. Pope, *An Essay on Criticism,* 1711.

tyrannical idol, threatens to warp our judgment or restrict our pleasure. No, if periods are considered merely as convenient means of analysis and classification.

The first use of the period idea is negative. It adds nothing to literature, but it helps remove causes of misunderstanding. We frequently attach the word period to the notion of style in clothes or furniture: the study of a period brings out the important fact that such things are mere fashions, and do not affect the essential man. We shall never fully know "what the poet tried to express and how he expressed it," unless we are acquainted with his *language*, that is to say with the conventions of his time. We might think that the French classics of the seventeenth century were highly artificial and pompous, because they wore impressive periwigs and wrote in heroic couplets. Greater familiarity with their costumes and customs makes us realize that Molière, Racine, Boileau, were men like ourselves. The realistic minds of the Middle Ages were not "naïve"; the critical philosophers of the Enlightenment were not "flippant"; they only seem so to the uninitiated. The work of the antiquarian, who revels in period differences, is of capital importance for the true historian, because it enables him to discount these differences.

If we thus eliminate what is "period" in an author, we discover his essential humanity, and also the uniqueness of his personality. We have to study the Elizabethan Age in order to disengage the true Shakespeare from his purely Elizabethan trappings and tricks of speech. For the period, which creates false differences between men of various centuries, also creates false resemblances among members of the same generation. We have to reconstitute the atmosphere of Paris and Versailles under the reign of Louis XIV in order to measure the full distance between Racine, Thomas Corneille and Quinault, and in order to discover that Racine is more akin to Shakespeare than to those men who wore the same elaborate uniform as he.

But the Period idea may also be used positively. All tendencies, we are ready to grant, are present at all times in the human race; but they do not always have an equal chance. A period is the moment when a particular tendency is favored and emphasized. In 1917, America was the Great Crusader; a few years later, the word was passed: "America's business is Business." The two strains coexist in us: in the country as a whole, and in the heart of every citizen. But the materialist was scorned in 1917, the idealist was jeered at in 1922: two different periods. These collective waves are interesting phenomena in themselves. Shall we say that they belong to the domain of history, not to that of literature? But they affect directly the essential problem of criticism: "What has the poet tried to express, and how has he expressed it?" For, according to the atmosphere of the time, the same man might be exulting, resigned, rebellious. A Napoleon could not have arisen in an age of profound stability: neither could a Byron or a Shelley. Even if we believe that their indomitable genius would have forced a new way, they would bear little outward resemblance to the Napoleon, the Byron, the Shelley whom we know.

It is impossible to survey our literary tradition, and not to be impressed with two facts. The first is the undeniable reality of change; the second is the unevenness of that change. We firmly believe that the permanency of human nature is a fact also, and of far greater moment: our whole conception of world literature is based upon it. But man, like Tennyson's God, "fulfills himself in many ways, lest one good custom should corrupt the world." We may be able to enjoy *Genesis*, the *Iliad*, Aristophanes, Lucretius, Dante, Balzac, on a broad human basis; but we are also aware—to our delight—that we are taken through the various circles of an infinitely complex world. But that change, which is unceasing, refuses to keep step with the calendar. If time is ever-flowing, history has pools and rapids. We find centuries of magnificent self-assurance and stability, and crises which, in a decade, transform the face of the world. The nineteenth century, itself an age of revolutions, technical, economic, social, artistic, asserted desperately "the inevitability of gradualness": wishful theorizing, which proved unable to avert catastrophes. These two considerations determine the basic problems of literary history. If there be change, is it possible to ascertain in what direction it is taking place? And why is it that change is so fitful—headlong and sluggish by turns? The first is the question of *progress;* the second the problem of *periods.*

To many readers, the first question will seem pure foolishness. Progress in science and industry is undeniable; a cynic would gladly admit that we can kill men more efficiently than ever before, and that vulgar nonsense can be transmitted to the very ends of the world with the rapidity of lightning. We have more power than our ancestors; but we are not sure that we have more sweetness and more light. In art and religion, the doctrine of progress, far from being commonly accepted, has ever been considered a paradox, if not a sacrilege. The orthodox view is that perfection was attained in ages remotely past. All our endeavor should tend to check the inevitable tendency to decay. Any apparent progress is only a partial recovery.

There is nothing absurd in this sharp contrast between material progress and spiritual immobility. When an individual learns a new technique, like driving an automobile, he becomes more efficient, he acquires new power; but he is not made thereby more intelligent or more virtuous. His new knowledge will not enable him to refute Spinoza, or prevent him from cheating his neighbor. Similar might very well be the experience of the race: mankind is increasingly skilled in the use of tools, with no sign of increase in mind or heart. It could even be argued that toying with innumerable and complicated gadgets is actually a hindrance to earnest thinking; it certainly is no help to righteous living; least of all is it able to enhance our enjoyment of beauty. This is no argument for primitivism. Since we have tools, and must have tools, let them be as perfect as possible; there is no virtue in the horse and-buggy as compared with a swift, smooth-running car. But let us not forget that they are only tools.

This is familiar, and even commonplace enough. But the

commonplace is not necessarily true. The opposite view is that mankind has acquired, not gadgets merely, but a method. This method does not alter the quality of the mind, but it immeasurably increases its capacity. Perhaps there is no living chemist who is the intellectual peer of the Greek natural philosophers; but, in comparison with our age, the knowledge of the Greeks was scant, and their very thought was crude. In the scientific field, this critical and experimental method has been applied for the last three hundred years with increasing rigor and with increasing success. In other fields, it is not applied at all, and the result is stagnation. The fact that it is not applied does not prove that it is inapplicable. We are beginning to feel that in political, social and economic organization, the laboratory spirit might be an efficient substitute for "the wisdom of our ancestors." Perhaps the same spirit would prove effective in the study and practice of art and literature.[1]

This great issue was debated two hundred and fifty years ago, in the famous Quarrel of the Ancients and the Moderns, which raged—mildly—in France and in England for a whole generation.[2] Unfortunately, this controversy blurred the prob-

[1] It may be objected that the scientific approach has been used in the study of literature, under the form of scholarly research. It has yielded much—quantitatively—but failed to affect in any measurable degree our understanding or enjoyment of the art. For this confessed failure, two causes may be suggested: (a) scholarly research is purely historical, even antiquarian, and not experimental; (b) it ignores the basic facts of literary experience, namely, the psychology of creation, the psychology of appreciation, the sociology of success. Textual criticism and proper dating are indispensable; but they are merely the collection of retrospective material, for a study which so far has barely been undertaken. Zola did write a book on *The Experimental Novel;* but he did not have in mind the experimental study of literary production. He wanted his novels to be considered as valid experiments in physiology and sociology; a claim which, if not altogether absurd, was at any rate overstated.

[2] Charles Perrault, *The Century of Louis the Great,* 1687; Sir William Temple, *Ancient and Modern Learning,* 1690; Jonathan Swift, *The Battle of the Books,* 1697; Houdar de la Motte, *Reflections on Criticism,* 1716. Also Boileau, Fontenelle, Fénelon, Madame Dacier, etc. Note that, in a purely scientific subject, the circulation of the blood, Boileau had vigorously taken the modernist side against the blind followers of Aristotle. His sprightly "Mock Decision of the Supreme Court of Parnassus, sustaining the doctrine of Aristotle," could easily be transferred from the medical to the literary field.

lem instead of focusing it. Both sides had ambiguous cases, and the battle was undecisive. The best men were on the side of the ancients; it is not certain that they had the best of the argument. Unfortunately, Pascal was dead, who had said so definitely that mankind, in its continuity through the centuries, was like a single man forever adding to his store of experience; and that antiquity represented therefore, not the wisdom of age, but the infancy of the race.

Our purpose is not to defend the theory of progress in literature; we only want to show how crude it would be to reject it offhand. It would deserve to be so rejected, if it involved the sacrifice of cherished masterpieces, if we were asked in its name to treat Shakespeare with the same amused contempt as we treat the popular books of a generation ago. But this is not implied in the theory of progress. Not only could we still admire the great works of the past *historically*, as we admire the ingenuity of the Ptolemaic system, although it has long been superseded; but they would remain, if truly great, a living part of our experience. Science does not grow simply by brushing away old errors; this is but a secondary process. It grows by discovering new truths which do not contradict the old, and new aspects of the old truths. The essential work of great scientists is absorbed, not destroyed; it is only the tricks of charlatans that disappear altogether. In the same way, the pseudo-classics would be left behind and forgotten; the true classics would remain and grow with us.

Neither the idea of decadence, nor that of progress, and still less that of aimless tramping about, can explain the uneven rate of change. It cannot be accounted for either by the alleged rhythm of youth and old age. "There are," said Taine, "but two parties: that of the men of twenty, that of the men of forty": impatient youth, sober maturity; radicals, conservatives. This oft-repeated assertion is at variance with plain facts. Everyone has met men who were conservatives at twenty, and men who were radicals at forty—or twice forty. There are even cases, and not a few, of men who, with advancing years, grew from conservatism to radicalism: Victor Hugo, Gladstone, Anatole France. But even if that rhythm were admitted as real, it would affect the individual, not the nation, in which all ages are represented. It would explain "periods" in the life of an author: Wordsworth's youthful and flamboyant Jacobinism, his long and gray Toryism; it would not explain "periods" in the development of Europe. And, if we accepted the bold and delusive metaphor that a race grows old like a man, we should be faced with the absurdity of a radical and even revolutionary Enlightenment six hundred years older than the conservative Middle Ages.

Nor can periods be determined by the natural reaction of one generation against its immediate predecessor. Of course, our fathers are invariably "naïve," either in their enthusiasm or in their cynicism, in their simplicity or in their sophistication; we have outgrown all that; we have attained "the only possible method" in criticism, in history, in fiction, in lyric poetry. This tendency is widespread, but it is not universal; there always are young people who attempt the impossible feat of "walking in their fathers' footsteps." But these wavelets of reaction are the same through the ages; the surface of history is uniformly rippled with them; they do not create periods. Physically, there is no such thing as a generation. America today is composed of men of all ages, as it was thirty and sixty years ago. What we call a "generation" is a vogue, or, more nobly, a prevailing ideal. There was a romantic generation in France between 1820 and 1830 (side by side with a larger, if less brilliant, un-romantic generation). It followed the inspiration of Chateaubriand, who was thirty years older, and of Jean Jacques Rousseau, who had died fifty years before. Our "Lost Generation" after the war was "lost" (vociferously) because it had followed a few old men attached to eighteenth-century ideas. Had they been "their own age," they would not have been lost at all. Periods are collective phenomena; they affect the individual, they may have an individual as a leader or as a symbol, but they are not created by purely individual causes.

A tempting explanation is offered by the *ethnic* theory. Each race or people that steps on the stage of history brings with it some new element, its own particular gift to human culture. This element is crude at first; then it reaches a point of perfection; then it disappears, absorbed into the common stream; or else it exhausts itself ingloriously in endless repetition. Thus the Greeks brought beauty and reason in subtle harmony; the Romans represented the triumph of the practical will: conquest, order and law; the ancient Hebrews gave a fierce sense of righteousness, or active conformity with the will of an intensely personal God; the later Jews and Syrians contributed a religion of meekness and love. With the Nordics, the ideas of force, heroism, loyalty, freedom, received a new life, a wilder coloring; and with the Celts came the sense of romance: adventure, mystery, dreaminess, and fatal love as the greatest of adventures and the greatest of mysteries. If we had the eloquence of a Bossuet, or simply the assertiveness of a Spengler, this could be made to sound very impressive; but no eloquence could make it even mistily true.

It may happen that an idea is prominent at the time when a particular people is at the height of its influence; but this does not prove that "idea" and "people" are naturally and inseparably linked. Heroism, for example, is a factor common to practically all civilizations; the sense of law was expressed by Socrates as strikingly as by the Romans; and if there were periods of Greek, Roman and Nordic supremacy, there never were any corresponding moments of political predominance for the Hebrews, the Syrians or the medieval Celts. In any case, this theory would cease to operate as soon as all the characters had appeared on the stage, that is to say by the end of the Dark Ages: for the last thousand years, no new ethnic element has been introduced. If we attempt to identify those complex and ever-shifting groups, the modern nations, with this or that ideal, we shall find ourselves lost in utter confusion. Neo-Classicism, which assumed a French form, was of Italian origin; the Enlightenment was Anglo-French; Romanticism,

Anglo-German; Realism, Russo-Franco-Anglo-German; Symbolism, Russo-Germano-Franco-Scandinavian. No doubt there is a lag between various national cultures, so that an idea may reach maturity, or secure recognition, ten years earlier in one capital than in another; but all these movements, which were also periods, affected the whole of European civilization.

Professor Louis Cazamian offers an extremely interesting theory of periods, based upon what he calls "the collective Psychological Rhythm." He recognizes that Pluralism is a fact: all forms of literary taste coexist at the same time and in the same country; but there always is one of these forms which may be recognized as dominant, and the season of its dominance is a *period*. The shift from one particular taste to another is due to the constant swing of the pendulum between intellect and sentiment, that is to say between Classicism and Romanticism.

This theory, expounded in several essays, is the subject of a very searching book, *L'Evolution Psychologique et la Littérature en Angleterre, 1660-1914*. There the hypothesis is confronted with definite facts, by a man whose knowledge of the field is matched only by the subtlety of his mind. So the examination of Professor Cazamian's theory should at any rate be a stimulating mental exercise.

Why, in the first place, should the coexistence of intellect and sentiment create a "rhythm," a regular swing from one to the other? We are all compounded of conflicting elements in precarious equilibrium. We are body and soul, therefore materialists when we are hungry or tired, idealists when we read Plato or the Psalms. We have at times at least the vigorous delusion of freedom, at times an overwhelming sense that we are determined by forces which we cannot control. We do "swing" indeed from one tendency to its opposite, but sanity consists in preserving a constant adjustment between them. We can easily understand how even a well-balanced man may be swayed now by his head, now by his heart. But in order to synchronize those innumerable individual rhythms into a collective movement, into a period, there must be some outside force, which Professor Cazamian does not define. Yes—if we are willing to oversimplify—the abstractions called Europe, or England, may be coolly rational today, and tomorrow wildly passionate. This states the fact, but does not attempt to explain it.

Second objection: of the three old-established "faculties of the mind," intellect, sentiment and will, Professor Cazamian tells us that only the first two are important sources of mental activity and of esthetic pleasure; we are not satisfied with this rejection of the will as a psychological and artistic factor. Many authors were first of all "Poets of the Will." It is a commonplace of French criticism to give that very title to "great Corneille." He is not lacking in intellectual power, nor in genuine pathos; but the true Cornelian ring comes with the assertion of the indomitable ego. "I, myself, alone, and that is enough!"—the defiant cry of his Medea could have been uttered by all the most impressive among his characters. We find the same element in Stendhal and in Balzac, who were both affected by the example of Napoleon, "professor of energy"; in Schopenhauer, who at the same time magnifies and combats the will, in which he sees the cause and the curse of life; in Nietzsche, apostle of ruthlessness; in Ibsen, with his rugged anarchism. These are not mere exceptions: there are moments when will power for its own sake becomes a collective ideal. About 1900, chiefly as a reaction against a decade of sophistication and exquisite decadentism, red-blooded men like Rudyard Kipling, and strenuous Theodore Roosevelt, were national and international idols. No, it will not do to ignore the will; but, if we restore it to coequal rank with intellect and sentiment, our psychological rhythm will lose much of its convincing simplicity.

Finally, we challenge the assertion that Classicism is intellectual, Romanticism sentimental. This is plausible, but not accurate. If we accept the common definitions of Romanticism as the desire for indefinite expansion, of Classicism as the willing acceptance of restraint, we shall see that each of these tendencies can find its manifestation in the intellect, the sentiments, or the will. There is a Classicism of the intellect, which is the rule of pure reason; but there is a Romanticism of the intellect, which is the predominance of imagination. The pioneers of thought are not sentimentalists; they are men who dare to venture into uncharted seas. There is a Classicism of the sentiments, which is the love of duty; men whose lives are well ordered are not necessarily heartless. There is a Romanticism of the sentiments, according to which passion is justified by its very sincerity and intensity. There is a Classicism of the will, which seeks power through "self-reverence, self-knowledge, self-control." And there is a Romanticism of the will, which spurns every check. Tristan and Isolde were romantics of the heart; but Milton's Satan was a romantic of the will, Coleridge in *Kubla Khan* a romantic of the intellect, and in neither is there any trace of sentiment.

Perhaps the safest approach would be to consider first those periods which are indisputable, or at least undisputed, and which stand out as patterns for the less definite divisions. The first that come to our minds are the three classical ages, often named, after the rulers, the Ages of Pericles, of Augustus and of Louis XIV. Not only do they stand out because of their magnificent achievements; they are more distinctive still because of their self-assurance. They have attained conscious maturity. That impression of maturity does not result merely from the perfection of individual works, but from the harmony between all the manifestations of life; they are, to borrow a useful term from the early socialist Henri de Saint-Simon, *organic* periods. The Athens of Pericles, racked as it was by philosophical controversies, party strife and merciless war, still offers to our eyes a harmonious picture, in which the Parthenon, Pheidias, the tragic writers, the historians, Socrates, assume their natural place. Even when they differed most fiercely, the Greeks of that golden age belonged together; there is among them an unmistakable unity of style. Everything is Augustan in the Augustan world: ruler, art, society, literature. The Age of Louis XIV is a model of well-balanced composition. In the center, the king, revered as the living law, the symbol of unity, discipline and power; at his right hand, Bossuet, at his left, Colbert: religion and economics bearing the same stamp of assurance, solidity, grandeur—bourgeois common sense purged from bourgeois pettiness. The artists, Mansard, Lebrun, Lulli, the poets, Boileau, Molière, Racine, find their appointed place in the glorious pageant. Even nature, under the hands of Lenôtre, proudly conforms to the stateliness of the whole.

With this pattern of the organic periods in our minds, we can discern a few others which, less obviously perhaps, also deserve the name. Classical critics recognized four great "centuries"; to the three we have mentioned was added that of the Italian Renaissance, which, for the sake of symmetry, was called "the Age of Leo X" after the great Medici pontiff. We believe that the thirteenth century offers the same character of essential unity; the concepts of papacy and empire, the Christian monarchy of St. Louis, Gothic art and the *Summa* of St. Thomas Aquinas are parts of a grand synthesis. Personalities may clash, and it is a scandal; but principles and institutions fit together. Even those elements which are of a different origin, feudalism, the communes, the guilds, must repeat the formulae and adopt the trappings of Catholic civilization, which dominates the whole. Unlovely no doubt, but marked with undeniable organic unity, was the period of Realism, in the second half of the nineteenth century. Whoever dissented was a spiritual exile: Realism was supreme. In philosophy, with Utilitarianism, with the Positivism of Auguste Comte, and most of all with the triumph of the scientific outlook; in economics, with the Manchester School; in painting, in literature, with Manet, Courbet, Flaubert; in the state, with the *Real-Politik* of Bismarck. Even Napoleon III, a romantic dreamer, succeeded only because his regime served realistic ends, assured material order, and promoted material prosperity.

Every one of these ages did believe, and was apparently justified in believing, that it had reached at last the eternal verities, even though the truth thus attained, in the case of Realism, be harsh and somber. It is a disconcerting fact that these moments of certainty were fleeting. The "organic periods," far from covering the major part of history, are but a few luminous points in the confused annals of mankind. These ages are often called "centuries"; but these centuries never covered more than a few decades. The Periclean age did not extend much beyond the personal rule of Pericles. The medieval dream of a City of God on this earth was soon shattered: pope against emperor, pope against king, pope against pope. Leo X died in 1521: six years later, the sack of Rome tragically and permanently obscured the splendor of the Italian Renaissance. The "Century of Louis XIV" began with the accession of the king to personal power in 1661; it was over with the death of Colbert in 1683, or with the Revocation of the Edict of Nantes in 1685. The realistic synthesis did not triumph until the collapse of the Romantic Revolution of 1848; by 1880, certainly before 1890, Realism was on the defensive in every domain.

Epochs of organic unity are few and brief; the long intervals between them are "times out of joint": science at odds with religion, the social order not in keeping with the political system, art unable to express itself in the terms of its own day. The impressive harmony of the great ages is so precarious only because it never was absolute, nor even perhaps profound. When a conqueror enters a city, he may be hailed by enthusiastic throngs. But his opponents are overawed, not destroyed; the masses shout for him, because they would invariably shout for the victor; his own partisans are ready to carp and to squabble; disillusion begins on the very day of apparent triumph. So it goes when the conqueror is, not an individual, but a principle. Every great movement is a chance coalition; the various elements that fought under the same flag are expecting incompatible things from their common victory. The Neo-Classical synthesis of Louis XIV was a compromise. It harnessed together ancient authority and free reason, Christian faith and a literature rooted in paganism, absolutism and the "liberties" or traditional privileges of classes and provinces, bourgeois realities and the brave show of an aristocratic court. Of all these elements, some were survivals, and already on the wane; others were gathering new strength. The inner balance of the coalition could not be preserved, and its disruption was inevitable.

Inevitable, but not sudden. The process of dissolution is gradual. We start with the organic period in all its self-confidence, the new synthesis promising and producing wonders, a Golden Age. It is followed by a Silver Age, still unquestioning in its faith, still productive, but with a touch of lassitude, a dimming of hope. Then comes the generation of the Epigoni: the imitators, the pedants, the *pseudo* or *would-be*, who strive to preserve the forms all the more scrupulously because the spirit is no longer in them. With them are often found the *dilettanti*, for whom the forms themselves have lost all meaning, and yet who continue to cultivate them, because their mastery of empty forms sets them apart as the connoisseurs, the erudite, the initiated, the acrobats of technique.

Before that point of utter vacuity is reached, a movement of protest has already started. It may begin with the *dilettanti* themselves, as pure skepticism and self-irony: a period of elegant anarchism and refined decadence. It may assume the form of sheer despair, in a world grown stale and unprofitable. Unmitigated, despair is seldom productive. It must be illuminated by hope, however distant and vague. Then it turns into rebellion, rebellion still uncertain of its aim, almost rebellion for rebellion's sake. The best example of this is the German *Sturm-und-Drang* ("Storm-and-Stress"), and its motto might be Schiller's epigraph to his drama *The Brigands: Quae medicamenta non sanant, ferrum sanat, quae ferrum non sanat, ignis sanat* (Hippocrates): What remedies fail to cure, iron will cure; and, if not iron, then fire. But rebellion, being active, needs principles of action, and evolves them in the course of battle, if they were not clear before. This is the period of pioneers, forerunners, pre-this and pre-that, obscure and confused fighters, sometimes destined to be half-forgotten, like Johann Georg Hamann, the Magus of the North, sometimes hailed as the Fathers of a Revolution which their eyes did not see, like Jean Jacques Rousseau. A decisive campaign, and the old is supplanted by the new; another synthesis assumes control, and bears in itself the germs of its own destruction.

This is of course merely a schematic outline. It describes fairly accurately the transition from Classicism to Romanticism in the eighteenth century. But, even in that particular case, it does not take into account many disturbing elements. An ideal survives longer, naturally, when it has become incarnated in a man of commanding genius. Thanks to Shakespeare, Elizabethan Romanticism never completely disappeared in English literature; and unswerving Classicism, by which Shakespeare would stand condemned, only made Thomas Rymer ludicrous. Then the whole field of battle may be shifted. In the eighteenth century, while the change from Classicism to Romanticism was slowly taking place, the main issue was no longer literary: it was the struggle between reactionaries and liberals in the realm of thought. A man like Voltaire could be intellectually in the vanguard, artistically an Epigone. We are not attempting like Spengler to provide a single pattern for all the cycles of cultural evolution. No attempt at tracing a general trend can hope to account for the innumerable eddies. In the second half of the eighteenth century, for instance, while the tendency to romantic medievalism was already apparent, there was in art and even in literature a sharp revival of interest in the antique. It is odd that the most purely romantic of all poets, Blake, should in many of his engravings stand so close to the arch-classicist Flaxman.

We are only endeavoring to show that literary history is not a kaleidoscope, in which the whole design is completely changed when we jerk the instrument; it should rather be likened to a series of dissolving pictures. Yet the "jerk" theory should not be completely dismissed. A great event in the non-literary field may accelerate and clarify the process of change, or on the contrary it may retard and confuse it. The course of the Renaissance was undoubtedly deflected by the Reformation; and the French Revolution, absorbing all energies, deferred by several decades the advent of Romanticism in France.

SUMMARY

Periods, like tendencies and genres, are abstractions and conventions. A rigid conception of a period might be called "chronological totalitarianism": all people living at the same time are supposed to think and feel alike. This is a fallacy; a man remains in many cases a fossil of his formative years; different opportunities determine a different rate of development; there are inborn differences that no "Spirit of the Period" can overcome; and the individual himself lives on several chronological planes.

This is most evident in terms of Literature; that is why we are able to move, in our readings, up and down the centuries, feeling ourselves the contemporaries today of Job, tomorrow of Cervantes.

To isolate "our times" or any other "times" from the rest of time is a delusion. But periods are convenient means of analysis and classification. The first use of the period idea is negative: by eliminating from an author everything that is "period" in him—the conventions of his time—we realize better both his essential humanity and the uniqueness of his personality. The second is positive. A period is the moment when a particular tendency is emphasized; we are thus enabled to explore this tendency more thoroughly, under the most favorable circumstances.

A brief survey of literary tradition impresses two facts upon us: the reality of change, and the unevenness of that change. Hence the two essential problems: (1) is it possible to ascertain whether change is effected in a definite direction? This is the question of *progress*. (2) Why is that change so fitful, headlong and sluggish by turns? This is properly the question of *periods*.

In science and industry, progress is undeniable. But in art and religion, the doctrine of progress has ever been considered a paradox. Perfection, it is believed, was attained in ages remotely past. Man has acquired new power without growing more intelligent or more virtuous. The opposite view is that mankind has acquired, not gadgets merely, but a method, which, while it does not alter the quality of the mind, immeasurably increases its capacity. In the scientific field, this method has been applied for three hundred years with increasing success. In the fields in which it is not applied there is stagnation. A new spirit, experimental and not antiquarian, might prove equally efficient in the study and practice of literature.

Neither the idea of decadence nor that of progress will explain that uneven rate of change which determines the period. This cannot be accounted for either by the rhythm of youth and old age, in men or nations: some young people are conservatives, some old men are radicals. Still less by the reaction of one generation against its immediate predecessor: such reactions are constant ripples on the surface of history, they do not create periods.

One favorite explanation is the *ethnic* theory: each race or people that steps onto the stage of history brings its peculiar gift to human culture. But nothing proves that any *idea* is exclusively linked with any one race or people; and in the last thousand years, no ethnic element has been added to the composition of Western Europe.

Cazamian's theory of periods is based on the *collective psychological rhythm* from intellect to sentiment, i.e., from classicism to romanticism. But (1) why should the coexistence of intellect and sentiment create a rhythm between them? (2) Why neglect the will as an element in literature? (3) Why identify the intellect with classicism, sentiment with romanticism? There is a classicism of the intellect, of the sentiment, of the will; and forms of romanticism to correspond.

We start realistically with the periods best established in tradition, unmistakable, undeniable: the three classical centuries, those of Pericles, Augustus, Louis XIV. They offer a well-ordered picture, they have organic unity. The thirteenth century, the Italian Renaissance, the realistic synthesis in the second half of the nineteenth century, present the same character of integration.

But these periods are few and brief: the long intervals are "times out of joint." This is because any synthesis, deeming itself eternal, is in fact artificial and precarious, and begins crumbling in the very moment of victory. A Golden Age is followed by a Silver Age; then a generation of Epigoni or imitators; possibly the dilettanti and the elegant anarchists. Against empty forms a protest is growing: at first sheer rebellion, with melancholy or despair; then the pioneering of a new synthesis, which, when victorious, will believe itself final.

This schematic process is modified of course by innumerable causes. The two most important are the influence of commanding geniuses, which retards the dissolution of their ideal; and that of great events in the non-literary field, such as reformations, revolutions and wars.

CHAPTER XVII

PERIODS IN LITERATURE

II. SURVEY OF THE PERIODS

W E SHALL now pass in rapid review the periods generally recognized in world literature. It will be noticed
at once that they do not fully coincide with the conventional divisions in any one of the national literatures. They
are broader, and cannot take into account purely personal
groups, like Ronsard's Pléiade in France, Johnson's circle in
England, or the Court of Weimar in Germany. But the discrepancies are due to other causes as well. First of all, we suffer from the lack of a common terminology. The habit of calling an age by the name of a ruler is confusing. We bracket together as Victorians, for example, writers who, like Macaulay,
Carlyle, Thomas Hardy and Oscar Wilde, had practically nothing in common. If "Victorian" has a definite meaning, as a spirit,
not as a chronological division, it closely resembles the school
of bourgeois common sense in mid-nineteenth-century France.
The local names imply false affinities and conceal real ones.[1]

But the difficulty lies deeper. Although we firmly believe that
European culture is one, we have repeatedly admitted that the
rhythm of change varies in the different countries. The literatures of England and France have for centuries kept in such
close touch that they are indeed inseparable. Yet any attempt to
synchronize their development too closely would be foolish.

---

[1] Another source of confusion is the ambiguity of the word *classic*. Calderón, for instance, is the last of the great Spanish Classics, but he is not a
classicist. Schiller and Goethe are the German Classics par excellence; but *The
Brigands*, *Werther*, *Faust*, are striking examples of Romanticism.

327

The two nations have the same problem to meet, and go, at their own proper time, through the same phases; but it is almost a miracle if at any moment, in art or in politics, they are able to see eye to eye.

Of these departures from the European norm, the most striking examples are the Italian *Trecento* (fourteenth century) and the Spanish *Siglo de Oro* (seventeenth). The Italy of Dante, Petrarch, Boccaccio, was at least a hundred years ahead of the Northern countries. The Spain of Lope de Vega and Calderón was not, as we should expect, part of the Neo-Classical era, but a glorious and unique blend of the medieval and Renaissance spirits. Yet the Pan-European periods are not wholly delusive. Ultimately, every country adapts itself to the general evolution; the pioneers pause for a while, and the laggards catch up with the main body.

We feel that we are on fairly safe ground when the periods are self-determined, when the contemporaries themselves are conscious of entering upon a new era. Even if they were deluded, their state of mind itself is an undeniable historical fact. The hymns of triumph which, North of the Alps, hailed the Revival of Learning, are indications which we cannot ignore. "O times, O century!" cried Ulrich von Hutten, "it is a joy to be alive!" And in Rabelais, Gargantua writes to his son Pantagruel: "The dark calamitous night of the Goths is over. Through heavenly grace, in my own lifetime, dignity and light have been restored to humane letters." But the still greater Renaissance of the eleventh century, which actually changed the face of the world, came in unheralded. No single date, no event, no masterpiece, no great personality, marked the turning point. So even today, we are still tempted to think of the whole millennium between the downfall of Rome and the dawn of modern times as a single period; we call it the Dark Ages, which is absurd, or the Middle Ages, which is meaningless. The greatness of a change does not wholly depend upon contemporary awareness. Revolutionary France, in 1792, had no doubt but she was inaugurating a new epoch, and embodied that belief in a new calendar; Goethe claims to have said, on the battlefield of Valmy: "At this time, in this place, a new era begins in the history of the world." We now consider the French Revolution only as a confused episode in a much vaster process. On the other hand, when Newcomen, in the first decade of the eighteenth century, constructed crude but practical steam engines, he was probably not conscious that he was starting "the Industrial Revolution."

It must be remembered that we are limiting our survey to Western World Literature: the masterpieces of the East have not yet been fully integrated with our tradition. Even the Bible does not find a logical place in the accepted divisions of literary history: for centuries, its sacred character precluded a full appreciation of its artistic power. Our periods therefore are those of classical antiquity and modern Europe.

Inevitably, we must begin with Homer. We start, as Horace advised, *in medias res*. In other arts, we have vestiges of primitive times, and we can trace man's progress from his crudest attempts; but the long evolution which must have led to Homer has left no trace. This first period offers a curious contrast: it is sharply defined on a background of impenetrable mist. No poems could be more clear-cut and sunlit than the *Iliad* and the *Odyssey*; and through them, the Homeric world is extremely real to us. But we know nothing of the author himself, of his predecessors, of his rivals; we know hardly anything about his immediate successors.

After this Homeric period came the age of the great lyric poets, Sappho, Alcaeus. This period also is dimly known; and it merges with the following one, which was marked by the sudden flowering of the dramatic art. For lyricism continued to flourish long after Sappho, with Anacreon, Simonides of Ceos, Pindar; and Pindar was almost exactly the contemporary of Æschylus.

We thus reach the Golden Age, the fifth century before Christ: supreme in drama, supreme in history, it was also the time of Socrates, wisest of mortals. Before the death of Pericles, the greatness of Athens had already waned; but the fourth century B.C. still offers names of unrivaled splendor: Plato and Aristotle in philosophy, and Demosthenes, who has remained the very symbol of eloquence.

With Alexander, Hellenism spread with fabulous ease, even as far as India. This incredible adventure did not dissolve like a dream: the Eastern Mediterranean remained Greek for a thousand years. Greek in language, Greek in tradition: but the fearless spirit which had given Athens its unique and perilous greatness had already disappeared when Macedonia assumed leadership. Alexandria, perpetuating the founder's name, became the capital of Hellenism, and the period was called after the city. A weakened culture could provide very brilliant forms for the vast and complex Hellenic world, but not a principle of life: "Alexandrian," in art and literature, evokes the idea of sophistication and learning, rather than originality and power. It was no longer the expression of the whole community, but the refined amusement of an élite. Alexandrian culture was a prolonged and fading shadow; but so great was Periclean Greece that its very decadence still had extraordinary vitality. It survived for centuries, kept its vigor under Roman rule, assimilated even the Jews, evolved a heady synthesis of Platonism, Biblical tradition and Oriental mysticism. It did not die of senile weakness: it had to be killed by uncompromising Christianity.

Greek culture, as we have noted, remained active under the hegemony of Rome, in Athens itself, with its famous schools, in Alexandria, second city in the ancient world, even in distant provincial centers like Massilia (Marseilles). It produced writers who have taken their place in our tradition: the biographer Plutarch, who crystallized for the Renaissance and the Neo-Classical Age the conception of the ancient hero; Lucian, whose witty skepticism found expression in the purest Attic style; the mysterious Longinus, whose treatise On the Sublime should be the charter of all Romantic criticism; Longus and his delightful idyllic romance *Daphnis and Chloë*. Late Greek passed into Patristic Greek, which in its turn lost itself into the Byzantine: the twilight of the Greek world lasted a full thousand years.

But, by the first century B.C., Rome had already become supreme in letters as well as by the force of arms. There was no revolution: Greece and Rome offered two aspects of the same culture, and the relations between the two were unique. To the end, Rome acknowledged the intellectual primacy of subjugated Greece. The basis of education was the study of the Greek classics; young Romans went to Greek schools and had Greek tutors; the emperors Hadrian, Marcus Aurelius and Julian wrote in Greek. Far more striking is the fact that many of the greatest works in Latin literature were deliberate attempts to rival Greek models. The two comic writers Plautus and Terence adapted Greek themes and plots to Roman conditions; the most powerful of all Roman poets, Lucretius, translated into Latin verse the philosophy of Epicurus. Catullus could be accounted one of the Alexandrians. Vergil confessedly pasticized Theocritus and Homer.

Yet this imitative literature is far from second-rate. Thanks to the survival of Latin as the universal language of the Church and of the learned, the great writers of Rome were far more directly known in medieval and Neo-Classical Europe than their Greek originals. Later ages revered Homer, Sophocles, Aristophanes, Demosthenes: but it was Vergil, Seneca, Plautus, Cicero, who served as patterns. Latin is not the source of our culture, but it remains its center.

It is customary to divide Latin literature, after its modest and halting beginning, into a Golden Age and a Silver Age. The former extended from the time of Sulla (ca. 100 B.C.) to the death of Augustus (14 A.D.) It comprises Lucretius, Cicero, Caesar, Sallust, Livy, Catullus, Vergil, Horace, Tibullus, Propertius, Ovid: an array second only to the matchless constellation in Periclean Athens. The second closes with the death of Trajan in 117. This Silver Age offers names which had long echoes in our culture: Seneca, Petronius, Lucan, Statius, Persius,

Martial, Juvenal; and one at least that fears no comparison, the historian Tacitus.

Perversely enough, unmistakable decadence set in with a ruler who was devoted to letters, Hadrian. This decadence was not checked during the three weary and tragic centuries before the final catastrophe. Scholars could quote the names of many Pagan writers during that long period of gathering darkness; the general reader remembers only two, and they almost belong to the Silver Age. The first is Suetonius, who, in his *Lives of the Twelve Caesars*, gave excellent models of realistic, damaging biographies, a curious counterpart to the work of Plutarch. The second is Apuleius, whose spirited and entertaining medley, *The Golden Ass*, is a hybrid between the old *genre* of mythological metamorphoses, and the realistic, satirical, almost picaresque narrative. At last the complete triumph of Christianity, and the collapse of the Western Empire before the barbarians brought to a close the long history of pagan Rome. We have alluded to the self-determination of periods: but the very last poets of the old dispensation, living as they did amid catastrophes, seemed to have no inkling that the end was near. Claudianus, a vigorous and passionate writer, no mere pseudo-classical ghost, had undimmed faith in the Eternal City, although his hero, Stilicho, was himself a Barbarian. And never did the conquering and civilizing greatness of Rome inspire a more ardent tribute than is found in the *Itinerary* of the Gaul Rutilius Namatianus, in the anxious dawn of the fifth century.

Already the New Rome had come to life, the Christian Rome. Latin as the language of the Church is still alive; as the chief vehicle of religious thought, it had an active history of at least twelve hundred years. If we limit ourselves, as we must, strictly to literary considerations, we are bound to acknowledge that this enormous period yielded very little of supreme value. At first, Christian culture, even with a man of genius like St. Augustine, had difficulties in freeing its originality from pagan influences. It developed long after the Golden Age was past, at a time when the language itself was threatened with decadence. It triumphed at the very moment when the whole of Roman civilization collapsed under the impact of the barbarians. When the world recovered confidence and energy, in the earlier and greater Renaissance, that of the eleventh century, Latin had to face the rivalry of the vernaculars. And when the Italian Renaissance restored the prestige and purity of the Latin language, it also revived the worship of *pagan* antiquity. From the literary point of view, the Latin of the Church was thus constantly handicapped, and, as a result, its vast literature remained disappointing. Its indirect influence was great; but, even in a large collection of World Classics, it would be represented by very few titles: *The City of God* and the *Confessions* of St. Augustine, an anthology of hymns and canticles, and, at the very end, *The Imitation of Christ*.

The half millennium that followed the downfall of Rome (500-1000) is palpable darkness. It affords a wealth of materials for the historian and the philologist; but for the student of literary tradition, there is nothing except a few Anglo-Saxon poems. Apart from its venerable character, *Beowulf* has undeniable power; but, except in the English-speaking world, it has not become a classic. Life did not stand still; the future nations and their vernaculars were obscurely emerging out of chaos. The figure of Charlemagne hovered, vast and vague, with an ill-fitting saintly halo, in the imagination of Western Europe. But the feeble revival of letters under his reign was only a false dawn. The Scandinavian *Eddas* and the *Song of Roland* were not to appear, or to assume definite form, until the eleventh century, and the *Nibelungenlied* even later.

When these rugged masterpieces took shape, the Dark Ages were over at last, and the great Renaissance of the eleventh century manifest. We have noted that it came without a date and without a sponsor. Hundreds of years later, romantic historians like Michelet dramatized the terror which, about the year 1000, preyed upon the minds of men. This, at any rate, has some symbolical value. The fatal date went by: men saw that God's wrath had been averted, and that they were spared for yet a little while; they began again to hope, to work, to build. "It seemed," wrote the Burgundian Raoul Glaber, "that the world was shaking off the rags of its old age, and clothing itself anew with a white mantle of churches."

Few periods have more reality than the one which thus began almost unperceived. But it has no birth certificate, and never received an acceptable name. The term *Middle Ages* was of course applied much later; it is ambiguous, for it is supposed to span the whole interval between the ruin of ancient culture and its conscious revival. It was the *Christian* epoch *par excellence:* never had the Church been invested with so much authority and so much splendor. Even the emperor bowed to the pope, and every institution, monarchy, feudalism, universities, cities and guilds, received at least its coloring from the one universal light. We are reluctant, however, to reserve the name Christian Age, or Age of Faith, for five only out of the nineteen centuries since the death of Our Lord. The clearest symbol of the period would be its glorious architecture. It developed late in the eleventh century, and was not supplanted in Northern Europe until the sixteenth. But that great art itself is wrongly named. *Gothic,* of course, had nothing to do with the Goths of history; it was a term of contempt which simply meant *rude* or *barbaric.* We are reconciled, through long habit, with the absurd expression Gothic Cathedrals; we should not like to call St. Thomas Aquinas a Gothic thinker, or Dante a Gothic poet. The *Feudal Age* will not do, for feudalism is only one aspect of the epoch. So we are compelled to fall back upon the equivocal and conventional expression, *Middle Ages.*

Within these five hundred years, we can descry vaguely three main divisions. The first (eleventh and early twelfth centuries) is full of rough vigor. It is an age of eager monks and warriors: the first Crusade, the only one that deeply moved all classes, the only one that achieved its end, was their great adventure. After the middle of the twelfth century, with the general economic and intellectual progress, civilization grew far more subtle, and attained extraordinary refinement and brilliancy in the Southern Courts. Provençal culture was brutally crushed, but it had already transmitted its achievements. This second period is an age, no longer of simple faith, but of elaborate theological reasoning. The ideal of courtesy permeated that of physical prowess. The knight was still the soldier of the Cross, but he was also the servant of his lady. The romance of chivalry gradually superseded the epic of fighting deeds. The age of St. Louis, although more complex than that of Godfrey of Bouillon, had not lost sincerity and power: but the medieval synthesis was growing too rich to remain stable.

So in the third division, the fourteenth and fifteenth centuries, the various elements of medieval culture began to fall apart. Each, because it was out of touch with the others, insisted upon its own technique rather than upon the common spirit. Flamboyant Gothic indulged in veritable tricks of ornamentation. Theology lost itself in the excessive refinement of late Scholasticism. Chivalry became a set of gorgeous trappings and a complicated code. It would be an injustice to see nothing but decadence in that uneasy but very active period: it was an age of uncertainty and conflict, with a tragic background of war and pestilence. Here, as we have noted, a sharp cleavage appeared. North of the Alps, Europe, in confusing twilight, was seeking a blurred path; but Italy, in the *Trecento* (fourteenth century) had already rediscovered antique culture, and was consciously emerging out of medievalism.

The Renaissance, in the late fifteenth century and the early part of the sixteenth, began with great definiteness. It was hastened by political events—the downfall of Constantinople, the Italian wars; and also by discoveries and inventions, the greatest of these being the printing press. This suffices to indicate that the Renaissance was not purely a revival of ancient learning; it was a movement of expansion in all domains, and classical scholarship was only one of them. It is not the rediscovery of Plato that inspired Gutenberg, Vasco da Gama or Christopher Columbus. The keynote of the early Renaissance was Humanism in the larger sense; not the grammarian's delight, but a new joy in human life, a new faith in the human spirit. Of this, Rabelais even more than Erasmus is the exulting prophet; and the aptest symbols of that age are the encyclopedic giants of Italy, Leonardo da Vinci and Michelangelo.

In spite of the dramatic change in atmosphere, the medieval synthesis did not suddenly disappear. Men like Skelton and Clément Marot were still medieval: the one paraphrased, the other edited, the great classic of the Middle Ages, the *Romance of the Rose;* but both were touched with the light of the Renaissance. Rabelais, the scientist and humanist, borrowed his theme from medieval folklore, and stuffed it with medieval tales; as we have noted, the delightful châteaux of the French Renaissance are purely Gothic in general outline, Italianate in ornamentation.

We must emphasize the word: Italianate. The Renaissance honestly believed itself to be Greco-Latin: but it received ancient art and learning refashioned by Italian hands. Pindar was far less influential than Petrarch; and, when Northern critics did obeisance to Aristotle, they were really bowing before his Italian commentators. Italy, disunited, invaded, subjected, was the light of the modern world.

It is easy to assign a definite beginning to the Renaissance. Its end is far less certain. Walter Pater felt justified in giving *The Renaissance* as a title to a series of studies which included *Aucassin and Nicolette,* a delightful narrative medley of the late twelfth century, and Winckelmann, the great Hellenist of the eighteenth. German scholars often close the Renaissance proper with the sack of Rome (1527), and call the succeeding period *Barockzeit.*[1] For the French, the Renaissance was over with the sixteenth century and the end of the Religious Wars; then the founder of the Bourbon line, Henry IV, restored peace and order in the state, and Malherbe in literature: "At last

---

[1] Barock, Barocco, Baroque: a highly decorative, theatrical, almost tormented style which culminated with the architecture and statuary of Bernini in the seventeenth century. Certain aspects of Roman decadence already had a definitely Baroque quality.

Malherbe came!" Our Elizabethan Age is usually counted part of the Renaissance. In Italy, Tasso is its last great representative. As we have noted before, the Spanish Golden Century, the seventeenth, has a strong Renaissance element.

The Renaissance clearly illustrates our theory that all great moments in the history of mankind represent the triumph of heterogeneous and precarious coalitions. All contradictions are effaced for a while in the radiance of enthusiasm; when this rapture begins to cool, conflicts inevitably appear. The Renaissance was both prospective and retrospective. It represented an expansion of the spirit, a boundless adventure; but progress was sought through a return to the main highway, that of the ancients. Which was the more essential, the progress, or the return? To the present day, "Humanism" hesitates between the two answers. The Renaissance had fought medieval superstitions. For some, that fight led back to paganism; for others, to untrammeled free thought; for others still, to a purer, re-vitalized Christianity. In that clash of ideals, the splendid spirit of confidence and joy found in Rabelais was destroyed. All that was left was the weary skeptical smile of Montaigne: no opinion is of such inestimable value that we should roast people alive for its sake. As a minor result of this skepticism, there was everywhere in Europe an epidemy of sheer formal cleverness. Nothing matters, but the skill in expressing nothing: Marinism in Italy, Gongorism in Spain, Euphuism in England, Preciosity in France.

This was the ultimate dissolution of the true Renaissance spirit. The next synthesis was the *Neo-Classical Compromise*, which dominated the whole of the seventeenth century, and, nominally, most of the eighteenth. Man cannot live by skepticism, and still less by preciosity, alone. Some order is needed: provided it be order, let us be satisfied. So tradition and reason were brought to co-operate in restoring discipline. Art sought its precepts and its models in the pagan world, but remained scrupulously Christian. It was a masterpiece of unconscious cultural diplomacy; incompatibilities were so nicely balanced that,

selves, with no lasting success. There are brief relapses into weary anarchism. After the fever of the Dreyfus Case, there was in France one of those moments when the futility of all striving appears with irrefutable clearness, so that futility itself seems the only available wisdom. A little later the whole Western world, and particularly America, went through a phase of disenchantment, after national selfishness had killed Wilson's dream of an organized world. Then in *Ecclesiastes* was found the sole preacher to whom men would hearken: "Vanity of vanities, and all is vanity." "Get drunk and be dismal, for tomorrow we die" became the sole gospel of the sophisticates. But this reign of disenchanted skepticism was the merest episode: not a "period," barely a mood. The ironists and "futilitarians" of yesterday are now serving causes; and the clash of collective wills for the conquest of power is as brutal as ever.

It takes no prophet, only the most elementary kind of historian, to assert that this "dynamic" synthesis cannot last. Unreasoning, unfeeling will-to-power leads only to the abyss. Reason and gentle sympathy must reassert themselves. We must again view the world "realistically," and not through a lurid nightmare. When some degree of sanity is restored to the world, we shall enter upon a new age, and we shall proclaim that it is eternal. But this "only possible solution" also will be compounded of crumbling facts and fading dreams: "Our little systems have their day; they have their day, and cease to be."

SUMMARY

The periods in World Literature do not exactly coincide with the conventional divisions in national literatures. There is a confusion due to the over-emphasis placed upon individuals—rulers or leaders; due also to the lack of an accepted common terminology; and above all to the lag in the evolution of various countries. It must be borne in mind that we limit ourselves to *Western* World Literature.

SYNOPSIS OF THE PERIODS

A. Classical Antiquity

I. Greece

1. Primitive and Homeric
2. Lyrical (Alcaeus, Sappho)
3. Golden Age (500-350 B.C.) (Age of Pericles: 460-429 B.C.)
4. Alexandrian (330-100 B.C.) (with long twilight)
5. Greco-Roman (Plutarch, Lucian, Longus, etc.)
6. Late Greek, Patristic and Byzantine

II. Rome

1. Early
2. Golden Age: Sulla to death of Augustus (100 B.C.-14 A.D.) Augustan Age (40 B.C.-14 A.D.)
3. Silver Age: from death of Augustus to death of Trajan (14-117)
4. Pagan Decadence (117-400)
5. Christian Latin Literature (200-1500)

B. Dark Ages and Middle Ages

1. Dark Ages (500-1000)
2. Early Middle Ages: Crusades, Epic (1000-1150)
3. Flowering of Medieval Culture: theology, chivalry, courtesy, city life (1150-1300)
4. Late Middle Ages: transition. In Italy: *Trecento* and *Quattrocento*: Pre-Renaissance. In rest of Europe: mingling lights, confusion.

C. Modern Times

1. Early Renaissance, Italian Hegemony (1453-1527)
2. Disruption and Conflict (end of sixteenth century); leading to skepticism (Montaigne) and preciosity. Great flowering in England and Spain.
3. The neo-classical compromise, tradition and reason, pa-

gan art and Christian faith. Milton, Racine. Unquestioned until Quarrel of Ancients and Moderns, 1687.

4. Eighteenth century: transition
   a. Twilight of classicism; post- and pseudo-classicism; with sharp revival at the end
   b. Enlightenment: Voltaire, Gibbon, Lessing
   c. Rise of Bourgeoisie: novel and drama
   d. Pre-Romanticism, *Sturm-und-Drang*, primitivism
5. Romanticism: from pre-romanticism to post-romanticism (1750-1850). Main period of romantic activity: 1800-1830.

D. *The Contemporary World*
   1. Realism: Positivism, science, industry, pessimism (1850-1890) and naturalism
   2. Anarchism: decadence, symbolism, estheticism. Conflicting influences of Nietzsche, Ibsen, Tolstoy.
   3. Dynamism: cult of strenuousness, energy; anti-intellectualism, anti-sentimentalism (1900-19—?). (Eddy of skepticism and sophistication, lost generation, post-war decade.)

PART THREE

MAIN PROBLEMS IN WORLD LITERATURE

CHAPTER XVIII

THE SOCIAL APPROACH TO
THE STUDY OF LITERATURE
I. RACE, ENVIRONMENT AND TIME

IN CONSIDERING the periods in World Literature, we have insisted upon the fact that they have no objective existence. A nation has frontiers, a language has a grammar and a vocabulary, a political regime has a constitution, a social regime has a code: a period is merely a collective state of mind. Such a state of mind is invariably complex, frequently confused. It imposes no absolute uniformity upon those who live and work under its dispensation: in the seventeenth century as today, men differed in temperament, ability, taste, training. And a period is not rigidly self-contained, an *autarky* cut off by impassable barriers from other ages; we are able to enjoy the masterpieces written centuries ago.

With these qualifications, the periods possess undeniable reality. It is obvious that the works of Shakespeare would not have been exactly the same, if he had been born in the murky seventh century, or in the twentieth. The most independent genius is subjected to innumerable influences. They are the material, if not the spiritual, conditions of his being. He may manifest his originality through them, in spite of them, and even against them: he cannot escape them altogether. He may use language as no one did before: he cannot create for himself a language absolutely his own. Granted that a man is fundamentally *man*, and that he is also his own unique self: between these two extremes, the human race and the individual, we cannot ignore

345

intermediate divisions: group resemblances and group differences. These we must study, if only for the purpose of discounting them. We should be obscuring our conception of Shakespeare, if we were to substitute "the Elizabethan" for the poet himself; but we shall better understand the poet, if we are clearly aware of those things in him which are "Elizabethan."

Thus the history of Civilization—the political, religious, social, economic conditions, the collective psychology of a period—can be of great assistance to the study of literature. It can never be a substitute for purely literary criticism. Literature is an art; like all the other arts, it is meant to be enjoyed; and knowledge, by itself, does not create esthetic pleasure. But it can deepen that pleasure, by removing obstacles to comprehension. This is what we call the social approach to the study of literature; we propose to examine some of its problems in the next three chapters; and we shall consider, first of all, the general influences which affect both the writer and his public, as members of the same community.

This social approach is surprisingly venerable, and has already gone through many phases. It goes back, at any rate, to that strangely isolated genius, a very Melchisedek among philosophers of history, Giovanni Battista Vico. In his *Principles of a New Science* (1725), he maintained that primitive literature was "poetic wisdom," the unconscious manifestation of a people's soul. Vico had no direct disciple; but the same idea was expressed again by Herder, half a century later. We have seen what important part this conception of poetry as "folk voice" had played and is still playing in literary theory. When critics insist that literature in America should be unmistakably American, they show themselves the disciples of Vico and Herder.

Here we have literature considered, not in the light of general esthetic principles, and not in terms of individual achievements, but *socially*, as the manifestation of a whole culture. If the "folk song" reveals the "folk soul," it follows that, reciprocally, the study of the "folk" is a key to poetical expression. The mystic notion of a "people"—*Volkstum*, folkdom—as blood, spirit, culture, inseparably united, is part of Herder's romantic legacy. It has dominated German thought throughout the nineteenth century; it is the foundation of Adolf Hitler's ideology.

But the social approach was also attempted by less adventurous minds than Herder's. Voltaire, a genuine, and at times a profound historian, believed, as a good prophet of the Enlightenment, in the unity of mankind and the universal validity of reason. But he was also struck, far more than his predecessors, by the extreme differences between various ages and various nations. These differences he ascribed, not to irremediable antinomies, but to traditions, customs, manners. Human progress consists in seeking unity in spite of these historical hindrances. But the realistic reformer must know the obstacles he has to overcome. He is a relativist; civilization is not a miracle, but an achievement; genius, powerless in isolation, would not even have the chance of manifesting itself in an age of barbarous darkness. The connection between literature and the other forms of human activities is thus clearly established.[1]

From Voltaire's position to Madame de Staël, there is but an easy step. In the Introduction to her *Literature Considered in Its Relations with Social Institutions*, she writes: "My purpose has been to examine the influence of religion, manners and legislation upon Literature, and the influence of literature upon religion, manners and legislation. . . . Hitherto, the moral and political causes which modify the spirit of a literature have never been sufficiently analyzed." No modern apostle of the sociological method could be more explicit. And, in her book on *Germany*, she gave a definite application of her principles to a great cultural group. She was among the first to discover that the Germans were Germans, and not simply benighted human beings who, through sheer perversity, refused to speak French.

---

[1] Such was the lesson of his great universal history, the *Essay on the Manners and Spirit of Nations*. The political enquiry of Montesquieu, in his *Spirit of Laws*, was guided by a similar thought.

(This, by the way, seems to have been Frederick the Great's idea of his own subjects.)

The social approach therefore was not "discovered" by Hippolyte Taine in the age of Realism. Taine simply provided, in the *Introduction* to his *History of English Literature*, a vigorous summing up of a theory which had been growing for fully a hundred years. Because Taine was the younger contemporary of Karl Marx, and because like Marx, he had a rather unquestioning faith in materialistic science, we are inclined to consider him as antiquated. But we must repeat that he did not invent *"la Race, le Milieu, le Moment"* in the year of grace 1863. Race, environment and time were already with us in the eighteeenth century; and there is no sign of their being banished from the interpretation of literature in the twentieth.

The main objection to Taine's formula is not that it is outmoded, but that it is ill-defined. It is impressive in its imperious brevity. It is defended with a fine show of realistic toughmindedness. "Vice and virtue are products, like vitriol and sugar": how could we fail to trust a critic so free from idealistic nonsense? The combination of vehement logic with a scientific vocabulary and a colorful style is well-nigh irresistible: seldom was confusion of thought more brilliantly camouflaged. Unfortunately, the successors of Taine have not clarified his doctrine. It must be understood at the outset of this discussion that our purpose is not to discredit, but to define, the social approach. We are fully aware of its possibilities. But, as it claims to be scientific, it should be stated with scientific definiteness, and applied with scientific caution.

When we have to deal with *race*, the first element in the sociological approach, scientific caution is usually flung to the winds. No subject, not even religion, seems to call for such passionate affirmations and denials. It would be easier to discuss the problem reasonably, if we defined our term. *Race* belongs to the domain of biology. It denotes a group with certain permanent traits in common, traits which are "in the blood" and are transmitted with the blood: race is the manifestation of collective heredity. This is clear enough, although, as we shall see, by no means simple. But few are the theorists of race willing to remain on purely biological grounds. In Taine's own work, we pass, without warning, from "the Anglo-Saxon Race," presumably a biological group, to "the English People," an historical entity, not coextensive with any stock or breed. It may be said that Taine was only an amateur in this field, and that, three quarters of a century ago, anthropology was still in its infancy. But professional scientists today are not a whit more careful. In a very thorough investigation of the Hawaiian Islands—which provide such a unique laboratory for the study of races—we have seen the Portuguese and the Porto-Ricans listed as "races": race here was loosely used to denote a national, or ethnic, element.

This is a manifest confusion, and yet it seems to be absolutely ineradicable. We speak airily of a man as being "of French blood," without enquiring whether he is a Breton, a Basque, a Fleming or an Alsatian. "French" has a very definite meaning: but it is purely a political and historical term. All French citizens are French, whatever their race or color may be; anyone who is naturalized becomes French without transfusion of blood. That is why we find prominent "Frenchmen" called Macdonald, Clarke, Mac-Mahon, Thompson, Hennessey, Archdeacon; de Brazza, Gambetta, Zola, Giovanninelli, Gallieni, Viviani; Kleber, Kellermann, Hirschauer, Zurlinden, Siegfried, Schrader, Schneider, Scherer; Strowski, Zyromski and Oualid. Frenchmen on the various frontiers resemble their neighbors across the border far more closely than their compatriots at the other end of the country. Offhand, it might be difficult to tell apart a Frenchman from Saargemünd and a German from Saarlouis: it would be much easier to see the difference between a Norman and a Corsican. It must be remembered that we are not questioning the importance of nationality as a historical and cultural factor. But nationality is based on a common tradition, not on blood relationship. The families which stood for so long as the symbols of the nations, the royal houses, were also the most cosmopolitan of all. All kings were cousins, and the "princes of the blood" were emphatically not of the same blood as the commoners.

A second and even deeper confusion is that between race and language.[1] We are apt to forget that terms like Celtic, Latin, Teutonic, Slavic, refer to linguistic families, not to biological groups. In primitive, isolated tribes, a common language may be the sign of common blood; but this has long ceased to be the rule. For untold centuries, conquests and migrations have been taking place. In some cases, the victor imposed his speech, as Rome did in Gaul and Spain: obviously, the natives of these countries were not exterminated and replaced by Latin settlers. In other cases, the invaders adopted the tongue of the land they had overrun: only a few score of Frankish words survived in the Kingdom of the Franks, *Frankreich*, modern France. In one case at least, that of the Norman Conquest, the result was a compromise, the hybrid wrongly called English. For individuals and even for families to change their language is a comparatively simple affair: it has been happening in our country for a hundred years. For a compact group to adopt a different tongue is a much more difficult process: long-established, well-knit minorities, like the French-Canadians, may survive indefinitely. But enough changes have taken place, on a vast scale and over centuries, to destroy any definite connection between blood and speech. An extreme example may serve as a symbol. One Negro slave from West Africa may have been shipped to Brazil, another one to our shores; this will not turn the descendants of the first into "Latins" and those of the second into "Anglo-Saxons."

[1] Incidentally, linguistic and political boundaries seldom coincide, although desperate efforts are made to bring them together. Territories are claimed on the basis of common speech; the "national" language is forced upon minorities, as in Southern Tyrol. Conversely, linguistic groups seek to organize themselves into autonomous nationalities (Catalonia) or even into independent nations. Nations conscious of a separate existence strive to foster a separate language, like Ireland and the Philippines. In this, literature often plays a great part; the literary revival of a neglected dialect may lead to the disruption of a state.

One should blush to rehearse such truisms, if they were not challenged by such formidable powers. It is plain to the dispassionate observer that "Germany" is essentially a language and culture group; secondarily, and only for the last three quarters of a century, a national state; never, in any intelligible sense of the term, a race. That some "Germans" should acknowledge Bern instead of Berlin as their capital is no hardship at all; that Lessing's *Nathan the Wise*, a great lesson in tolerance, should cease to be a German classic; that Heinrich Heine should be exiled from the Germany of the spirit: these are humiliations and mutilations that no foreign victor could impose.

These words must make it plain that we have no thought of minimizing the language factor. Even more emphatically than in the case of nationality, we recognize its existence and its immense power. Linguistic boundaries, we must repeat, are far more real and far more difficult to overcome than the most bristling military frontiers. Radio waves ignore formidable Maginot lines; but no radio has yet been devised with the Pentecostal gift of tongues. Our only contention is that *language* is not *race*. Language is an instrument of culture, and culture is greater than its instrument. Race divides, language divides, on totally different lines; culture unites. It creates a free commonwealth of the spirit, superior to any one of its provinces.

Brushing aside the confusion between nationality, language and race does not destroy the validity of any of the three. There are nations, there are languages, there are races. In reaction against the excesses of the racialists, it is sometimes asserted that race is a myth: yet race is a fact, among human beings as among animals. There are freaks in nature; but normally, out of a long, unmixed line of Chinese ancestors, you do not expect a child with Negroid or Scandinavian characteristics. There is a science of genetics: a science still in the making. It will be full-fledged when, like the other sciences, it considers every one of its assertions as a working hypothesis to be checked by observation and experimentation, not as a dogma to be enforced. In its popular, political and journalistic forms, the pseudo-science of genetics is a mass of such un-verified dogmas, the most blatant of which is the dogma of Nordic superiority. In such cases, the terms *racial myth, preju-dice* or *superstition,* apply with particular force.

Our World Literature, we have repeatedly confessed, is *Western* World Literature, that is to say predominantly Euro-pean and "White." Our main problem therefore is the racial division of the white inhabitants of Europe and of European settlements. In this respect, it will be well to bear in mind two elementary facts. The first is that the standard distinction be-tween *Nordics, Alpines* and *Mediterraneans,* without being wholly false, is at best merely a crude convenience. These three types do exist; but there are far more than three distinct types in that small, bewildering and distressing continent. The second fact is that, whatever list of types you choose to adopt, the people who conform strictly to these specifications are a minor-ity. Most Europeans are hybrids, and hybrids of hybrids, ad infinitum.

For these mixed strains, orthodox racialists use the con-temptuous term *mongrels.* This is not simply bad manners: it is bad science. The idea of racial purity is one of those dogmas which, if not severely tested, remain mere prejudice. This notion is borrowed, not from science, but from the breeder's art. But the breeder knows that his finest products are the stabilized results of a successful mixture. The best example, the English "thoroughbred" horse, combines Arabian elegance and spirit with the greater size and sturdiness of native stock: the hybrid is superior to both lines of its progenitors. Dog fanciers create breeds at will, some of which become fashion-able because of their very absurdity. A "mongrel" is simply an undesirable experiment.

Applied to human beings, "race" or "blood" [1] is the founda-

[1] *Blood,* the blood that "will tell" and is "thicker than water," is of course a metaphor. In actual fact, "blood" belongs to several different types, deter-mined by counting red and white corpuscles; and these types have nothing to do with class, nation, language or even race.

tion of hereditary aristocracy: the Social Register should be a stud book. Logically, this would tend to create, within the same country, a caste system: certain "breeds," royalty, nobility, gentry, yeomanry, could mate only within their own hermetically closed limits. When that great eugenic experiment has been carried out with some degree of thoroughness, as in the case of certain royal houses, the result has been manifest degeneration. The British aristocracy has been saved from such a fate because it has been constantly refreshed by new blood from energetic men and handsome women. As a result, people of the best "blood" in England are very far from Nordic racial purity: brown eyes, for instance, are more frequent among them than among commoners. In the exclusive Prussian aristocracy were found the names of French Huguenot refugees. There are physical elites, and intellectual elites, and it would be well if, through eugenic measures, we favored their increase; but they coincide neither with races nor with classes.

With hereditary physical traits should go, we must surmise, intellectual and moral predispositions. "There are naturally varieties of men, as there are of bulls and horses, some brave and intelligent, others timid and stupid," says Taine in his *Introduction*. But the terms of the problem are so complex that so far we have not been able to trace the connection. Brothers, with exactly the same heredity, often present the widest discrepancies in ability. Jean Jacques Rousseau remains a disturbing force to this day; François Rousseau lived and died in perfect obscurity. Of the Bonaparte brothers Napoleon had demonic energy; Joseph was mediocre and easy-going; Louis a hypochondriac; Jerome an amiable libertine. It is impossible to determine intelligence or virtue by skull measurements or blood counts. The *genes* that correspond to greatness as a lyric poet or as a dramatist have not been isolated. The Jews, so universally considered as the best example of a strongly characterized race, further bound together by their religion, and by centuries of suffering, have produced the Prophets, *Ecclesiastes*, Spinoza, Heinrich Heine, Jacques Offenbach, Marcel Proust: trace the family likeness if you dare. No one could guess from their works that Pushkin and Alexandre Dumas were Negroes.[1]

So much for the racial interpretation of literature. Under *environment* or *milieu* may be considered first the natural or geographic factor, the habitat; and then the social factors, political regime, structure of the community, economic system. All of these influence human development: even the most extreme racialists profess that race is not enough, and that the finest breed will not thrive under adverse circumstances. Everything that affects human life obviously affects literature; where no man can exist, it would be vain to look for art. This is a truism, not a problem. But the truism turns into a fallacy, if we admit without further proof that between a particular kind of habitat or regime, and a particular kind of literature, there is a definite, traceable, measurable relation. No fallacy, however, is more popular. In schematic form, it might be stated as follows: "Literature is inconceivable apart from man; man needs ground to tread upon; therefore geology is the foundation of literature, and the study of Shakespeare should begin with that of Jurassic rocks."

Now this may be an extremely fruitful hypothesis, and we do not want to bar out any avenue of thought. But a hypothesis it must remain, until it has been properly checked. Most of the assertions that we encounter in "the geographical interpretation of literature" are not even assumptions, but only loose metaphors. We take it for granted that Hindu literature should be "dank" and "torrid," Nordic literature "rugged" and "gloomy," Mediterranean literature "sharp in outline" and "sunlit." Walt Whitman and Thomas Wolfe worked deliberately on the principle that the vastness of our continent should

---

[1] The Jews—this is the greatest paradox presented by that paradoxical people—are not a race according to the standard tests for the determination of races, i.e., build, coloring and skull measurements. There are blond Jews and dark Jews, round-headed Jews and long-headed Jews. Antisemitism is a religious and social phenomenon, not a form of racial enmity; for *antisemitism* is most pronounced among the Arabs, who are as "Semitic" as the Jews.

find expression in loose, sprawling verse or prose; it was flippantly suggested that, by the same token, the literature of Chile should be thin and elongated. If the reader will watch for this strain, even among the most reputable critics, like Taine himself, Renan, Matthew Arnold, André Maurois, he will repeatedly come across solemn affirmations more humorous than any parody.

The field of investigation remains open; we should not be discouraged because, so far, the yield has been so meager. Very few facts are established beyond dispute; and they are of such a general nature as to be of very slight interest. We may take it for granted that, until now, our civilization has developed best in the temperate zone. Iceland, the Northernmost territory on the literary map, is inside the arctic circle; and the West Indies just below the Tropic of Cancer. There are literary centers nearer the Equator, like Santa Fé de Bogotá: but there the altitude corrects the influence of latitude. Natural resources determine economic possibilities which in their turn have some bearing on literature. But even this, vague as it is, is not wholly true, and poor countries, like Iceland, Ireland and Norway, can boast of admirable work, greater than that of far richer regions, like the English Midlands. Except for such generalities, we are left groping. Certain things that we are tempted to take for granted are palpably false. From the sunny Mediterranean zone have come some of the most austere and even somber masterpieces in the history of man's spirit: the great angry prophets of Israel, Æschylus, Lucretius, Dante, Leopardi. Glum Puritans and gay Cavaliers lived under the same skies. Scotland the bleak gave us writers of a lovable sunny disposition, Robert Burns, Sir Walter Scott, Robert Louis Stevenson, J. M. Barrie.

Man adjusts himself to his material environment. This does not mean that he is modified in essentials by external circumstances, but only that he yields a little, so as to remain more fully himself. To a large extent, he conquers circumstances, reshapes his environment: it is the task of civilization to provide him with clothing, shelter and artificial heat, as a substitute for the warmth of the sun. In many cases, he reacts triumphantly against the pressure of the material world. A gloomy scene may depress him; it may also challenge him to energy and cheerfulness. The geographical factor is real, but not decisive, and it operates in many subtle and even devious ways. For these reasons, we find it impossible to trace on the map an area for ode or sonnet, as we do for palm or pine. Any type of literature can be produced anywhere and be enjoyed anywhere. Almost at the same time, the short story flourished with Maupassant in France, with Kipling in India, with O. Henry in Texas and New York, with Chekhov in Russia. The Bible and Shakespeare are read over the whole earth, with little regard for local weather conditions. Bonaparte, the typical "Mediterranean," took with him to sun-scorched Egypt his favorite Italian version of Macpherson's *Ossian*.

The political atmosphere is, we believe, of far greater importance than the geographical. We used the word *atmosphere*, not *regime:* actual constitutional forms matter very little. Our country went through a number of cultural changes in the nineteenth century, without any radical modifications in the mechanism of government. France, during the same period, had two distinct Empires, three Republics, and two different brands of kingship. She also had waves of Classicism, Romanticism, Realism, Symbolism. But, between literary evolution and political events, there is no exact correspondence. Romanticism fought and won its battle against Classicism under four different regimes; Realism yielded to Symbolism without creating a flutter in the drab life of the Third Republic. We have noted before that Europe grew "realistic" in the harsh and cynical sense of the term when the idealistic movement of 1848 collapsed. But the change had occurred in literature years before: Romanticism had been sharply defeated as early as 1843; and, since 1830, Balzac had been writing realistic masterpieces.

This lack of correspondence does not prove a total lack of connection. It only proves that the connection is not immediate.

Both literature and politics are influenced by vaster trends. There may be a lag between different forms of collective activity, in the same way as there frequently is a lag between nations. At times, the literary upheaval precedes, at times it follows, the political one. Rousseau came twenty years before, Byron twenty years after, the French Revolution. In the perspective of centuries, this imperfect synchronization loses much of its significance.

The wording of the Constitution, we repeat, counts for very little in this respect. Liberia has done us the honor of borrowing our political forms; but their influence on Liberian literature is slight. The fundamental distinction, whatever the institutions may be, is that between autocracy and liberty. Naturally, we are tempted to think that autocracy must be deadly to literature. Then we remember that the most brilliant epoch in Latin letters was not the Republic, but the reign of Augustus; and that the golden age of French culture was the absolute monarchy of Louis XIV.

These undeniable facts, however, should not be accepted at their face value without closer scrutiny. In these two cases, the lag that we have mentioned before is manifest: the great writers under the two autocrats had been formed earlier, under the influence of a stormier and freer age. It is important to note that, after Louis XIV had ruled for twenty-five years, there was a marked decline both in the political world and in the cultural. Napoleon, far more efficient a despot, killed French literature outright: the only writers who counted under his reign were in opposition or in exile.

But there is a more important consideration. "Autocracy" and "liberty" are themselves vague terms. The real issue is between the totalitarian state and the pluralistic. Pluralism implies that men can differ on vital questions, and live peaceably side by side; the sole duty of the state is to guarantee their right to differ. Totalitarianism means that all men must think alike on all subjects. Now, the government of Louis XIV was autocratic, but not totalitarian. The privileges, immunities, franchises, of social classes, provinces, cities, historical bodies like the Parliaments, were not wholly destroyed. During the successful years of the regime, the Jansenists and the Protestants were tolerated. Louis XIV admitted that his "divine right" did not extend to Parnassus. When Boileau told him that Molière was the greatest writer of the time, the autocrat answered, sensibly and meekly: "I did not think so: but you know about these things better than I do." Under Louis XV, the "tyranny" was in the hands of a half-ironical monarch, spiritually an absentee, who seldom interfered with state affairs except to play tricks on his ministers. The state, at the behest of this or that faction, could swoop down upon an individual author, capriciously, brutally: it was a fitful Enlightenment no doubt; yet no age was ever freer in thought.

A "tyranny" may tolerate pluralism, or be unable to suppress it: the Tsar was compelled to respect Tolstoy. Totalitarianism, on the other hand, may prevail under liberal forms. To borrow Hilaire Belloc's image, public opinion may become a thick gluey substance against which it is impossible to swim; this limits our freedom far more efficiently than any statute or any police force. Our own ideal of a few years ago, "one hundred per cent Americanism," was totalitarianism of a particularly insidious kind. Any thought might be stifled, under the plea that it was "un-American." We have at last wakened to the saving truth that nothing is so un-American as enforced conformity.

It would seem plain that, in a totalitarian milieu, literature could not thrive. Our one desire, in this study, is to keep our mind open; this forces us at times into the uncongenial position of Devil's advocate. We know that totalitarianism today is hurting many of the noblest among literary men; we do not know for certain that the ultimate triumph of totalitarianism would crush out literature. The experience of the main totalitarian states has been too brief. If they produce great art in this generation, their enemies might ascribe it to the "lag," the heritage of the liberal state before the flood; if they do not produce great art, their defenders will offer as an explanation that they are engaged in the terrific task of rebuilding a world. Only the achievements of the second, or third, generation would enable us to judge.

If through ruthless education, all men were so conditioned that in all essentials they would automatically think and feel alike, they would only have reached the ideal professed by our best citizens for ages past: "one hundred million minds with but a single thought, one hundred million hearts that beat like one." Vast numbers, in England and in America, accept without dispute our respective constitutions, the profit motive and evangelical Christianity. Naturally, we are persuaded that our Anglo-Saxon synthesis is far superior to the Italian, German or Russian syntheses. But this is beside the point. The essential fact is that in all cases, theirs as well as ours, there is a synthesis or ideology, which has to be "defended," that is to say enforced. Many of us do not believe that it is in the least an advantage for the state that there should be people seeking to destroy, even by peaceful means, the Constitution, the profit motive, or orthodox religion; unanimity on these fundamental points is considered a blessing; we are at heart "totalitarians." Our ideology is easy-going because it does not feel itself seriously challenged. We are tolerant for the same reason that we are peace-minded: in both cases, we are satisfied. We have attained what others are struggling for. If our essential unity were threatened, we could be ruthless.

Every system is both an incentive and an obstacle to thought. The dispassionate observer, while himself an enemy of all rigid system, cannot affirm that a new age of barbarism is threatening the world. It is not inconceivable that the human spirit will find its way under the new disciplines. It is practically certain that it will find new ways, which will make the new disciplines obsolete. To the question: "Would a totalitarian regime destroy literature?" we are compelled to give an evasive answer. In the past, no regime has been totalitarian enough, or, if fully totalitarian, has endured long enough, to stifle art and thought. In the future, we do not mean to give it a chance.

In discussing the social environment, we have placed the political factor first, not because it is the most essential, but because it is the most obvious. The organic structure of society, its division into definite groups with separate rights and separate interests, is at least as important, but is also far more difficult to define. In America, we have a written Constitution, but we are not quite sure whether we have classes.

We may conceive, at one extreme, of a classless society: Shelley's ideal in *Prometheus Unbound* (III, 193-7):

> The loathsome mask has fallen, the man remains
> Scepterless, free, uncircumscribed, but man
> Equal, unclassed, tribeless and nationless,
> Exempt from awe, worship, degree, the king
> Over himself. . . .

At the other extreme, we could imagine a system of absolutely closed castes: Plato's Republic, Brahmanic India. Between these two ideal types, our civilization offers a loose division into classes. If the classes are extremely fluid, they almost disappear; if they are rigid at all, they tend to turn into castes. Hereditary rights, in titles, functions or wealth, constitute an incipient caste system. As noted above, we in America have never been able to make up our minds on this all-important subject. We reject with horror heredity in empty titles, the formal aristocracy of Europe; but we defend heredity in economic power. At times we deny the existence of classes altogether, as un-American; at other times, we urge that they should co-operate harmoniously, which implies that they are a reality.[1]

[1] It is sometimes asserted that a perfect tyranny is classless: all equal under the yoke. A fallacy: there are two classes, the leader, the led; and, inevitably, there grows a privileged class of the leader's immediate henchmen. The race idea, as we have seen, is linked with that of caste. The Nordics, for instance, are thought of as a huge aristocracy that should keep itself pure.

Loosely, the classless society is called democratic, the hierarchized society represents the aristocratic ideal. What bearing does this have on the understanding of literature? For centuries, and particularly since the Renaissance, art has demanded a long and elaborate initiation, which implies a leisure class. The numberless hidden allusions, the felicities of speech, the classic and philosophical overtones, the very reticences in Racine and Milton are exquisite flowers which presuppose a rich humus of tradition, and prolonged, sedulous "culture." That is why there are not a few delicate minds, from Renan and Matthew Arnold to Ortega y Gasset, who dread the "classless society," democracy unconfined, as the destruction of art and the triumph of vulgarity. On the other hand, there has been, ever since the middle of the eighteenth century, a revival of faith and interest in "folk art." If the disciples of Vico and Herder are right, the classless society, the *folk*, would destroy conventions, despise sophistication, ignore connoisseurship, but liberate vital art.

Perhaps we might restore the conditions that prevailed under Pericles: a classless society among free men, sustained in comparative leisure by the labor of slaves; only, in the twentieth century, our slaves would be machines, not human beings. The modern state can provide for all its members the opportunities that once were rare privileges: a democracy of aristocrats is well within our reach.

The most dangerous fallacy in this respect is the confusion between *class* and *élite*. The idea of class, like that of race, implies that, generally speaking, *all* the members of the higher group are in *all* things superior to the members of the lower group. This is a manifest absurdity. Instead of such a simplified hierarchy, reality offers the fact of "pluralistic élites": each of these should be freely open to the best in its particular line, without any implication of superiority in other lines. There is an élite of pugilists as there is an élite of grammarians, an élite of cooks and an élite of architects. No Pico della Mirandola, no Admirable Crichton, can hope to belong to all of them. Only the élite can reap unusual rewards: even in crudest terms, a third-rate prize-fighter wins less fame and money than a great classical scholar; an inspired hairdresser, like Marcel of the Waves, can attain a distinction denied to many poets. This is as it should be: honor to those who, in any field, are not merely successful imitators, but are able to push back the limits of human endeavor. The best state will be the one which, leaving the commonplace to take care of themselves, shall best reward its various élites. And, in Utopia, a proper hierarchy would be established among the different élites: philosophy, for example, would rank above baseball or salesmanship. Far from being synonymous, élite and class represent antagonistic conceptions. For classes, like races, create false equalities among their members: the idea of free élites restores the essential fact of natural inequalities.

Fortunately these ideas, far from being revolutionary, have always prevailed in the interpretation and appreciation of literature. Villon the gangster, Bunyan the tinker, Rousseau the vagabond, outrank the aristocrats of their days. If the sociological approach were to make us class conscious, it would confuse the literary issue instead of clarifying it.

We now turn to the most pressing and the most controversial aspect of the environment problem: *the economic interpretation of literature*. Its main thesis is well stated in a *Primer of Instructions* published by the International Revolutionary Theatre Society in Moscow: "According to Marxist principles, the economic conditions of the country in the historic period in which the author has placed his scene must first of all be analyzed. Before the play is produced a careful study should be made of the relations of the classes, the conditions of the class war, the peculiar forms and solutions employed in the social struggles of the period, and all ideas concerned with class war."[1]

---

[1] Thomas H. Dickinson and others: *The Theatre in a Changing Europe*, Henry Holt, 1937, p. 89.

The reader must bear patiently with us, if the discussion of this familiar thesis takes us away for a while from the field of pure literature. Before we can apply economic principles to the criticism of letters, we must at least dispel a few ambiguities. The adoption of an economic terminology is no guarantee of clearness, if that terminology remains vague in our minds.

In current controversies, as in the passage quoted from the Moscow *Primer*, the class problem and the economic problem are almost invariably considered to be one and the same. Neither history nor logic will justify such an assumption. Very sharp class conflicts existed in the eighteenth and nineteenth centuries between elements—nobility, bourgeoisie, common people—who were all committed to the same economic principles. No one was more attached to the idea of private property and to the sanctity of the profit motive than the peasant or the small shopkeeper. On the other hand, an impoverished nobleman, a priest, a military officer, an important civil servant, even a successful artist, could all be members of the "upper class," while a rich manufacturer might remain "socially ineligible."

It is a fact that "society" has a tendency to stratify according to wealth: friendly intercourse is hampered by excessive differences in resources. But this has nothing to do with the "class war." A modest, unsuccesful investor, the owner of barren land, the proprietor of a run-down shop, will find it hard to join a good country club, although, in theory, all three are "capitalists." On the other hand, the employee with an ample salary, the doctor, lawyer or artist who can command munificent fees, may be admitted to play golf with a financial magnate. It may be inevitable to use the word *class* for such widely different notions as *aristocrat* and *capitalist;* at any rate, we should be warned that the two meanings do not coincide. The "tyranny of words," denounced by Stuart Chase, is chiefly the result of confusion. If instead of *classes,* we used *social strata* in one case, *economic interests* in the other, a few ambiguities would be removed.[1]

We must also remember that it is impossible to describe the atmosphere of a period, the state of a society, exclusively in economic terms. American life, the background and condition of American literature, is by no means solidly capitalistic. There are many elements, like love, work and play, which are decidedly pre-capitalistic; and others, like religion and patriotism, which may at times be associated with capitalism, but which at other times stand squarely against it. No Christian and no patriot will acknowledge that his ideals are colored by the profit motive.

Finally, we often fail to realize that, even in the economic field, "systems" or "regimes" are abstractions which oversimplify reality. Our world does not conform to a single set of blue prints. At one time, the army and the judiciary were "capitalistic": one bought a regiment or a seat on the bench, as an investment; today, they are "communistic," that is to say, run for service and not for profit. We can send a package through the capitalistic express companies, or through the communistic parcel post; if we circle the globe, we go through the capitalistic Suez Canal and the communistic Panama Canal; some cities drink capitalistic water, others communistic water. On Market Street in San Francisco, capitalistic and communistic street cars run on parallel tracks. We may be told that all the above examples are not genuine communism, but only state capitalism. Granted: then Soviet Russia is not communistic, only state capitalistic. Pure communism exists only in the convents and monasteries.

We are not taking sides in current controversies; least of all do we maintain that these controversies are futile. Our point is that the field of literature is life as a whole, and cannot be re-

[1] It is inexcusable, for instance, that the same word *bourgeois* should denote: the city dweller as opposed to the countryman; the middle class as opposed to the aristocracy; the civilian as opposed to the military; and the philistine as opposed to the artist.

stricted to a single set of considerations. The study of literature should not be made a footnote to *Capital* or *The Wealth of Nations*.

Economic conditions, however, are not irrelevant to our purpose; if they do not determine literature, they undoubtedly affect it. But these conditions should be stated in terms of general stages or aspects of economic development, and not reduced to a single eighteenth- or nineteenth-century system. These stages are the pastoral, the agricultural, the commercial and the industrial. These are part of the atmosphere in which literature lives and moves.

The pastoral and, in a lesser degree, the agricultural states have a great tradition in literature—as themes for sophisticated city dwellers. In the actual creation of art, they play a very minor role. When agricultural countries like medieval England, classical France, pre-war Russia, or Ireland to the present day, have produced masterpieces, it was because they possessed urban centers. Recorded literature is a form of civilization; civilization, in etymology and history, is of the city; and the city is built on trade. From ancient Athens to modern New York, the arts have grown, not with the fields, but with the harbor, the market place, the counting house. Artists may go into lyrical ecstasies about nature: but that is eminently characteristic of the urban spirit.

In the commercial state, industrial production does of course exist, but only on a local and restricted sale. The man of large interests, the man with vision and power, is the merchant or the banker, not the manufacturer. This is still largely true of our civilization. When we think of *business*, it is financing and merchandizing that we have in mind, rather than industrial production. Industry simply provides articles for the trader to sell: the trader is still king.

Gradually, the Industrial Revolution is making itself felt. Very slowly indeed: nineteenth-century England, although thoroughly industrialized, still preserved the trappings of feudalism, and was governed alternately by the country squires and by the merchants, but not by the manufacturers. We are entering upon a conscious Industrial Age, in which production and consumption will have to be directly adjusted, without relying overmuch upon the haphazard and gambling processes of trade. Industry on an enormous scale cannot afford to guess, and match wits with a rival: statistical methods are taking the place of unlimited competition. A commercial polity can be founded upon rugged individualism: the industrial world is collectivistic. Although we may call them by the same name, a regime of individual farms, workshops and stores, and a regime of nation-wide corporations are poles asunder. Of this growing collectivism, America gave the first decisive examples; Russia is the country which follows most enthusiastically the American model. France, on the contrary, is striving to preserve economic individualism: apparently a losing fight. The other nations stand between these two extremes. How does the economic environment, thus defined, influence literature?

From the days of Pericles to the present, our literature has been chiefly one of the commercial state. When insecurity killed all trade beyond local barter, culture ceased: and yet Europe had the right *race* in command, the Teutons, the right faith prevailed, Christianity, and the geographical conditions were unchanged. With the revival of business, letters flourished again. What the coming Industrial Age will do to our arts, we do not know, and for a while, we shall not be able to tell. The conditions of the problem are still blurred in America, for the commercial element remains strong; and Russia, which has frankly subordinated commerce, cannot be used as an example, for all her energies are absorbed, and will be absorbed for decades, by her gigantic effort toward Americanization. So prophecy will have to outrun the safe anticipation of facts: mankind is attempting a new path.

To most observers, it seems obvious that the industrial state will imperil our individualism: such was the meaning of Georges Duhamel's little book: *America the Menace*. If this be granted, three hypotheses are possible. The first—sheer pessimism—is that the Industrial Age will herald the decline of culture; men will degenerate with the arts, and material civilization itself will no longer be safe in their hands. The industrial state will keep progressing for a while on momentum, then will slow down, and ultimately collapse into barbarism. The second hypothesis—rank optimism—is that the industrial state will indeed kill our individualistic culture, but also evolve a culture of its own: anonymous, collective, communal, but no less vital than the old, and truer perhaps to the very origins of the arts. The third hypothesis is that man will, be able to resist "totalitarianism," or the rule of a single formula for all the varied activities of life; that he will be frankly collectivistic in the material world, since that is manifestly the key to efficiency; but that he will be no less staunchly individualistic in matters of the spirit. In such a case, art would be, not a mere ornament of life, but the citadel of those values which are beyond the range of mechanical production. But this implies a dualism repellent to the totalitarian mind, and the vigorous denial that economic conditions determine cultural life.

The third factor is called by Taine *"le moment,"* which is usually translated "time." The term is so general that it is not always easy to distinguish *time* from *environment*. If we want to study the *time* in which an author lived, the Elizabethan Age for example, we shall have to list the political, social and economic conditions then prevailing; in other words, we shall simply describe the *milieu*. But we shall describe these conditions as simultaneous: we shall give a still picture of the Elizabethan scene. Now these elements exist in a *time sequence*. The present is to a large extent determined by the past. It is this continuity, this inseparable unity of past and present, that Taine wanted to denote by the word *time*, or, more accurately, *momentum*. It might also be called history, evolution, tradition, custom, habit: all these terms imply that our activities are not isolated, instantaneous; that every gesture, word or thought, casual as it may seem, is the result of some cause, obscure or manifest; and that, link by link, the chain of causation reaches back into remote centuries.

In literature, this element of *time* is of the utmost importance. Even the most elementary, the most ephemeral form of communication among men demands a code, a set of conventions, a language, which cannot be created afresh on every occasion: language is the living past. And by language, let us repeat that we must understand not merely the plain meaning of simple words, but their implications, their associations, their connotations. So, without our being aware of it, language embodies acquired wisdom and acquired unwisdom, preconceptions and prejudices. The man of today is never able to think and speak in terms of today. He must constantly adjust the words that he has inherited to the changing conditions. If we are able to understand this morning's paper, it is because author and reader have, substantially, the same tradition.

Languages, nationalities, religions, thus exist not merely on the map, in the spatial world, but also in the historical chart, in the world of time. All this is evident enough. The consequences which are commonly drawn from this truism are not invariably quite so convincing.

The traditional or historical spirit is often interpreted as resistance to change. But this itself is un-historical. Change is of the very nature of the time-flow: with absolute immobility, time itself would cease to exist. History tells us that we are the heirs of our ancestors; but it tells us also that we are different from them. Change is a fact: the only matter in dispute is the proper rate of change, in so far as that is under our control. This is the issue between Toryism and Progressivism: but the urge to change is as historical, as traditional, as the desire to retard change. On this point, no one is or can be wholly consistent. A man will be enthusiastic about the sudden progress of our age in matters of transportation, and combat the modifications in government that this very progress has made possible and desirable. We have known conservatives, deeply attached to the past, who yet hoped to convert the world to their religious faith in this generation: thus expecting a miraculous acceleration in the development of mankind. The tempo varies in the different fields; it varies in different epochs. Centuries of stagnation may be followed by decades when progress rushes like a cataract. Untold ages had dreamed of artificial flight; and the present writer was a full-grown man when the first aeroplanes left the ground.

This time element affects literature in many ways, but especially through language and nationality. Both, we repeat, are historical products, traditions. They are often mistaken for *race;* but, in shaping works of art, they are far more influential than race: Dumas the Negro takes his place in the French tradition, Heine the Jew in the German tradition.[1] A tradition is a very effective reality: a treasure house which may also become a prison. Through tradition, a group of people know certain things, and deliberately ignore other things. In particular, they entertain beliefs about themselves, which act as checks and as norms. In this way, group consciousness again affects literature far more than race; every American strives to be, in his own line, the typical, the ideal American; but every American, blond, medium or dark, does *not* strive to be the typical Nordic, Alpine or Mediterranean.

Tradition is therefore a fact of collective psychology; and we have already admitted more than once the potency of collective psychology, even when it takes the form of a psychosis or mental disease. But, if we accept it pragmatically, we refuse to accept it uncritically. First of all, the national tradition is a vague entity. It is by no means homogeneous. Everything that exists has its root in the past, and is a tradition. There is a tradition of vice as well as of virtue, of stupidity as well as of intelligence. Woodrow Wilson, William Randolph Hearst,

---

[1] According to Taine, race itself is a product of time; but it is the result of "myriads of centuries"; its rate of change is so slow that it may be considered negligible. Franz Boas, on the contrary, believes that race characteristics can alter in a single generation.

James Branch Cabell, Harold Bell Wright, H. L. Mencken, the Rev. William Sunday, Calvin Coolidge and Granville Hicks are the variegated flowers of the great American tradition. In France, the tradition of Rabelais, Montaigne, Molière, Voltaire, Renan, is no less real than that of Bossuet, Joseph de Maistre, Veuillot and Charles Maurras.

What we usually mean by tradition is the kind which, for the time being, seems predominant. But, for all its assertiveness, it may be surprisingly recent and singularly precarious. The Germany described with great acumen and sympathy by Madame de Staël was sentimental, artistic, philosophical, unpractical, unmilitary, and with no sense of political unity. Fifty years later, the Germans believed that they had been Bismarckians to a man ever since the days of Arminius. The British glory in their muddle-headedness as one of their most ancient and most cherished traditions. But this treasured possession is an illusion. All the clear-cut ideas which have ruled European thought for the last three centuries came from England, the home of lucid, systematic thinkers. It was Bacon who gave the rules of the inductive methods; Hobbes who created the formula of the state as Leviathan; Berkeley who stated most cogently the doctrine of absolute idealism; John Locke who was the teacher of all Enlightenment philosophers; Adam Smith who reduced political economy to a definite system; Malthus who focused the problem of population. All Europe, for a century, had groped for the idea of evolution: it took a Darwin to state it in unmistakable terms. Everyone felt vaguely that war is bad business: it was an Englishman, Norman Angell, who gave an irrefutable demonstration of that great and impotent truth. We may conclude that the muddle-headedness of the British, like the dreamy melancholy of the Irish, has been greatly exaggerated.

The fact that traditions are mere states of mind, and frequently delusive, accounts for the rapidity with which they can alter. There are phenomena of mass conversion, revolutions in thought. This is not contrary to the historical process;

it simply means that fabrics of thought, like political regimes, when they grow obsolete, may collapse with dramatic suddenness. The Islamic world literally burst into being; the time may come when it will dissolve as rapidly. Medieval and isolated Japan disappeared overnight; Turkey changed from obstinate reaction to determined progressivism; the age-long loyalty of Holy Russia to her tsars left not a wrack behind.

Such catastrophes are possible only because the traditions they destroy are superficial. This is the case with all *conscious* traditions: they are artificially fostered, not in accordance with the facts, but in defiance of the facts. We must keep clearly in mind the distinction between a tradition and an ideal. A tradition is based upon the past, and is limited to a particular group; an ideal looks toward the future, and is freely open to all. When we fight for a tradition, as distinct from an ideal, it implies that, left to natural forces, that tradition would die. The traditions that are truly irresistible are those which are unchallenged, because they are unconscious. A nation will fight for its language; it will not fight, it will have no cause to fight, for *language* in general, which no one tries to suppress. Yet the tradition of articulate speech, which separates us from the brutes, is immeasurably more vital than the differences between Polish and Ruthenian.

Clashing traditions are merely interchangeable costumes for the same human feelings. *France d'abord! America First! Sacro Egoismo, Rule Britannia, Sinn Fein, Deutschland über alles!*—these defiant phrases simply prove that men can express exactly the same thing in many different ways. The experience of World Literature enables us to appreciate this fundamental unity. That is why, in reading the masterpieces of other ages and of other nations, we can so easily transpose their sentiments into the terms of our own life. We can sympathize with the alien patriotism of William Tell, with the alien religion of Antigone, even with the alien moral code of the *Nibelungenlied*.

In attempting to prove that all *conscious* group differences are superficial, we are not seeking to demonstrate that all men are alike. On the contrary, our point is that all men are different. Races, classes, languages, nationalities, create in our minds abstract entities, *the* Aryan, *the* aristocrat, *the* capitalist, *the* Latin, *the* Belgian, which over-emphasize minor resemblances. No doubt Thomas Hardy and Anthony Hope were both "Anglo-Saxon" and both "Victorian"; but the one thing to remember is that they were not interchangeable.

Race, environment and time have a place in the study of literature: when we are interested in an author, we want to learn all we can about him, and Taine's formula provides an acceptable program of investigation. For the determination of esthetic values, the "social approach" is worthless. The Preacher (*Ecclesiastes*) was a Jew; he wrote in Hebrew, many centuries ago, in far-off Judea; he was a great capitalist, sadly boasting of his possessions. Yet we, who have not a single point in common with him, often feel in closer touch with his thought than with the thought of some writer in our own community. The one profit of the social approach is to establish—indirectly —the infinite variety of men, the essential unity of mankind.[1]

SUMMARY

The Periods represent a common denominator, "the spirit of the time." The consideration of this collective element is the *Social Approach to the Study of Literature*. It originated rather obscurely with Vico and Herder: if you would understand literature, study the folk, for literature is the spontaneous voice of the folk. On a different basis, Voltaire was also interested in the customs and manners of nations, as affecting their thought and expression. This social approach was clearly defined by Madame de Staël, and finally by Taine, who suggested the convenient formula: race, environment and time.

By *race* is meant collective heredity, transmitted with the blood. It is often confused with nationality and language; but

[1] A fuller treatment of these problems, with a Bibliography, will be found in the author's *Literature and Society*, Part I.

there is no *French* race, no *Latin* race. Among Europeans, the standard division—Nordics, Alpines, Mediterraneans—is misleading. There are more than three basic types, and the vast majority of Europeans are complex hybrids. It has not been found feasible to trace any relation between race and individual superiority. World Literature is compelled to ignore these distinctions altogether.

Under *environment* or *milieu*, we first consider the *geographical* habitat. Its influence is shown to be uncertain, if not negligible. Men of radically different abilities and tempers live under the same skies.

The *political* atmosphere is not a matter of formal constitution. The essential difference is that between liberty and tyranny, i.e., between pluralism and totalitarianism. Many "liberal" states are totalitarian in their heart without confessing it. Would totalitarianism destroy culture? The problem is stated, but no solution is offered as final.

More important than the political is the *social* structure of the commonwealth: the hierarchized *vs.* the classless type of society. So far, definite art and literature have relied upon the existence of classes. It would be well to keep clearly in mind the distinction between *classes* and *élites*. Our hope might be an aristocracy embracing the whole people, with the machines as the only servile class.

The *Economic* environment, over-emphasized by modern theorists, does not coincide with the *class* structure. It does not depend upon doctrines: Colbert *vs.* Adam Smith *vs.* Karl Marx. All systems and all alleged regimes are too simple and too rigid to account for the complexity even of economic life, *a fortiori* for the richness of cultural life. The most general and easiest classification of economic conditions would be, according to the chief source of wealth: the pastoral, the agricultural, the commercial, the industrial states. So far, art and literature have been chiefly associated with the commercial state. The industrial state, even in America and Russia, is still in the making. Its meaning for culture is uncertain. The function of art might be to serve as a center of resistance against the tyranny of the machines.

By *time*, we mean momentum the past still alive in the present. The historical, traditional element is manifested chiefly through three agencies: language, nationality, religion, all of which deeply affect literature.

Their commanding importance is fully acknowledged, with the following qualifications:

1. The historical spirit is the recognition of change; nothing so un-historical as the refusal to change.

2. Tradition should be tested critically; it seldom is as unanimous and as ancient as its defenders maintain. When it becomes artificial, it may crumble with catastrophic suddenness.

3. For the student of World Literature, permanent and universal elements stand out; traditions are found to be costumes and customs rather than ineradicable differences.

CHAPTER XIX

THE SOCIAL APPROACH TO THE STUDY OF LITERATURE

II. AUTHOR AND PUBLIC

WE HAVE so far examined race, environment and time as they affect the whole community, author and public alike. If literature were pure folklore, the spontaneous expression of the whole people, our task would be ended. The situation, however, is not so simple. An author may be the mouthpiece of a group: thus Tennyson, as choir leader, bringing tribute to Wellington or Victoria. But an author is also an individual, and sharply distinct from the mass.

He is not, however, an isolated individual. Anyone may have poetic dreams, anyone may even give his dreams definite form, for his own exclusive satisfaction, and this creative urge is the very essence of art; but, if it is not recorded and transmitted, it perishes with the creator, it is art only in his own private universe. We are willing to grant that the unknown, even the unwritten, masterpiece is none the less a masterpiece, that the "mute inglorious Milton" evoked in Gray's *Elegy* may have had greater genius than the author of *Paradise Lost;* but such an admission remains purely theoretical. The poems that exist only in your own mind, the manuscripts jealously kept under triple key, are, as yet, only potential literature. In order to be turned into actuality, they have to be communicated, were it but to a single friend. The reader, the student, the critic, can deal only with the known. The three specifications for authorship are a mind (or a soul, if you prefer), an

deal only with the living. In this sense, we are justified in saying that the body of literature is selected, and therefore *created*, by the public out of the amorphous mass of published and unpublished writings. But what is this formidable master, the public, and how does it exercise this decisive power?

In good democratic doctrine, there should be no exclusion and no hierarchy: the whole of mankind is the ultimate judge. And it is enabled so to judge through an inherent sense of right and wrong which is a basic human quality. This is no invention of modern demagogues. Descartes asserted that "good sense" is universal; Rousseau, that conscience, found in every heart, is an infallible guide; Blake, that all men have taste, when they are not "connoisseured out of their senses." The plain man is the sane man: it is only pedants, cranks and fanatics that would lead him astray. Not for long: "You cannot fool all the people all of the time." Thus we have a very definite system: let the people rule, in politics and in letters alike.

But Lincoln's pregnant phrase implies that "the people" can only be fooled or refuse to be fooled, can only endorse or reject, but not initiate, action. There is no spontaneous collective mind. When we affirm that the country has "made up its mind," it means that individuals have formed themselves into definite groups, and that one of these groups appears definitely stronger than its rivals, because it is more numerous, because it occupies a strategic position, or because it is more vociferous. At the nucleus of these groups will be found a small, compact organization; at the very center of the organization, a few individuals, perhaps a single leader. It is not necessary that these be giants: when public opinion is sufficiently bewildered, it will accept a leader of inconceivable crudity; that is how "all the people" may be fooled "some of the time." Even what we call a "mass movement," a panic, a stampede, is not wholly spontaneous, but rather the blind following of particularly inept leadership. There must have been some fool to cry before the rest, at the crucial moment: "All is lost!" or "Kill the rascals!" Without some leadership, the mass, however seething with energies, is aimless and inert.

We are not here expounding the philosophy of modern dictatorship. The idea is as ancient as human society; it prevails in all domains, and under every regime. The old world had tyrannies, monarchies, aristocracies, which we have discarded. The new world has party machines, pressure groups, lobbies, propaganda. In no case do we expect the truth to arise, automatically, out of the collective mind. *Vox Populi* has only two words at its command: Yes or No. It is always a conscious, organized minority that propounds the question, which, stripped of all verbiage, is invariably this: "Have you confidence in us?" In a traditional regime, the answer is taken for granted, and assent goes by the flattering name of "loyalty." In a democracy, any group may call for the question, even in awkward terms and at awkward times. In a dictatorship, the leader sees to it that he alone should ask the question, at his own time, in his own terms, and that the *Noes* be sternly discouraged. This saves a great deal of confusion.

We are only beginning to realize that the essence of political science is the study of public opinion: the laws of collective psychology and the methods of propaganda. We have now a number of very interesting books on the subject, the most accessible being those of Walter Lippmann. We have not yet fully applied the same method to the discussion of literary problems. Yet the conditions are not radically different from what they are in politics. America will not draft for the Presidency an admirable, but totally unknown person, until a few men have discovered him and spread the good news. Exactly in the same way, America will not spontaneously rush to the bookstores and discover the Great American Masterpiece, if no one, not even a publisher's reader or book agent, had passed the word that it was a masterpiece. In art as in politics, success depends first of all on an active minority. When *Vox Populi* has answered *Yes*, that success may be challenged again and again, in good democratic fashion: but it will have to be challenged by an active minority. Left to its own devices, *Vox Populi* would continue to acclaim, in a half-hearted way, works which have long lost all savor. In literature as in politics, again, there are some traditions which, in a well-established state, it is not lawful to challenge: a gentleman accepts unquestioningly the Dynasty and the Classics. This fine, restful, undemocratic virtue is called sterling loyalty in the one field, mellow culture in the other.

There are in literature also pressure groups, lobbies, machines, conscious and organized minorities which make up the public mind. The last word, *Yes* or *No*, is with Demos; but meanwhile, you can fool a good many people for a very long time. Eighteenth-century France was particularly modern and sprightly; yet it put up with dismal pseudo-classical tragedies which did not in the least correspond to its real taste. Why? Because those in authority had decreed that this fossil genre was the highest possible form of serious drama. Many impressive successes were scored, simply because no alternative was allowed. The alternative may have been ready: but the groups which acted as nominating committees refused to have it considered. In literature as in politics, it frequently happens that "we repair to the ballot box, and vote for Harding or for Cox." Ultimately, these artificial celebrities fade away. The lists of the best-sellers in any country, the roll of Academicians in France, offer a very large percentage of forgotten mediocrities. But the better work that was not given a chance is even more deeply forgotten. It is not certain that Dr. Pangloss was right, that "all is for the best in the best possible world," that all kings, all presidents, all generals, were the most efficient men available at the time; and in the same way, there is nothing to prove that our collection of acknowledged masterpieces represents the highest attainments that man could have reached.

Of these conscious minorities, some definitely claim authority, as bodies of trained and recognized experts: the professors, the academies. Others consider themselves as the natural leaders of the reading public, the epitome of the educated classes, the élite of society: Court circles and drawing rooms. The authors themselves, anarchical as their temper may be, do unite to form "pressure groups": the literary schools and the cliques. In our plutodemocracy, all these elements, without disappearing altogether, have lost much of their influence. On the contrary, the business of publishing has enormously grown in importance. The publishers profess, not to dictate public taste, but only to guess its trend. Their guesses, however, have a formative influence. *Vox Populi* cannot answer *Yes* when no question is asked; in other terms, the readers cannot demand books that are not offered for sale. So the public taste is limited to what the publishers guess it to be. It is these various agencies in the formation of literary opinion that we shall now pass in rapid review.

The nearest approach to a constituted authority in literature is the professorial body. Ideally, it should be the clergy of the literary church, the keeper of sacred tradition, the upholder and interpreter of sound doctrine. These lofty claims, in modern America, will not even elicit a smile: we are persuaded that the influence of the professors on living literature is imperceptible. We are conscious of it only when we react against it: there is, among publishers, critics and readers alike, a dread of the "highbrow" taint which is a real force.

Yet the professors may assert without conceit that they have shaped the literary conscience of the people far more definitely than is usually allowed. "What droll creatures these professors be!" exclaimed Gustave Flaubert. But Flaubert himself was the reverse of a young barbarian, untainted by schooling: he was a sedulous pupil. In his spirited correspondence with George Sand, he wrote in the vernacular; in his novels, he used a decidedly academic French, and seemed to be in constant dread of the teacher's blue pencil. How many masterpieces, from *Paradise Lost* down, depended for their creation, and still depend for their preservation, on the scholarly attitude! If the professors and their textbooks were to disappear altogether, and if the new generation had an absolutely free start, much would be lost that we now deem precious. Perhaps posterity would rediscover the classics for itself; but in the process, it would evolve a new brood of professors.

The "Mandarin dialect," as Cyril Connolly calls it,[1] is not a dead language. It plays a great part in the writings of our own generation. Many are the authors whose power is based on allusiveness; and allusions are drafts on the treasure house of literary tradition. Aldous Huxley denounced very wittily the snobbish element in "culture";[2] but his own works, delightful for the initiated, cannot be fully relished by the man in the street. Perhaps the most extreme products of the professorial influence are the bewildering "novels" of James Joyce, particularly *Ulysses* and *Finnegans Wake*. There we find an array of erudition that would appall Andrew Lang, Sir James Frazer, James Branch Cabell, Oswald Spengler and Cardinal Mezzofanti. No wonder the effect is slightly nightmarish.

By the "professors," we do not mean exclusively those who happen to earn a scanty living by teaching classes: we mean all the followers of the scholastic didactic tradition. Dr. Samuel Johnson was among the Fathers of the Professorial Church; Matthew Arnold, Ferdinand Brunetière, Irving Babbitt, T. S. Eliot, would be "professors" to the marrow of their bones even if they had not been attached to Oxford, the Ecole Normale, or Harvard University. The professorial attitude is based on three assumptions: that knowledge of the past is indispensable to the enjoyment of the present; that there are definite rules for the appraising of literary works; and that individual preferences should bend in obedience to these rules. As Brunetière bluntly put it: "It may be *wrong* to be amused, and *wrong* to be bored." It implies an orthodoxy of belief, and, in conformity with it, an orthodoxy of conduct. Without the Professorial Church, there is no salvation.

Academic refers both to the teaching profession, and to those august bodies which elect to membership the most distinguished

[1] Cyril Connolly: *Enemies of Promise.*
[2] Aldous Huxley: *Music at Night.*

men in scholarship, science and the arts. This is no mere coincidence: the aim of universities and academies is the same. It may be said that the first are the Church Militant, the second the Church Triumphant: in both cases a Church, preserving the ideals of discipline and tradition. In the old world, at any rate, they are eminently conservative agencies: the radical individualist and the reckless pioneer have no place in the *academic* scheme. We may add, irrelevantly, that the word *academic* is sometimes used in the sense of "divorced from practical life."

This conservative influence of the academies may be illustrated by a famous example: of all these institutions, the one which, in the realm of literature, has enjoyed the greatest prestige is the French Academy, and it was founded by Cardinal de Richelieu as part of his great effort for the restoration of order. Richelieu's method was at the same time *authoritarian* and liberal; he desired to suppress anarchy in every domain, but he was willing that every domain should enact and enforce its own laws. In his mind, his Academy was to be endowed, not merely with prestige, but with power. It was to codify and interpret the law, as it had descended from the ancients; and for that purpose, it was expected to issue treatises on rhetoric and poetry, a dictionary, and a grammar. It was also to apply the codes thus promulgated: Corneille, found guilty of violating the Aristotelian rules in his tragedy *Le Cid*, was courteously but firmy reprimanded, in spite of his acknowledged genius.

This is a conception which remains very attractive: no wonder it was so strongly advocated by Matthew Arnold. In the welter of literary production, ephemeral, sensational or vulgar, we long for expert guidance. We want the rules of the game to be drawn up, in accordance with the experience of the race; and we want to see those rules applied in definite cases by the best qualified judges. Thus we hope to have standards, and by these standards, to tell, infallibly, right from wrong. If Richelieu had had his imperious way, France would have provided a veritable Utopia for the literary world.

That is why the long and honored career of the French Acad-

cial. A living museum, the Academy has become the trustee for several museums, including the princely collections of Chantilly. It awards a number of prizes, with commendable caution; it even offers, with a smile of embarrassment, prizes for "virtue." The Academy is self-recruiting; an election seldom fails to cause a flutter in the drawing rooms, because it has almost invariably been prepared in the drawing rooms. Ladies are not eligible to membership: they find consolation in the thought that their influence in this sphere, although unofficial, is generally decisive.

This eminently *social* and unprofessional character of the Academy is, in our opinion, a strong point in its favor. A body composed exclusively of professors would not have enjoyed the same prestige; and it is doubtful whether a gathering of great original writers could have offered any *esprit de corps*, any corporate consciousness. Literature is the meeting ground of authors and public: it is excellent that there should be a joint committee uniting the élites on both sides.

The danger is not that literature should be dominated by society; but that society, that is to say the commonwealth, should be identified with "Society," that is to say the privileged classes. During the first half of its career, the Academy was actually ahead of the times. As conceived by Richelieu, it was the one institution where class distinctions expired: within its precincts, nobility and educated middle class associated on terms of complete social equality. Had the ancient regime been as liberal in other fields, there would have been no revolution in 1789. The situation is very different now. Forgetting the intentions of the founder, the Academy has become, very consciously, a class citadel. Every prominent conservative is certain of a seat among the Immortals; every leader of the Left is *ipso facto* debarred from the society of gentlemen. It suffices to compare the literary claims of Raymond Poincaré, Paul Deschanel, Alexandre Ribot, members of the Academy, with those of Jean Jaurès, Edouard Herriot and Léon Blum. In England, a peerage may be conferred upon a man of noted

Liberal tendencies; the Academy is far more exclusive than the House of Lords.

We have insisted upon the case of the French Academy, because it offers a clear-cut symbol of our general problem: the social approach to the study of literature. It is hard to separate cultural from social values, and "social" is a willfully ambiguous term which may refer to the interest of the community as a whole, or to the preservation of an established hierarchy. "The best literature is the one which is enjoyed by the best people, and the best people are those who move in the best circles": the present temper of the French Academy is an example of this confusion.

The influence of Royal Courts and aristocratic drawing rooms is exactly of the same nature. A Court, like the Academy, is supposed to be a place where all superiorities congregate, in the service of the realm; and such an ideal was *almost* realized under Louis XIV. A Court is an exalted salon, and a salon is a private court: minor courts, like that of the Grand Duke of Weimar, and princely circles, like that of the Duchess of Maine at Sceaux, are intermediate stages which reveal the kinship. *Courtesy* and *étiquette* prevail in both cases. A sovereign, if he knows his trade, will adorn his court with great dignitaries, field marshals, cardinals, and, if possible, a few men of genius. Exactly in the same way, an ambitious hostess will seek out, to grace her drawing room, celebrities of all kinds, leaders of church and state, artists, writers.

This "social" influence was already great in the late Middle Ages; greater still in Renaissance Italy; it was the brilliancy of the Italian Courts that induced northern kings and nobles to become patrons of all the arts. It was a luxury becoming a sovereign and a gentleman: art and aristocracy borrowed luster from each other. This factor does not explain the whole of literature; but it is far from negligible. Rousseau, for instance, the primitivist, the rebel against sophisticated society, was himself a product of that society. When he was only a provincial

bourgeois wives, who might be out of place in a skirmish of wit. Thus the social life of literary men often had for its center the inn, the tavern, the coffee house, the café, or even the lowly wineshop or cabaret. The *Mermaid* and the *Cheshire Cheese* will immediately come to mind, as indispensable items in the biographies of Shakespeare and Samuel Johnson. They do not merely provide a picturesque background and a few entertaining anecdotes: they have a significance in literary history, for the convivial group, even without striving, becomes a force. Dr. Johnson the author would be favorably remembered by scholars: but it is Dr. Johnson as the massive center of a circle that has become a familiar and beloved figure. The club founded by Sir Joshua Reynolds with Dr. Johnson's co-operation (1764) wielded extraordinary powers: its approval signified instant success.

A coterie is not invariably a clique; the clique is narrow and unscrupulous, ready to deny any wit to the unfortunates outside of the charmed circle; [1] but the coterie also is exclusive, and very legitimately implies mutual help among its members. It may sound sacrilegious to suggest "consolidated advertising" in the case of the glorious quartet, Boileau, Molière, La Fontaine, Racine; yet it is not indifferent to their fame that they stood so staunchly together; and they admired one another a little more warmly for the pleasant bouts they had at the *Pomme de Pin* (At the Sign of the Fir Cone).

These four men, it would seem, were members, not merely of a group, but of a school: they were all classicists. But who was not a classicist in those days? It is true, however, that the informal group passes, by very easy stages, into the recognized *school*. It did not happen in the case of Dr. Johnson: much as his friends admired the sage, they kept their own counsel; and, at the very height of his prestige, his Neo-Classicism was a lost cause. It did not happen either in the case of Chateaubriand: like Napoleon, with whom he loved to compare himself, the

---

[1] "*Nul n'aura de l'esprit que nous et nos amis*"; Molière, *Les Femmes Savantes*, III.

great romanticist had too lofty a sense of his own uniqueness.
But, frequently, people gather together because they have
tastes and tendencies in common; and, as a result of their getting together, these tendencies assume greater definiteness.

If there be among the members one with an instinct for
leadership, these tendencies will harden into a doctrine; the
doctrine will be embodied in a manifesto, and receive a formal
name; and the literary world will be enriched with one more
school. Thus the young poets meeting at Charles Nodier's
formed a *Cénacle*; but Victor Hugo walked away with the
Cénacle, carried it to his own home, and turned it into the
French Romantic School. His elders, Chateaubriand, Stendhal,
Lamartine, could only stand by in amazement. Thus again,
although the Goncourt brothers had already given the formula
of naturalistic fiction, and although they entertained very freely
in their famed *Grenier* [1] at Auteuil, it was Zola who organized
the troops and appointed himself their general. One may regret
that material and psychological circumstances made it difficult
for James Joyce to found a school: there was in *Ulysses*, apart
from the author's individual genius, a formula which should
have been worked out by a whole team of writers, instead of
remaining an almost unique experiment, abandoned by the
master himself.

It is possible for a school to have its origin, not in a social
gathering, but in a common enterprise: thus the great *Encyclo-
pédie* of Diderot and d'Alembert (1740-51-76); and *Le Par-
nasse Contemporain*, an anthology of poetry (1866-76); *En-
cyclopédiste* and *Parnassien* have remained definite terms in
the history of thought and art. The process, however, may be
reversed; the group seeks to assert its existence and to make its
power felt through some collective activity; and this usually
takes the form of a magazine. Thus, especially in the last half-
century, the ideas of clique, doctrine, school *and review* are
almost inseparable in the public mind. Best remembered perhaps is *The Yellow Book*, associated with the Decadentism of

[1] *Grenier:* literally hayloft; actually attic, and in this case studio.

the 'nineties; not with full justice, for it did not reflect exclusively the spirit of Oscar Wilde and Aubrey Beardsley. Few of these valiant publications last long: Miss Gertrude Stein shed one tear over "the little magazines that died to make verse free." One only, to our knowledge, has performed the miraculous feat of evolving from cliqueishness to business permanency: *Le Mercure de France*.

Of recent years, the creation of schools has frankly become a game in younger literary circles. Commendable ingenuity is displayed in the invention of names and tenets: Unanimism, Futurism, Vorticism, are good samples. If the supply should fail, there is always the possibility of tagging *Neo-*, *Post-*, or *Super-* to some ancient *-ism*. Dadaism should have been "the school to end all schools," the formal proclamation of absolute anarchy, an excellent *reductio ad absurdum* of Romantic individualism. But Dadaism itself lived only "the space of a morning"; and the cafés of Montparnasse remember it no more.

It is easy to smile at these youthful pranks: most of them were perpetrated with a smile. But there are serious aspects to the conception of a school, even the latest and most lively caricature. In the practical realm—for there is a practical side even to mystification—a school is, as we said, "consolidated advertising," a pressure group. In unity there is strength: seven isolated individuals would create less stir than a *Groupe des Sept*. Ronsard knew this full well, when he formed a constellation of Renaissance poets under the name of *Pléiade*. On the positive side, a school is a method for emphasizing some element in literature that had been overlooked, and for exploring its possibilities. In this respect, Unanimism and Futurism were at least interesting working hypotheses, and the experiments were well worth performing. A school, in this case, should be destroyed by its own success: the valid results of the experiment are incorporated into the general life of literature.

But the schools also foster elements which are inimical to art as well as to good manners: dogmatism (every school has discovered "the only possible method"); superciliousness ("We have done with the old fogeys"); cliqueishness ("No one shall have wit, but ourselves and our friends"). A school imposes upon a writer a false consistency. It is a great pity that Zola, as head of the Naturalistic School, should have felt obliged to be so steadily "naturalistic"; if it brought out and sustained certain aspects of his talent, it warped or repressed others. In many cases, this enforced conformity is altogether alien to the spirit of the man. It frequently happens that poets, in their earlier works, speak with two voices, that of their school and their own; and the voices may be discordant.

These dangers are great when a school holds sway for a long period, as was the case with Classicism, Romanticism and Realism. We shall never know how much originality they have thwarted or distorted. The present multiplicity of cliques and movements is a blessing in disguise. These groups are too numerous and too short-lived to be taken tragically. In a circuitous, paradoxical and entertaining manner, they are leading us back to tolerance and catholicity.

There is therefore a manifest waning in the influence of schools: when there are too many dictators, public taste is free. Free, but more helpless than ever. If the much-touted "new ways" offer us a maze instead of a well-marked path, if we cannot follow even the Greenwich Villagers, whither shall we turn?

The decadence of the old aristocracies in Europe left the field clear for plutocracy, which does not quite know what to do with its power. Similarly, the crumbling down of all conscious minorities, the keepers of the scholarly tradition, the academies, the courts, the drawing rooms, the schools and cliques, simply increases the power of "plutocracy" in letters, the commercial element, the book trade. At present, the publishers are the only organized influence in the literary world. *Vox Populi* is as inarticulate as ever: it can only grunt a confused assent. The publishers alone decide what is to be submitted to that rough plebiscite.

This situation, in the long perspective of history, is comparatively new. Before the printing press was invented, the "publishers" played a very small part in the selection of literature; any man could recite his poems to his friends, or circulate his manuscripts. Even in the sixteenth and seventeenth centuries, an author's reputation was made in and by the select groups; printing was almost incidental.[1] To address the general public directly, and through commercial channels, was chiefly an eighteenth-century development: the middle class no longer submitted in all things to the dictation of the élites. But its emancipation was gradual; today the process is practically complete. No one has the right to tell Demos what to read, and there is no way for Demos to make his desires known. The publishers can only hope that they have correctly anticipated his taste: a right guess is gain, a series of wrong guesses spells bankruptcy.

In describing the publishers as "plutocrats," in other terms as devotees of the profit motive, we have no thought of casting any slur upon them. They are performing an indispensable service. In most cases, they genuinely love literature; they would rather sell books than real estate, and sell good books rather than indifferent ones. It would be a grotesque misconception to imagine the author as invariably the idealist, the publisher as the sordid materialist. But, like all other plutocrats, they have to follow the rules of the trade, or go under. And, again like other plutocrats, they are bewildered. For, in that guessing game with Demos, Demos is likely to prove unaccountable. You cannot eternally offer him the standard article: at any moment, he may turn away in disgust. You cannot safely rely upon the spice of novelty: for novelty may strike him as foolish eccentricity. So publishing, according to the ad-

---

[1] Something of this survives today, when a sermon, an address, a poem, having met with the approval of their intended public, are "printed by request" for wider circulation.

mission of the best authorities, is a gamble.[1] In terms of the trade, you need at least one best-seller to make up for the expected ten or twelve *flops*.

With an inarticulate, unorganized public, there is little chance for gradual education. In the old days, it was possible for a book to "take" slowly, for an author to widen his circle in the course of many years. This is becoming increasingly difficult; the book which fails to "catch" in its first season is almost invariably doomed. The publisher cannot even hope to alter this condition through advertising. Advertising on an effective scale is used to help the book which is already well launched; in other words, advertising seldom *creates* success, it only *advertises* incipient success, and thus increases its momentum.[2] Thus massive and instantaneous success becomes the goal; and to reach that goal, there seem to be but two ways, both unsafe: the commonplace and the sensational. A book paradoxical and revolutionary to the point of absurdity will have a sporting chance; a book that is unobtrusively new and unobtrusively good cannot move the thick sluggish mass of "public taste."

Does this imply the death of all fine literature? We do not believe it. Among the books that we have described as "commonplace"—more courteously, safe and sane—some may possess delicate qualities. At first sight, one might see in Arnold Bennett and John Galsworthy only the perfection of the ordinary; yet it is not inconceivable that they will retain a place in literature. Among the "sensational" books, some may reveal enduring power. The present method, or lack of method, is not absolutely destructive of all values: it is only infinitely wasteful, like nature itself. Many excellent manuscripts are rejected, many works far superior to the average are stillborn: but so enormous is the number of books thrown upon the market that a few of them are bound to be both successful and good. For

[1] O. H. Cheney: *Economic Survey of the Book Industry*, 1930-31, a particularly shrewd and informative book.

[2] George Stevens, *Lincoln's Doctor's Dog and Other Famous Best-sellers*, 1939.

sells to us articles that are still unpublished and even unwritten. It is the method of the Book Clubs; and the earliest of these, like Charles Péguy's famous *Cahiers de la Quinzaine* (Notebooks of the Fortnight) in Paris, were halfway between the regular magazine and the series of independent volumes. By grouping together a small band of like-minded people, they were able to bring out works which would have had no chance in the general trade; they were associations for the defense of cultural minorities. The Book Clubs in the United States soon lost this character, if ever they offered it. They are simply a convenience for the general public; like any other form of commercial publishing, they have to provide books acceptable to the million. Their record has been creditable, but certainly not sensational.

The third way is to recognize excellence through the award of prizes, with or without formal competition. This is a very ancient method, for it goes back to the Greeks. We have at present three different kinds of prizes. The first are those offered by *publishers*. However lofty their professed aims may be, they are purely and simply a commercial device. They present two distinct advantages: the names of the judges are given, which is a guarantee of competence; and the winner is better advertised than other beginners. But the main object remains, very naturally, profitable sales. The most independent judges are aware of that essential condition. They will not select a book which seems to them excellent, but unlikely to be popular.

The second kind are those awarded by non-commercial bodies, but in *confirmation* of success already attained; to this category belong the Pulitzer Prizes. Motives and results are alike unexceptionable: it is meet that good authors should receive additional distinction and profit. But the effect on literature is negligible; no Pulitzer award has revealed a new writer to the world, none has directed public taste into unfamiliar channels, none has corrected the fundamental injustice of applying business criteria in matters of art. We were looking for leadership; we find only intelligent followers.

The third kind are the *discovery* prizes, given to unknown authors by a disinterested, non-commercial authority. Of these the best-known example is the Goncourt Prize. It is awarded by a permanent Committee of Ten, the endowed, self-perpetuating Goncourt Academy. In this case, the influence upon literature has been noticeable. The Goncourt Academy has actually brought to the world's notice authors who otherwise might have missed their chance altogether. Marcel Proust was wealthy, well-known in cultured circles; yet he had reached middle age without finding his public. It took the Goncourt Prize to make him famous. Every winner of that coveted distinction is assured of at least one brilliant success, not merely with the Parisian *literati*, but with the world at large: Goncourt Prize novels command large sales, and are usually translated into several languages. Yet, even in this most favorable case, it is obvious that the prize method offers no panacea: dust is gathering thickly over many prize-winning works. The ten Goncourt Academicians have proved less infallible than old Boileau, whose judgments on his contemporaries have never been reformed.[1]

Whichever way we turn, we find that there must be, at some point, a decision taken by a small group: the general public can only confirm or ignore that decision. The group may be the publishers' readers, the managers of endowed presses, the directors of book clubs, the judges of literary contests, the committees for the awarding of prizes: responsibility always rests with the few. Usually, these groups sin through timidity. Called to a position of influence, they abdicate. Their rule of conduct might be that of the French Revolutionary chieftain, in 1848: "Where are we going? I don't know: *I am their leader: therefore I must follow them.*" They try hard to find what the people want; what the people want is expert and

[1] The Nobel Prize usually means *confirmation* within the author's own country, *discovery* without; in this it fulfills a very useful purpose.

courageous leadership. In literature, such leadership has a name: it is called *criticism*.[1]

SUMMARY

All art that we can appreciate and discuss implies a public. We do not deny the existence of the "mute inglorious Milton"; but, with this bare admission, the matter must end. The public determines literature in two ways. Even the most aloof and rebellious author does think of a public, however restricted or hostile: the public is his "tacit interlocutor." And that public, out of the loose mass of mere writing, creates, because it selects, the body of what we know as *literature*.

What is this *public* then? All men? No; the mass is inert, and *Vox Populi* can only answer "yes" or "no." Public opinion is determined by conscious minorities.

Of these conscious minorities, some definitely claim authority as bodies of trained and recognized experts: the professors, the academies. The influence of the Professorial Church is deeper than present-day America is ready to admit; but it is not, and never has been, decisive. The most successful of academies, the *Académie Française*, has not become the Supreme Court of Correct Taste that Richelieu had in mind. The prestige of universities and academies is social, not dogmatic; it is due to long association with a ruling class.

Other minorities consider themselves the natural leaders of the reading public, the epitome of the educated classes, the élite of well-bred society: court circles and salons. Their power has waned in Europe, and disappeared in America. It survives, infinitely diluted but ubiquitous, in the literary clubs.

The writers themselves have a social life of their own, and combine into cliques, coteries and schools. These turn easily into consolidated advertising and pressure groups, with results which are not uniformly to the best interests of art. This also is a recessive influence.

[1] A fuller treatment of these problems, with a bibliography, will be found in the author's *Literature and Society*, Part III.

In our pluto-democracy, the publishers are the sole fully conscious and organized minority able to determine literature. They claim to be mere purveyors: they do not attempt to dictate public taste but only to guess its trend. Their guesses, however, have a formative influence. They alone frame the questions to which *Vox Populi* can answer only "yes" or "no."

The publishers are intelligent and well-meaning men. But, by their own admission, they are nonplused, and resort to gambling. They need massive and sudden successes (best-sellers) to recoup many wrong guesses. This puts a premium on the conventional or the sensational. The slow growth of an unobtrusively delicate book becomes increasingly difficult.

How could these chaotic conditions be remedied? (1) Through a deeper study of collective psychology on the part of the publishers, resulting in less crude and more efficient advertising; (2) through publishing purged from the profit motive: state, universities, endowed presses; (3) through the subscription-, series-, or book club method, so long as it does not itself become big business; (4) through the award of disinterested prizes, aiming at the *discovery* of new talent rather than at the *confirmation* of established success.

In all cases, responsibility rests with the few. The few sin through timidity. They seek only to find what the people want. What the people want is expert and courageous leadership, which in literature means able and honest *criticism*.

wearily because they have prevailed too long, when the clash of ideals leads to their mutual destruction, then Art becomes more sharply aware of its independence. It takes refuge in the ivory tower, its own exclusive domain.[1] Not out of cowardice; but, surveying all "sakes" and causes, it decides with Landor that none is worth its strife.[2]

The ivory tower need not be an abode of inglorious ease; life there may be no less strenuous and more ascetic than in the market town. It stands for an escape, not from responsibility, but from compromise. It is, on another plane, the equivalent of the monastic life during the Dark Ages: there must be some place on earth where the flame is preserved in its purity. It is not art that is decadent: it is art alone that retains its integrity in a decadent world.

If this interpretation be accepted, art for art's sake is not a rare disease, but a permanent tendency; it will be hidden or revealed according to circumstances, in history and in the life of the individual. Every man knows moments when it seems right, not to relax, but to escape; at times, to escape, not from failure, but from success, not from loss, but from profit: "for what shall it profit a man, if he shall gain the whole world and lose his own soul?"

Art for art's sake is therefore a quest for the strength that is in purity. It is the rejection of tainted alliances. Even when these alliances seem to "pay." The reader will remember our definition of *Kitsch*, or spurious art: the use of non-artistic means to secure pseudo-artistic effects. *Kitsch* is a kind of esthetic hold-up: the *Kitsch*-artist points a worthy purpose at

---

[1] This famous phrase is found in the *Song of Solomon*, VII-4: "Thy neck is a tower of ivory." It passed into the Litanies of the Virgin: *Turris Eburnea.* It denotes the strength that is in purity. Sainte-Beuve applied it to Alfred de Vigny (*Pensées d'Août*, 1837, A Villemain). Note that Vigny, the reverse of a decadent, was a stoic, and among the noblest of philosophical poets.

[2] I strove with none, for none was worth my strife,
  Nature I loved, and next to Nature, Art;
  I warmed both hands before the fire of life,
  It sinks, and I am ready to depart.
  —Walter Savage Landor, *On his 75th Birthday.*

you, and challenges you to deliver your approval. If you refuse to applaud when he waves the flag, you will be denounced as unpatriotic; if you smile when he rolls his eyes piously to heaven, you will be branded as irreligious; if you yawn when he sings of home with a sentimental tremolo in his voice, this argues that you are, by your own confession, a heartless son, a faithless husband, an unnatural father.[1] True art refuses to submit to such a hold-up; in its own name, and in the name of the ideals thus prostituted. This rejection requires courage: it is far safer to be enthusiastic or indignant, outwardly pious or properly tearful with the crowd. Cordelia refused to turn her filial love into a stage performance: she was not understood.

But there is a problem more complex than that of *Kitsch*, and on a higher plane. One may refuse to borrow, yet be ready to lend. Art may spurn the success that goes to the cause, not to the art; but can it not legitimately come to the aid of the cause? For the clearness of the argument, let us present the two attitudes with a definiteness they seldom offer in real life. On the one hand, we find the *Gospel of Usefulness*. The first test applied to anything should be: "What is it good for? What does it mean? What purpose does it serve?" Obviously, that purpose need not be grossly material: the utilitarians do not propose to abolish all music and all statuary. But there must be some clear gain: art must be relaxing like a warm bath, or bracing like a cold shower, or, and above all, "elevating." If it does for us none of these things, it is futile and stands condemned. "If it attempts any of these things," say the upholders of art for art's sake, "it becomes business, hygiene or education, and ceases to be art."

The utilitarian attitude is sometimes called *philistinism*. Like

[1] The non-artistic means used by *Kitsch* are not necessarily borrowed from virtuous sources. As we have noted, *Kitsch* is all the more *Kitsch* when it appeals to the gorgeous, the cryptic, and especially the meretricious. It is well known that Art, in certain publications and spectacles, and in the works of Pierre Louÿs, is only a diaphanous veil for pruriency: *Kitsch* of an aggravated kind.

almost every term beyond the designation of simple material objects, this one is equivocal. It originated in the German universities: the "philistines" were the outside world, as opposed to the Lord's own people, the students themselves. Goethe lent prestige to this bit of college slang, and Matthew Arnold gave it currency in English. It is frankly a term of contempt: it connotes the petty materialism of the lesser bourgeoisie. But this is only a caricature. Not all philistines are stupid. Queen Victoria's Consort, Prince Albert, was clever as well as good; yet his philistinism is beyond dispute. Macaulay was a brilliant philistine; Voltaire was in every respect, high and low, the monarch of philistines; and George Saintsbury dared to call Goethe himself "a Philistine of Culture." This seems rank sacrilege: yet the essence of culture is to be disinterested, and Goethe asked himself the philistine question: "How can this help us?"

The notion of philistinism is of the utmost importance for our purpose, but in a negative way: the philistine represents exactly all that the "Artsakist" strives not to be. It will therefore be sufficient to pass in review all the "sakes" for which art can be attempted by the philistine—art for the sake of money, art for the sake of social prestige, art for the sake of information, art for the sake of a cause—and then to deny the validity of every one of these "sakes": the residue will be art in absolute purity, art for its own sake only.

Art for the sake of money seems to be an obvious case. We feel that when the thought of gain mingles with any one of the higher values, its effect is corrosive. Love for the sake of money is prostitution, religion for the sake of money is simony: there is an equivalent for these in the field of art. It has always been felt that art is a gift of the spirit, and should not be put up for sale.

True: but not without qualifications. If we were to admit that the slightest admixture of the profit motive were sufficient to destroy the possibility of art, we should be compelled to rule out of the literary field Shakespeare and Molière, who were decidedly "in the business" of writing plays, just as Balzac and Dickens were "in the business" of writing novels. And yet we should be reluctant to lose even Alexandre Dumas, who was running a romance-factory of unexampled efficiency. Our theoretical puritanism will have to adjust itself to very palpable facts.

A man must be pronounced guiltless, for one thing, if material success comes to him as a surprise. A suspicious critic might accuse Santayana of having given sales more than a passing thought when he wrote *The Last Puritan;* but no one dreams that Robert Bridges was seeking pelf and popularity, when he composed his lofty and austere *Testament of Beauty.* Gain, in that case, was "an act of God" for which no man can be held responsible. We are apt to be unjust on this score. Abbé Dimnet, for instance, did not shrewdly forecast and engineer the phenomenal sales of his *Art of Thinking.* If *The Bridge of San Luis Rey* had not taken so well, Thornton Wilder would have been hailed by the *literati* as a subtle and delicate author, incapable of truckling to the crowd.

Guiltless also is the "folk" writer, who writes in the popular taste because it is his own taste. We take it for granted that Homer did not try to set himself apart from the Greeks of his day, or Shakespeare from his Elizabethan audience. Dumas enjoyed for himself exactly the kind of romance that he gave the public; and the blend of melodrama, sentiment and caricature in Dickens, if it was "lower middle-class Victorian," was also, and even more, genuinely Dickensian. A man is not to be despised for writing popular stuff unless he first despises it himself.

Then there is the possibility of financial gain as the mere inevitable accompaniment of recognition. For lack of an organized, hierarchized public, the author who wishes to reach a few congenial minds must cast his net very wide. If he has a hundred thousand readers, he stands a chance of reaching the three or four thousand to whom his work was essentially addressed. The case is even clearer when the author has a "message," like Victor Hugo in *Les Misérables*, Tolstoy in *Resurrection*, Henri Barbusse in *Under Fire*. Then it is his duty to reach the widest possible audience. Most publishers are so honest, that it is difficult for a writer to be successful without collecting sizable royalties. *Profit* there is: but the profit motive is present only in harmless doses, like poison in beneficial remedies.

Finally, authors must live. If their activity is legitimate, and indeed valuable, they should be supported by their chosen labor, in the same way as priests and doctors. Here the historical and social approach to the study of literature proves of great value: it enables us to take changing conditions into account. We cannot blame a penniless writer, in the Classical Age, for accepting aristocratic patronage. Even sturdy Dr. Johnson, in his scathing letter to the Earl of Chesterfield, did not object to the principle: he refused patronage which had been denied in the hour of need, and was proffered only when it would do credit to the giver. Today, this dependence upon wealthy individuals would be considered demeaning. Other ways are open, and the alternative which developed in the eighteenth century was a direct appeal to the public, on a business basis. Writing for profit then meant liberation, and not servitude. It is quite possible that we shall grow beyond the present stage. We could easily draw up a Utopia in which no one would preach, comfort, heal, protect, judge, for promotion or pay; and in which the same disinterestedness would prevail among those who carve, draw, paint or write. Until this millennium has dawned, and all men are free from worldly care, writers should not be singled out for blame if they accept compensation. Provided always that the compensation be merely a necessity, not the ruling motive.

Art for the sake of social prestige also seems a travesty of pure art. Success, of course, is flattering to an author's vanity; it is sweet to hear one's name on the lips of men. And artistic success, in all ages, has opened the gates of exclusive society. Horace and Vergil were the Emperor's friends; Charles IX went out of his way to flatter Ronsard; Voiture, son of a wine merchant, was "the little king" of Madame de Rambouillet's aristocratic salon; Boileau and Racine had more direct access to Louis XIV than many a noble lord; Goethe was a great personage at the Court of Weimar; Balzac flirted with Duchesses and married a Countess; D. H. Lawrence, a miner's son, was sought after by titled ladies, and their American equivalents. Even today, a few poems or short stories will open doors which are closed against mere wealth.

This appeal, frankly, is but a refined form of snobbishness. An author who works with such an end in view is a social climber, a "Would-be Gentleman," like Molière's Monsieur Jourdain. Yet here again we find it difficult to draw an inflexible line. Should an author reject all honors and distinctions, bits of ribbon, titles, membership in prestigious bodies like the academies, the old Italian Senate, or the House of Lords? Not unless he is such a revolutionist that he considers the existing order as topsy-turvy, and the social élite as the enemy. The desire for distinction is the same under ludicrous and under exalted forms. One wishes to attain prominence, then celebrity; to be invited to meet the lions, then to be a lion with a mane and a roar of one's own. What is celebrity but incipient fame, and what is fame but the foretaste of glory? There is little chance that your name will reach posterity, unless it has been at least whispered by influential contemporaries. And what proof is there that *glory*, the favor of our great-grandchildren, is better worth having than *celebrity*, the approval of living men? When we are pursuing either, we are setting the opinion of outsiders above intrinsic values. For the "pure" artist, his own satisfaction should be the sole test. All else is vanity.

Yet we know that many artists of the highest order have confessed, proudly, their desire for fame. It is not merely the last infirmity of noble minds: it belongs to the very nature of art, if we conceive of art as a fight against death. The same yearning cry echoes through the generations: "I shall not die altogether," claims Horace; "Read me, do not let me die!" pleads Edna St. Vincent Millay. Art exists, not solely for the sake of beauty, but for enhancing our consciousness of life.

Art for the sake of information might be dismissed with a smile. Everyone knows that literature is not an encyclopedia of useful knowledge. Pedagogical romances, like *Telemachus, Emile, Leonard and Gertrude, The Swiss Family Robinson,* hover on the borderline of art, but are very far from its center. Even in the case of history, art would be out of place when the purpose is pure information, as in epitomes, chronologies, annals, dictionaries. History as *literature* is judged by literary standards. That is why we still read and enjoy Livy: not as a textbook, but as a masterpiece of narrative eloquence. Not that we are willing to condone willful inaccuracy. Our point is that, in historical writing, art, philosophy and information are inevitably mingled, and that, while enjoying the rich combination of these three elements, we are justified in striving to separate them in our reflective mind. Factual errors, regrettable as they may be, will not invalidate brilliant art or cogent thinking; on the other hand, art and thought at their very best will never establish as true a fact which is not so. Information should be checked by the most rigorous methods available to scholarship; art should be judged for art's sake.

The information purpose appears, at times blatantly, in genres which claim to be strictly literary: historical, geographical, and realistic fiction. There are far too many people who believe they have acquired authentic knowledge about the French Revolution from *A Tale of Two Cities.* There may be a few who consider *Moby Dick* as a valuable treatise on the whaling trade. Zola, in each volume of his monumental series, *The Rougon-Macquart,* took up some aspect of French society under the Second Empire, and gave a severely documented report on the subject. As an instance of his scrupulously scientific attitude, it is mentioned that, when he was preparing a handbook of railroad practice (with a bit of melodrama thrown in), he went from Paris-St. Lazare to Mantes in the cab of a locomotive, a distance of fully thirty-seven miles. And if we read *The Grapes of Wrath*, we shall know everything about the migrants, from the dust bowl of Oklahoma to the jealously guarded earthly Paradise of Central California.

As in the case of history, we have here a blend of motives. But the proportion is reversed. History, by its very nature, should conform to reality, although it presents reality in an artistic light. *Fiction* is not plain truth: the "realists" compel us to reassert this elementary fact. In fiction, the essential purpose is artistic, and the use of accurate details is but an artistic device. Information given solely for the sake of information is actually a blemish. The sole advantage of "realism," historical or contemporary, is to create an atmosphere. We rarely enjoy characters who move in an abstract world, or in a world remote from any known reality: even Poictesme must evoke the land of the Troubadours. The choice of a definite milieu provides from the outset the thrill of strangeness or the comfort of familiarity; it suggests the mood that the author wishes to rouse in us. Its chief effect is not to impart information, but to tap the resources of information stored in the reader's mind. But, once more, it is merely a device, and like all devices, it defeats its purpose when it becomes obtrusive. It is not enough that the facts be true: they must have suggestive power. We do not care whether the picture is rigorously accurate, so long as it is convincing.

Thus Gustave Flaubert's Carthaginian story, *Salammbo*, was worked up with the same care as a doctor's dissertation, and, on that very account, provides singularly heavy reading. As science, it has no standing, since it is, avowedly, fiction. As art, it is redeemed by flashes of romantic imagination: an intense vision of a strange city, teeming, cruel and remote. But Victor Hugo, Leconte de Lisle, James Thomson, Lord Dunsany, obtained exactly the same effect without Flaubert's crushing load of erudition.

Information as an artistic device is therefore a powerful but dangerous instrument: the slightest excess repels. And the blend of reality and fiction is precarious. if truth is an asset, if it strikes a responsive note in the reader's memory, by the same token an anachronism will cause an unpleasant jar, a flagrant liberty taken with the accepted facts will ruin the effect. It is not impossible to compose a picture with actual bits of clothing, real hair, photographic features for certain characters, while others are treated with a free brush: but it would take miraculous skill to make it a success, and the result is more likely to be a nightmare. Yet this is exactly what historical and realistic fiction attempts to do. We resent it when Zola brings together an authentic Napoleon III, and, as his prime minister, a semi-fictitious Eugène Rougon. We are expected to live in two discordant worlds.

Shall we conclude that the historical novel is indefensible because it is *not* historical, and the realistic novel indefensible because it is *not* realistic? Fortunately perhaps, this is not a logical world, and these "indefensible" kinds are still thriving exceedingly. Art is a dream world compounded of oddly definite facts and the freest of fancies. When we have entered the magic realm, we are ready to accept anything, even the "coasts of Bohemia," even the monstrous White Whale which is a symbol of all evil, even the Octopus in *Toilers of the Sea*, even the secret of the Iron Mask, even, as in Zola, the "spontaneous combustion" of a drunkard. But, before we reach that blissful "suspension of disbelief," there must be magic: the magic of art. Is not that another way of saying that in art, information as such is irrelevant, and that our final judgment is invariably given "for art's sake"?

Art for the sake of a cause is a very controversial subject, and requires particularly careful definition. It is obviously legitimate for the defender of any cause to employ the best tech-

nique at his command; and there are many points upon which
the rules of art and the laws of effectiveness are in complete
agreement. On an elementary plane, no one denies that a plea
before a court of justice, a political speech, a sermon, will be
none the worse for being well constructed and lucid. If literary
art were identical with the art of English composition, it could
and should without question be placed at the service of any
cause worth defending. Virtue is not best served by awkward
syntax or clumsy diction. On a higher plane, art is not simply
a *language*, but, like science, a method of exploration. It actually discovers facts, and the relations between facts, through the
artist's acuity of vision and power of sympathy. Like science,
it performs experiments, although never with the same degree
of certitude. It takes a hypothesis—character, passion, situation
—and works out its possibilities, striving to arrive at a credible,
a convincing solution. Now, any "cause" will profit by making
use of the artistic method, as well as of the scientific. In so far
as they are, not exclusively achievements, but instruments, science and art can be made to serve. And whatever the purpose
may be, the results of the artistic method properly applied cannot be anti-artistic.

This leads us to our second point, no less obvious in principle, but a little more delicate in application: both art, and
the cause which uses art as a tool, are bound to suffer through
dishonesty. When we speak of art sacrificed to politics or morality, we generally have in mind art prostituted to propaganda,[1] an attempt to sway opinion through willfully distorted
information. A drama that will invariably present one class or
party as a set of villains is rank propaganda, and deplorable art.
The simplest and most ubiquitous case of willful distortion is
that of the alleged "poetic justice"—vice punished, virtue rewarded—which mars so many works of art, including some of

[1] We are here using *propaganda* in the very unfavorable sense it has acquired in this generation. We do not forget that, *per se*, propaganda means
simply the diffusion of truth: *"de propaganda fide."* In this it is not different
from the missionary spirit, education and advertising.

the highest. We feel that the author is not playing fair; he deflects the logic of circumstances for the sake of deluding us, or himself. Wishful thinking is not good morality. The world has always had to face the problem of the just man suffering and of the wicked flourishing: hence the craving for another life, to redress the manifest wrongs of this one. It is immoral to pretend that it is not so. Only one thing could be worse: to twist, not the material facts, but the moral values; to claim that right always triumphs, because whatever triumphs is right.

Let us suppose, however, a man who is thoroughly honest with himself, both as an artist and as an apostle. Will it be possible for him to serve both his art and his cause? We do not see how he could keep them separate, if both of them are himself. If there is anything in his art that is not identical with his inmost thought, that something is spurious art—mere display of technical skill, lifeless tradition, sophistication for the sake of prestige—and should be eliminated. If there is anything in his cause that his conscience cannot approve, that something is prejudice, self-interest, partisanship, and must be purged away.

Thus the purity of art would not suffer in the service of a "pure" cause—if one could be found. This is such a counsel of perfection that it sounds like cynical irony rather than wisdom. Yet it has definite significance. It means that art, even when it knows it not, is an eternal protest against those "sakes" that do not embrace humanity in their scope. Every exclusion is a mutilation, to which artists may submit, but which art condemns. Art enlisted and drilled under the banner of tribe, myth or party is a little less than art. Shakespeare was at times a ranting jingo, but "if so, the less Shakespeare he." In its narrower meaning, a "cause" is an organization for promoting an idea which, for its supporters, it is no longer lawful to question: Art stands outside of all such causes, and, if need be, against them, in order to avoid being captured by them. This is not a purely negative attitude: it denies only those limitations that would turn man into an automaton. Such is the meaning, cautious rather than defiant, that can be attached to the phrase "art for art's sake."

This attitude, we repeat, is not negative; but it is defensive. Pressed to join this or that organization, art escapes into the ivory tower. But the remedy might be worse than the evil: few "causes," however narrow, could inflict such a deadly mutilation on an artist as complete exclusion from the world of men. The ivory tower is justified as a retreat; not as a permanent dwelling place. Constantly, artists have sallied forth from their fortress; not seldom because they were reduced to spiritual starvation; not seldom also in order to carry an aggressive campaign.

For—this is the second and more elusive meaning of art for art's sake—art itself can be turned into a cause, exclusive and jealous as all causes must be. The artists do not want art merely to live and to be free, but to rule. They attempt to reshape the world on an esthetic basis. Instead of asking of a thing, with the philistine, "Is it useful?"; with the scientist, "Is it true?"; with the moralist, "Is it good?"—they want us to inquire only, "Is it beautiful?" Beauty becomes the first and greatest commandment.

Art—and the world—for beauty's sake! This sounds at first like an outrageous paradox; in practice, most men arrive at a workable, sensible, and thoroughly illogical compromise. Beauty is a term hard to define, and, before they are through with the discussion, people generally manage to reintroduce truth, goodness and even utility, all the better for appearing in esthetic garment. If Keats said: beauty is truth, he also said: truth is beauty. Some Platonist, ages ago, declared beauty to be "the splendor of truth"; and the Psalmist reminds us repeatedly of the mightier beauty that is in holiness.

Beauty-worship as the highest of causes, as the only cause to which art can legitimately be devoted, has never been the central element in literature. Every great writer has always professed to have other ends in view: religion, love, happiness, national grandeur, social justice, truth; even Keats, who pondered tragically over "the giant sorrows of the world"; even Baudelaire, who claimed at times to be an impassive scientist, at other times to be an orthodox Christian, tortured with the sense of sin. In literature, beauty is not so much a motive as a sign: the sign of profound harmony between personality, purpose and technique. Apparent beauty of image and sound, without the things that beauty signifies, is like the pitiful emblems of victory worn when there is no victory. There is no more abundant source of *Kitsch*.

Philistinism, as we have defined it, is the attempt to introduce into art the notion of utility. *Estheticism* is a curious revenge of the artistic spirit: it appraises the practical world exclusively in terms of beauty. Beauty, in this conception, is not merely independent of use, but incompatible with use; it is enhanced when it destroys philistine "values." Nero set Rome on fire: a conflagration is a thing of beauty, far above the cost of sticks and stones, far above commonplace human existences. This state of mind is most tersely summed up in the phrase *"beau geste."* Lives had been sacrificed in an anarchistic outrage: the decadent poet Laurent Tailhade defiantly declared: "Who cares for the death of vague human beings? *The gesture is beautiful!*" [1]

The *beau geste* attitude is perhaps the most striking example of the interaction between literature and life. It is hard at times to decide whether artists are prophetic voices or sonorous echoes: the responses of poets and public are inseparably woven together. Both have their origin in esthetic appreciation. The humdrum is sensible, and we submit to it—but we submit reluctantly, wistfully. Every man is at heart a Don Quixote chafing under the yoke imposed upon him by Sancho Panza; every man seeks to escape from the deadly dailiness of life. Those characters, ideals, events, appeal most to him which offer the

---

[1] Through an impardonable abuse of poetic justice, Laurent Tailhade himself was the victim of an anarchist's bomb a few months later. He is not remembered, except for this one immortal phrase.

promise of a victory over the commonplace. Now these are ready themes for folklore; they are cherished before they are written down; they are vaguely desired before they have revealed themselves.

We can follow this *beau geste* motive—heroic, adventurous, romantic—in private morality, in politics and history, even in religion. It is this protest against philistinism that causes the eternal prestige of the Prodigal Son, who lived dangerously, as against his safe-and-sane brother. Hence also the fascination of the magnificent transgressor—brigand, outlaw, enchantress. The paradoxical extreme of this would be "murder as one of the fine arts," as in De Quincey, or "murder as a pure act," for the sake of disinterested energy, as in André Gide's *Vaults of the Vatican*. Hence the appeal, for our bourgeois mind, of a political economy based on struggle and gambling, offering the thrilling alternatives of glorious success, or bankruptcy and suicide. It makes for a colorful world, in which even such a prosaic transaction as selling soap or pickles assumes the character of a battle and a game. The great objection to socialism is that it would reduce the business of life to mere business: production, distribution, consumption, on a dreary statistical basis, stodgily sensible, with all the entrancing perilous fun eliminated.[1]

This same motive operates in the life of the nation as well as in that of the individual. Theorists offer an economic interpretation of history, but it is a mere theory; the living reality is the dramatic, the poetic interpretation. No one ever made war for purely economic reasons: even the Opium War had to be justified by a question of prestige. The purest economists, those of the Manchester School, were determined pacifists, because they knew that war is bad business. The most conscious business center in the world, the City of London, was per-

---

[1] Repeatedly, men with a literary turn of mind, George Moore, Aldous Huxley, Joseph Wood Krutch, have declared that *Utopia*, in the sense of a world based on order, justice, security, would be incompatible with the arts. Cf. "Literature in Utopia," in our *Literature and Society*.

suaded of that truth even before Norman Angell made it patent in *The Great Illusion.* "We are not all cotton spinners yet!" proudly claimed Tennyson. War is invariably a defiance against bourgeois common sense, a moment when the people are most intensely conscious of their collective life, when they raise themselves, in their own eyes, to the heroic plane; it is emphatically a *beau geste,* counting the cost as naught. Peace has seldom been sung by poets: war is the stuff epics are made of. Even stories about the horrors of war are tributes to its fascination. Collectively also, we are in romantic thrall to *"les Belles Dames sans Merci,"* the fatal beauties. "Had Cleopatra's nose been a little shorter," said Pascal, "the face of the world would have been changed": certainly the course of historical writing. Cleopatra, Messalina, Theodora, Mary Stuart, have seduced innumerable scholars. Burke and his followers passed judgment on the French Revolution in terms of Marie Antoinette's royal beauty. Professors echo unwittingly the words of the Trojan elders, when Helen passed by in her sovereign perfection: "For such a woman, it is meet that a city should perish."

The clearest example of the esthetic motive is the ineradicable prestige of Napoleon. To the good organizer, the sound financier, the efficiency manager, we do homage with our lips: but what thrills our hearts is the epic adventure, the mad and glorious gamble. Washington was sensible, and is universally revered; but the mass of art and literature inspired by Napoleon, even in this country, is immensely larger; common sense and patriotism together will not make Washington a best seller. What fascinates us most in the career of Napoleon are those "gestures" which were most "beautiful" because they were most senseless: the Egyptian expedition, the retreat from Moscow, the Hundred Days. The Russian campaign, as we know, was ill conceived, ill prepared, ill executed; out of six hundred thousand men of the Grand Army, only a few thousand returned in formation. But the story has epic magnitude, and the delectable appeal of horror: what matters it that vague human beings should die of hunger and cold?

The Napoleonic Legend was worked up by poets: it was part of the great romantic fever. It did not arise spontaneously from the masses; but it did not remain confined to the domain of art and poetry. *Vox Populi*, after some delay, echoed thunderously the concert of Béranger, Thiers, Dumas, Hugo; the Legend became practical politics; and it became responsible for the Second Empire. A "legend" also, the medieval glories of the Hohenstaufen, the promised return of Barbarossa, fired the imagination of Germany, and led to the Second German Empire. Bismarck himself might pose as a realist; but the regime he imposed upon the scientific and industrial Germany of 1871 was a bit of belated romanticism, a pseudo-Wagnerian opera. William II, the crowned Lohengrin, was a clear example of the would-be artist on the throne.[1] Post-war Germany dramatized herself into the passionate hatreds and millennial hopes of the Third Reich. The Weimar Republic died of the same congenital weakness as the bourgeois monarchy of Louis-Philippe: both were sensible regimes, and the countries grew desperately bored.

In religion also, there is a strong, at times an overwhelming element of Estheticism. *Credo quia pulchrum:* I believe because it is beautiful. Chateaubriand, the great apostle of Catholic Romanticism, who claimed to have restored religion in France after the orgies of impiety of the Enlightenment and the Revolution, had first entitled his work *Beauties of Christianity*. He finally called it *Genius*, or *Spirit*, *of Christianity:* but his system of apologetics remained the same. This argument, which lends itself admirably to poetry and eloquence, appears on three different planes. First of all, the splendors of nature declare the glory of God. When Rousseau wanted to expound, through his *Vicaire Savoyard*, the principles of free Christianity, or natural religion, he took his pupil to the foothills of the

---

[1] An even clearer case was that of Louis II of Bavaria; but he was too consistent in his policy of "government for art's sake," and was declared mad.

Alps: the admirable spectacle of lofty peak and fruited plain fills the soul with reverence. Ruskin thanked the Divine Craftsman for offering to our delighted eyes, *almost* every morning and evening, masterpieces of living art in the form of sunrise and sunset. The objection is that the beauties of nature appeal to us only in contrast with the commonplaceness of the rest. There is no beauty in a swamp under a leaden sky, in a vast field of dust or mud, in oppressive heat or numbing cold; yet these also were prepared for us by hands not our own.

The second level of argument is the sentimental and sensuous beauty of ritual. In this Chateaubriand reveled; and the solemn tolling of bells was in his mind proof irrefutable that his faith was true. This thought was an essential part of the ritualistic tendency in nineteenth-century Anglicanism: another manifestation of the romantic spirit and the Gothic revival. Strangely enough, it was best expressed by the poet in whom we see the prophet of Puritan austerity, John Milton. A few lines in *Il Penseroso* give in condensed form the full gospel of esthetic Christianity, and we may consider the phrase "dim religious light" as its perfect epitome.[1]

On the other hand, there has been constant dread, on the part of earnest souls, lest the sensuous appeal should conceal, distort and destroy spiritual truth. We know for certain that in all churches the deepest experiences have not been dependent upon the magnificence of the setting. No purer faith could be found than in the bare cell of the monk, the hut of the

---

[1] But let my due feet never fail
To walk the studious cloister's pale,
And love the high embowéd roof,
With antick pillars massy proof,
And storied windows richly dight
Casting a dim religious light.
There let the pealing organ blow
To the full voiced Quire below,
In service high and anthems clear,
As may with sweetness, through mine ear,
Dissolve me into ecstasies,
And bring all Heaven before mine eyes.   (1633)

missionary, the closet of the lonely wrestler with God. Pomp attended pagan sacrifices, and the courts of earthly kings; it is now most impressive in the great pageants staged by the totalitarian states; but the blare of ten thousand trumpets cannot silence the still small voice.

Finally, on the highest plane, we find the esthetic appeal of sacred story and dogma. While theologians, both Catholic and Protestant, St. Thomas Aquinas even more than John Calvin, insist upon expounding faith in terms of reason, there has been a constant tendency to justify faith because of its intrinsic beauty. Faith alone, it is argued, is able to convert a chaotic or ruthlessly mechanical universe into an epic drama of matchless grandeur. A creed reduced to Aristotelian syllogisms could compel our cool assent; it would not draw from the soul the great lyric cry of Psalmist and prophet; it would not evoke before our eyes the formidable visions of the Apocalypse. We have repeatedly stated that the test of literature is to be *convincing:* here the test applies with extraordinary literalness. There is a point, foreshadowed but not attained by Keats, where Beauty and Truth merge with irresistible power.

This argument may be advanced with full consciousness, or remain the secret armature of our thought. In James Branch Cabell,[1] it is stated with such directness that it sounds almost ironical: for the artist, Christianity is true, because it offers "a tremendous situation." G. K. Chesterton played round the same idea, with his bulky nimbleness, but never expressed it in such plain terms: he sought refuge in a cloud of delightful paradoxes. Chateaubriand's case is similar; he is a forerunner of Cabell, but he could not be brought to confess it. He found protection from the logic of his thought, not, like Chesterton, in dazzling wit, but in a softly luminous Romantic haze. In Pascal, the conception of the "tremendous situation" is present; there is in Pascal, by the side of the philosopher, the scientist and the mystic, a poet with a shuddering sense of tragic

[1] *The Cream of the Jest. Evolution of a Vestryman.*

conflict. For him, the Christian faith alone could bring the cosmic drama to its full *catharsis*, the purification of terror and pity. Milton did not separate in his mind the epic beauty of his narrative from its authenticity as spiritual truth; if truth deepened beauty, so did beauty in return confirm truth.

It is an ungrateful task to examine critically a conception which has inspired masterpieces, and imparted a richer glow to the faith of millions. Yet it cannot be denied that this blend of "literature and dogma" offers many dangers. If we adopt the esthetic standard, we shall be led to pick and choose among the sacred writings, and decide that *Deuteronomy* and *Leviticus* are not "beautiful" in the same degree as *Genesis* or the *Book of Job*. And we shall be tempted also to rank certain pagan works above some of those which embody our own faith. *Prometheus Bound* offers a greater "situation" than the story of Samson. The beauty of a myth is proof of its validity *as a myth*. The convincingness of literature is not literal: it merely implies a possibility. Yes, Schiller, through his art, gave us an idea of the way in which William Tell might have thought, spoken, acted; he gave us also a great symbol of the spirit of freedom, and we carry the inspiration from his drama into practical life. Thus he has served well the cause of spiritual truth; but Schiller's masterpiece does not prove that William Tell ever existed in the flesh.

Then the mind of the true estheticist will not be the temple of a jealous God, but a Pantheon: whatever is beautiful is right. That is why Christian poets like Camoëns found it impossible to discard pagan mythology, which was still, for them, a never-failing source of beauty; so that we find in *The Lusiads* Olympian deities, medieval enchanters, the Virgin and the saints, appearing in the same pages in delightful and baroque confusion. That is why also even Dante and Milton added to their sacred authorities, and apparently on the same plane, the products of their own imagination. For the scrupulous believer, such "improvements" are sacrilegious. Perhaps Boileau revealed both his earnest faith and his vigorous common sense when he declared that "pleasing ornaments" were not compatible with "the awe-inspiring mysteries of our religion."

The worst danger is that the esthetic attitude, in its purity, is indifferent, not only to literal truth, but to goodness also. If rarer flowers can be plucked from the garden of evil, let evil be our good. There is no beauty, for an exclusively artistic mind, in tame acquiescence: the original *"beau geste"* in spiritual history was that of Satan daring to rebel against eternal law. In private life, as we have seen, the prodigal, the outlaw, even the murderer, are more appealing as literary subjects than the stodgy conformist; in collective life, our favorites are the audacious gamblers, rebels, revolutionists, and those great anarchs the conquerors. The equivalent of this on the cosmic plane is Satan-worship. As Blake, with the fearless irresponsibility of genius, frankly proclaimed: "The reason Milton wrote in fetters when he wrote of Angels and God, and at liberty when of Devils and Hell, is because he was a true poet and of the Devil's party without knowing it." [1] We know that this Byronic-Baudelairian strain is not the whole of Milton's art. But it is the exaggeration, the caricature, that brings into strong relief an element of corruption; outwardly condemned and repressed, it is the object of our secret indulgence. It would be far safer for religion to let art go its own way: faith would thus be liberated from a contaminating influence. Perhaps the greatest service of art for art's sake would be to purify for us the thought of religion for religion's sake.[2]

[1] *Marriage of Heaven and Hell.*

[2] The difficult question of art and religion has been made worse confounded in two ways. On the one hand, there has been in certain circles what seemed a deliberate quest of ugliness; this implies the consciousness, as well as the fear, of beauty; it is a perverted form of estheticism. On the other hand, we must note the use, at times the lavish use, of spurious art for religious purposes: sham Gothic or decadent Baroque in church architecture, and, in literature, a conventional, sentimental, edifying tone: if we must have art, let us have the best, and not *Kitsch.* For the serious-minded believer, architecture and literature are like the garments of his body: they must be honest, adequate and neat, without a thought for sheer ornament. This austerity of taste, as we shall see, is not incompatible with beauty: beauty comes unbidden, modestly, in the form of the "functionalist" ideal.

We have attempted to present the essential facts of the case; we do not claim that, as presented, they lead irresistibly to a single, unequivocal verdict. On the whole, we decided against the philistine in art: art may be associated with utility, but utility should never be its main purpose. And we decided also against the Estheticist: the cult of beauty has no right to force itself as a rule of life, because beauty, as the estheticists understand it, has a narrow, formal connotation. To give it autocratic sway would be a willful distortion of our nature; and that distortion would ultimately destroy the very beauty art is seeking to serve.

If we attempt to reach more specific conclusions, we shall have to distinguish between three meanings, and three levels, of art; and this distinction might be the chief profit to be expected from this survey.

First of all, we have art frankly as relaxation, as entertainment. Few people will be so ascetic as to deny the legitimate place of this element in life; fewer still will be so futile as to claim that this place ought to be central and dominant. This is the level of play, games, sports, masquerades, ornament: if it amuses you, it needs no other justification. In literature, it includes all those works, mostly narrative fiction and drama, which we read solely as an agreeable pastime. Amusement need not be coarse and cheap: Alexandre Dumas, Gilbert and Sullivan, Offenbach, who are obviously entertainers, are also genuine artists. Even poetry may come under this head: songs, humorous ballads, nonsense, society verse, technical acrobatics. This art, so modest in its purpose, must be kept very "pure": it would be a breach of taste, and a loss in effectiveness, if the dancer should stop and give us a lesson in patriotism, morality or piety. In its purity, this art is irresponsible and completely autonomous. If you play a game of chess, the opinions, past deeds or sinister projects of your opponent are irrelevant: nothing matters but the rigor of the game.

But in literature, it is extremely difficult to remain within the strict confines of a game. Literature represents human beings, and expresses feelings and thoughts. Only a very philosophical mind will be able to keep an impassable barrier between entertaining literature and practical life. Charles Lamb asserted that Restoration comedies were not immoral; they presented colorful, amusing, life-size puppets, strutting in a fantastic world of their own. But we know from the memoirs of the time that the vices thus depicted existed in real society; their presentation in an attractive light gave them the force of an example; and Jeremy Collier was justified in denouncing "the Immorality and Profaneness of the English Stage."

On the second level, art is purely a method of expression, a technique. In this case, it is invariably linked with a purpose: the incessant drilling of a pianist's fingers is not music in itself, but a preparation for music. But, if it does not exist for its own sake, technique can be detached for a moment, and examined separately. A professor in a theological seminary will criticize the diction and delivery of a sermon, even though its orthodoxy be unimpeachable. When, taking the major issues for granted, we discuss only the means, we are, for the time being, dealing in art for art's sake. To the uninitiated, this serious attention given to minute points may seem futile or heartless. A surgeon may speak of a "beautiful" operation, although the patient broke the rules and died: among his fellow surgeons, this apparent callousness is no crime. He knows that his one purpose is to save lives; he need not reiterate in pious tones that noble profession of faith; but it is through faultless technique that he can best accomplish his task.

There again, we see the danger. If the layman is apt to criticize unjustly, he may also blunder upon an essential truth, that the professionals are tempted to forget. For there are technicians, in letters as in all other arts, who prize their skill above its purpose, and who would rather achieve a futile thing to perfection than a great thing through clumsy or "vulgar" means. Fortunately true art is in constant rebellion against the pedantic tyranny of the connoisseurs.

In so far as art is technique, its ideal is to disappear: *Ars*

forgetting, however, that it remains his true home. And his message is to induce every one of us to seek and find, beyond the toil and squabbles of the day, our own ivory tower. Thus art, as communication, points the way to the art that transcends communication, art for art's sake.[1]

SUMMARY

In the study of literature, there are two antagonistic tendencies. One interprets art in terms of some other activity, seeks to subordinate art to some other discipline: religious, social, scientific. The other, in protest, asserts art's independence: art for art's sake.

At times, the doctrine of art for art's sake has assumed a decadent tinge; but the taint was in the man, not in the thought itself. Frequently, art for art's sake appears in epochs of decadence: then it is art alone that retains its integrity in a corrupt world. The ivory tower represents the strength that is in purity.

So art for art's sake is the rejection of tainted alliances: the spurious art, or *Kitsch*, that steals pseudo-artistic effects from non-artistic sources; the Philistinism that would place art at the service of some *useful* purpose. What remains when these alien "sakes" have been purged away is pure art.

First of all, the "pure" artist condemns *art for the sake of money*; yet there are cases in which gain does not destroy artistic value. To be condemned also is *art for the sake of success*, i.e., social prestige: prominence, distinction, celebrity, fame, glory, "the higher snobbishness." Yet the desire for fame as a triumph over death is human, and not always inartistic. *Art for the sake of information* is frequently present in historical and realistic novels: all too often treatises made palatable with a few grains of fiction. True information may be excellent material for the purest art; but it is not the purpose of art. Information for its own sake ruins art for its own sake.

Art for the sake of a cause is the most controversial of all

[1] A fuller treatment of these problems, with a Bibliography, will be found in the author's *Art for Art's Sake*.

subjects. Art is an instrument: any cause is free to use the artistic method of exploration and presentation, as well as the scientific. Nor will art be degraded, provided the cause itself be "pure." Both art and the cause that uses it as a tool will suffer through any dishonesty, any willful warping of thought or fact, any "propaganda" in the pejorative sense of the term. A man can serve both his art and his cause, if they are truly himself. Any cause that requires insincerity is unworthy of art.

Art, to flee the Philistine, retreats to the ivory tower; but sallies forth to conquer. This is *estheticism*, the desire for art not merely to be free, but to rule, the effort to reconstruct the world on the basis of beauty. This is the *beau geste* attitude: whatever appeals to our esthetic sense is right.

In private morality, this leads to the extolling of the picturesque or dramatic transgressor at the expense of the stodgy conformist; in politics and history, to the worship of war and war heroes (every war is a *beau geste*): witness the indestructible prestige of Napoleon. In religion, it becomes *credo quia pulchrum*, I believe because it is beautiful; because *nature* is beautiful (Rousseau, Ruskin); because *ritual* is beautiful (Milton); because *dogma* itself is beautiful (Chateaubriand, Cabell). A dangerous heresy: it would lead to the conclusion that all beautiful myths are true; it has actually led to Satan-worship: the *beau geste* of rebellion is more poetic than tame acquiescence: "True poets are of the Devil's party." Let us have art for art's sake, and religion for religion's sake.

In order to reach a conclusion, we shall have to distinguish three meanings, and three levels, of art.

1. *Art as relaxation*, mere entertainment. In its purity, and within its modest sphere, such art is autonomous, responsible to itself alone.

2. *Art as technique*. The experts among themselves may enjoy the technique for its own sake. But a technique implies a purpose: it is a way of doing *something*, and the something counts for more than the way. The highest quality of such technique is perfect adequacy (*functionalism*); its ideal is to

disappear: "art conceals art." To have style is a virtue; to be a stylist is a fault.

3. Beyond all purposes, art is a protest against death, and the reassertion of the unique. This art does not serve. At most, it acts as a warning and a check: whatever is *ugly* cannot be *right*.

In its affirmation of life, art is akin to love and to mystic communion; but this experience is ineffable: "The sole language of the mystic is silence." Yet art is communication. The artist cannot manifest himself to us, and even to himself, without abandoning his ivory tower. But the ivory tower remains his true home. The artist thus points the way to the art that transcends communication, art for art's sake.

CHAPTER XXI

THE PROBLEM OF CRITICISM

SUMMARY AND CONCLUSION

I F ART were nothing but spontaneous self-expression, the author would write as a healthy man breathes, unconsciously. There the matter would rest, and there would be no field for criticism. But art is also communication; the author is conscious of the self he wants to express; and he desires to convey that consciousness to others. *Criticism registers how completely that communication has been established.* It is not therefore an alien or parasitic element which art is able to ignore: "I am I: all critics be confounded!" It is an essential part of the artistic process.

When the author is composing, he does not jot, automatically, all the chaotic thoughts and incoherent images that whirl through his brains; he selects and orders them in the most effective fashion. There are a few cases of masterpieces written *as if* in a trance: some of the Prophetic Books of Blake, Coleridge's *Kubla Khan;* but even then, the poets had enough conscious self-mastery to organize their visions according to the rules of English syntax, with an intelligible vocabulary, and a recognizable prosodic scheme. *Finnegans Wake,* which is supposed to reproduce the amorphous structure of a dream, demanded many years of effort on the part of James Joyce, a trained and scrupulous artist. The author assumes control; he shapes his own thoughts. The work of creation is mostly rejection: of his teeming fancies, he knows that some are irrelevant, and even harmful, to his essential purpose. In this sense, we can accept without demur Croce's paradoxical phrase: the identity of *genius* (creation) and *taste* (selection). The author thus passes judgment upon his own imaginings; and his test for acceptance or rejection is whether the result will be *communicable* to a public, however limited. If he feels that his words will not bridge the gulf between himself and his reader, why should he write at all? Silence is a most effective means of non-communication. To compose is therefore to measure in advance the probable response; *and this is an act of criticism.* The author should be his first and most pitiless critic: so ruthless indeed that others could have no choice but to confirm his verdict.

From the moment the work reaches its very first public, it elicits a response. The response may be purely negative: the reader closes the book at once, because he fails to understand, or because, understanding too well, he is bored. This simple gesture, a yawn, a heaviness in the eyelids, are forms of criticism, unspoken, but of deadly effectiveness. On the other hand, the desire to read on, the reluctance to drop the book until the last page has been devoured, are also criticism, of the approving kind. State these plain facts in plain terms to a friend, and you have turned into a literary critic without knowing it.

Under modern conditions, books have to be printed and sold; this is *business;* but business is *criticism* at every turn. The work is submitted to a publisher, who decides upon the probable response on the part of the public. If he accepts it, that means that in his opinion, the book is good of its kind, whatever the kind may be, cheap thriller or *Testament of Beauty:* and that is an act of criticism. Through advertising in the trade journals, through circulars and the personal appeal of agents, the booksellers are induced to confirm the publisher's judgment; they are converted by his favorable criticism from indifference to optimism. If customers buy the book on the bookseller's recommendation, it is because they believe, naïvely perhaps, that the bookseller is a good judge, or that he had access to authoritative information. Then, as we have seen above, the individual reader inevitably criticizes the book by liking or failing to like it; and, frequently, he communicates his impression to a friend. Thus at every step in the creation, manufacture, and distribution of the book, we find acceptance or rejection, that is to say criticism, even before a single word of blame or praise has been formally uttered by a professional critic.

Once again, we have been compelled to reassert, at wearisome length, what no one seriously thought of denying. But if everybody admits that criticism is indispensable to literature, few people have a good word to say for the critics. The general public is satisfied to ignore them altogether; the writers treat them, not as their allies, but as their enemies; and the critics themselves pour contempt on one another. "Criticism of Criticism" is a flourishing branch of essay writing. Such unpopularity must be deserved; yet it should not be accepted uncritically. If criticism is right, and the critics are wrong, someone should teach them, courteously, the error of their way.

Critics are arraigned under many counts. They are accused of being surly pedants, blind to beauty, and devoting their whole energy to fault-finding. They pass judgment when there is no law to justify their verdict. They are a breed of parasites, preying on the actual creators of literature. As their craft is easy as well as unpleasant, it is practiced mostly by mediocrities. At its best, criticism, through analysis, could only spoil our esthetic pleasure. The one extenuating circumstance in favor of the critics is that they have no power whatsoever. Let us take up in detail the various points of this truly devastating indictment.

The first count is that criticism, in the popular mind, is inevitably associated with *"carping."* Critics are accused of following too literally St. Paul's stern injunction: "Reprove; rebuke"; and nothing is so disagreeable as eternal fault-finding. This, however, is a confusion excusable in common speech, but which should have no standing in the literary world. To criticize does not invariably mean to condemn: it means to judge,

prurient and to repel the healthy-minded, we are venturing a hypothesis in collective psychology which is as explicit as any formal condemnation. The critic, in this conception, is not a supreme judge, but an assayer. "This sample which you brought to me is gold, or copper, or silver, or lead. All have their uses; there is a market for each; but let us not palm off the one for the other. And it is my duty to report also the tenor of pure metal in the ore, the presence of other elements difficult to eliminate, so that you will be able to decide whether the claim is worth exploiting."

This interpretation disposes of the third objection to criticism, namely, that it is *a parasitical activity*. So it is, like the work of the inspector or the assayer, which, obviously, is not productive; or, to put it more paradoxically, like the function of the judge, which presupposes the "creative activities" of the lawbreakers. No form of work is to be accounted inferior, because it uses as its raw material the finished product of some other trade; the baker receives his flour from the miller, the miller gets his grain from the farmer, but it is the earth that actually grows the wheat; does that make the baker inferior to the miller, the farmer, or the soil? Flaubert's *Madame Bovary* stands on a higher plane than the sordid and commonplace story that he borrowed from real life (for Flaubert himself was a "parasite" preying upon newspapers, court reports and gossip); a book on how Flaubert came to write *Madame Bovary*, although technically classified as criticism, would have a subtler and deeper theme than the original work. It is not inconceivable that a piece of criticism should be a more important contribution to literature than the work it discusses. Sainte-Beuve devoted many articles to minor figures, remembered only because he took notice of them. Criticism, according to this conception, is "parasitical" only because it represents a further step in a refining process. "Nonsense!" the reader will impatiently exclaim; "no book about a novel will ever have the same appeal as that novel itself." Not the *same* appeal, we are ready to grant. The original story—divorce, murder, suicide—is read by millions in the newspapers; the psychological novel that it inspires is read by tens of thousands, with cooler and deeper appreciation; it is not impossible that the critical analysis of the novel should be itself a work of art, although it might reach only a few hundreds. Neither the size of the audience nor the intensity of the thrill is a valid test of literary excellence; and the public that enjoys good criticism is the most critical of all.

There is an ineradicable prejudice that "criticism is easy, art difficult." As if criticism were not a particularly delicate form of art! And as if much alleged "art" were not imitative, slipshod, "easy" in the most contemptuous sense of the term! "He who can, does; he who cannot, teaches," is a very neat epigram, but it is very little more. Many prose writers, philosophers, historians, dramatists and novelists, count among the great critics: Aristotle, to begin with, Pascal, Molière, Burke, Stendhal, Tolstoy, Zola, Anatole France; but also an even greater array of poets. Not merely those who could be accused of being sturdily or elegantly pedestrian, like Boileau, Dryden, Pope or Voltaire; but those in whom the divine lyrical gift is undeniable, Horace, Dante, Du Bellay, Sir Philip Sydney, Schiller, Goethe, Blake, Coleridge, Wordsworth, Poe, Victor Hugo, Matthew Arnold, Baudelaire, Swinburne, Mallarmé. It would be possible to compile a magnificent anthology of criticism, including only the work of acknowledged masters in creative art. That there are bad critics as well as worthless rhymesters must of course be accepted as a truism.

Two facts of literary history, however, cannot be denied. The first is that criticism is poorly rewarded. No honest man grows rich on critical work alone, whereas fiction and drama open up at any rate a distant prospect of making a fortune. On that very Philistine basis, criticism stands below the popular and profitable kinds of writing, but far above esoteric poetry. It is obvious that criticism may legitimately refuse to be appraised by the financial test. The second, and far more important fact, is that no critic so far, *purely as a critic*, has achieved a rank comparable to Shakespeare's or Balzac's. Boileau outranked all his contemporaries—with the exception of five or six; and we cannot help placing him appreciably lower than even La Fontaine, who was but the most delightful of minor poets. Coleridge wrote abundantly, learnedly, cogently, on criticism; but his fame rests on three or four poems. The writer who attained the most notable position, solely for his critical work, is probably Sainte-Beuve. His poetry and his novel, although not negligible, are read only because they are by the author of *Causeries du Lundi* and *Port-Royal*. Like Boileau, he stands head and shoulders above the innumerable company of poets, dramatists, novelists in his own time; but not on a level with Victor Hugo, Vigny, or even Baudelaire. There is still, unjustly or not, a hierarchy of the genres; the very greatest critics have not yet reached equality with the very greatest poets. Perhaps the greatest poets are insurpassable because, as we suggested above, they were, intuitively or deliberately, the most ruthless critics of their own work.

But if "Rhadamanthus," in all likelihood, is not the universal monarch of wit in his generation, it would be rash to assume, as Cabell does, that he is *ex officio* a mediocrity. He may be like Sainte-Beuve a good novelist shrewd enough to give up novel writing because he found that he could do something else even better. Cabell pours ridicule on those puny scribblers who dare to criticize "genius": "You do not, I suppose, imagine in uninspired hours that your position in letters compares favorably with the position of, let us say, Ellen Glasgow?" There is a profound element of truth in this jibe, but also a fallacy which might be very harmful to literature.

The truth it contains is that authors are entitled to courteous, even to respectful treatment. It is of course painfully ludicrous when a fledgling assumes a supercilious attitude towards writers who have become important facts in the realm of art, like Ellen Glasgow, or, for that matter, James Branch Cabell himself. We should like to go further, and affirm that the veriest beginner has a right to expect sympathetic attention from critics of the highest standing, if they deal with his work at all. To have written a book should not be considered as a presumption of guilt, but as a praiseworthy attempt, an evidence of creditable pertinacity. Only plain malicious lying, and that aggravated kind of artistic lying, pretentiousness, call for ruthless castigation. The authors seek to reach the public; the critics are but a vanguard or a delegation of the public; so authors and critics should meet in a friendly spirit. It is a fact, which Mr. Cabell has a right to expose and to condemn, that many critics have deplorable manners. As a rule, this is not due to surliness of temper: it is a survival of the classical tradition. Critics preserve the attitude and tone of the dogmatic period in an age when dogmatism is no longer accepted. Whenever there is a plain, accepted law, the judge is not "pedantic" or "overweening" if he simply applies the law. "I am not posing as your superior in all things; but I know my Castelvetro, and you have flagrantly broken the Rule of the Three Unities. This is *wrong.*" At present, all criteria are hypotheses, interpretations or impressions. The critic speaks in his own name, not in the august name of the law; and therefore he should speak with becoming modesty.

But he has a right to speak. Let him, if you insist, use Chinese forms of self-depreciation, and refer to himself as "this most insignificant person": humble or not, he may candidly state the fact that he is not amused, not thrilled, not awed. This is a privilege that any reader purchases with the book. And, with all possible courtesy, the critic should be no respecter of vested interests. Mr. Cabell, who belongs to the old South, thinks too exclusively in terms of "established position." He would have everyone duly "know his place," be ever fearful of "presuming," and show proper deference to his "betters." In the democracy of art, there is no position, however exalted, that is not open to challenge. What is it that confers "position"? Surely not the brutal statistics of sales? Yet sales record "public opinion" backed by the willingness to part with a few dollars. "Position," we feel sure Mr. Cabell would agree, is the result of enlightened, formulated opinion, that is to say of intelligent criticism.

And what criticism has given, criticism can also take away. Many are the writers, great in their own eyes, and in the eyes of their cliques, who have been tumbled down from their pedestals to the applause of posterity. Boileau wasted few shafts on poets who were generally despised; those whom he attacked were of high standing in the professional, academic and social world. Edgar Allan Poe has been "established" as a great poet for three generations: a "truth" which is solidly imbedded in most of our textbooks. Yet who could blame Aldous Huxley (*Music at Night*) or Yvor Winters (*Maule's Curse*) for submitting *Ulalume* to the most searching criticism, which in this case proved extremely damaging? A healthy life of the spirit demands a constant revaluation of all values. This is not a revolutionary, an iconoclastic process; we hope that the works we revere will triumphantly stand any test. But we must be ready to submit them to the test. Else our apparent respect would be only a veil for our lack of genuine faith.

The last of the common objections to criticism is that it *destroys the immediacy, and with it the purity and intensity, of our pleasure.* Art is akin to love and faith; criticism to their enemy, doubt. In love, faith and art, there is a moment when you must let yourself go—uncritically. This is as true of enjoyment as it is of creation: ultimately, art appeals to the emotions, and emotion, *per se*, is not critical. "Letting oneself go" means freeing oneself from the fetters of critical common sense; or, in other words, the artistic experience in absolute purity is possible only during "temporary insanity."

But the "insanity," the silencing of reasonable objections, the lifting of all critical checks, must be "temporary." To use again Coleridge's pregnant phrase, if there must be a "willing suspension of disbelief," disbelief, i.e., critical doubt, is only suspended, not annihilated; and the will that suspends it is also expected to restore it at the proper time. When disbelief disappears altogether, we have to deal, no longer with art, but with hallucination. Don Quixote read *uncritically:* romance, to him, was sober fact. To create such a delusion would seem the highest possible triumph of art; yet it would not permanently satisfy the artist himself. For in such a case, his own contribution, his inventiveness, his style, his whole personality, would be obliterated: Don Quixote gave no thought to the authors of the books he so avidly devoured. If the writer were a pure propagandist, an apostle immolating, without question, his own self to the cause he is serving, then he would want to be believed and followed, not admired; admiration for his skill would actually irk him, and many believers resent the praises lavished on the Bible "as literature." But the *artist,* living on a less exalted spiritual plane, does not want us to forget that it is he who "makes it up," that his "art" is something different from the reproduction of objective truth. In other words, he wants us to remain critics.

The literary experience, whether in creation or in enjoyment, thus necessitates the co-operation of two contradictory factors, faith and disbelief. We compose, and we read, with two minds, the one unquestioning and naïve, the other sharply conscious that we are in the domain of art. There is no fixed proportion for the blending of these two elements. The reader may abandon himself completely to the book, which, for the time being, creates for him another universe. He may weep, shriek with terror, flush with anger, grab for his sword; then he wakes up from his trance (if he be sane, and not a Don Quixote), and enjoys his emotions in retrospect, *as art,* that is to say critically. If the author does not possess that magic power, or if the critical sense is very strong in the reader, the enjoyment will result from watching, from page to page, "how it is done." According to the popular phrase, it is fun to be fooled, and it is fun to know. In most cases, the two states of mind alternate with such rapidity that they practically merge: we live in the world of the book, but also in our own. This creates an impression which can never be quite so vivid as direct reality, but which is richer and subtler. *Awareness, i.e., criti-*

And their basis of selection is not purely artistic, but predominantly commercial. There is room, therefore, for a second series of advisers, sifting again the choice of the publishers' readers. These advisers are the critics properly so-called. They are known by name, and responsible for their opinions; they are not guided by thoughts of sales; they are free to voice disapproval. In a closely knit community like ancient Athens, or even like Paris and London in the classical centuries, "word-of-mouth comment" might be sufficient; with an enormous and unorganized public like ours, it is a woefully haphazard method. *Purchasers' Guides* are at least a great convenience; if we want to secure competent service, it is not good policy to ignore or deride them. Nations get the politicians and the critics they deserve; there is room for improvement in both fields; and it is for us, the common voters and the common readers, to demand and to effect this improvement.

Not that we suggest that the public should abdicate in the hands of the critics, and obediently buy, read and *like* the recommended books, forsaking all others. We have no faith in the divinely appointed authority of the critics, and we believe in the virtue of "eternal vigilance." Every man *is* the ultimate judge: no expert can *like* a book for you. He can only direct you to the books you would probably like. He can so direct you if you have confidence in his consistency. Once you know your critic, you are able to make allowances for his "aberrations," as physicists do even with their finest instruments. It is impossible that he should not have a personal equation; but he should have a definite personality, that is to say that his equation should be fairly constant. He may not share your prejudices: all that is needed is that his thought be cogent, not capricious. We might even show our trust in a critic by reversing automatically every one of his judgments: if we know that, without fail, he calls black what to us is white, we shall find him a very reliable guide.

But this demands that we should know our critics, and that we should know our own critical minds: two different ways of saying that we should care for criticism. Every baseball fan likes to read the sport section of his paper; every noted sport writer has an extensive following; this is the sign of intelligent interest: hence the thriving state of baseball in our commonwealth. There is something a little discouraging in a literary world in which capital works of criticism, if they are not spiced with gossip, have no audience at all. This reveals two contradictory aspects of our public mind. The one is a proud refusal to take competent advice: "I know what I like when I like it: why should I go to a critic to tell me?" The second is a modest diffidence to exercise our rights as responsible citizens in the republic of letters. We dare not "like what we like" until we have been assured that everybody likes it. We do not want to be guided, and we are not prepared to steer our own course: the result is that we are stampeded.

We have so far advanced a plea for recognizing the place of criticism in the life of literature, and a defense of those very unpopular writers, the professional critics. We repeat that criticism can operate only when there is some common ground upon which the critic can induce author and public to meet. They must, in the widest sense of the term, speak the same language; that is to say, they must, in essentials, hold the same principles. Are there such principles available today?

We need not reject *a priori* the hypothesis that there are in our world irremediable differences. If there were no principles accepted by all, it would not mean the negation of all art; it would only imply that, instead of a single literature, we had a number of independent, interpenetrating literatures. This would be *Pluralism*, a doctrine which has manifest appeal in religious and political matters; for, although the name is not universally familiar, our whole conception of American freedom is based upon Pluralism. Freedom, in the eyes of its defenders, never is the liberty to do wrong, but the liberty to do that which is right in our own eyes, the sole limit being the freedom of others. Under a pluralistic dispensation, criticism would not disappear; it would on the contrary assume greater importance. Not only would it exist, in obvious and familiar form, within each of the separate literatures, but it would help the bewildered reader to discriminate between the various worlds which coexist in the American scene. The critic would report. "This book is meant for citizens of Commonwealth D; and under the laws of D, it is a very competent piece of work." There are times when peace and friendliness depend upon a clearly defined boundary.

But criticism would not merely take cognizance of frontiers: it would also assist us in crossing them with safety and comfort. The critic is an interpreter: from nation to nation, from age to age, from group to group. Not all differences are irremediable. In many cases, they result, not from the essential facts, but from a system imposed upon the facts, an *ideology;* and an ideology itself can frequently be reduced to a vocabulary. If we do not speak the same language, this does not prove that we do not think the same thoughts. No one denies that the great function of criticism, when applied to works of the past, is to reveal human values under a puzzling variety of forms. Criticism makes us realize that men were men in the days of Pericles, although they spoke a tongue unfamiliar to us, and worshiped alien gods. The critics can perform the same service for Commonwealth A or Commonwealth D. Our next-door neighbor may seem more remote from us than the contemporaries of Pericles; still, under the bristling array of his prejudices, he is (presumably) human. Thus the recognition of Pluralism helps us transcend Pluralism, and reassert Humanism: a Humanism which is liberal, and not totalitarian.[1]

But even though our Pluralism need not destroy faith in fundamental unity, it does preclude the adoption of a single method as exclusive and infallible. It makes us realize that there are many varieties of literary experience, each valid

---

[1] Not seldom a paradox, pressed too hard, turns into a harmless truism. Can we not translate the baffling assertion: "There are many interpenetrating universes" into the homely truth: "It takes all kinds to make a world"?

within its own domain; and that, in consequence, there are many types of criticism. We shall list, in an appendix, those most generally recognized: to discuss or even to define them with any completeness would require a separate volume. We shall only attempt a rough classification, which corresponds with the main conceptions of literature.

For the sake of convenience, these may be reduced to four. The first is all-embracing: *Everything written is literature.* The second is idealistic: *Literature, even when it does not give formal expression to eternal principles, the True, the Good and the Beautiful, is determined by them and must be judged in their light.* The third is empirical or pragmatic: *Literature is that which appeals to those who are consciously interested in the subject;* it is therefore defined in terms of its public. The fourth is purely individualistic: Out of the mass of mere writing, with no reference to abstract principles, with no regard for the opinion of others, *literature is that which gives me personal pleasure.*

To the all-embracing conception of literature corresponds *scientific criticism;* and it corresponds to nothing else. By scientific criticism, we mean the kind which seeks to elucidate, not to judge. Science ascertains and observes facts. A fact *is* or *is not:* but it cannot be right or wrong. Science may analyze a complex fact into its elements: but this establishes no hierarchy of worth, this confers no superiority upon the atom, because it is *pure,* or upon the compound, because it is *rich:* they are what they are. Science may classify the facts: but classification cannot introduce the notion of value. Therefore the scientific study of literature can pile up facts about Shakespeare and John Doe; it cannot establish, and does not seek to establish, that Shakespeare is *better* than John Doe. All the explanations that it can offer operate in both cases. If Shakespeare was affected by race, environment and time, so was John Doe; possibly by the very same race, environment and time, if John Doe happened to be an obscure kinsman and contemporary of Shakespeare. In all this, there is no possible criterion of excellence. Philology, geography, biology, psychology, economics, can be used to "elucidate" anything written; and, conversely, anything written is a fact, and may serve as a document.

If the scientific critics tell us that they will consider excellence itself—Shakespeare's supremacy in the drama, for instance —as a basic fact, and investigate that fact by strictly objective methods, we shall reply that they are begging the question: they have no right to take excellence for granted. What they can measure is, not intrinsic worth, but the response of a given public. Popularity can be reduced to figures and graphs: the book sells. Durable fame can also be translated into concrete terms: Shakespeare is taught, performed, demanded, in the public libraries. These are facts, but they are statistical facts. Fechner evolved, through a series of tests, a *Golden Rectangle* of such proportion that it would be "most pleasing." Most pleasing to whom? To a majority of Fechner's guinea pigs; but there is no proof that the minority were wrong.

Whatever we want to know, we should attempt to know as accurately as possible. All assertions that claim to be factual should be corroborated through rigorous research. So far scientific criticism is on the firmest possible ground. More: we cannot deny that knowledge clarifies understanding, and that understanding deepens appreciation. Knowledge thus liberates appreciation, which was hampered by ignorance. It liberates; it does not create. Scientific criticism, the sum total of the *auxiliary* sciences, brings information, often of the most valuable kind; but, in itself, it is not criticism at all.

To the idealistic conception of literature corresponds *dogmatic criticism*. The "eternal principles," if they are not to remain pious platitudes, must be formulated definitely; they are thus embodied into a doctrine. If the doctrine is fundamental, if you believe in it with sufficient faith, it becomes a dogma. A dogmatic tone may be bad manners; but no disparagement should attach to dogma itself, for it simply implies *certitude*. Particular dogmas may be wrong; any dogma may be applied wrongly; but this does not condemn the man who is in possession of the truth. All believers and all judges must be dogmatic, or give up the law they live by.

Any school of thought, in philosophy or religion, creates a dogma: a professed skeptic is a dogmatist, if he denies *absolutely* the possibility of absolute knowledge. So it is in literature. We are apt to associate *dogmatism* with *Classicism*, because of the trenchant manner in which classical rules were proclaimed and enforced. This does not tell the whole truth. Curiously, the great masters of classical doctrine were very far from rigid dogmatism. Aristotle had a scientific mind; he enquired rather than taught. Horace was a man of the world, who, in a rambling familiar Epistle, gave many shrewd bits of practical advice. Longinus *On the Sublime*, if he could be classified at all, would be a romanticist; the Classicism of Boileau is a reasonable compromise. On the other hand, there is a manifest romantic dogmatism, with all the appurtenances of a literary church: fundamental beliefs, traditions, authorities; and, in the name of romantic orthodoxy, men did not hesitate to damn or praise. There is an even stricter realistic dogmatism, before whose implacable judgment seat all romantic works were tried and found guilty. And every minor school, down to the most ephemeral clique, sets up a little court of justice: secret tribunals are reputed to be the most pitiless, and esoteric law is the most rigid of all.

Scientific criticism is but an expert witness; it reports on questions of fact, but should not presume to judge. To judge is on the contrary the essential function of dogmatic criticism, and the source of its undeniable appeal. In the aimless flow of dissolving appearances, it is a great relief to discern here and there certain fixed points; and to hear, over the confused hubbub of the multitude, voices which speak in tones sharp and assured. A critical dogma requires a system of thought: even when we cannot accept it, it throws a welcome challenge to our reasoning power. If the system be truly a system, it constitutes an intelligible language, which, if we choose, we can translate into our own idiom. So the most profitable and also the most enjoyable of critics are those who have a consistent mind, and speak it out consistently. It is extremely easy not to agree with Brunetière or with Irving Babbitt; but the very act of disagreement is a stern pleasure.

The obvious objection to dogmatic criticism is its exclusive character. Each school believes itself to be in possession of absolute truth, and unhesitatingly condemns everything that is not in accord with its tenets. No matter what set of criteria we adopt, we are compelled to dismiss, as unworthy to be called "literature," many works which the world agrees to call great. To do this requires intellectual courage; but it involves no absurdity. The believers in any religion are convinced of its exclusive claims, although they know full well that their faith is professed only by a minority of mankind. We repeat that nothing in the realm of the spirit is settled by a majority vote: Copernicus and Harvey had the bulk of the learned against them. If a bolder Thomas Rymer dared to excommunicate Shakespeare from the literary fold, he might be hailed by later ages as the Copernicus of criticism.

However, scientific truths, such as those propounded by Copernicus and Harvey, can be tested by experiment; artistic truth is hard to separate from the subjective fact of appreciation. It is easy enough to decide that the majority of your fellow men are "wrong" in admiring, as the case may, Shakespeare, or Racine, or Rousseau, or Edgar Allan Poe. It is a little harder to preserve your orthodoxy unsullied if, in the teeth of your formal creed, you admire the "wrong" things yourself. There are few dogmatists so consistent that their experience rigorously coincides with their doctrine; few courageous enough to pluck out their right eye lest it should cause them to offend. The dogmatist proclaims his rule to be absolute, but he is loath to give up the beloved exception.

This imperils the exclusive pretensions of dogmatic criticism; it does not compel us to give up the method altogether. A literary doctrine may profitably be used, not as an infallible criterion, but as a working hypothesis; with such an instrument, we shall find it easier to think, to express ourselves, and to be understood. We may also consider a literary dogma as a shaft of light, more powerful when it is concentrated, which, trained upon a masterpiece, brings out its salient points in bolder relief. We are free to use another light later, and from a different angle. *Absolutism* is a safe method—in the hands of the relativist. All that we have a right to require is that the criticism be *honest*. If, in the name of his doctrine, a critic praises with his lips that which he despises in his heart, then he stands surely condemned, and brings discredit upon his faith.

Few dogmatic critics are as intolerant as strict dogmatism would require them to be. They acknowledge the importance, and even the greatness, of work which disregards all their rules. Thus Voltaire, steeped in classical prejudices, but too intensely Voltaire to be swayed by any set of prejudices, spoke of Shakespeare's "monstrous farces," declared that at times Shakespeare wrote like a "drunken savage," and yet recognized Shakespeare's genius. No one dares to dismiss altogether the masterpieces of the past; so dogmatism is almost invariably tempered with *pragmatism:* "What has been accepted as literature by a sufficient number of people over a sufficient period of time must be literature."

This conception is so self-effacing that it seldom is frankly admitted. More prestige is to be gained by expounding an eternal truth, or voicing one's inmost thoughts, than by attempting to gauge and define public taste. Yet pragmatic criticism is probably the most important in bulk, and not necessarily the least in value. It comprises, first of all, every literary history that does not claim to be exhaustive.[1] From the modest high school textbook to a mighty collective enterprise like the *Cambridge History*, the spirit is the same: the basis for selection is general agreement. Many authors are included who do not follow the critic's favorite doctrine, or who do not appeal to his personal taste; he may treat them with extreme severity,

---

[1] An "exhaustive," i.e., all-inclusive history, gathering all available facts, would belong to "scientific," not to "pragmatic," criticism.

but, as a historian, he cannot afford to ignore them. He has to admit them, at any rate, into his literary *Purgatorio;* he cannot consign them to outer darkness, the *Inferno* of oblivion.

The same method is used with reference to current productions. The pragmatic critic treats by preference of those works which command attention, of those authors who "count": Shaw, Thomas Mann, André Gide, Gertrude Stein, James Joyce. They are part of the historical scene. He also deals, no doubt, with unknown authors, new or neglected; but it is in anticipation of their coming fame. His chief function is not to examine the book on its own merits, but to introduce authors to the right readers. "Merit," under this conception, could be defined as "appeal to a given public": for the thought of the public is never completely absent from the pragmatic mind. It is on this basis that most reviewing is done, and should be done.

The pragmatic critic is thus a social secretary, a middleman, a literary agent; and, if competent, a most useful person. Under ideal conditions, the success of his activity should be marked by increased sales: to *forecast* a public correctly is to *create* that public, and the critic who does it well deserves authority. There is nothing wrong about sales, if they are not made under false pretenses, if they lead to the mutual satisfaction of producer and consumer. The highest praise that the pragmatic critic can confer is the promise of glory, which means extensive and prolonged recognition. The danger of pragmatic criticism is to mistake this social test—sales, popularity, fame, glory—for intrinsic value. Napoleon's renown is overwhelming; but it does not prove that the man was great, or that his work was good. Pragmatic criticism is legitimate within its own limits: the prophecy and measurement of *success.* But we refuse to accept success as the final criterion.

Finally, to the individualistic conception of literature corresponds *Impressionistic Criticism.* As in several other cases, the usual connotation is less than fair to the term. Impressionism evokes too easily the damning epithet *slapdash.* To end a long study with a defense of impressionism would seem a confession of defeat. What need is there of an *Introduction to World Literature*, if every man is a good judge of books, so long as he has not been "connoisseured out of his senses"?

We have to recognize that there are degrees in impressionism, as in all the other kinds of criticism. To say: "You are wrong" may be dogmatic; but it is not the whole of dogmatism, nor the best. To say: "The book sells" is pragmatic; but on a low level. To say: "I like this" is impressionistic; but in a most rudimentary form. In all fairness, we should consider each method in its most comprehensive development.

Impressionism, in a critic, means honesty. It means that he will not *pretend* to admire or despise a book, because a theory or an influential group order him to do so. If he yawns, he yawns, nor makes it a matter of pride or shame. His motto is Luther's: "So help me God, I cannot otherwise." To the radical impressionist, all other forms of criticism appear as an evasion of plain duty. It takes a Luther, or the child in Andersen's allegorical tale, to state simply what he actually thinks or sees. Most of us shirk this responsibility. We want to entertain the *right* opinions, that is to say those which are taught us by the right people. This is most commendable, if it can be done with complete sincerity: then impressionism, orthodoxy, good taste, unite in happiest harmony. If not, we deceive ourselves, and the truth is not in us.

Ultimately, every form of criticism must seek its foundation in impressionism. Scientific esthetics, for instance, will tabulate reactions to this or that artistic stimulus. But the elementary facts which it tabulates are the assertions of individuals: "I like this, I do not like that." Classical dogmatism imposes rules upon us, but recognizes the existence of Genius, which is superior to all rules; and the presence of genius can be felt only through the reader's personal response. Although there is a romantic dogmatism, it should be a contradiction in terms: Romanticism is the expression of the individual, and appeals to the individual. Even realistic dogmatism admits that "art is nature seen through the temperament of the artist," and should add that "criticism (appreciation) is the work of art seen through the temperament of the reader." Collective taste, which is the field of pragmatic criticism, is but the findings of private taste accumulated into a blurred composite picture: it would be impossible for "everybody" to enjoy a book, if no single individual did enjoy it.

The responsibility is yours, reader; you cannot escape it. Use all forms of criticism to their full extent; each one of them can be of service; but it is *you* who are using them. Pragmatic criticism will roughly sift for you, out of the unwieldy mass, those things which you are most likely to appreciate; scientific criticism, without judging, will strive to explain whatever you think needs explaining: they are both good servants, if you keep them in their place. Even dogmatic criticism, less manageable in temper, will be of great assistance in helping you organize your thought, in suggesting the questions you should ask yourself. But when William Lyon Phelps, Sir Sidney Lee, and Aristotle in all his might, have done their best to help you, still you are yourself, and not an automatic registering machine.

The problem of impressionism is: "What is this elusive self, which flees from its responsibility, but is inevitably brought back to its seat and compelled to *judge?*" We have no hope of answering a question which philosophy has asked in vain throughout the ages. We shall simply note that this mysterious self exists on at least three different planes; each implies a different psychological approach; and each determines a different kind of impressionistic criticism.

First of all, self is a mere bundle of sensations, of responses to stimuli. In art, this is the self which actually shudders or weeps at melodrama, is convulsed with laughter by rough-and-tumble farce, yawns at the first difficult sentence, tingles at the beat of martial drums. If you state candidly these elementary facts, you have a form of psycho-physiological impressionism, "slapdash" if you please, but perfectly valid so long as it does not trespass beyond the boundaries of its domain. This impressionism should not say: "I like," but only "I cry," "I laugh." Perhaps even this contains an unwarranted assumption, and the proper form should be: "It cries," "It laughs," as we say: "It rains."

But there is another self, conscious of these animal reactions, and attempting to control them; a self which represents a precarious victory over chaos; a self which possesses memory, reasoning power, foresight, purpose; a self which organizes chance impressions into consistent patterns. Its instrument is understanding, and not mere sensation. It does not ignore or destroy the data of the senses: it interprets and co-ordinates them; it is aware of optical delusions, and does not reach for the moon. In many cases, interpretation and co-ordination will actually intensify the spontaneous reaction: for example, the moon whose magnitude and remoteness we understand is far more impressive than a silver disk almost within our grasp. In other cases, understanding will minimize the impressions, rob them of their crude intensity, rule them out of the critical field. I may admit unblushingly that a sentimental scene brought tears to my eyes, if my understanding self is not fooled by my lachrymatory glands.

This understanding self may be an inborn gift: certain it is that experience enriches and sharpens it; and literature is concentrated experience. So literature and the understanding self constantly assist each other. It is the self, and nothing else—no science, no law, no conformity to usage—that ultimately appreciates literature. It is literature that enlightens and trains the self, and deepens its consciousness. This is a very sweeping claim: we mean it literally. All other disciplines would abolish individuality, reduce man to an anonymous particle, a unit in a statistical table: literature is the assertion of the life that is within you.

The impressionism of this understanding self is not a crude fact; it depends for its validity upon the development, the culture of the individual. Not all impressionisms are of equal value, because no two individuals are ever equal. Your own hasty, casual, unreflective impressionism is not the best that you can achieve. You can, by taking thought, add more than a cubit to your mental stature. On this level, it will not suffice to say: "I like what I like": snap judgments have no standing here. You are led to ask: "What is it in me that likes this thing? In what manner? To what degree?" This criticism is *exploration:* of literature through the self, of the self through literature.

Finally, deeper than sensation, and beyond the range of consciousness, there are forces within you, which by their very nature elude definition, and which our halting vocabulary calls daimonic or divine. They reveal themselves, from below through instinct, from above through intuition. They are the dynamic element without which we should be inert; but I doubt whether they can be called self. They are forces placed *at our disposal:* it is our own will, our own intelligence, that are called upon to direct them. They are powers; but so far as we *know,* blind powers. Use them, do not abandon yourself to them; do not let your self go, beyond recall. That is why I firmly believe that the impressionism which claims to voice the unconscious is illegitimate. The unconscious is not communicable; all we can express is the conscious self carried, in rapture or in horror, by unconscious forces. Even if these forces should urge us irresistibly into the abyss, it is the glory of intelligence, to the very last, to keep her eyes open. No capitulation to chaos: art is awareness in creation, criticism is awareness in contemplation.

SUMMARY

Art demands communication between author and public; criticism registers how completely that communication has been established. There is criticism, therefore, at every stage of the artistic process. The writer, when he composes, uses self-criticism; the reader, when he manifests boredom or interest, acts as a critic; the intermediary, the publisher, is a critic also when he accepts or rejects a manuscript. It is strange that, while criticism is so evidently indispensable, critics should be treated with scant respect by authors and public alike.

They are arraigned under many counts. They are accused of being surly pedants, blind to beauty, and devoting their whole energy to fault-finding. They pass judgment when there is no law to justify their verdict. They are a breed of parasites, preying on the actual creators of literature. As their craft is easy as well as unpleasant, it is abandoned mostly to mediocrities. At its best, criticism, through analysis, could only spoil our esthetic pleasure. The one extenuating circumstance in favor of the critics is that they have no power whatsoever.

The various points of this truly formidable indictment are taken up in some detail. The most controversial of all is that critical analysis impairs our enjoyment. It is shown that *uncritical* acceptance, on the contrary, would destroy our artistic pleasure. To appreciate a work of art, we must remain conscious that it is a work of art. There must be, as Coleridge said, "a willing suspension of disbelief"—which implies a constant interplay of belief and disbelief.

As for the lack of influence of formal criticism, it is regrettably true. We follow advertising, which is one-sided paid criticism; word-of-mouth comment, which is hasty, irresponsible, gossipy criticism; but too often we ignore or spurn the best qualified criticism. The state of our literature would be healthier, if expert knowledge enjoyed more prestige.

Criticism could play a useful part, even if this were a pluralistic literary commonwealth, if we had several independent literatures instead of one. Then the critic would warn us that such a book is intended for Commonwealth D, not for Commonwealth A; he would also interpret D to A, just as it has been his task heretofore to interpret remote ages and distant countries. Pluralism is an avenue to humanism.

To every conception of literature corresponds a type of criticism, valid within its field. To the all-embracing definition: literature is everything written, corresponds *scientific criticism*, an expert witness which can elucidate, but neither select nor

APPENDIX I

BIBLIOGRAPHICAL NOTE

There is no single bibliographical instrument in the field of World Literature that is indispensable and sufficient. The two books of Professor Charles Mills Gayley would need to be reorganized and brought up to date:

GAYLEY, Charles Mills, and SCOTT, Fred Newton: *An Introduction to the Methods and Materials of Literary Criticism:* the Bases in Aesthetics and Poetics. Boston, Ginn, 1899. 587pp.

GAYLEY, Charles Mills, and KURTZ, B. P.: *Methods and Materials of Literary Criticism:* Lyric, Epic, and allied forms of Poetry. Boston & New York, Ginn, 1920. 911pp.

MAIN DIVISIONS

I. *General Conceptions of World Literature*
IIa. *Histories of World Literature*
IIb. *Other Instruments: Dictionaries and Periodicals*
III. *The Body of World Literature: Collections and Anthologies*

I. *General Conceptions of World Literature*

The study of these conceptions is equivalent to the history of critical theories. Among the basic works:

SAINTSBURY, George: *History of Criticism and Literary Taste in Europe.* Edinburgh & London, W. Blackwood, 1900-1904. 3 vols.

MENÉNDEZ Y PELAYO, Marcelino: *Historia de las Ideas Estéticas en España* (general discussion, not limited to Spanish literature). 2nd ed., Madrid, 1890-1907. 7 vols. in 9.

SPINGARN, J. E.: *A History of Literary Criticism in the Renaissance.* 2nd ed., New York, Columbia University Press, 1908. 350pp.

CROCE, Benedetto: *Estetica,* tr. by AINSLIE, Douglas: *Æsthetic as Science of Expression and General Linguistic.* (Historical as well as theoretical.) London, Macmillan, 1909. 403pp.

Brunetière, F.: *L'Evolution des Genres:* la Critique. Paris, Hachette, 1898. 283pp.

Dabditt, Irving: *Masters of Modern French Criticism.* Boston, New York, Houghton Mifflin, 1912. 427pp.

Scott James, R. A.: *The Making of Literature.* New York, Henry Holt, 1929. 396pp.

Anthologies of Criticism

Saintsbury, George: *Loci Critici:* Passages illustrative of critical theory and practice from Aristotle downwards. Boston, Ginn, 1903. 439pp.

Smith, James Harry, and Parks, Edd Winfield: *The Great Critics.* New York, W. W. Norton, 1932. 564pp.

Lewisohn, Ludwig: *A Modern Book of Criticism.* New York, Boni and Liveright, 1919, 210pp.

Foerster, Norman: *American Critical Essays,* Nineteenth and Twentieth Centuries, World's Classics, Oxford University Press, 1930. 520pp.

Bowman, J. C.: *Contemporary American Criticism.* New York, Henry Holt, 1926. 330pp.

Babbitt, Irving & al. (Van Wyck Brooks, W. C. Brownell, Ernest Boyd, T. S. Eliot, H. L. Mencken, Stuart Sherman, J. E. Spingarn, George E. Woodberry): *Criticism in America.* New York, Harcourt, Brace, 1924. 330pp.

IIa. Histories of World Literature

There are many one-volume histories of World, and even of Universal, Literature on the market, particularly in German. Some are frankly and proudly drier-than-dust; others appeal to the general reader. Not one of these, however, has attained the same immense popularity as H. G. Wells: *The Outline of History,* or Will Durant: *The Story of Philosophy.* No slur is implied, either way.

The two following books are purely reference works, and convenient:

Botta, Ann C. Lynch: *Handbook of Universal Literature.* Boston, Houghton Mifflin, 1923. 530pp.

Van Tieghem, Paul: *Outline of the Literary History of Europe since the Renaissance.* New York, The Century Co., 1930. 361pp.

(If the impossible task could be done at all, Professor F. Baldensperger, late of Harvard, would be the man to do it. At the time of going to press, his *History of Universal Literature* has not yet appeared.)

Our advice would be to use as a foundation, not a history of literature, but a general history of Western Civilization; then to proceed directly to the study of particular periods, genres, themes or authors.

On a larger scale: As we started with the statement that Goethe is the godfather of World Literature, we should like to mention:

BARTELS, Adolf: *Einführung in die Weltliteratur von den ältesten Zeiten bis zur Gegenwart im Anschluss an das Leben und Schaffen Goethes.* München, Georg D. W. Calwey, 1913. 3 vols., 916-815-890.

SAINTSBURY, George, Editor: *Periods of European Literature* (from the Dark Ages to the end of the Nineteenth Century), 12 volumes. New York, Charles Scribner's Sons, 1907.

(Each "period" volume is divided, in most cases, into "national" chapters, and the "World Literature" point of view is forgotten. The general Epigraph is worth quoting: "The criticism which alone can much help us for the future is a criticism which regards Europe as being, for intellectual and spiritual purposes, one great confederation, bound to a joint action, and working to a common result."—Matthew Arnold.)

The most ambitious of these collective undertakings is

WALZEL, Oskar (Editor): *Handbuch der Literaturwissenschaft.* Berlin, Akademische Verlag Athenaion, 1923 seq.; in course of publication. One volume, by the editor: *Gehalt und Gestalt im Kunstwerk des Dichters,* Berlin, 1929. 412pp., is of a general nature. The work is profusely and handsomely illustrated.

More important for our purpose than General Histories of World Literature are special studies which bring out the spirit and method of this discipline. Four notable examples are:

WENDELL, Barrett: *The Traditions of European Literature from Homer to Dante.* New York, Charles Scribner's Sons, 1920. 669pp.

HAZARD, Paul: *La Crise de la Conscience Européenne, 1680-1715* (a model of integral cultural history). Paris, Boivin, 1934-35. 3 vols. (Vol. III: Notes & References).

BRANDES, George: *Main Currents in Nineteenth Century Literature* (the testament of bourgeois Liberalism). London, Wm. Heinemann; New York, Macmillan, 1906. 6 vols.

CROCE, Benedetto: *Poesia e non Poesia.* Bari, Laterza, 1923. 329pp. Tr. by Douglas Ainslie: *European Literature in the Nineteenth Century.* London, Chapman and Hall, 1924. 367pp.

IIb. Other Instruments: Dictionaries and Periodicals

Dictionaries

HARVEY, Sir Paul: *The Oxford Companion to English Literature.* Oxford, Clarenden Press, 1933. 866pp.

A convenient epitome of what one should know in order to understand *English* literature: (a) the salient facts of that literature itself; (b) the social background; (c) not least, those elements in foreign literatures which have influenced our own

(Sir Paul Harvey has also compiled a *Companion to Classical Literature*; a *Companion to American Literature* is in preparation.)

MAGNUS, Laurie: *A Dictionary of European Literature*, designed as a companion to English Studies. London, George Routledge; New York, E. P. Dutton. 2nd Impression, revised, 1927. 605pp.

Does not include items of a non-literary nature, as the Oxford Companion does; excludes antiquity, the Orient, and America. "Briefly, it comprises general articles on movements or topics continuous through several centuries and countries; concise surveys of the literary history of the chief countries; critical and biographical accounts, with a minimum of bibliography, of major and minor writers, and definitions of such literary terms as the student or general reader is likely to encounter" (from the Preface). A marvel of condensation; some articles are brilliant miniatures. Errors of facts, which survived a first revision, are not so numerous and so shocking as might have been feared.

SHARP, R. Farquharson: *A Short Biographical Dictionary of Foreign Literature*. Everyman's Library, London, J. M. Dent; New York, E. P. Dutton, 1933. 302pp.

(*Foreign* understood as *European not English*; leaves out antiquity, the Orient and America. 550 authors. Inexpensive and convenient.)

Periodicals

HELICON: Revue Internationale des Problèmes Généraux de la Littérature (in five languages). Editions Académiques Panthéon, Amsterdam, 1938 seq. 3 times a year. (The Editorial Board might be called the general staff of World Literature studies.)

REVUE DE LITTÉRATURE COMPARÉE, Paris, Boivin; quarterly (sponsors also an excellent collection of studies in Comparative Literature).

BOOKS ABROAD, University of Oklahoma, Norman, Okla.

Numerous brief reviews of current literature in European languages other than English; increasing importance given to longer articles; documents and discussions. Extremely useful.

MERCVRE DE FRANCE, Paris.

A general magazine, predominantly but not exclusively devoted to literature. Contains periodical surveys of various national literatures.

DIE LITERATUR (das literarische Echo), Monatsschrift für Literaturfreunde, Stuttgart.

INTERNATIONAL LITERATURE, Moscow.

Frank propaganda, but contains useful indications.

III. The Body of World Literature: Collections and Anthologies

1. Collections

World's Classics, Oxford University Press.

Everyman's Library, London, J. M. Dent; New York, E. P. Dutton.

The Modern Library, New York (including Giants).

The Harvard Classics, President Charles W. Eliot's Five-Foot Shelf of Books, New York, P. F. Collier, 50 vols.

(Everyman's Library includes several reference works and a Reader's Guide; The Harvard Classics have a supplementary volume of Lectures and a Reading Guide: Fifteen Minutes a Day.)

2. "Monumental" Anthologies

The International Library of Famous Literature, edited by Dr. Richard Garnett, Léon Vallée, Alois Brandl, London, The Standard, 1900, 20 vols.

The Universal Anthology, same editors, London, Clarke Co., 33 vols.

Library of the World's Best Literature, Ancient and Modern, edited by Charles Dudley Warner. New York, J. A. Hill Co., 1902, 46 vols.

3. One-Volume Anthologies

BUCK, Philo M.: An Anthology of World Literature. New York, Macmillan, 1934. 1016pp.

(Does not include literatures of England, America or the Far East.)

CROSS, Ethan Allen: World Literature. New York-Cincinnati, American Book Company, 1935. 1396pp.

ROBBINS, Harry Wolcott and COLEMAN, William Harold: Western World Literature. New York, Macmillan, 1938. 1422pp.

(Includes Antiquity, England and America, but not the East; selections from the Bible in Appendix.)

VAN DOREN, Mark: An Anthology of World Poetry. New York, A. & C. Boni, 1923. 1318pp.

(All inclusive. An extremely valuable collection.)

VAN DOREN, Carl: An Anthology of World Prose. New York, Literary Guild, 1935. 1582pp.

SHAW, Charles Gray, editor: 101 World Classics. New York, Literary Guild of America, 1937. 823pp.

"THE BEST WHICH HAS BEEN THOUGHT AND SAID IN THE WORLD . . ."

Making up a list of the best books is a pleasant art. A bibliography of this subject would fill—unprofitably—a large pamphlet. Columbia University (Studies in Library Service), The National Council of Teachers of English, and the General Federation of Women's Clubs are prepared to offer assistance. So we shall mention only two items:

LUBBOCK, Sir John: *The Best Hundred Books*, containing Sir John Lubbock's list and additional suggestions by Ruskin and others. New York, E. L. Kellogg and Co., 1887. 62pp.

HAINES, Helen E.: *Living with Books*. The Art of Book Selection. New York, Columbia University Press, 1935. 505pp.

The following lists do not represent our personal taste, but a consensus. Their sole interest is as documents on the present state of the literary world. It must be remembered that we exclude: (a) works written originally in English: Shakespeare obviously does belong to World Literature, but if he did not, we should read him all the same; (b) Oriental works which have not become part of our heritage.

Separate lists will be submitted for: (a) World Classics (before our own times); (b) Contemporary World Literature; (c) "decisive" books not purely of a literary nature. The mode of selection will be stated before each list.

I. WORLD CLASSICS

We have compared four collections: Oxford Press World's Classics, Everyman's Library, Modern Library, Harvard Classics; and the three anthologies by Philo Buck, E. A. Cross, and Robbins & Coleman. We consider that inclusion in such a series, as it involves effort and money, is a more weighty and responsible nomination than inclusion in a mere list. We give the names of all writers who received at least two votes.

Unanimity was complete only in the cases of Homer, Dante, Cervantes and Goethe.

GREEK

HOMER	ca. 900 B.C.	Epic	Iliad, Odyssey
AESOP	ca. 620-560 B.C.		Fables
AESCHYLUS	525-456	Tragedy	Prometheus Bound
			Oresteia
SOPHOCLES	496-406	Tragedy	Oedipus King
			Antigone
EURIPIDES	480-406	Tragedy	Iphigenia
			Alcestis
THUCYDIDES	ca. 460-399	History	Peloponnesian War
ARISTOPHANES	ca. 448-385	Comedy	The Frogs, The Birds
PLATO	429-347	Philosophy	Republic, Dialogues
DEMOSTHENES	ca. 384-322	Oratory	Philippics
ARISTOTLE	384-322	Philosophy	(Encyclopaedic)
THEOCRITUS	ca. 310-245	Lyric	Bucolics
PLUTARCH	46-120 A.D.	Biography	Parallel Lives
EPICTETUS	ca. 60-145	Philosophy	Encheiridion (Manual)
MARCUS AURELIUS	121-180	Philosophy	Meditations

(Familiar names absent from this list: the early poets Sappho, Anacreon and Pindar; the historians Herodotus and Xenophon; Lucian the Satirist; Longinus *On the Sublime*, Longus, *Daphnis and Chloe*.)

LATIN

CICERO	106-43 B.C.	Philosophy, Oratory	On the Nature of the Gods Against Catiline
CAESAR	102-44	History	Commentaries (Gallic War)
LUCRETIUS	98-55	Philosophical Poetry	On the Nature of Things
VERGIL	70-19	Poetry	Aeneid, Bucolics, Georgics
HORACE	65- 8	Poetry	Odes, Satires, Epistles
OVID	43 B.C.-18 A.D.	Poetry	Metamorphoses, Art of Love
PETRONIUS	1st Cent.	Satirical Medley	Feast of Trimalchio
TACITUS	55-117?	History	Annals
JUVENAL	60-140	Poetry	Satires

(Regrets: The comic writers Plautus and Terence; the poets Catullus, Propertius, Tibullus; the historians Sallust, Livy, Suetonius; the philosopher and dramatist Seneca; the romancer Apuleius; and St. Augustine.)

ORIENTAL (ASIATIC)

1. (Sanskrit)	1500 B.C.?	Religious Poetry	Vedic Hymns
(Sanskrit)	500-300 B.C.	Epic	Mahabharata
VALMIKI (id.)		Epic	Ramayana
KALIDASA (id.)	c. 375 A.D.	Drama	Sakuntala
2. Hebrew and Greek	10th cent. B.C.-1st A.D.	Religious	Bible
3. Arabic	10th cent. A.D.?	Tales	1001 Nights
4. Persian: OMAR KHAYYAM	d. 1123	Poetry	Rubáiyát

(The above received proper nomination, and are duly included. Personally, we do not believe that Sanskrit literature has become part of our

468 APPENDICES

tradition. *The Arabian Nights* as we know them are mostly Antoine Galland's, and the Rubáiyát Edward Fitzgerald's.)

MEDIEVAL LITERATURE

Author	Language	Dates	Kind	Masterpieces
?	French	c. 1100	Epic	Song of Roland
?	French	12th cent.	Romance	Aucassin and Nicolette
?	German	c. 1200	Epic	Nibelungenlied
DANTE	Italian	1265-1321	Religious Epic	Divine Comedy
PETRARCH, Francesco	Italian	1304-1374	Poetry	Canzoniere (Sonnets)
BOCCACCIO, Giovanni	Italian	1313-1375	Tales	Decameron
THOMAS À KEMPIS	Latin	1380-1471	Religion	Imitation of Christ
VILLON, François	French	1431-?	Poetry	Ballades, Testaments

(A shockingly brief list, especially if we consider that the great Italians were not purely medieval. We regret the absence of some of the Minnesinger, particularly Walther von der Vogelweide; and of some of the Chroniclers, Joinville, Froissart. The great "classics" of the Middle Ages, Chrétien of Troyes, the Romance of the Rose, are no longer definite forces.)

RENAISSANCE AND NEO-CLASSICAL AGE

ERASMUS, Desiderius	Latin	1467-1536	Moral Philosophy	Praise of Folly, Colloquia
MACHIAVELLI, Niccoló	Italian	1469-1527	Politics	The Prince
RABELAIS, François	French	1494-1553	Philosophical Romance	Gargantua and Pantagruel
CELLINI, Benvenuto	Italian	1500-1571	Artist	Autobiography
MONTAIGNE, Michel Eyquem de-	French	1533-1592	Moral Philosophy	Essays
CERVANTES Saavedra, Miguel de	Spanish	1547-1616	Satirical Romance	Don Quixote
CALDERÓN de la Barca, Pedro	Spanish	1600-1681	Dramatist	El Mágico Prodigioso, La Vida es Sueño
CORNEILLE, Pierre	French	1606-1684	Dramatist	Le Cid, Polyeucte, Nicomède
LA FONTAINE, Jean de	French	1621-1695	Poet	Fables
MOLIÈRE, J. B. Poquelin	French	1622-1673	Dramatist	Misanthrope, Tartuffe
PASCAL, Blaise	French	1623-1662	Religious Philosophy	Thoughts
RACINE, Jean	French	1639-1699	Dramatist	Andromaque, Britannicus, Phèdre, Athalie

VOLTAIRE, F. M. Arouet	French	1694-1778	Polygraph	Candide, Essai sur les Mœurs
PRÉVOST d'Exiles, Antoine (Abbé)	French	1697-1763	Novelist	Manon Lescaut
ROUSSEAU, Jean-Jacques	French	1712-1778	Philosopher	Nouvelle Héloïse, Contrat Social, Emile, Confessions
LESSING, G. E.	German	1729-1781	Dramatist, Critic	Minna von Barnhelm, Nathan der Weise, Laokoon, Dramaturgie

(Perhaps the most glaring omission in this list is that of the delightful Ariosto. We understand that the *baroque* mixture of incongruous elements in Tasso and Camoens discourages the modern reader. Lope de Vega is a prodigy: but there is no single commanding masterpiece that crystallizes his enormous production. This is true also of Diderot the Encyclopedist, and it might have been true of Voltaire if he had not written Candide. As for Montesquieu, he might be considered as more important in the history of thought than in pure literature. The supremacy of French literature for nearly a century (1660-1760) comes out very clearly.)

FROM THE REVOLUTION TO THE GREAT WAR

GOETHE, Johann Wolfgang v.	German	1749-1832	Universal	Werther, Wilhelm Meister, Faust I & II
SCHILLER, Friedrich	German	1759-1805	Drama, History, Poet	Die Räuber, Wallenstein, Wilhelm Tell
BÉRANGER, P. J. de	French	1780-1857	Poet	Popular Songs
HEINE, Heinrich	German	1797-1856	Poet, Essayist	Lieder
BALZAC, Honoré de	French	1799-1850	Novelist	Comédie Humaine (Père Goriot, Eugénie Grandet, Cousine Bette)
HUGO, Victor	French	1802-1885	Poet, Dramatist, Novelist	Notre Dame de Paris, Les Misérables
DUMAS, Alexandre	French	1803-1870	Dramatist, Novelist	Trois Mousquetaires, Monte Cristo
SAND, George	French	1804-1876	Novelist	Indiana, Lelia
SAINTE-BEUVE, C. A.	French	1804-1869	Critic	Lundis, Port-Royal
ANDERSEN, H. C.	Danish	1805-1875		Fairy Tales
GOGOL, N. V.	Russian	1809-1852	Novelist, Dramatist	Dead Souls, The Inspector-General
TURGENEV, Ivan	Russian	1818-1883	Novelist	Fathers and Sons
DOSTOEVSKY, Fedor	Russian	1821-1881	Novelist	Crime and Punishment, Brothers Karamazov

470 APPENDICES

FLAUBERT, Gustave	French	1821-1880	Novelist	Madame Bovary, L'Education Sentimentale, Salammbô
Rbham, Ernest	French	1823-1892	Religious Philosopher	Life of Jesus, Souvenirs
IBSEN, Henrik	Norwegian	1828-1906	Dramatist	Peer Gynt, Brand, Ghosts, Wild Duck, Hedda Gabler
TOLSTOY, Leo	Russian	1828-1910	Novelist, Dramatist, Apostle	Anna Karenina, War and Peace
DAUDET, Alphonse	French	1840-1897	Novelist	Tartarin, Sapho, Petit Chose, Nabab
ZOLA, Émile	French	1840-1902	Novelist	Rougon-Macquart Series: Germinal, l'Assommoir
NIETZSCHE, Friedrich	German	1844-1900	Philosopher	Also sprach Zarathustra
CHEKHOV, Anton P.	Russian	1860-1904	Novelist, Dramatist	Short Stories, The Cherry Orchard

(The survival of George Sand came as a surprise and that of Béranger as a shock. On the other hand, we had fully expected that Manzoni (*I Promessi Sposi*), once as popular as Walter Scott and Alexandre Dumas, would have kept a more faithful following. The absence of personal favorites like Kleist, Hebbel and Alfred de Vigny could not be resented; but it is high time that the international influence of Stendhal (Le Rouge et le Noir, La Chartreuse de Parme) and Charles Baudelaire (Fleurs du Mal) be acknowledged by the editors of Collections and Anthologies.)

II. CONTEMPORARY WORLD LITERATURE

To give an objective inventory of contemporary world literature, we have used three methods:

A. Nobel Prize Winners in Literature
B. Literary Works of Foreign Origin among the "best sellers" on the American market since the World War
C. Works not in the two categories above, but frequently mentioned in responsible discussions

A. NOBEL PRIZE WINNERS IN LITERATURE, 1901-1938

1901	Sully-Prudhomme	1839-1907	Poet	French
1902	Theodor Mommsen	1817-1903	Historian	German
1903	Björnstjerne Björson	1832-1910	Novelist, Dramatist	Norwegian
1904	Frédéric Mistral	1830-1914	Poet (Provençal)	French
	José Echegaray	1833-1916	Dramatist	Spanish
1905	Henryk Sienkiewicz	1846-1916	Novelist	Polish

1906	Giosuè Carducci	1836-1907	Poet	Italian
1907	Rudyard Kipling	1865-1936	Poet, Story Writer	English
1908	Rudolf Eucken	1846-1926	Religious Philosopher	German
1909	Selma Lagerlöf	1858-	Novelist	Swedish
1910	Paul Heyse	1830-1914	Story Writer	German
1911	Maurice Maeterlinck	1862-	Poet, Dramatist, Essayist	Belgian
1912	Gerhart Hauptmann	1862-	Novelist, Dramatist	German
1913	Rabindranath Tagore	1861-	Poet	Hindu
1914	No award			
1915	Romain Rolland	1866-	Novelist, Dramatist	French
1916	Verner von Heidenstam	1859-	Poet	Swedish
1917	Henrik Pontoppidan	1857-	Novelist	Danish
	Karl Gjellerup	1857-1919	Novelist	Danish
1918	No award			
1919	Karl Spitteler	1845-1924	Poet	Swiss
1920	Knut Hamsun	1859-	Novelist	Norwegian
1921	Anatole France	1844-1924	Novelist, Essayist	French
1922	Jacinto Benavente	1866-	Dramatist	Spanish
1923	William Butler Yeats	1865-1939	Poet	Irish
1924	Ladislas Reymont	1867-1925	Novelist	Polish
1925	Bernard Shaw	1856-	Dramatist	Irish-English
1926	Grazia Deledda	1875-1936	Novelist	Italian
1927	Henri Bergson	1859-	Philosopher	French
1928	Sigrid Undset	1882-	Novelist	Swedish
1929	Thomas Mann	1875-	Novelist	German
1930	Sinclair Lewis	1885-	Novelist	American
1931	Erik Axel Karlfeldt	1864-1931	Poet	Swedish
1932	John Galsworthy	1867-1933	Novelist, Dramatist	English
1933	Ivan Bunin	1870-	Novelist, Story Writer	Russian
1934	Luigi Pirandello	1867-1936	Dramatist	Italian
1935	No award			
1936	Eugene O'Neill	1888-	Dramatist	American
1937	Roger Martin du Gard	1881-	Novelist	French
1938	Pearl Buck	1892-	Novelist	American
1939	Frans Eemil Sillanpää	1888-	Novelist	Finnish

(Incidentally, this list takes care of a delicate problem: that of the intermediate generation, the great writers who are no longer on the battle line, and yet are not secure in their "classical" immortality: Maeterlinck, Hauptmann, Romain Rolland.)

B. TRANSLATIONS ON THE BEST SELLERS LISTS IN AMERICA

Name	Nationality or Language	Representative Book
ANDREYEV, Leonid	Russian	Seven That Were Hanged; He Who Gets Slapped
ARTZIBASHEF, Mihail	Russian	War, Tales of the Revolution
ASCH, Sholom	Yiddish-Polish	The Three Cities
BARBUSSE, Henri	French	Under Fire
BAUM, Vicki	German	Grand Hotel
BLASCO IBAÑEZ, Vicente	Spanish	The Four Horsemen of the Apocalypse
BUNIN, Ivan	Russian	The Gentleman from San Francisco
ČAPEK, Karel	Czech	R. U. R. and other plays
CÉLINE, Louis	French	Journey to the End of the Night
CHEVALIER, G.	French	Scandals of Clochemerle (? !)

Name	Nationality or Language	Representative Book
DINESEN, Isak	Danish	Seven Gothic Tales
DUHAMEL, Georges	French	Civilization, Salavin, The Pasquier Chronicles
FALLADA, Hans	German	Little Man, What Now? [Josephus
FEUCHTWANGER, Lion	German	Jew Süss, The Ugly Duchess, Success,
FOLDES, Jolan	Hungarian	The Street of the Fishing Cat
FRANCE, Anatole	French	Complete Works in translation
FRENSSEN, Gustav	German	The Pastor of Poggsee
GIBRAN, Khalil	Syrian	The Prophet
GIDE, André	French	The Counterfeiters, Two Symphonies
GIRAUDOUX, Jean	French	Amphitryon 38 (not best sample)
GORKY, Maxim	Russian	Bystander, The Magnet
GULBRANSSEN, Trygve	Norwegian	Beyond Sings the Wood
HAMSUN, Knut	Norwegian	Growth of the Soil
HEMON, Louis	French	Marie Chapdelaine
KAFKA, Franz	German	The Castle
KEYSERLING, Hermann	German	Travel Diary of a Philosopher
KUPRIN, Alexander	Russian	The Swamp, Yama
LAGERLÖF, Selma	Swedish	Gösta Berling, Ring of the Löwensköld
LUDWIG, Emil	German	Napoleon (etc., etc.)
MADARIAGA, Salvador de	Spanish	Englishmen, Frenchmen, Spaniards
MALRAUX, André	French	Man's Fate
MANN, Thomas	German	Buddenbrooks, Magic Mountain, Joseph and His Brothers, Stories of Three Decades
MARAN, René	French	Batouala
MARTIN DU GARD, Roger	French	The Thibault
MAUROIS, André	French	Ariel, Byron, Disraeli, etc., etc.
MEREZHKOWSKI, Dmitri	Russian	The Romance of Leonardo da Vinci
MEYER-MEYRINK, Gustav	German	The Golem
MOLNAR, Ferenzc	Hungarian	Liliom, The Swan, The Devil
MORAND, Paul	French	Black Magic, etc.
MUNTHE, Axel	Swedish	Story of San Michele
NEUMANN, Alfred	German	Another Caesar; Gaudy Empire
NEXÖ, Martin Andersen	Danish	Ditte, Girl Alive
PAPINI, Giovanni	Italian	Life of Christ
PIRANDELLO, Luigi	Italian	Six Characters in Search of an Author, and [other plays
PROUST, Marcel	French	Remembrance of Things Past
REMARQUE, Eric Maria	German	All Quiet on the Western Front
ROLLAND, Romain	French	Jean-Christophe (popular editions)
ROLVAAG, Ole	Norwegian	Peder Victorious, Giants in the Earth
ROMAINS, Jules	French	Men of Good Will
SCHNITZLER, Arthur	German	Anatol, Fräulein Else, Rhapsody
SHOLOKHOV, Mikhail	Russian	And Quiet Flows the Don
SILONE, Ignacio	Italian	Bread and Wine
SOKOLOF, Boris	Russian	Vitality
SOLOGUB, Fedor	Russian	Little Demon, The Scented Name
SPENGLER, Oswald	German	Decline of the West
TAGORE, Rabindranath	Hindu	Gitanjali, 100 Poems of Kabir
TYNAIRE, Marcelle	French	To Arms!
UNAMUNO, Miguel de	Spanish	The Tragic Sense of Life
UNDSET, Sigrid	Norwegian	Kristin Lavransdatter
VERCEL, Roger	French	Tides of Mt. St. Michel
WASSERMANN, Jakob	German	World's Illusion
WERFEL, Franz	German	The Forty Days of Musa Dagh
ZWEIG, Arnold	German	The Case of Sergeant Grisha
ZWEIG, Stefan	German	Amok, Fouché, Marie-Antoinette, etc.

C. AMONG THOSE ABSENT

The above list is very arbitrary, for the term "best-seller" has no definite meaning. But even if it were more complete, it would fail to give a full idea of the cosmopolitan character of our reading. We should add the following elements:

1. Those foreign authors who write directly for the American public, like Abbé Ernest Dimnet (*The Art of Thinking; What We Live By; My Old World; My New World*), the historian Bernard Faÿ, the Chinese scholar Lin Yu Tang (*My Country and My People; The Importance of Living*).

2. American writers of foreign *birth* (we do not mean of foreign ancestry, for that would extend beyond computation). This would include many well-known names, including perhaps the greatest in American letters, George Santayana.

3. It was found difficult to distinguish between popular history, or philosophy, or political science, such as Ludwig's *Napoleon*, and history, philosophy, political science accessible to the general reader. We should gladly have listed such names as André Siegfried (*America Comes of Age*), Giuseppe Antonio Borgese (*Goliath*); the readable as well as thorough historical works of Count Egon Corti, particularly his *Maximilian and Carlotta in Mexico*; those of Octave Aubry, the best of the popular and orthodox historians in the Napoleonic field (*St. Helena, The King of Rome, The Second Empire*); E. A. Rheinhardt, more unconventional; the searching and delicate work of Paul Cohen-Portheim (*The Discovery of Europe*); Friedrich Sieburg, journalistic, but with very fine elements (*Who Are These French? Robespierre*); the sensationally good memoirs of Caulaincourt (*With Napoleon in Russia, No Peace with Napoleon*). The purely literary merits of Leon Trotzky's work are evident. Those of *Mein Kampf*, by Adolf Hitler, require a larger dose of faith.

4. A number of writers (translated) had a definite influence and devoted followers, although they were not reported among best-sellers. Among those Benedetto Croce should be mentioned first, chiefly in the field of esthetics and criticism, but also in pure philosophy, the theory of history, and modern Italian history (on the other hand, no one would count Vilfredo Pareto a *literary* force); Ortega y Gasset, for his *Revolt of the Masses*; the French poet Paul Valéry as an essayist (*Variety*); the French Ambassador J. Jusserand (*What Me Befell*); the French Ambassador Paul Claudel, religious poet and dramatist (*The Tidings Brought to Mary*).

Our nets failed to catch great writers of an intermediate period: not yet established classics by 1914, but not strictly our contemporaries in the post-war era, even if they are still alive and writing. We have noted that the Nobel Prizes helped us in this respect, as in the case of Henryk Sienkiewicz, Maurice Maeterlinck and Gerhart Hauptmann.

The two most striking omissions are those of Guy de Maupassant, who seems safely acknowledged as a minor classic; and Gabriele d'Annunzio, Principe de Monte Nevoso, who is at least a picturesque, indeed a flamboyant, figure; important in history, as revealing the esthetic background of the New Imperialism. The key to the Dictatorships is to be found less in doubtful economics than in questionable literature (cf. note on *Kitsch*).

Among those who failed to find a place in the above lists, but who had—or still have—a position in world literature, we may mention: Johann Bojer, Norwegian novelist; Paul Bourget, French psychological novelist, the friend of Henry James and Edith Wharton; A. Fogazzaro, Italian novelist (*The Saint*); Rémi de Gourmont, French critic (*Mercure de France*); J. K. Huysmans, French novelist (*A Rebours;* converted to Catholicism); Pierre Loti, French novelist, exotic and sentimental; B. Pérez Galdós, Spanish historical novelist and dramatist; Edmond Rostand, French dramatist (*Cyrano de Bergerac, L'Aiglon*); Matilde Serao, Italian novelist (*The Land of Cockayne*); Hermann Sudermann, German dramatist and novelist (*Magda, Dame Care*); Emile Verhaeren, Belgian French poet (*The Cloister, Belgium's Agony*).

III. DECISIVE BOOKS

In the two foregoing series of lists, we have attempted to remain as strictly as possible within the limits of literature as an art. There are, of course, borderline cases: Thomas à Kempis would scorn to have *The Imitation of Christ* discussed in terms of composition and style. A number of winners of the Nobel Prize for idealistic literature are manifestly philosophers rather than literary men. But the general line of demarcation is clear enough: Milton's *Paradise Lost* and Spinoza's *Ethics*, which belong to the same period and show the same preoccupation with the highest problems of man's destiny, cannot be appraised by the same standard.

In order to clarify our ideas about the relation between influence and literary value, it is an excellent exercise to draw up a list of the most vital works in human experience, irrespective of their esthetic merit. President Stringfellow Barr, of St. John's College, Annapolis, has devised a curriculum based on the co-ordinated study of "The Hundred Best Books," scientific and philosophical as well as literary. The idea is extremely attractive; but we doubt the advantage of having undergraduates approach science through the mighty works of the past, which are at the same time difficult and obsolete.

The interest of this exercise is in the discussion, not in the results, which vary with the experience of each individual, and with every wind of doctrine. The clearest results are that "decisive" is one of those polite terms which are all things to all men; and that we are never quite sure that any book is actually "decisive." We submit two samples of such symposia: the first with a triple halo of authority; the second, carried on by a modest group of graduate students at Stanford University.

LIST OF THE TWENTY-FIVE VOLUMES THREE NOTED SCHOLARS CONSIDER TO HAVE HAD THE MOST INFLUENCE ON THOUGHT AND ACTION DURING THE LAST HALF-CENTURY

JOHN DEWEY *Professor Emeritus of Philosophy at Columbia University*	EDWARD WEEKS *Editor of the* Atlantic Monthly Press	CHARLES A. BEARD *Historian*
1 K. Marx: Das Kapital	K. Marx: Das Kapital	K. Marx: Das Kapital
2 E. Bellamy: Looking Backward	E. Bellamy: Looking Backward	E. Bellamy: Looking Backward
3 Sir James Frazier: The Golden Bough	Sir James Frazier: The Golden Bough	Sir James Frazier: The Golden Bough
4 Wm. James: The Principles of Psychology	Wm. James: The Principles of Psychology	Alfred Mahan: The Influence of Sea Power upon History, 1660-1783
5 Henrik Ibsen: Hedda Gabler	L. Tolstoy: Kreutzer Sonata	Rudyard Kipling: Barrack-Room Ballads
6 T. Hardy: Tess of the d'Urbervilles	A. Mahan: Influence of Sea Power upon History	Thorstein Veblen: The Theory of the Leisure Class
7 T. Veblen: Theory of the Leisure Class	Conan Doyle: Sherlock Holmes	John Atkinson Hobson: Imperialism
8 G. B. Shaw: Man and Superman	Rudyard Kipling: Barrack-Room Ballads	Upton Sinclair: The Jungle
9 Samuel Butler: The Way of All Flesh	G. B. Shaw: Plays Pleasant and Unpleasant	Sir James Jeans: The Mathematical Theory of Electricity and Magnetism
10 Henry James: The Golden Bowl	Havelock Ellis: The Psychology of Sex	Norman Angell: The Great Illusion
11 Bertrand Russell and A. N. Whitehead: Principia Mathematica	John Dewey: The School and Society	Marie Carmichael Stopes: Married Love and Wise Parenthood
12 Franz Boas: The Mind of Primitive Man	Ida M. Tarbell: History of the Standard Oil Company	Vladimir Ilich Lenin: Imperialism, the State and Revolution
13 Henry Adams: The Education of Henry Adams	Sir James Jeans: The Mathematical Theory of Electricity and Magnetism	John Maynard Keynes: The Economic Consequences of the Peace
14 Carl Gustav Jung: The Psychology of the Unconscious	Henry Adams: The Education of Henry Adams	H. G. Wells: Outline of History
15 Albert Einstein: Relativity, the Special and General Theory	Marie Carmichael Stopes: Married Love and Wise Parenthood	Sinclair Lewis: Main Street

JOHN DEWEY	EDWARD WEEKS	CHARLES A. BEARD
Professor Emeritus of Philosophy at Columbia University	*Editor of the* Atlantic Monthly Press	*Historian*
16 H. G. Wells: Outline of History	Vladimir Ilich Lenin: Imperialism, the State and Revolution	Frederick Jackson Turner: The Frontier in American History
17 Marcel Proust: Remembrance of Things Past	John Maynard Keynes: The Economic Consequences of the Peace	Sinclair Lewis: Babbitt
18 Sinclair Lewis: Babbitt	Albert Einstein: Relativity, the Special and General Theory	Vilfredo Pareto: Treatise on General Sociology
19 Sigmund Freud: The Interpretation of Dreams	Romain Rolland: Jean-Christophe	Oswald Spengler: The Decline of the West
20 Oswald Spengler: The Decline of the West	Sinclair Lewis: Main Street	A. S. Eddington: The Internal Constitution of the Stars
21 James Joyce: Ulysses	Sigmund Freud: The Interpretation of Dreams	Sir Philip Gibbs: Now It Can Be Told
22 Thomas Mann: The Magic Mountain	Oswald Spengler: The Decline of the West	Sidney B. Fay: Origins of the World War
23 Charles and Mary Beard: The Rise of American Civilization	James Joyce: Ulysses	Eric Maria Remarque: All Quiet on the Western Front
24 Niels Bohr: The Atomic Theory and the Description of Nature	A. S. Eddington: The Internal Constitution of the Stars	Leon Trotzky: History of the Russian Revolution
25 K. E. L. Planck: Lectures on the Theory of Heat Radiation	Eric Maria Remarque: All Quiet on the Western Front	Adolf Hitler: My Battle

—From *The English Journal,* June, 1936, pp. 496-8.

(I can only say, as Louis XIV told Boileau: "I did not think so: but you know better about these things than I do.")

THE FIFTEEN DECISIVE BOOKS OF THE WORLD

Consolidation of a series of symposia among graduate students of *Literature and Civilization,* Stanford University.

The title was borrowed from Sir Edward Creasy's famous book: *The Fifteen Decisive Battles of the World.* Books which do not affect us directly, like the Sacred Books of the East, or books whose influence was limited to one definite historical issue now settled, like *Uncle Tom's Cabin,* were ruled out. The books are presented in order of obviousness; but the obviousness may not be apparent to every reader.

I. The Bible

II. Rousseau (*Omnibus:* 2 discourses, New Heloise, Social Contract, Emile, Confessions)

III. Karl Marx (with Adam Smith as a Preface): Capital

IV. Machiavelli: The Prince

V. Darwin: Origin of Species

VI. Bacon: Novum Organum (father of scientific experimental method)

VII. Descartes: Discourse on Method (scientific rationalism)

VIII. Plato: The Republic, and Dialogues (both in his own name, and in the name of Socrates)

IX. More: Utopia (Principle of a planned Society)

X. Montaigne: Essays (Radical Skepticism. Individual man as measure and center of all things. Tolerance)

XI. Locke: Essay on Human Understanding (Father of the Enlightenment, Montesquieu, Voltaire; bourgeois liberalism)

XII. Herder (with Vico as forerunner): Ideas on World History (links philosophy with history and poetry. The unconscious and subconscious in national life. More definitely than Rousseau, father of Romantic-Nationalistic Democracy: "Herder rules the Reich")

XIII. Malthus: Principle of Population (the first to state and face the problem definitely. Pessimism: no "guiding hand" as in Adam Smith. Influence on Darwin and Marx: Struggle for Life and Iron Law)

XIV. Hegel: Logic (Dialectical method. Restores sense of motion by breaking Aristotelian circle. Philosophical basis of Evolutionary theories—including Bergson's—and of Marxism. Also the all-powerful concept of the State)

XV. Nietzsche (Challenge to Christian virtues. Concept of superman. Ruthlessness. Will-to-power)

(Considered: Kant: essence of critical attitude already in Descartes. Reconstruction of the world on moral basis (categorical imperative) already in Calvinistic-Rousseauistic notion of conscience. Freud? Perhaps. Gave definiteness to elements present in Medieval Christianity and romantic psychology.)

TYPES OF NARRATIVE FICTION

No dogmatic value is attached to these classifications. They simply represent some of the angles from which narrative fiction may be viewed. Every method that ever was practiced is still in use today. There is no such thing as "the only possible way."

Only the types commonly accepted as "standard" narrative fiction are here considered. The formal epic and epic romance, the pure allegory, the fable, are not included.

I. CLASSIFICATION ACCORDING TO TECHNIQUE

A. *Verse or Prose:*
  1. Novel in verse: Chaucer: Troilus and Cryseide; E. B. Browning: Aurora Leigh
  2. Prose: standard type
  3. Poetical prose: H. Melville: Moby Dick
  4. Mixed: Aucassin and Nicolette

B. *Length:*
  1. Anecdote and "short short story": cf. magazines
  2. Tale, short story: Boccaccio, Maupassant, Chekhov, K. Mansfield
  3. "Long short" (German *Novelle*), merging with the novelette and short novel: Prévost, Manon Lescaut; Mérimée: Carmen; Edith Wharton: Ethan Frome
  4. "Full length," standard type; 60,000 to 120,000 words
  5. *Giants:* "three-deckers," *romans-fleuves*, etc. Richardson: Pamela; Hugo: Les Misérables; Tolstoy: War and Peace
  6. This runs into the *Series* of connected novels: Dumas: Valois Romances, Musketeers Romances, Balsamo Romances; Galsworthy: Forsyte Saga; Jules Romains: Men of Good Will; Balzac's Human Comedy and Zola's Rougon-Macquart are extreme examples. (Cf. also Romain Rolland: Jean-Christophe; Proust: Remembrance of Things Past; Thomas Wolfe)

C. *Method of Presentation:*
1. Third-person narrative (standard type)
   a. omniscient-objective (factual report: Hemingway)
   b. omniscient, objective and subjective (factual report, plus feelings and motives of all characters): standard
   c. from the point of view of one character only: biographical method
2. First-person narrative
   a. Pseudo-autobiography, Memoirs, Confession, Diary: De Foe, Lesage
   b. A tale within a tale: first person narrative of events relating to third person (parts of Conrad: Lord Jim)
3. Interior Monologue, merging with "stream of consciousness" (formless, uncontrolled monologue): parts of Joyce: Ulysses
4. Epistolary: Richardson, J. J. Rousseau
5. Dramatic form (in the words of the characters only)
   a. Series of monologues: Browning: The Ring and the Book
   b. Dialogues: La Celestina; Roger Martin du Gard: Jean Barois
   c. Crypto-drama: mostly conversations, but with narrative and descriptive passages: Book of Job; Meredith: The Egoist
6. Mixed (not blending, but conscious use of different techniques in different parts of the work): Wilkie Collins: The Moonstone. James Joyce: Ulysses (narrative, parody, dialogue, stream of consciousness)

D. *Emphasis on:*
1. Setting, milieu (cf. Part II)
2. Plot (from the *all-plot* narrative-detective, mystery, romance of adventure—to the *plotless:* Flaubert: Sentimental Education)
3. Problem:
   a. psychological
   b. social
4. Character
5. Style: Pierre Louys, A. Machen, James Branch Cabell, Donn Byrne, James Joyce, Gertrude Stein
Partaking of 1 and 4, setting (milieu) and character, is the Family Saga:

E. Zola: Les Rougon-Macquart: "Natural and Social History of a Family under the Second Empire."
John Galsworthy: The Forsyte Saga: dirge on the passing of "the Man of Property," the Victorian Bourgeois.
Thomas Mann: Buddenbrooks: Refinement and decline of Lübeck merchant family.
Mazo de la Roche: Jalna: a great estate in Canada.
Georges Duhamel: The Pasquier Chronicle (lower Parisian bourgeoisie).
Roger Martin du Gard: Les Thibaut (upper Parisian bourgeoisie).

II. CLASSIFICATION ACCORDING TO SUBJECT

A. *Location in Time*
   1. Past
      a. Indefinite: fairy tales, romances, allegories, cf. Cabell: Poictesme series
      b. Definite: "period" setting: all historical romances, from the prehistoric to "only yesterday"
   2. Present (actually immediate past) with reference to time of writing. Standard type
   3. Future: anticipations, prophecies, many Utopias. H. G. Wells, Michael Arlen, Aldous Huxley (Brave New World)

B. *Location in Space*
   1. Imaginary: fairy tales, fantastic romances, allegories, Utopias. Hudson: A Crystal Age
   2. Exotic: i.e., describing a civilization radically different from our own. Melville: Omoo, Typee; R. Kipling: Kim; Pearl Buck: The Good Earth
   3. Foreign: country different from that of author and intended public, but within same group of civilization, i.e., for us the European (urban, Hispanized Mexico is *foreign*; rural, Indian Mexico is *exotic*). Romain Rolland: Jean-Christophe, Part I
      a. Expatriate, cosmopolitan: P. Bourget: Cosmopolis; R. Rolland, Jean-Christophe, Part III; E. Hemingway: The Sun also Rises; R. Briffault: Europa
   4. Home Country: standard type (a "home" novel, like Anna Karenina, becomes "foreign" in translation, just as a "contemporary" story becomes "historical" for the next generation. Time and Space are here stated relatively to the writer and the immediate public)
   5. Within any one of the above divisions, we may have:
      a. Countryside: Thomas Hardy: Far from the Madding Crowd
      b. Small town: Flaubert: Madame Bovary; Sinclair Lewis: Main Street
      c. Large city: Sinclair Lewis: Babbitt; J. Farrell: Studs Lonigan
      d. Metropolis: London (Huxley: Point Counterpoint); Paris (Jean-Christophe, Part II); New York: John Dos Passos, etc.

C. *Social Environment* or *Milieu*
   1. Upper Classes:
      a. Royalty: Thomas Mann, Royal Highness
      b. Aristocracy (long the favorite *milieu*: Madame de Lafayette: La Princesse de Clèves; Ouida, Paul Bourget, Henry James, Edith Wharton, Sackville-West (The Edwardians), Marcel Proust

2. The Professions:
   a. The clergy: Willa Cather: Death Comes for the Archbishop; G. Bernanos: Diary of a Country Priest; A. Trollope: Barchester Towers
   b. Army and navy (Capt. Marryat)
   c. Artists, writers (often with touch of Bohemianism)
   d. Physicians (a great favorite at present)
   e. Academic, both from students' and teachers' points of view
   f. Politicians and officials
3. Business life, large and small: Balzac, Zola, Dreiser, Frank Norris, Sinclair Lewis, etc. (an enormous field)
4. Industrial Life: occasionally from the employers' point of view (J. R. Bloch: & Co.; A. Maurois: Bernard Quesnay). Usually from the workers' (Dickens: Hard Times; Zola: Germinal; and the innumerable proletarian novels)
5. Agricultural life: Rolvaag: Giants in the Earth; L. Reymont: The Peasants; John Steinbeck: The Grapes of Wrath
6. The transgressors: prostitutes ("pornographic" in literal sense) Zola: Nana. Rogues, thieves, murderers, gangsters, dope peddlers, smugglers, spies: the underworld, including the picaresque, old and new, and much detective fiction
7. Odds and ends: out-of-the-way, ill-defined or not fully respectable occupations: circus performers, pugilists, toreros, etc. (E. Hemingway)

III. CLASSIFICATION ACCORDING TO THE AUTHOR'S ATTITUDE

A. *Author's Motive*
   1. Money: "pot-boilers." Cf. discussion in Ch. XX, "Art for Art's Sake"
   2. Entertainment: Alexandre Dumas. A. Hope: Prisoner of Zenda
   3. Fame and/or Art for Art's Sake: Gustave Flaubert
   4. Investigation, deepening sense of life: Henry James, Thomas Mann
   5. Service of a Cause:
      a. Propaganda: Ibañez: The Four Horsemen
      b. "Mission": Hugo: Les Misérables; Tolstoy: Resurrection
      c. Purposeful satire: Aldous Huxley, Richard Aldington, etc.

B. *Motif or Chief Source of Interest*
   1. Religious (may be ethical, and not theological). The Book of Job (cf. H. G. Wells: The Undying Fire); Shorthouse: John Inglesant; Mrs. Humphry Ward: Robert Elsmere

2. Heroic:
   a. Adventure, discovery: Kingsley: Westward Ho!
   b. Patriotic and military (positive, negative or dubious): Stephen Crane: The Red Badge of Courage; H. Barbusse: Under Fire; E. Hemingway: Farewell to Arms
   c. Revolutionary: André Malraux: Man's Hope
3. Idyllic: innocent love: Daphnis and Chloe, Paul and Virginia; Hardy: Far from the Madding Crowd
4. Passionate and guilty love: Tolstoy: Anna Karenina, Kreutzer Sonata; Abbé Prévost: Manon Lescaut
5. Materialistic:
   a. Avarice: Balzac: Eugénie Grandet
   b. Ambition: Dreiser: The Titan

C. *Tone Adopted by the Author:*
   1. Dramatic: Hugo, Dickens, Thomas Wolfe, Faulkner
   2. Sentimental: Richardson, Rousseau, McKenzie, Goethe (Werther)
   3. Dispassionate: Stendhal, Mérimée, Hemingway (with tendency to systematic understatement)
   4. Ironical: flippant: Michael Arlen, Evelyn Waugh
      a. Urbane irony: Voltaire (Zadig, L'Ingénu); Fielding (Jonathan Wild), Thackeray, Rose Macaulay, James Branch Cabell
      b. Savage irony: Swift; Voltaire: Candide; A. France: Penguin Island

APPENDIX IV

TYPES OF CRITICISM

There are few critics pedantic enough to be, like Thomas Rymer, rigorously "true to type." Even those who have discovered the only possible method cheerfully use many impossible methods as well. So, in most cases, we should substitute for the word Type less rigid terms such as "elements in criticism" or "aspects of criticism." For instance, the geographical element is found everywhere ("The English," said André Maurois, "do not like clarity of thought because their climate is foggy," etc.), but I do not know of any reputable essay in criticism that is solidly geographical.

It is important, however, to analyze these various elements in order to avoid a common temptation: to justify a judgment, a prejudice or an impression, valid in themselves, in terms of a science or of a philosophy which may likewise be valid, but which are not relevant. ("Shakespeare used a discursive, episodic method because he was a Goth," said Edith Wharton.)

I. SCIENTIFIC CRITICISM

A. The *basic facts:* text, authorship, date. Scholarship, preparation of a critical edition. Cf. Morize, André: *Problems and Methods of Literary History,* a Guide for Graduate Students, Ginn, 1922.
Author's biography.
Literary History as a collection of such data.
(These problems and methods are not radically different from those of history proper; an *Introduction to Historical Studies,* such as Ch. Seignobos and Ch. V. Langlois would serve very well.)

B. *Psychological Criticism:*
1. Psychology of the author (Sainte-Beuve, Gamaliel Bradford)
2. Psychology of composition, a very promising branch: cf. Pierre Audiat: La Biographie de l'Œuvre Littéraire
3. Psychology of character or situation. Very frequent; cf. Goethe's interpretation of Hamlet. Usually a re-creation on the part of the critic; personal, non-scientific elements then appear.
4. Psychology of reception, by the individual reader. Cf. impressionistic criticism.

5. Psychology of reception, collective. Cf. pragmatic criticism, history of (collective) taste.

Psychological criticism may use any brand of psychology:
  a. Analytical and descriptive (classical): Sainte-Beuve
  b. Psycho-physiology: cf. Dr. Toulouse on Emile Zola
  c. Psychoanalysis,
and any other kind, normal or abnormal.

C. *Sociological Criticism:*
  1. Race: ubiquitous, especially when race is confounded with nation, ethnic group or language group. Long a favorite, and now official, in Germany
  2. Environment: climate, political regime, social regime, economic regime (V. F. Calverton, John Strachey, Granville Hicks; limits of the method ably discussed by Max Eastman, Edmund Wilson, James T. Farrell)
  3. Time (momentum, i.e., tradition), purely literary tradition: conservative taste
  4. Nationalism as tradition: national interpretation of literature. Ubiquitous

II. DOGMATIC CRITICISM

A. *Classical:*
  1. Antiquity
  2. Renaissance and Neo-Classical
  3. Modern: Matthew Arnold, Brunetière, T. S. Eliot and the Neo-Humanists

B. *Romantic:* Blake; August-Wilhelm and Friedrich Schlegel; Coleridge (to some extent); V. Hugo; A. C. Swinburne.

C. *Realistic-Naturalistic:* Zola. Widespread for last fifty years. Often masquerading as "scientific."

D. *Sociological:* When social conception is used, not to explain, but to judge. Has political and moral aspect.

E. *Moralistic:* Long universal. Censorship.

F. *Expressionistic dogmatism:* Benedetto Croce. Probably the most dogmatic of all.

III. PRAGMATIC CRITICISM

(Study of collective taste)

A. Retrospective: all literary history beyond the material facts (selecting authors who "counted"), especially the history of an author's fame: Frederick Blanchard: Fielding the Novelist. Studies of influences and collective movements have a pragmatic basis.

B. Study of effectiveness and success. On the stage: Aristotle on Euripides; Francisque Sarcey: "Ca, c'est du théâtre!" George Baker: "Such popularity must be deserved." All advertising on basis of sales.

C. Prospective: forecasting nature, extent and duration of probable success.

IV. IMPRESSIONISTIC CRITICISM

A. Purely factual: note reactions. May be "scientific."

B. Expression of personality. Worth what personality is worth, from slapdash and incoherent to thoughtful and organized. Autobiographical: "the adventures of a sensitive soul" (Anatole France).

V. PSEUDO-CRITICISM

(Using the work criticized as a pretext or as a document)

A. Writing an essay on same subject as the book, but not on the book itself (Macaulay).

B. Literature as document on psychology, history, sociology: "Literature as the Mirror of Society"; social conditions in the Middle Ages according to contemporary romances; French bourgeoisie in the plays of Eugène Brieux, etc.

A CRITIC'S GLOSSARY

This is not a technical dictionary of literary terms. Words about which there is complete, objective agreement, such as *sonnet, couplet,* are not included. This list might be called a *Lexicon of Debatable Connotations.* In most cases, these connotations are discussed in the body of the book. It is to be understood that such a glossary is only a sample and a challenge. Anyone interested in literature should "know what he is talking about"; he should take stock of his own equipment, an important part of which is his critical vocabulary.

ACADEMIC: referring (a) etymologically and distantly to Plato's school of philosophy; (b) to institutions of learning; (c) to learned bodies. Formal, remote from practical life.

ADJECTIVES derived from authors' names. Adjectives in *ese, esque, ian, ic* can be formed with the names of any author, living or dead; only a few, however, have passed into common speech; and, in many cases, with a connotation which is somewhat arbitrary. Examples: *Æschylean:* rough-hewn and somber grandeur.

anacreontic: lightsome spirit; wine, easy love, and song.

apocalyptic: weird and terrible visions.

Baudelairian: perverse, decadent.

Byronic: romantic pose; rebellion with a touch of dandyism.

Dantesque: visions of horror, less fantastic, more realistic than the Apocalypse.

Homeric: not so much epic grandeur as majestic simplicity. Special connotations: Homeric laughter; Homeric similes: comparisons elaborated at full length, a device imitated by many classical poets; Homeric epithet: the descriptive epithet, often compound, inevitably attached to certain names: e.g., swift-footed Achilles; a device revived by *Time* and Damon Runyon.

Miltonic: majesty coupled with consummate art; less primitive and sunny than Homer, less somber than Æschylus.

Molièresque: comic in the large sense, verging on the broadly farcical: *M. de Pourceaugnac* is more "Molièresque" than *The Misanthrope.*

Rabelaisian: jollity on an enormous scale; with a touch of grossness; gluttony; obscenity (very unjust).

Shakespearian: emphasizing the more somber aspect of Shakespeare's art, particularly madness and death; often with a blend of the grotesque. The Witches in *Macbeth*, the last scene in *King Lear* are specifically "Shakespearian."

Shavian (semi-humorous term): pertaining to G. B. Shaw: paradoxical wit with a background of earnestness.

Vergilian: not the epic side of the poet, but the bucolic, idyllic and almost elegiac; gentle melancholy dignified by classic beauty.

Voltairian: irreverent, destructive, cynical irony; best example *Candide;* by no means the whole—or the best—of Voltaire.

AESCHYLEAN, cf. Adjectives.

ALLEGORY: simile (comparison) developed into a narrative; e.g., *Romance of the Rose, Pilgrim's Progress.* Merely a prolonged figure of speech; does not imply *real* connection between the two terms of the comparison. Cf. Symbol.

AMATEUR: a person fond of an art, but not practicing it; at least not professionally; hence AMATEURISH: hasty, superficial.

ANACREONTIC, cf. Adjectives.

ARCHAIC: in art: ancient, early (archeology); in style: obsolete, no longer used.

ARCHAISM: (a) an obsolete form; (b) deliberate revival of such forms.

ART: (a) materially: technique, the manner or way of doing anything: "the gentle art of making enemies"; thus opposed both to Nature and to Science (theoretical knowledge); (b) the quest of beauty as created by man: a beautiful landscape is not art; a landscape painting is; (c) that which quickens (enhances) our consciousness of life.

ART FOR ART'S SAKE: refusal to place art at the service of any motive or cause.

ARTSAKIST: abbreviation for believer in the doctrine of art for art's sake.

ATMOSPHERE, cf. Elements.

BABBITT, Irving and George (Follansbee): humanism and philistinism, both with an American accent.

BAROCCO, BAROCK, BAROQUE: a highly decorated, overemphatic, dramatic style; chiefly in architecture and painting; the "flamboyancy" of the classical age; in French: odd, bizarre, absurd.

BATHOS: a caricature of *pathos;* excessive appeal to the feelings; more intense and in worse taste than sentimentality.

BAUDELAIRIAN, cf. Adjectives.

"BEAU GESTE": judging an act by its esthetic (artistic) appeal.

BEAUTY: (a) the splendor of truth (wish it were so!); (b) harmony between personality, subject and form in art; (c) beyond art: sign and promise of pleasure, inspiring respect. (Compare: Prettiness: sign and promise of pleasure, not inspiring awe; Meretriciousness: sign and promise of pleasure, with tinge of contempt.)

BOMBAST: exaggerated eloquence.

BOURGEOIS: (a) town dweller vs. country man; (b) middle class vs. aristocracy and common people; (c) civilian vs. military; (d) philistine vs. artsakist; (e) capitalist vs. socialist. Feminine BOURGEOISE; corresponding Class: BOURGEOISIE. "Petit (petty) bourgeois," "petite (petty) bourgeoisie": lower middle class, as opposed to merchant princes, captains of industry, magnates of capitalism, etc.

BOVARY(I)SM: from Flaubert's heroine; Byronic rebellion on a *petit bourgeois* plane.

BYRONIC, cf. Adjectives.

CARTESIAN: pertaining to the philosophy and method of René Descartes.

CATHARSIS, KATHARSIS: in Aristotle's *Poetics*, "purification" of Terror and Pity achieved in tragedy. The most obscure term in literary theory.

CHARACTER, cf. Elements in a Work of Art.

CIRCULUS: constant interchange in a closed circle or cycle.

CLASSIC, -AL: standard; long-established; superior; Greco-Roman.

CLASSICISM: (a) the norm; sanity, discipline, harmony; (b) study of, and conformity with, "classic," i.e., Greco-Roman, tradition. Ultra- and Pseudo-Classicism, including certain aspects of humanism (q.v.): the form without the spirit of classicism; restraint for its own sake, and worship of dead tradition.

CLICHÉ: stock expression, once of some literary value, unaware of its own triteness. (A frank commonplace or truism is not a cliché.)

CLIQUE: mutual admiration group, with suspicion of intrigue.

CLOSET DRAMA: intended for reading, not for the stage.

COGNOSCENTI, cf. Connoisseur.

COMIC, cf. Spirits.

COMPARATIST: student of Comparative Literature, i.e., relations between various national literatures.

CONCEIT: (a) style (Italian *concetto, concetti*); affected mode of expression, form of preciosity; (b) moral: the *sine qua non* of authorship; name given by the philistines to the noble self-confidence of artists.

CONNOISSEUR, modern French Connaisseur: "one who knows"; a judge of fine points, chiefly in connection with wine and the arts; may be blind to larger values; obsolete. The Italian Cognoscente, usually in the plural Cognoscenti, is also archaic.

CRITERION (Greek), CRITERIUM (Latin), pl. CRITERIA: test, gauge, standard, by which a thing is judged. Measurement is effected by means of units; judgment by means of criteria (Standard may be used in both cases). A rule or law defines a criterion, but is not itself the—criterion. A Shibboleth (q.v.) is a purely formal and superficial criterion.

CRITICISM: process of examining, discriminating; appraising, evaluating; judging. Only incidentally: carping, fault-finding. (a) *Literary Criticism:* gauging communication between author and public; (b) *Scientific Criticism:* fact-finding, elucidating; (c) *Dogmatic Criticism:* judging in the name of a doctrine; (d) *Pragmatic Criticism:* registering public taste; (e) *Impressionistic Criticism:* registering personal taste.

CRYPTIC: with a hidden meaning, hard to decipher.

CRYPTO-: concealed; e.g., crypto-drama, drama under the form of a novel.

CULTURE: (a) refinement, admission to the ranks of the connoisseurs; (b) erudition in artistic and literary matters; "getting to know the best which has been thought and said"; (c) an inward process, liberation from inferiority complexes, consciousness coupled with ease.

DANDYISM: foppishness raised to the level of a doctrine and an art; elegance as a sign of exquisite refinement (Byron, Beau Brummell, Musset, Disraeli, Count d'Orsay).

DANTESQUE, cf. Adjectives.

DECADENCE: decline in vitality, artistic or moral; increasing refinement of the form when the spirit is gone.

DECADENT-ISM: the glorying consciousness of decadence (sheer perversity, or self-defense, or love of excessive refinement); the neo-barbarians may call Decadent anything that is not crude or brutal.

DEUS EX MACHINA (Horace): Lit.[1] a god out of a (stage) machine; illogical intervention of some external power in the development of the plot: disease, accident, unexpected return, as *Deus ex machina.*

DILETTANTE, plural Dilettanti, Ital.: lit., those who take pleasure in art or literature; usually connotes indifference to all other values, and little seriousness even in artistic interests. Cf. amateur, connoisseur.

[1] Literally.

DISCOURSE: *in this book:* mere communication through words, as opposed to poetry. Prose and Verse refer to technique; Discourse and Poetry to spirit.

DOCTRINE: a system of thought (or the central idea of such a system) so definite, so certain that it can be *taught* ao the truth. E.g.: "Texas barred out Evolution as a doctrine, not as a hypothesis."

DOGMA: a doctrine supported by an authority which it is not lawful to dispute: *Magister dixit,* the Master said so.

DRAMATIC: cf. Spirits.

ELEMENTS in a Work of Art. Intellectual: (a) *Purpose,* intention, such as entertainment, edification, information, inspiration, profit (fame or money). In strict art for art's sake, there should be no purpose; according to Kant, art is adequacy to purpose without purpose (Zweckmässigkeit ohne Zweck); (b) *Theme:* general interest treated, such as: love, glory, revenge, pride, jealousy, avarice; work, travel, war, politics, etc.; (c) *Thesis:* the proposition that the author is seeking to establish; in pure art, should not be obvious; but is seldom lacking; (d) *Subject:* the actual events narrated or represented. E.g.: in *Othello,* Shakespeare's purposes were entertainment, profit (fame and money) and, secondarily, edification. His main theme: jealousy (secondary: love and revenge). His thesis: warning against jealousy. His subject: the events leading to the deaths of Desdemona and Othello.

Technical (working out of the above): (a) *Situation:* the problem affecting the heroes of the work; (b) *Plot:* a sequence of situations, leading to a solution of the original problem; (c) *Characters,* Characterization: convincing depiction of the persons involved in the action; (d) *Motivation:* proper interworking of characters and plot; (e) *Atmosphere:* the background: geographical, historical, social, moral; (f) *Tone:* the expression of the attitude adopted by the author: solemn, sentimental, light, flippant, dispassionate; (g) *Mood:* actual feelings of the author when writing; usually, the feeling he is attempting to create in the reader (not always with success: an author in solemn mood may induce a frivolous mood in his readers). *Tone* and *Mood* are frequently in harmony. When they are not (tragic events narrated with apparent dispassionateness or even levity; frivolous events reported with solemnity), we have a form of *Irony* (q.v.). (h) *Technique* proper: the tricks of the trade.

ÉLITE (French): the elect, the chosen, the "happy few." Should be identical with aristocracy or upper class, but is not.

ELOQUENCE: power to convince through logic and passion; Rhetoric: the technique of eloquence; pejorative: emphasis on mere technique;

Bombast: eloquence strained for immediate effectiveness; the exaggeration or caricature of eloquence.

EPIGONE, pl. -NES, -NI (Greek): a second generation, presumably inferior to the first; hence: uninspired followers and imitators.

ESOTERIC: secret teaching, reserved for the initiated. For the outsider, *esoteric* lore is *cryptic*.

ESTHETE: a devotee of art; one whose practical life is ruled by esthetic principles. Frequently a pose: hence: the pharisee of beauty-worship, ineffectual, tinged with immorality, decadent.

EXPRESSIONISM: "the identity of content and form," according to Benedetto Croce.

ESTHETIC: pertaining to art and/or beauty.

ESTHETICS: the science or philosophy of art and/or beauty ("Snakes in Iceland").

FALLACY: both the method and the result of plausible but faulty reasoning. "*Un-English* is a perfect fallacy in a single word," said Walter Bagehot. The *Pathetic Fallacy:* ascribing to nature the emotions of men; denounced by Ruskin, who was guilty of the *Esthetic Fallacy:* there is a God, because nature is (sometimes) beautiful.

FARCICAL, cf. under Spirits (Comic).

FLAIR (French): "scent," as of a dog. Instinctive discrimination; fact-finding rather than judicial.

FOLK (in literature, usually with the force of the German VOLK): the people; blending race, language, customs, traditions. *Folkways, folksay, folklore* vs. *definite* literature; *folk* epic, *folk* ballad vs. *art* epic, *art* ballad. *Volkstum* (folkdom): a form of romantic primitivism, responsible for many fallacies.

FUTURISTIC: as a doctrine or school, originated with the Italian F. T. Marinetti. Ideally: liberated from dead hand of tradition; looking freely toward the future. Practically: strenuous, defiant departure from the accepted, even, or rather chiefly, when the accepted is safe and sane.

GENIUS: acknowledged, but unaccountable superiority. A few interpretations: I.Q. (Intelligence Quotient) 140 and over; exceptional (not miraculous) attainments: the prodigy; Inspiration; "Infinite capacity for taking pains"; a "mutation" or new departure; the creative vs. the imitative-derivative; beyond the safe and sane (which may imply either insanity or mysticism); acceptance, recognition; and especially, a residuary word to conceal our ignorance.

GENRE: historical and conventional grouping of works which have in common definite elements of spirit and form. E.g., the tragedy.

GNOMIC: (Greek) lit. "wisdom" literature; proverbs, maxims, aphorisms; at lowest level, popular saws; at highest, ethical *sententiae*.

GOTHIC(K): in literature only, a tale of mystery and terror, often with elements of the supernatural; formally started with Horace Walpole's *Castle of Otranto*, 1764; still going strong.

GROTESQUE: willful blending of the terrible and the ludicrous. Particularly monsters; cf. *Faust*, I and II, Medieval and Classical Walpurgis Nacht; strong in Victor Hugo. Pirandello used a psychological brand of the grotesque. (Often, in common speech, merely ludicrous.)

HUMANISM: (a) sympathy with mankind as such. Terence: I am a man, and nothing human is alien to me. Leads to philanthropy and humanitarianism; (b) Philosophy according to which man is the end and measure of all things; often blending with *philosophical* (not with *literary*) Naturalism, q.v.; e.g., Rabelais; (c) Culture of human values through the classics of antiquity. Sometimes narrowed (unduly) to Greek and Latin scholarship. No *mere* grammarian can be a *true* humanist; (d) Neo-Humanism: man is man, neither an Angel (supernaturalism) nor a beast (materialism). A doctrine of enlightened discipline; often with a conservative tinge (Irving Babbitt).

IMMORTALS, the Forty: title ironically given to the members of the French (literary) Academy, most of whom are forgotten in their own lifetime.

IMPRESSIONISM: immediate reproduction of images derived from the senses, the intellect acting as a transmitting medium, not as a modifying influence. (These *images* need not be purely material.) Both analysis and synthesis avoided. Compatible with Romanticism and Realism. Symbolism is no part of Impressionism, but may be superadded.

IMPRESSIONISTIC CRITICISM: "So help me God, I cannot otherwise" (Luther at the Diet of Worms). Refusal to pretend for dogmatic or social reasons.

INTELLIGENTSIA (Russian): the intellectuals. A term which may have had a meaning in Russia; now antiquated jargon.

IRONY (lit. questioning; Socratic method): (a) condensed *reductio ad absurdum*; agreeing with opponent better than he agrees with himself; e.g., "Every nation should have a navy equal to all the other navies combined." (b) Conscious discrepancy between tone and mood: apparent agreement covering satire (the reverse, less frequent, is also a form of irony).

IRONY AND PITY: excellent phrase coined by Anatole France; unfortunately turned into a *cliché*.

IVORY TOWER (origins—Song of Solomon; Litany of the Virgin; poem of Sainte-Beuve, referring to Alfred de Vigny): refuge of the artist from the practical world. At worst: escapism, flight from responsibility; at best: refusal to compromise; the strength that is in purity.

JARGON (in literature): the conventional vocabulary of a clique or set (e.g., the jargon of the Précieuses); used with conscious pride, as the badge of initiation or "sophistication"; ceases to be esoteric only to become cliché: e.g., fate of word *bromide*. This has impaired the usefulness of excellent words and phrases, like *Irony and Pity* (above). Samples of jargon: devastating, stark, sophisticated, suave, subtle, rhythm, pattern, values, vital, etc.

JOURNALESE: the jargon of a vigorous tribe; forcible, but short-lived.

JOURNALISTIC: unscrupulously vivid ("'tis a pity it is true").

KITSCH (German slang): spurious art; deriving pseudo-artistic effects from non-artistic sources of appeal: gaudy, bathetic, sentimental, meretricious, etc.

LITERATI (Latin, plural only): semi-humorous: those interested in letters. Cf. Pharisaism.

MASOCHISM: cf. Sadism.

MELODRAMA, -TIC: cf. Spirits.

MILTONIC: cf. Adjectives.

MNEMONIC, MNEMOTECHNIC: aid to memory (one of the bases of verse).

MOLIÈRESQUE: cf. Adjectives.

MYSTIC-ISM: in direct communication with the Divine. The mystic cannot express himself directly: his intuition is "ineffable," beyond words; so he must use symbols. As a result: often seems vague and irrational.

NATURALISM: (a) frank, and often joyous, acceptance of nature, both physical and human; opposed to supernaturalism and the metaphysical; e.g., Rabelais. George Brandes called the nature-worship of the English poets Naturalism. (b) The same principle, interpreted as rebellion against corrupting influence of society, the arts and civilization, leads to "Return to Nature," Primitivism: J. J. Rousseau. Both optimistic. (c) Scientific Realism; so named by analogy with the *Natural* sciences; frequently a materialistic, cynical, sordid view of the world: Tennyson denounced "the troughs of Zolaism."

PARADOX: opinion contrary to common belief, and apparently contrary to common sense and common experience. May be true or false. The rotation of the earth once was a paradox. The Gospel is full of paradoxes.

PARODY: the caricature of a style; imitation of an author's tricks so as to make them ludicrous. A form of irony. At times a valid form of criticism.

PASTICHE: deliberate and faithful imitation of a style. Conscious (Thackeray: *Esmond*) or unconscious. No satirical intent as in parody.

PATHETIC, cf. Spirits.

PERIOD: in literary history, time during which certain principles, ideologies or fashions prevail. "Period," used particularly of decoration: the style of the time: Queen Anne, Colonial, etc. By analogy: "Period" pieces in literature: either clear-cut examples of the work of a time: to "date" or "be dated" becomes an element of charm; the antiquated becomes an antique. Or a careful reproduction of such work: Thackeray: *Esmond*; Rostand, *Cyrano de Bergerac*; Eugene O'Neill: *Ah, Wilderness!* (Faked antiques).

PERSONALITY: consistency in thought and action, which determines taste and style.

PHARISAISM, PHARISEE: self-righteous, thanking the Lord that he is not as other men, or even as this (Babbitt, Yahoo, etc.). When the desire to belong with the righteous is stronger than the consciousness of belonging, we have (literary) snobbishness. The following words have a decided Pharisaical or snobbish overtone—self-confessed or not: Clique, Cognoscenti, Connoisseur, Cultured (in formal sense) Dilettante, Élite, Esoteric, Esthete, Happy Few (Stendhal's formula), Highbrow (a lowbrow cliché), Intelligentsia, Literati, Sophisticate. Cf. "The Smart Set, for Minds that are not Primitive."

PHILISTINISM: the utilitarian spirit in art: "What is it good for?" The alternative is Art for Art's Sake.

PITY: cf. IRONY AND PITY; PITY AND TERROR: the two passions which, according to Aristotle, should be excited and purified (reconciled into acceptance of fate) in tragedy. SOCIAL PITY: *misericordia*, love for the humble: the Gospel, Hugo, Dickens, Tolstoy. The spiritual reality back of "dialectic materialism" and the proletarian novel.

PLAGIARISM: literary theft of subject or form. Edmond Rostand was twice condemned in Chicago for "plagiarism."

PLOT, cf. Elements.

POETRY: not verse, but "awe and wonder"; revealed by the tremor that attends discovery or intense realization.

POPULAR: not vulgar, but accessible. (a) "in a tongue understanded of the people"; (b) a general favorite. Shades, but no radical difference, between popularity, celebrity, fame, glory. Popularity so long-continued as that of Alexandre Dumas amounts to glory. Milton never was "popular" in any sense of the term; Homer and Shakespeare were and are.

PORNOGRAPHIC (Greek): lit. describing the life of prostitutes; usually: indecent, obscene.

PRAGMATIC: in modern philosophy, William James, John Dewey: radical empiricism. Implies confessed ignorance (not denial) of absolute realities. In the practical world, whatever is, is; whatever works, works. Pragmatic Criticism: "such popularity must be deserved": cf. Aristotle on Euripides.

PRÉCIOSITÉ, PRECIOSITY, PRECIOUSNESS: from Précieuses, seventeenth century social-literary set of sophisticates. Cleverness, affectation in expression.

PRESTIGE: authority, influence or fame accepted *uncritically*.

PRIMITIVISM: (a) optimistic: Rousseau's return to the original goodness of man; cf. Naturalism (b), the myth of the noble savage; (b) pessimistic: admiration for the crude, the brutal, as such; contempt for subtlety, refinement and scruples (Worship of the Rough-and-Tough). Both forms are romantic delusions (cf. Vico, Herder, etc.).

PROSE: expression without hard-and-fast rules (beyond the grammatical), as opposed to verse. May have qualities of euphony and particularly of rhythm not inferior to those of verse.

PROSE, POETICAL: an ill-defined medium, freer than free verse, but departing consciously from the practices of everyday language, so as to produce an effect akin to that of verse.

PROSODY: rules of versification, particularly those relating to meter (accent and/or quantity).

PSEUDO: false; deceitful imitation (an honest pastiche is not "pseudo"). "Fake": the pseudo-ruins of the eighteenth century. Unsuccessful, lifeless imitation: Pseudo-Gothic. Cf. a favorite word of D. H. Lawrence's: the *would-be*.

PURPOSE, cf. Elements.

RABELAISIAN: cf. Adjectives.

REALISM (in medieval philosophy: belief in the reality of general ideas): Seeing things as they are, in and for themselves; accuracy, dispassionateness. Often (in reaction against wishful "Idealism"): sordid, pessimistic, cynical. The confusion between Realism and Cynicism is the most dangerous of fallacies.

RHETORIC: (a) the art of persuasion, generally through the spoken word (oratory, eloquence); (b) by extension: the art of composition in general (obsolete); (c) unfavorably: conscious, excessive use of the tricks of rhetoric; insincere, fulsome eloquence: "mere" rhetoric.

RHYTHM: regular recurrence (in events as well as in sounds: the *rhythm* of history). In its purity, would be mechanical, and therefore anti-artistic; becomes art only when combined with, and subordinated to, other factors.

ROMANCE: (in the most general sense) that which excites wonder: adventure, the unexpected, the indeterminate. Love, discovery, mystery. Modern science is the most thrilling of romances.

ROMANTIC: full of imagination, passion, picturesqueness.

ROMANTICISM: love of the romantic (as above); individualism (hence rebellion); intensity, intuition, mysticism.

SADISTIC: from Marquis de Sade, late eighteenth century novelist. Strictly: lust coupled with infliction of pain upon its object. Cf. Masochism (from Sacher-Masoch): lust coupled with infliction of pain upon oneself. Broadly: pleasure in the infliction of pain (Neronism); pleasure in describing suffering. (Easy descent from the tragic to the harrowing, from the harrowing to the sadistic.)

SAGA: Scandinavian, particularly Icelandic, epic legend. Extended to many non-classical epics. Semi-humorously: annals of a family: the Forsyte Saga.

SHAKESPEREAN, SHAKESPERIAN, cf. Adjectives.

SHAVIAN: from George Bernard Shaw. Cf. Adjectives.

SHIBBOLETH: A purely formal Criterion (q.v.). From *Judges*, XII-6: Kill any one who says Sibboleth for Shibboleth. Ostracize a man who eats peas with his knife, drops an H or splits an infinitive. Most "sophisticated" criticism is based on shibboleths.

SOPHISTICATE-D: lit. adulterated, departing from healthy simplicity. Frequently but wrongly used in favorable sense for subtle, urbane, civilized. More naturally connected with jargon, Kitsch and Pharisaism.

SPIRITS in Literature. (a) *Tragic:* that which arouses terror and pity, purged (purified) through a sense of moral inevitability. (b) *Dramatic:* the effect of successive, sharply contrasted events, not necessarily tragic: success may be *dramatic*. The tragic is inherent, and may remain passive; the dramatic may be fortuitous, and implies development. A perfect tragedy should be both tragic and dramatic. (c) *Pathetic:* realization of the tragic. (d) *Melodramatic:* exaggeration of the dramatic, both in fortuitousness and in sharp contrast. The *Melodrama* usually adds to the melodramatic proper an element of sentimentality. (e) *Comic:* that which rouses amusement; usually through some discrepancy: between aims and means; between sentiment and tone; between thoughts and words; between character and situation. (f) *Farcical:* elementary comic obtained through simple and excessive discrepancies. Comic caricature. Corresponds with the melodramatic on the tragic plane; but seems more capable of artistic treatment.

STYLE: (a) fashion, mode: *styles* in architecture and decoration; (b) including the *passing* fashion (in style, out of style); (c) personal mode of expression: consistency revealing personality: "Le style, c'est l'homme même" (Buffon).

STYLIST: one who willfully displays personal tricks of expression, and sins against the great commandment: "Art consists in concealing art."

SUBJECT: cf. Elements.

SYMBOLISM: attempt to express (or adumbrate) the unutterable. In its fullness: belief in secret harmony between sign and thing signified; thus differs from Allegory, which implies no such belief. Kinship with Mysticism.

SYMBOLIST: Movement, chiefly 1880-1900. Usually connotes vagueness (or the esoteric and cryptic); and unjustly associated with Decadentism.

SYNCRETISM: a philosophy(?) or a state of mind admitting incongruous elements. In Eclecticism, there is at least an attempt to unify or harmonize the heterogeneous (although the result is frequently mere syncretism). Synonym: Hodgepodge. Usually unconscious, thus incurable. The dominant "philosophy"; also called Collectionism and (by Irving Babbitt) Confusionism.

TACT: the anticipation and avoidance of conflict; out of prudence and/or kindness.

TASTE: (a) individual, spontaneous reaction of like or dislike; (b) a manifestation of personality: consistency in selection, as style is consistency in expression; (c) collective likes and dislikes (determining fashions and styles); (d) "good" taste: conformity with taste of a selected group; joining the right club, and not offending your fellow members.

TECHNIQUE: art in practical sense, i.e., the way of doing a thing (implies consciousness, and usually training: a fortuitous achievement is not a triumph of technique). In literature: the tricks of the trade. Should be concealed (cf. Stylist).

THEME, THESIS, TONE: cf. Elements.

TRADITION: not all that is transmitted from the past to the present, but only that which enjoys historical *prestige* (i.e., authority or influence accepted *uncritically*). A tradition submitted to fearless criticism disappears as a tradition, but may survive as a reasonable, permanent value. Admiration for the classics should not be a *tradition*.

TRAGIC: cf. Spirits.

VERNACULAR: home language, as opposed to learned or official language. If English was the vernacular as opposed to Latin and Norman French, dialects and slang are the vernacular as opposed to academic English.

VERSE: language with more obvious and mechanical pattern or rhythm than prose. Historically and psychologically associated with poetry, although the two can easily be divorced.

VICTORIAN: historically, everything pertaining to the Victorian Era, i.e., to England under Queen Victoria (1837-1901); subdivided into Early Victorian, Mid-Victorian, Late Victorian. Connotations (unjust as usual): Philistinism, with a little more Pharisaism than in the corresponding Bourgeois world on the Continent; and with a special emphasis on prudishness.

VIRGILIAN, cf. Adjectives.

VOLTAIRIAN: cf. Adjectives.

VULGAR: (a) lit.: of the common people: *vulgar* Latin, the *vulgar* tongue (in French: *vulgarisation:* popular science; *Haute Vulgarisation:* for the educated general public); (b) aggressively insensitive and coarse (vulgar display), *Kitsch;* (c) in the "Victorian" mind: ignorance of the proper shibboleths; freedom of thought or manner: to challenge respectability is *vulgar.*

WARDOUR STREET: the street of "antique shoppes" in London; hence: style reveling in archaisms.

WIT: quick realization, and terse expression, of a (comic) discrepancy. Humo(u)r: wit tempered with sympathy; Sarcasm, Sarcastic Wit: wit with sharp critical or satirical intent; Sardonic adds to Sarcastic a feeling of personal superiority; Cynical, Cynicism, gloats over the realization of a discrepancy, as a confirmation of a pessimistic philosophy. Irony has the same essence as wit; but, instead of denouncing the discrepancy directly, it exposes it through a *reductio ad absurdum.*

INDEX OF NAMES AND TITLES

A few names and titles mentioned in the text were omitted from the Index, because their relation to literature was casual or remote.

A few names are printed in CAPITALS, as of particular importance in the study of World Literature. This implies no judgment of intrinsic excellence, or of importance within the author's national literature. It indicates, for instance, that Byron's international position is more generally acknowledged than that of Keats.

American (Am.) and English (Eng.) names and titles have been kept separate. Usually, the indication French (Fr.), German (Germ.), etc., refers to the language group rather than to the nationality. Thus Irish and Scottish writers using the English language are listed as English; no distinction is made between Austrian, German-Swiss, Baltic German, etc.

The classification of *Genres* has been simplified to the utmost: thus *Poem, poet.*, covers anything from epic to epigram in verse; *novel* (nov.) includes tale, romance, etc.; *drama* (dr.) applies to tragedy, comedy, farce, etc.

Roman capitals (III, XII, etc.) stand for *centuries*. A.D. unless otherwise indicated.

As a rule, the date given is that of publication. When there are two or more dates, it implies continuation or reworking. In a few cases (Pepys' *Diary*, for instance) the date of composition seems more adequate.

(c: *circa*, about; f: and following.)

INDEX OF NAMES AND TITLES